The American Social Experience Series
GENERAL EDITOR: JAMES KIRBY MARTIN
EDITORS: PAULA S. FASS, STEVEN H. MINTZ, CARL PRINCE,
JAMES W. REED & PETER N. STEARNS

"A MIXED MULTITUDE"

The Struggle for Toleration in
Colonial Pennsylvania

SALLY SCHWARTZ

NEW YORK UNIVERSITY PRESS
NEW YORK AND LONDON
1987

Library of Congress Cataloging-in-Publication Data

Schwartz, Sally, 1952–
"A mixed multitude."

(The American social experience series ; 8)
Includes index.
1. Pennsylvania—History—Colonial period, ca.
1600–1775.   2. Religious tolerance—Pennsylvania—
History.   3. Pennsylvania—Ethnic relations.   I. Title.
II. Series.
F152.S34   1987   974.8'02   87-20386
ISBN 0-8147-7873-9

Book design by Ken Venezio

Contents

Preface

This study is concerned with the ideas, attitudes, and behavior of the men and women who settled in William Penn's province and, over the course of a century, brought together diverse ethnic and religious elements to coalesce into a pluralistic and broadly tolerant society. Because it is important to allow them to speak for themselves, quotations reproduce the often erratic spelling, capitalization, punctuation, and italicization of the seventeenth and eighteenth centuries. The use of *sic* has been avoided except in the few cases where a modern reader might question whether a typographical error has slipped into the text. Translations are mine, except where otherwise noted.

Readers interested in a formal bibliography and more extensive documentation are invited to consult the dissertation version, "'A Mixed Multitude': Religion and Ethnicity in Colonial Pennsylvania" (Harvard University, 1981). Constraints on the length of the book have made it impossible to include all of the relevant materials to the study in the notes.

I would like to thank the many librarians and archivists who provided access to collections in the following institutions and pointed me toward sources that might have been overlooked: American Philosophical Society, Philadelphia; Bucks County Historical Society, Doylestown, Pa.; Chester County Historical Society, West Chester, Pa.; Cumberland County Historical Society, Carlisle, Pa.; Dauphin County Historical Society, Harrisburg; Special Collections, Dickinson College, Carlisle; Evangelical and Reformed Historical Society, Lancaster, Pa.; Friends' Historical Library, Swarthmore, Pa.; Historical Society of Pennsylvania, Philadelphia; Lancaster County Historical Society, Lancaster; Library Company of Philadelphia; Library of Congress, Washington, D.C.; Lutheran Archives Center at Philadelphia; Archives of the Moravian Church, Bethlehem, Pa.; Pennsylvania Historical and Museum Commission, Harrisburg; Presbyterian Historical Society, Philadelphia; Quaker Collection, Haverford College, Haverford, Pa.; Schwenkfelder Library, Pennsburg, Pa.; and the Rare Books Room, University of Pennsylvania, Philadelphia.

The Charles Warren Center and History Department, Harvard University, and a CBS Bicentennial Narrators Scholarship provided financial assistance that allowed extensive research in Pennsylvania. A fellowship from the Deutscher Akademischer Austauschdienst permitted study at a Goethe Institute that improved my skills in German. Eastern Montana College assisted the final completion of the manuscript by making available supplies and photocopying services.

An earlier version of chapter 1 was published in *Social Science Perspectives*, 1 (1986); a preliminary version of chapter 2 appeared in *Pennsylvania History*, 50 (1983).

Donald C. Bellomy and Jefferson A. White read and critiqued various drafts of this manuscript, as did Bernard Bailyn, who guided it as a dissertation. I would like to thank them for their support, encouragement, and insight.

CHAPTER I

Prologue: Pennsylvania and American Pluralism

During the century following its establishment by William Penn in
1681, Pennsylvania became America's first self-consciously plural society. The 1790 census suggests that for the United States as a whole,
61 percent of the white population were of English origin. Approximately 9 percent were German, 8 percent were Scottish, 6 percent
were Scotch-Irish, and the remainder consisted of even smaller groups
drawn from several other nations and those whose origins could not
be identified. Because almost two-thirds of Americans were of English
descent, with usually only relatively small numbers of other cultures
present, "English" norms, institutions, and cultural patterns prevailed. In contrast, only 35 percent of Pennsylvanians were of English
descent, while 33 percent were German, 11 percent were Scotch-Irish,
and 9 percent were Scottish. Among the other components of the
Pennsylvania population were people of Irish, Dutch, Swedish, Finnish, French, and Welsh backgrounds.[1] Blacks and Native Americans, present in small numbers, added further to the diversity of provincial society.[2] Nor was the diversity of Pennsylvania wholly or even
primarily ethnic, for immigrants brought a variety of faiths with them.
Congregations affiliated with at least sixteen different sects and denominations were present in the colony by 1775.[3] The extremely het-

[handwritten margin notes:]
1790 61% Eng
9% Ge
8% Scot
6% Scot-Irish

Pa 35% Eng
33% Ge
11% Scot Irish
9% Scot

Relig & nat Diversity
fr. beg. in Del. River Valley   Holy experiment = relig freedom statutes in Const
                                 2 brief visits   ↓
                                 little   End of Const plan

2   "A MIXED MULTITUDE"

erogeneous population confronted Pennsylvanians with a unique set of problems that could have impeded the creation of a stable society. Nevertheless, despite the inevitable tensions, exacerbated by waves of new immigration, wars, and religious conflict, colonial Pennsylvanians managed to develop new ideals of pluralism and tolerance on which they built their province.

Religious and national diversity characterized the settlements of the Delaware Valley almost from the first arrival of Europeans. The problems involved in governing this complex region antedated the Penn regime, but the solutions reached by the earlier Dutch, Swedish, and English claimants to the territory before its grant to Penn were concessions granted for the sake of expediency. Policies included accepting aliens—especially those already present when a new power claimed control—as residents and according a limited measure of toleration to dissenters from their national churches. William Penn, in contrast, set forth a new, ideological basis for pluralism and tolerance that transformed the tentative pattern of relative harmony and toleration into one of official policy. Among Penn's goals was the establishment of a "holy experiment," a refuge where Western Europeans could live with minimal infringements upon their religious inclinations and enjoy the fundamental rights of English subjects. To accomplish this end, he drafted a series of constitutions that guaranteed religious freedom and promoted his colony not only in the British Isles but on the Continent as well.

Penn's ideals, ideas, and policies set into motion forces that would lead to an extremely heterogeneous province, and had significant effects on the development of the colony over the next century. But he apparently failed to consider the problem of devising ways in which individuals of different faiths, languages, and nationalities, who in Europe were in frequent conflict with each other, would live together peacefully. He made only two brief visits to his province, and exerted little control over it while he remained in England. It was thus the people of Pennsylvania who worked out the implications of his ideals and ultimately created a stable, pluralistic, and broadly tolerant society.

The uniqueness of Pennsylvania is therefore a consequence of the

R.W ≈ W P rthg tolcn,
W P col Del w/c pervovl, toler
or plurality

interactions among the ethnic and religious diversity (always present
in the province and greatly enhanced during the eighteenth century),
William Penn's ideology, and the colonists' transformation of these
ideals into reality. Although some of these characteristics were also
present, usually in lesser degree, in other colonies, no other province
had all three. Patterns of thought and behavior that evolved elsewhere
in British North America were thus unlike those of this distinctive
colony. All of the "middle colonies" had, to some extent, a population
drawn from many nations and religious beliefs, but only in Pennsylvania was there no clearly dominant cultural group. New York, with
its relatively large population at the time of the conquest, continued
to have a visible Dutch presence throughout the colonial period. Although anglicization was resisted, especially in the Hudson Valley,
English norms came to prevail. Roger Williams' views concerning religious liberty were similar to Penn's, but because Rhode Island did
not attract large numbers of non-British immigrants, its pluralism was
limited and the significance of its founder's ideas untested. Delaware,
also a proprietary colony owned by the Penn family, neither attracted
the great diversity of foreign immigrants nor adopted the principled
commitment to pluralism and tolerance that its neighbor to the north
did.

I

It is unclear why the unique nature of Pennsylvania society as a complex of diverse peoples who struggled to establish and maintain a stable society based on the principle of tolerance has not been more widely
recognized and studied. In recent years, the middle colonies have attracted renewed attention from historians, while scholars in many dis-
ciplines have studied immigration, ethnicity, and religious pluralism.
Nevertheless, virtually all studies of colonial Pennsylvania have been
narrowly focused. Most have concentrated on a particular religious or
national group. Older works are often filiopietistic and lack sustained
analysis. Although such studies are still often valuable, their major
weakness is a tendency to examine the history of one particular group
in isolation from other segments of society and from the larger issues

in colonial history. Recent studies of immigration have been more scholarly, but the quantitative methodology most have shared has imposed its own constraints. While it is helpful to know the magnitude of immigration and the sources from which it was drawn, such studies reveal little about the migrants' life or thought. Studies of redemptioners and indentured servants similarly provide material relevant to the experiences of many immigrants, yet because they are oriented more toward questions of class and frequently do not differentiate among the experiences of servants from different nations, their usefulness in understanding Pennsylvania society is limited.

Historians have occasionally attempted to be comprehensive in their investigations; however, they have generally limited their analysis to brief periods of time. For the most part, when they have considered group interaction, they have focused on the political realm. By concentrating on Quaker–Anglican relations, they have failed to give adequate consideration to other components of the population. While the presence of Germans or the Scotch-Irish is occasionally recognized, the implicit assumption has been that all Pennsylvanians—or at least all the ones that counted—were English. Some new investigations of political participation have revealed significant trends, such as a broadening of the national and religious groups that actively participated in politics or held office as the Revolution approached. But because such privileges were restricted, especially by wealth, and because politics was not a matter of great importance to most colonial Pennsylvanians, they, too, are limited.

In research that focuses more directly on the everyday lives of colonists, the interaction of different groups in several towns has recently been investigated. Social relationships, patterns of friendship and marriage, and membership in clubs or civic organizations do reveal much about the nature of provincial life. However, it is unclear whether the patterns discerned in one town apply to the colony as a whole, for the population mix of each town varied, while distinctions must also be made regionally and over the span of the colony's history. The central difficulty with all of the previous studies is that they have not analyzed people's ideas, their attitudes toward those who differed in national origin or religious belief, or the values that Pennsylvanians formulated to achieve unity in the midst of diversity and conflict.[4]

II

In many ways, colonial Pennsylvania prefigures the pluralistic Amer- <
ican experience of the nineteenth and twentieth centuries. Yet if the
colony's significance has been overlooked, perhaps this is due to a
discontinuity between the eighteenth and twentieth centuries. In
Pennsylvania diverse groups came together to create a new culture; in
the United States, newcomers were accepted into, or rejected from,
an already existing culture. In the national period, the paradigm to
which historians have been drawn is majority–minority relations in a
society in which important elements of the nature of the American
identity and its institutions have already been defined. In contrast, all
national and religious elements of colonial Pennsylvania were in a sense
"minority groups." There was no majority; nor was there a dominant
cultural group or strong institutions that could impose conformity.

Superficially, an "English" culture prevailed. Legal and political institutions were derived primarily from English precedents, and English was the unofficial language. But the less tangible aspects of provincial culture—especially the ways in which people thought and the
social and religious customs that governed daily life—evolved in ways
quite unlike those characteristic of England and its other colonies.
While Pennsylvania was an English province, its culture represents an
amalgam of different peoples, faiths, and ideas.

Moreover, the English culture transplanted to Pennsylvania was itself fragmented. Despite a commonality of language, Quakers and
Anglicans—the most important English-speaking subgroups—had very
different religious, social, and cultural values. Colonists from other
parts of the British Isles—the Welsh, the Scots, and the Scotch-Irish—
were all subjects of the same monarch and could migrate freely within
the Empire, yet they did not share common historical experiences or
cultures. Furthermore, religious uniformity did not characterize any
of these British groups.

To add further to the diversity, Continental emigrants were drawn
from a variety of states and principalities. For example, "Swedes" were
both Swedish and Finnish in origins and culture, and while they were
often designated "Germans" or "Palatines" by English-speaking Pennsylvanians, emigrants from the Rhineland spoke different dialects and

had little in common historically or culturally. Moreover, they were adherents of a broad range of denominations and sects; even churches in the Lutheran and Reformed traditions, of which the majority of non-English emigrants were at least nominal members, exhibited regional differences.

Because of the significant differences between the provincial culture and subsequent national culture, the questions that must be asked in order to understand each are dissimilar. However, the terminology and concepts, as well as the methodology, for understanding immigration, ethnicity, religion, and pluralism have been shaped by the national rather than the colonial experience. Because it is difficult to use a modern conceptual framework to interpret life in colonial Pennsylvania, studies of nineteenth- or twentieth-century society and social thought unfortunately do not provide the needed links between such issues in pre-revolutionary Pennsylvania and modern America.[5]

Assimilation, for example, is one of the most common concepts employed to analyze the immigrant experience, but it has little relevance for colonial Pennsylvania. The term has been used to describe several different, but related, modes of adapting to a new society. The most common definition involves minority groups yielding to the dominant culture, resulting in greater uniformity or homogeneity. Assimilation is thus a process by which pluralism is limited or reduced. But in Pennsylvania there was no single culture into which the colonials might assimilate, nor was there consistent pressure to conform to any particular language or cluster of customs. A second definition of assimilation posits a gradual submerging of ethnicity into a primary religious allegiance, which has slowly occurred with most American Jews and, to a lesser extent, Roman Catholics. This happened only to a limited extent in Pennsylvania. A third definition of assimilation has more relevance to Pennsylvania, although it must be modified. It involves the combination of people of diverse backgrounds into a new ethnicity or character—that is, a fusion of several ethnic backgrounds into a new one. If this may be interpreted as the formation of a new ethos, if not a new ethnic group, it does offer a key to understanding the Pennsylvania experience. For if immigrants to Pennsylvania—whatever their origins—assimilated, it was to an ideology of pluralism and tolerance that was often alien to their prior experiences or expectations.

Ethnicity has little relevance as a principle by which the Pennsylvania experience can be conceptualized. Not only is it anachronistic to speak of ethnicity prior to the rise of modern nationalism, but ethnicity also requires a consciousness of belonging to a particular group, a sense of social and cultural distinctiveness. While it might be accurate to describe the twentieth-century "Pennsylvania Dutch" as an ethnic group, eighteenth-century Pennsylvania Germans cannot be so designated. Individual identity was more complex than membership in one particular, narrowly defined category. Pennsylvanians did not, for the most part, define themselves or categorize others according to their state of birth. The seventeenth and eighteenth centuries were localistic in orientation, with allegiance not to a nation but to some subdivision of it. The very diversity of immigrants, as well as provincial settlement patterns that isolated individuals from others who might have a similar background, limited perceptions of belonging to an ethnic group, and perhaps hindered the development of ethnic consciousness. The national, religious, and cultural fragmentation of the colony, and the shifting allegiances to language, doctrine, or tradition, may have precluded a strong sense of group identity. In some instances, a sense of ethnicity may develop in response to hostility from a different segment of society. Because of the patterns of toleration and the interaction of different peoples, this was not the case in colonial Pennsylvania.

If nationality was not crucial in making distinctions among peoples, language was important and did help determine patterns of interaction. But language was not the issue of ideological concern it became for many nineteenth- and twentieth-century immigrants or for native-born Americans. Linguistic diversity was accepted as a matter of fact. Individuals seem to have drifted into a functional bilingualism as their personal interests indicated the advantage of learning a new language. There was little prejudice against those who could not speak a certain language; seldom was there pressure to adopt or to retain usage of a particular form of speech. In fact, English-speaking political and religious leaders sometimes aided groups in retaining their native language if they so desired or if circumstances dictated that a particular language be used. Except for one ill-fated experiment in the mid-1750s, Penn and his successors did little to hasten the process of anglicization.

Religion provided the foundation for most of the distinctions that provincial Pennsylvanians made. They tended to identify both themselves and their neighbors in terms of beliefs rather than nationality. However, most Pennsylvanians were undogmatic. Religious bigotry was seldom evident, either in such later typical manifestations in the United States as anti-Catholicism and anti-Semitism or, more broadly, as a prevalent opinion of "outside" groups. It is true that cooperation and interaction occurred primarily within the broad divisions of church and sect, for people associated with the territorial churches that developed because of the Reformation differed sharply from those who joined the sects that also sprang up after the collapse of a unified Western christendom. Yet to Pennsylvanians distinctions over minute points of doctrine or the language employed in worship were eventually of less importance than a perception that separate religious groups might have common interests to protect or to advance.

The variety of churches and sects, and the frequent drift of individuals from one to another, present difficulties in analyzing church adherence, or even in discerning the importance of religion to the colonists. To ask the questions of frequent concern to sociologists of religion, whether people were members of a church and how actively they participated in its rites, assumes that there were indeed churches and ministers available, and that Europeans had strong ties to institutional religion before they emigrated. Pennsylvania does, however, provide a good example of the voluntarism that came to characterize the later American religious experience. The reactions of Pennsylvania settlers to the complete separation of church and state, unusual in the colonial period but later guaranteed by the national constitution, are also of interest in the development of American religious and political thought.[6]

The concept of toleration, important for the national experience and for many of the other colonies, is of less significance for Pennsylvania. Toleration implies a concession of privileges by a controlling or dominant faction to a minority group, not the unhindered exercise of inherent rights. Pennsylvania was not founded on the principle of toleration, but of tolerance. Tolerance describes liberal attitudes toward members of other religious, national, or cultural groups, an acceptance of the right not to conform and to hold different beliefs. Although William Penn's goal was to establish, in almost absolute terms, religious liberty, with the expectation that mutual tolerance would prevail, Penn, Pennsylvanians, and contemporary observers often described conditions in the colony as "toleration," for it was the only frame of reference available in the context of eighteenth-century political theory.

Cultural pluralism, a concept occasionally advocated by some Americans since the late nineteenth century, reflects concerns alien to colonial Pennsylvanians. Cultural pluralists, who envision a tapestry of different, harmoniously coexisting cultures, are often romantic or simplistic in their lauding of "immigrant gifts" such as crafts, folk music, or new foods that enrich the basic culture but do not fundamentally alter the prevailing culture. In colonial Pennsylvania, in contrast, divergent groups joined together to create a new type of society in the wilderness. Each contributed ideas, customs, and institutions that blended together, if uneasily at times, to form the provincial culture, one that contemporaries knew was pluralistic, but rarely theorized about.

III

In recognition of the pluralism of Pennsylvania, this study attempts to be inclusive, to analyze the attitudes and behavior of colonists of all backgrounds and beliefs living throughout the province. It has, however, been pursued largely from the perspective of the overarching English culture, partly from necessity and partly from choice. Because Pennsylvania was a part of the British Empire, to which William Penn intended to transplant many aspects of English culture, a focus on "English" responses to and perceptions of the evolving society and culture is essential. And since other British colonies did not develop similar patterns, one must analyze the ways Englishmen understood and participated in the evolution of this new society in order to comprehend the uniqueness of the province. Nevertheless, because all peoples were welcomed and joined together to create a distinctive society, the responses of German, Scotch-Irish, and other Pennsylvania residents to their experiences are considered insofar as possible.

Unfortunately the source materials for this part of the study are not available to as great an extent as they are for people of English origins. Perhaps colonists from Wales, Scotland, Ireland, and the Continent corresponded less frequently with their friends in the homeland; perhaps letters are awaiting discovery in European archives. But then, few Pennsylvanians of any nationality or faith commented directly on their experiences of living in a pluralistic society. Their attitudes and behavior often must be inferred from brief references in letters or documents concerned with other matters. Official records for the province provide extensive materials relating to governmental or public concerns. Moreover, large collections of the papers of individual Pennsylvanians and for some religious groups, especially those that required regular correspondence from their missionaries or maintained close connections with their European counterparts, permit one to discern patterns. For other groups, especially some of the German sects, there is little available material. It is, however, reasonable to conclude that if immigrants of various nationalities and faiths did not find their experiences satisfactory on the whole, immigration would not have occurred on the scale that it did. Furthermore, conflict and dissension are more likely to be commented upon than are peace and harmony; silence is itself a testimony to tolerance.

Most of the material for this study, it must be admitted, has been generated by the articulate elite. Few ordinary colonists wrote letters or kept diaries that have survived. But if merchants, large landowners, politicians, and clergymen were not representative Pennsylvanians, they helped to shape the patterns of interaction and had the widest knowledge of the facts and issues involved in diversity and pluralism. Their letters, diaries, and church records therefore reveal much about the attitudes and behavior of their less articulate brethren. Moreover, the wealthy might have drafted petitions for defense, but they were signed by many others concerned about the province's welfare and ability to survive. Only upper class men might have run for office, but their campaigns appealed to men of lower status. And ministers might have reported on church affairs, but ordinary men and women filled the pews. For Pennsylvania to have developed into a pluralistic and tolerant society, a consensus was necessary.

This consensus did not come easily. William Penn prescribed novel ideas in founding his province, but his colonists discovered that it was easier to plan a pluralistic society devoted to liberty than to live in one. The interplay of ideas with reality, the evolution of new modes of thought and behavior in response to changing circumstances, and Pennsylvanians' attitudes toward their unique society constitute the main themes of this study.

CHAPTER 2

William Penn's
Ideals and Goals

W. shore Del 1681

America's first pluralistic society evolved from the colony established
by William Penn on the western shore of the Delaware River in 1681.
Although settlers of diverse ethnic and linguistic origins who professed a variety of religious beliefs and practiced different forms of
worship had been residing in the region before the organization of the
new regime,[1] the increasingly complex and unusual nature of the
province was a direct result of the ideas, and ideals, Penn articulated.

Because the Proprietor encouraged diversity and, more significantly, tolerance, these facets of provincial life became more than unthinking responses to shifts in European rivalries and the difficulties
of obtaining colonists. Penn's ideas were undeniably inconsistent, and
he sometimes compromised them to achieve pragmatic or immediate
goals; nor did he anticipate all of the practical implications of his
thoughts. Yet even without a clear vision for his colony, his ideas
concerning individual liberty of conscience and the role of the state in
religious matters, as well as his attitudes toward people of different
nationalities or beliefs, provided the foundation for the development
of Pennsylvania into a heterogeneous, and broadly tolerant, society.

I

Quakerism was among the most radical sects that sprang up in mid-seventeenth-century England. Many people in authority thought Quakers posed an imminent threat to social, political, and religious stability, for, among other manifestations of unacceptable ideas and behavior, they disrupted church services to proclaim their message, denounced the monarchy, and refused to conform to social customs that recognized class distinctions. Many early Friends suffered severely for their beliefs.

Quakerism had begun to stabilize by the time William Penn converted to its tenets in 1667, at the age of twenty-two. The extreme individualism of the early years was becoming subordinate to the structure of meetings and group discipline. The courting of persecution and martyrdom, and submission to it, were being replaced by legal challenges and political lobbying, while the hope of converting the world to Quakerism was gradually being replaced by the hope of obtaining toleration of religious dissent. Quakers had from the beginning often petitioned for relief from persecution for members of their own society; they continued to do so as circumstances required. But with the transformation of the sect, Friends broadened their demands for toleration and phrased them in more abstract terms. More precisely defined religious views, not persecution, fostered their concern about suffering for the sake of conscience.

Fundamental to Quaker religious thought was a belief that Truth had not been entirely revealed. The closely associated emphasis on the Inner Light, which enabled each person to search for and understand the will of God without the intermediaries of priests, liturgies, or sacraments, provided the basis for their emphasis on liberty of conscience and freedom from coercion in matters of faith and worship. Knowledge of God was individual and could not be judged by another. Thus, although Friends believed that they had found the way to salvation and had a responsibility to share it with others, they were also committed to a belief in the free individual quest for Truth and in its ultimate persuasiveness.[2] One of their most significant contributions to the concept of liberty of conscience was that they not only fought for their own privilege of worshiping according to their own fashion, but were also willing, even obligated by their theology, to extend this as a right to all individuals, regardless of their particular beliefs.[3]

Despite the Quaker emphasis on the equality of all individuals before God, Penn's superior education and social position were important to his recognition as a leading spokesperson for his sect, particularly in secular affairs dealing with the authority of the state.[4] The first instance of persecution for his beliefs,[5] imprisonment with others in Cork for attending a Quaker meeting,[6] brought forth his first exposition of the rights of individual conscience. Writing to the Lord President of Munster in an attempt to secure his and his fellow Quakers' release, Penn admitted that "To dissent from a Nationall sistem imposed by Authoritie renders men hereticks," but asserted that "diversitie of faith, and worships contribute not to ye Disturbance of any place" and that "morall uniformity is barely requisett" to preserve the peace. Liberty of conscience was not "riotous or Tumultuary, as by some vainly imagind"; on the contrary, freedom in religious matters offered an effective means "To improve or advantage This Country."[7]

Penn developed these themes in his subsequent writings, particularly in the pamphlets he wrote after 1670. His arguments became increasingly more sophisticated, and emphasized theological or moral justifications for toleration or liberty of conscience, constitutional arguments, and historical precedents that demonstrated the wisdom of respecting individual belief. His most important essays are those in which he argued systematically for liberty of conscience: *The Great Case of Liberty of Conscience* (written in Newgate Prison, 1670), *England's Present Interest* (1675), *An Address to Protestants of All Perswasions* (1679), and *A Perswasive to Moderation* (1686). The immediate needs of persecuted Quakers were deemphasized; Penn discussed more abstract questions and included the relief of all religious nonconformists in his pleas for toleration.[8]

Addressing his 1670 essay to the "Supream Authority of England," Penn criticized the government's harsh measures directed at Quakers and recommended indulgence for all dissenters as "not only most Christian and Rational, but Prudent also." Liberty of conscience was "not only a meer *Liberty of the Mind*, in believing or disbelieving this or that Principle or Doctrine, *but the Exercise of our selves in a visible*

Liberty of Cons ≠ only liberty to
believe or not but but meeting indep
of secular affairs
persec = illegal of immoral
∴ Anti- reason of nature

WILLIAM PENN'S IDEALS AND GOALS   15

Way of Worship." The legality of meeting for public worship extended
only "as it may refer to religious Matters, and a Life to come," that
is, to meetings "wholly independent" of secular affairs. "Imposition,
Restraint, and Persecution" included the requirement that stated doctrines be believed or denied, with penalties incurred by those who
could not conform, and extended to "any coercive Lett or Hindrance
to us, from meeting together to perform those Religious Exercises which
are according to our Faith and Perswasion."

Penn's central argument was that persecution was illegal, immoral,
and contrary to both reason and nature. When the state took upon
itself the responsibility of establishing beliefs or forms of worship, it
invaded the Divine Prerogative, set itself up as infallible, and prevented the operation of grace in each soul. The "Christian Religion
intreats all, but compels none." Enforced conformity subverted true
religion, for a person would believe or disbelieve merely out of obedience, regardless of the veracity of the tenet. "Force may make an
Hypocrite; 't is Faith grounded upon Knowledge, and Consent that makes a
Christian." The use of coercion in matters relating to conscience contradicted the nature and ends of government, which were justice, peace,
plenty, and unity. Persecution subverted liberty and property, fundamental English rights.

Penn disputed the contention that religious uniformity was essential
to maintain a government. On the contrary, civil disorders arose out
of a "Narrowness of Spirit, *in not Tolerating others to live the Freemen
God made them, in External Matters upon the Earth*, meerly upon some
Difference in Religion." He defended only religious nonconformists,
not political dissidents, for individuals were "unworthy of Protection
from the *English* Government, who seek the Ruin of it." But, he emphasized, "Contributors to the Preservation of it, (though Dissenters
in Point of Faith or Worship) are unquestionably intituled to a Protection from IT."[9]

England's Present Interest, an elucidation of Penn's interpretation of
the compact theory, Magna Carta, and the fundamental rights of liberty and property, focused on the nature of the English government.
Penn intended to "show that *Church Government* is no Essential Part of
the old *English Government*, and to disintangle Property from Opinion." The privileges granted in the great charter not only predated

Protestantism, but Christianity itself. Because dissent was not a civil crime, nonconformists could not be punished by an arbitrary deprivation of their property through fines, imprisonment, or similar measures.

Reviewing English religious history since the Reformation, Penn found that individuals had been forced to take repeated and contradictory oaths "under the Penalty of losing *Estate*, *Liberty*, and sometimes Life it self." But coercion of belief was sinful, for conscience was thereby "Debauch'd by Force, and Property toss'd up and down by the Impetuous Blasts of Ignorant Zeal, or Sinister Design." "*The sincere Promotion of general and practical religion*" was an obligation of civil authorities, but this he defined only as the Ten Commandments, the Sermon on the Mount, and other biblical teachings that guided behavior. He believed that if everyone lived a moral life in accordance with such basic tenets, peace and prosperity would come to the state.[10]

Penn's *Address to Protestants of All Perswasions* amplified his argument that morality was the basis of civil society. He argued that when "truth" became subject to human authority, most people would conform without critically evaluating the authorized opinions. Many would hold their beliefs from "*blind Obedience*" rather than from conviction if those who questioned or expressed doubt were harassed. Because people whose faith was not grounded in genuine belief might behave improperly, he proposed to "let some Plain, General and Necessary Truths be laid down in Scripture Terms, and let them be few," and offered a suggestion for reforming society and government: "*Let the Scriptures be free, Sober Opinion tolerated, Good Life cherish'd, Vice punish'd*: Away with *Imposition, Nick-Names, Animosities*, for the Lord's Sake, and let the Scripture be our *Common Creed*, and *Pious Living* the *Test of Christianity*."[11]

Concentrating on the expediency of toleration rather than on fundamental rights or the sinfulness of persecution, *A Perswasive to Moderation* represents a somewhat different line of argument. Penn declared that "worse Things have befallen Princes in Countries under *Ecclesiastical Union*, than in Places under divided Forms of Worship; and so Tolerating Countries stand to the Prince, upon more than equal Terms with *Conforming* Ones." While factors other than religion could produce social disorder, Penn insisted that, because a prince who granted liberty of conscience would be greatly beloved by his people, the state would become more secure. He advocated a balance of interests among the various churches and sects. If diverse forms of belief and worship were permitted, competition among them would lead to greater security for everyone's interests by preventing the destruction of liberties that might occur if one faction attained domination. Another advantage of tolerance was that it enlarged the pool of men eligible to hold positions of trust and honor. Penn thought that qualified persons were sometimes overlooked simply because of their nonconforming beliefs.[12] These pragmatic arguments for toleration were subsequently incorporated into the framework of Penn's colony.

Although an ardent proponent of religious toleration, Penn did not believe that liberty of conscience was absolute. He firmly believed that universally acknowledged standards of morality must be enforced by the state if people were to live together in a society. To an extent, he separated conscience ("the *Apprehension and Perswasion a Man has of his Duty to God*") and behavior: "I always premise this *Conscience* to keep within the Bounds of *Morality*, and that it be neither *Frantick* nor *Mischievous*, but a *Good Subject*, a *Good Child*, a *Good Servant*, in all the Affairs of Life."[13] Penn envisioned this foundation of civil society as Christian, and the people of such a state as Christians, although he did not hesitate to cite examples of toleration by pagans to strengthen his arguments. Implicit in his arguments for permitting conscientious dissent was an assumption that it should extend only to Christians who fell somewhere within the bounds of "orthodoxy."[14] Yet as a Quaker he should tolerate what others might call "heresy," confident that Truth would prevail by reasonable means. Demarkation of the limits of freedom of conscience was relatively abstract in the European setting, where Penn's principal concern was to obtain toleration for persecuted Christians; it became a more important question in the colony he established.

Penn did not respect equally all varieties of Christianity. There is a contradiction between his advocacy of liberty of conscience and his opposition to Roman Catholicism. In some instances, he suggested restricting the rights of English Catholics or requested concessions for Quakers or other Protestant dissenters that he would not extend to

Catholics.[15] He directed tracts to Protestants in which he urged mutual forbearance and a union of interests to prevent the spread of Catholicism.[16]

As a young man, Penn had strongly denounced the doctrines and practices of the Roman Catholic church. Like other reformers, he accused it of corrupting primitive Christianity from the simplicity of doctrine and worship established by Christ and His apostles. *"Papists, through many Generations, Received for doctrine the Precepts of Men."*[17] His main reasons for opposing the Church of Rome, however, were its persecution of dissent, its requirement of "blind obedience" from its adherents, and the spiritual—and civil—authority of the Pope. Penn had no doubt that the doctrinal and institutional structure of Roman Catholicism demanded uniformity and would permit no questioning of its teachings.[18] He therefore frequently compared Protestant establishments that oppressed dissenters with Catholic persecution of alleged heretics. He feared that the persecution of Protestants by other Protestants would encourage or provide a justification for Catholic repression of Protestants in countries where they held power. He believed it difficult, if not impossible, for Protestants to devise an argument for persecuting dissenters that could not be turned against them.[19]

Roman Catholicism was also a potential political threat to England. In an age in which religious factors often played a role in the origins of war and in alliances, there was reason to question the loyalty of subjects adhering to a faith that gave its leader civil as well as spiritual power and demanded an allegiance transcending that due their temporal ruler.[20] Penn believed that the "Principle which introduces Implicit Faith and Blind Obedience in Religion, will also introduce Implicit Faith and Blind Obedience in *Government.* . . . This is the *Fatal Mischief Popery brings with it to Civil Society,* and for which such Societies ought to beware of it, and all those that are Friends to it."[21]

Despite the fears Penn, and other Englishmen, expressed about Roman Catholicism, he recognized that "Violence and Tyranny are no Natural Consequences of *Popery,* for then they would follow every where, and in all Places and Times alike." Persecution was unknown in several countries "where that Religion is Dominant"; furthermore, "the People enjoy their Ancient and Civil Rights, a little more steadily than they have of late Times done in some *Protestant Countries nearer*

Home, almost ever since the Reformation."[22] He reminded his readers that Magna Carta had been obtained by *"Papists*, whom many think no Friends to Liberty and Property."[23]

Penn's thoughts about Roman Catholicism were inconsistent, if not confused. He once wrote that "I am by my Principle to write as well for Toleration for the Romanists,"[24] and was a close friend of the Catholic James II.[25] Nevertheless, because his first priority was to relieve Quakers' sufferings, he would on occasion compromise his demands for toleration of Catholics.[26] There was a difference, he averred, between a Quaker who refused to take a loyalty oath to the King simply because his religious beliefs precluded swearing any oath, and a Catholic who refused to take it for political reasons. Thus he could request alterations in the test laws so that Quakers could take them, but include provisions that made it impossible for Catholics to subscribe to them.[27] But despite his annoyance at accusations that Quakers were Catholics and that he was a Catholic or Jesuit in disguise,[28] he declared, "I would not be mistaken: I am far from thinking it fit, that *Papists* should be whipt for their *Consciences;* because I exclaim against the Injustice of whipping *Quakers* for *Papists;* . . . for we have Good Will to all Men, and would have none suffer for a truly *Sober* and *Conscientious Dissent* on any Hand."[29]

Penn's concern for liberty of conscience, religious toleration, and the sufferings of religious people in consequence of their beliefs led him beyond the English Channel. There he preached the message of Quakerism, lobbied rulers who required uniformity of faith or practice and tried to suppress dissent, and eventually recruited non-English immigrants for his colony. It did not matter that the people on whose behalf he worked were not Quakers, spoke a different language, and had a different culture. The issue that concerned Penn was persecution.

Penn undertook his first missionary journey to the Continent in 1671. His purposes were to meet with Dutch Quakers and to attempt to convert a group of Labadists living in Herford, Germany, to Quakerism. The most important outcome of this trip was the friendship that developed between Penn and Benjamin Furly, an Anglo-Dutch merchant living in Rotterdam, who was to play a major role in the

WP he will org
WP internat appeal   Furthy recd Gvr much dt immg
to tol R. of Poln   Col Faw Jersey

20   "A MIXED MULTITUDE"

recruitment of German, Dutch, and French emigrants to Pennsylvania.[30] Penn made two subsequent missionary journeys to Holland and the Rhineland, in 1677 and 1686. These travels were devoted not only to preaching Quaker doctrines and advocating religious toleration but also to recruiting colonists for the Quaker provinces of East and West Jersey and Pennsylvania.[31] Some of Penn's religious essays were translated into Dutch and German, and he once addressed an exhortation to return to the true spirit of Christianity specifically to *"all people in the High and Low-Dutch Nations."*[32]

In 1674 Penn wrote to the council and senate of Emden complaining of fines, imprisonment, banishment, and other forms of persecution visited upon Quakers residing in that city. Arguing that persecution of dissenters from an established church was unchristian, he pointed out that the magistrates were assuming an infallibility not unlike that for which they castigated the Church of Rome. The sectarians were "Men as well as your selves, born free, and have equal Plea to Natural and Civil common Priviledges with your selves"; their differences in opinions regarding things of another world "neither unmans nor uncivilizes them."[33]

Penn appealed to the King of Poland to grant religious toleration to the people of Danzig during his 1677 visit to the Continent. He explained the central tenets of Quakerism, informed the King that "True Religion" does not persecute, and bluntly asked for *"that speedy and effectual Relief which becometh Christian Magistrates to give to their own Sober and Christian People."*[34] Penn also wrote to the Elector Palatine during this journey, primarily to commend him for the indulgence he had granted to dissenters as both prudent and Christian. He suggested that the Elector inculcate such wise principles into his son and probable successor.[35]

Writing in behalf of Friends in Crefeld, who had been banished for their nonconformity to the Reformed religion, Penn addressed an appeal for toleration to the Prince of Orange in 1680. He declared that it was impossible to compel belief by force and unchristian to attempt to do so, and concluded with a request that, if no offenses could be proved against them "but w^t relates to Faith & worship so liberally allow'd in ye 7. provinces under thy Command, they may enjoy ye liberty of y^t their native country" and be permitted to return to their homes.[36]

Perhaps Penn's interest in people of other nations was quickened by his study of the history of dissenting movements and enforced conformity. He frequently cited precedents to prove his contention that a diversity of interests could strengthen the state and that intolerance might be a source of instability or disorder. Most of his examples illustrated religious diversity; once he indicated that cultural diversity could be a source of stability.[37] His most practical and immediate example of the prudence of toleration was contemporary Holland, "that *Bog* of the World, neither Sea nor dry Land, now the *Rival* of tallest Monarchs." Its wealth came not as a result of conquest, marriage, or other methods of building an empire, but from the industry of its people. When people were assured that their beliefs would not be questioned and that they would not be fined or otherwise lose their property as a result of religious nonconformity, they would work industriously to support themselves and their families. The nation would thereby be enriched.[38]

Penn thought that some of England's economic problems could be resolved if it adopted the more tolerant views of the Dutch. The swarms of beggars and poverty evident in England were attributable, at least in part, to the high cost of dissent and the dislocations caused by the civil wars. Because the fruits of the labors of dissenters as well as those of churchmen benefited the nation's economy, the former ought not to be discouraged or hindered.[39]

Moreover, persecution fostered emigration. Although Penn, of course, took advantage of this when settling his colony, he argued that it was in England's interest to preserve and if possible augment its population through liberal policies, for the population of a country enhanced its wealth. He was convinced that under the "antient Laws of this Kingdom," in which property rights had been carefully guarded, no English subjects were "ever tempted to transplant themselves into other Countries." On the contrary, "Strangers" oppressed in their native lands had been invited to emigrate to England. England, which had benefited from the immigration of persecuted Protestants from France and the Low Countries who had instructed Englishmen in the techniques of cloth manufacturing, could again take advantage of intolerance on the Continent. By the 1670s, however, "many whole Families of the industrious & trading subjects of this Kingdom for the preserving of their properties, & avoyding of the grivous penalties of the before mentioned [Penal] Statutes, have been induced to forsake this Kingdom, & to go, & plant y^mselves with their Estates & fortunes in other Countries."[40] Although some went to the colonies, where they might find a greater measure of toleration, Penn feared that the magnitude of this emigration would weaken England.[41]

II

The ideas that Penn had been developing began to take a more definite shape when he became involved in colonial projects, first in concert with other Quakers in West New Jersey and then with his own colonies of Pennsylvania and Delaware.[42] His policies reflect a conjunction of his ideas about the inviolable rights of conscience and the separation of church and state, his belief that government should establish and uphold basic standards of behavior or morality, ambivalent attitudes toward Roman Catholicism, and a decade of involvement with oppressed Christians of various beliefs and nationalities. Yet Penn was vague about the nature of the "holy experiment" he proposed to establish. His thoughts focused more on attracting settlers, devising a properly constituted government, and selling land than on the details of the settlement. Nevertheless, Penn's ideas, expressed in his polemical writings, promotional tracts, and letters, were the foundation upon which the colony was organized, settled, and subsequently developed.

Although one of Penn's goals in acquiring his territory was "to lay ye ffoundation of a free Colony for all Mankind, that should go thither," the Proprietor was not entirely altruistic; "Though I desire to extend religious freedom, yet I want some recompense for my trouble." Nor did he assume that settlers would have only religious motivations, for colonization offered an opportunity for poor but industrious people to improve their material condition. His mixture of motives shaped the early years of the colony's existence, and provides an explanation for some of the confusion of thought and inconsistency of policy.[43]

Penn's knowledge of the land he acquired in 1681 and 1682 was limited. Shortly after receiving his grant he assured the residents that "you shall be govern'd by laws of y^r own makeing & live a free & if you will, a sober and industreous People. I shall not usurp the right of any, or oppress his person."[44] His plan to sell large parcels of land and to reserve sizable manors for himself seems to reflect an implicit assumption, however, that his colony consisted predominantly of virgin land. His agents discovered that the settlers who had preceded them claimed much of the desirable land along the Delaware River and other streams, including the most suitable sites for the city Penn planned to establish.[45] Initially, Penn was apprehensive about the way the inhabitants would greet the change of government, and seemed to think that they might prove "hard or griping, takeing an advantage" of the new circumstances.[46] He was probably relieved at the warm welcome he was accorded upon his arrival in 1682.[47] The original residents were rarely considered in later years, except as another faction to be balanced.[48]

The pamphlets Penn authored, and other promotional writings he helped to distribute, were the most important factors involved in recruiting settlers. Advertisements informed people that there was a refuge for those suffering persecution and a place of opportunity for those willing to work. In part Penn was being pragmatic in advertising his colony, for there were other provinces, such as New Jersey and Rhode Island, in which a speculator could invest or where a Friend could be assured that his religious beliefs would be respected;[49] in addition, other colonial sponsors, particularly the Carolina proprietors, were actively searching for settlers.[50] Both this competition to sell land and his belief that emigration from England would weaken its power in Europe may have provided incentives to publicize his colony abroad.

In 1681 Penn prepared or sponsored the publication of four tracts which provided generalized descriptions of the province and its prospects for development, conditions for settlers and purchasers, and directions for obtaining passage and then establishing oneself in the colony. He was also responsible for translations of *Some Account of the Province of Pennsylvania* into Dutch and German. Translations of his 1674 letter to the Emden officials were included in the Dutch and German versions of this pamphlet. Although *Some Account* did not specifically mention his guarantee of liberty of conscience, this letter explained Penn's views about religious toleration to those unacquainted with his ideas.[51]

Pamphlets and letters by Penn and others written after they had visited or resided in the colony offered more specific information to prospective emigrants. Promotional tracts were widely distributed; in addition, some personal letters were published, while others were copied and circulated in manuscript.[52] On the Continent, Benjamin Furly seems to have taken the lead in publicizing the colony,[53] although in at least one instance Penn relied on the Quaker historian Willem Sewel to superintend a pamphlet through the Dutch press.[54] Letters from emigrants, whether or not they were intended for publication or circulation, focused on individual experiences. Writers described the Indians, the rapid improvement of the colony, and the opportunities for industrious people; they also included practical advice concerning the journey. Some mentioned that many people from Holland or German-speaking states had emigrated, and that they were welcome in the colony. Little emphasis was placed on the Proprietor's guarantee of religious toleration, although several writers mentioned the variety of religious beliefs observed in Pennsylvania.[55]

Penn appointed agents in London, Dublin, Edinburgh, Rotterdam, and elsewhere to assist him in providing information and selling land. His connections on the Continent, and in the British Isles through the organizational structure of the Society of Friends, helped to disseminate information about his province and to attract colonists from many lands.[56] Furly helped to make transportation arrangements for several emigrants from the Rhineland, while merchants in English ports assisted others to obtain passage to the colony. Penn personally interceded when he heard a rumor that a party of Swiss Mennonites might be hindered on their journey by Dutch officials.[57] He was particularly concerned with creating a favorable impression in the minds of visitors to the colony who were not Friends. Aware of the importance of informal reports received in Europe about the colony, Penn was disturbed by reports "that there is no room for any but Quakers &c[.]"[58] He repeatedly told his officials to "be kind to the people" and to aid immigrants by lending them supplies or providing other assistance.[59]

Penn recognized that publicity and generous concessions were the best means to ensure rapid land sales and colonization. He preferred to sell land in large tracts to wealthy individuals or to companies. Because

[handwritten margin note: welsh ok o/s co syol b ut grt debate Titles & quit rints]

he did not seem to give much thought to the ways in which different groups of settlers would form a unified society, he made or apparently made concessions to groups who wished to create ethnic enclaves. He seems at first to have agreed with—or at least not opposed—such proposals, but he subsequently refused to make grants in accordance with such designs.[60]

Early Welsh purchasers were particularly interested in establishing a settlement separate from their non-Welsh neighbors. Several companies were formed that, with a few other investors, purchased 40,000 acres in the province, which would then be sold in smaller parcels to their countrypeople.[61] This land was to be laid out contiguously, that "we might live together as a Civill Society to Indeavour to decide all Controversie & debates amongst o^{r}selves in a Gosbell order & not to Intangle o^{r}selves wth Lawes in an unknown Tongue, as allsoe to pserve o^r Language y^t we might ever keep Correspondence wth o^r friends in the Land of our Nativitie." Whether or not Penn accepted all these stipulations, he assured the Welsh before they left Europe that they could manage their own affairs outside of the county system. The Welsh would enforce provincial laws in their own courts with their own magistrates, and would be liable to taxation and jury service only within their own settlement. They were required to support their own representatives in the provincial assembly and council.[62] On several occasions he or his property commissioners ordered that the land be laid out contiguously, and as late as 1690 Penn agreed that, although the Welsh must be incorporated into a county, they "shall be a Seignory or Corporation of themselves."[63] However, as a result of difficulties over surveys, as well as Penn's interest in obtaining quit-rents and his modifications of the conditions under which they were assessed from the original agreements—in addition to grants to outsiders within the tentative Welsh bounds and the settlement of individual Welshmen elsewhere because of problems in obtaining secure titles within the tract—acrimonious relations developed between Penn and the leaders of the Welsh settlements.[64] Whatever the nature of his promises, Penn did not take effective measures to help the Welsh retain the unity they desired.[65]

Early Continental purchasers also thought that their lands would be laid out within a single tract where the colonists could maintain the language and customs of their homelands. When several Quakers from Crefeld purchased land in the colony, Benjamin Furly wrote out each deed separately, but promised, as Penn's agent, that the land would be surveyed in a single unit so that the emigrants would not be scattered among the English colonists.[66] Similarly, Penn promised that 18,000 of the 25,000 acres purchased by the German Society, or Frankfort Company, in 1683 would be laid out in a single tract called "New Franconia."[67] The company apparently later received some form of written guarantee that its land would be located in one block, provided that thirty families settled there within a year. Francis Daniel Pastorius, the company's agent, urged the company to send over the requisite colonists, "that we High-Germans may maintain a separate little province, and thus feel more secure from all oppression."[68]

The new conditions were more difficult to fulfill than those of the original contract, and were a source of contention between Penn and his German-speaking colonists.[69] Penn only reluctantly assigned land to the German and Dutch purchasers, and eventually combined the lands held by the Frankfort Company and the Crefelders into one "German Township."[70] Germantown was chartered as a borough, but its legal status, especially its relation to the county system of taxation, judicature, and representation in the provincial legislature, was imprecisely defined. Within a decade these settlers had lost even token isolation and control over their own affairs.[71]

The owner of a vast amount of real estate, Penn tried to sell it rapidly in large quantities. Often conditions were attached to require the purchaser to settle a certain number of colonists or tenants upon it within a fixed period of time, which could be an efficient method of disposing of land and peopling the country. By the time Penn arrived in his colony for the first time, 875,000 acres had been sold, and he thought there were approximately 4000 inhabitants.[72] Nevertheless, although he continued to sell land to people from various parts of Europe, he does not seem to have promised isolation after the confusion that occurred during the early years of his venture with the Welsh and Crefeld settlers and the Frankfort Company.[73]

Penn was enthusiastic about the success of his recruitment policies. He recognized that he was acquiring "people of all sorts of nations &

perswasions,"[74] yet he tended to act as though the colony were settled by Englishmen alone. He does not appear to have thought clearly about the implications of his efforts to recruit alien immigrants or the motivations people might have for emigrating. Since few other colonial promoters had attempted to tap non-English sources for prospective settlers, and the efforts of Sweden and Holland to encourage their subjects to emigrate to their colonies had produced meager results, Penn probably wondered about the success of his activities. He seems not to have realized that security of property might be as important an attraction to the colony as liberty of conscience.

Thus in 1682, after studying several of Penn's proposals for the provincial constitution, Furly commented on several issues "For the Security of Foreigners." His primary concern was with the property of aliens who died before they could be naturalized. If their property escheated to the Proprietor, as in England it would escheat to the King, Furly proposed that Penn freely restore it to the rightful heirs. He also suggested that purchase of land and subscription to the constitution be considered sufficient to guarantee an alien's right to his property; that thousand-year leases be granted, renewable to heirs who were aliens; or that Penn post bond to pay heirs the value of land declared forfeit for want of naturalization.[75]

In the early drafts of his frame of government and proposed conditions for settlers, Penn was vague about the meanings of the terms freeman and citizen and the differences between naturalization and denization, which he did not always use according to their legal meanings.[76] He defined freemen—those "capable of electing or being elected representatives of the people"—by property qualifications alone. There was a proviso that freemen be inhabitants, but not that they be British subjects.[77] Property holdings in the colony and pledges of fidelity to the King and to Penn defined freemanship in the Great Body of Laws, approved by the first provincial assembly.[78] Not until the 1696 frame of government were those who had the right to vote or to serve in office required to be "free Denizens of this government" who had resided in the province for two years.[79]

Naturalization was one of the first issues considered on Penn's arrival in the colony. At the first meeting of the assembly, Swedish, Finnish, and Dutch residents petitioned the governor "to make them as free as other Members of this Province, and that their Lands might be entailed upon them and their Heirs for ever[.]"[80] A naturalization act passed the following day. Recognizing that some of the inhabitants and other potential immigrants were "Forreigners, & so not Freemen, according to yᵉ Acceptation of yᵉ Law of England," a status that might prove detrimental to these men's "Estates and Traffick" as well as retard the colony's economic development, the legislature declared that all resident aliens who owned property and who would promise allegiance to the King and obedience to Penn within three months "shall be held & reputed Freemen of yᵉ Province & Counties aforesᵈ, in as ample & full a manner as any Person residing therein." The religious beliefs of those who wished to be naturalized were not questioned. Aliens who subsequently settled in the colony and requested freemanship were to make similar declarations before a county court and would be granted the same privilege on the payment of twenty shillings; there was no residency requirement.[81] In March 1683 this law was declared fundamental, not to be "Altered, Diminished, or Repealed in whole or in part," except with the consent of the governor and six-sevenths of the assembly and council.[82]

The revised frame of government of 1683 included a provision, added perhaps as a result of Furly's recommendations,[83] to protect aliens' estates. Penn guaranteed that foreign land purchasers who died prior to naturalization would not suffer the escheat of their property. Land would descend to their relations "In as free and ample manner to all intents and purposes" as if the alien had been naturalized. This provision, which applied to aliens who purchased land but did not emigrate as well as to those resident in Pennsylvania, was included "for the satisfaction and encouragement of all aliens."[84]

Penn was an early proponent of a uniform naturalization law for the colonies, for it might help to encourage immigration. He suggested that aliens declared freemen by an act of assembly in any province be granted all of the rights and privileges of Englishmen anywhere in the Empire, except for acting as the master or commander of a trading vessel.[85] A simple, general naturalization procedure was essential, for "'tis the Interest of england to improve & thicken her Colonys wᵗʰ people not her own, but as they become hers by Settling in those Colonys or Plantations."[86]

Penn tried to establish liberal procedures in his own colony, but

was thwarted by English officials. In 1700 Pennsylvania enacted two
laws to benefit aliens. A naturalization act declared everyone who had
resided in the province or territories prior to Penn's grant to be "fully
and completely naturalized." Like the earlier statute, religious beliefs
formed no part of the qualifications. Later immigrants who promised
loyalty to the Crown and to the Proprietor could be naturalized by
the governor, again without residing in the colony for any fixed period. Within the colony, those who took advantage of the law were
entitled to all of the privileges of natural-born subjects except those
expressly denied to aliens in the plantations by act of Parliament.[87]
The assembly also enacted a law to safeguard property owners and
their heirs.[88] The Crown rejected both acts, the former because "the
proprietor hath no such power [to naturalize] by his grant,"[89] the latter because a clause it included "for the satisfaction and encouragement of aliens coming into this province" extended to aliens the same
protection they would have if naturalized.[90]

Property rights were the most important consideration involved in
naturalization.[91] Penn had long believed that security of property was
a fundamental English right. Because the invasion of property rights
through the operation of penal laws imposed upon dissenters was one
of the important principles upon which he advocated toleration, he
recognized his colonists' concerns, once it became evident that many
might not be British subjects. While he reassured aliens after the repeal of the 1700 law that "they are safe from me & mine by my
charter," he did try to obtain naturalization or denization for a few of
them in England.[92] Rumors that their titles might be questioned had
led a group of Dutch and German colonists to petition the assembly
for clarification of their rights even before this law was repealed,[93] but
the assembly did nothing until 1709, when it naturalized several long-
time residents. They were required to prove that they were Protestants, probably in conformity with a 1709 English law which eased
naturalization procedures but applied only to Protestants. This law, a
private act that named each individual who would benefit from its
provisions, was allowed to stand.[94]

Penn gave more thought to the religious foundations of his province
than to problems that might arise from a heterogeneous population or
to the question of how various ethnic, linguistic, and religious groups

could live together peacefully. Yet despite his concern with toleration and the persecution of religious dissenters, he did not emphasize religious freedom in his promotional tracts. His public writings concentrated on the practical, economic, or imperial aspects of colonization rather than on the more idealistic ones evident in some of his private correspondence. He was aware of the appeal his colony had to dissenters and that persecution could be a motive for emigration, and once admitted that he "plead[s for toleration of Friends in Ireland] against my interest, for ye severitys of thos parts encrease the plantation & improvem^t of these."[95]

Penn's immediate goal was to secure the rights and privileges of Englishmen to his fellow Quakers, "not that I would lessen ye Civil Liberties of others, because of their perswasion."[96] Pennsylvania was to be more than a Quaker colony where other religious practices were tolerated. Freedom of conscience with equal civil rights for all, not a more limited toleration, was Penn's goal.[97] The royal charter contained only one religious provision. Added at the insistence of the Bishop of London, it stated that if twenty inhabitants petitioned for an Anglican clergyman, and the bishop sent one to the colony, he must be permitted to "reside within the said pvince, without any deniall or molestacon whatsoever."[98] Given Penn's well-known views, this clause was superfluous.

Guaranteeing the fundamental right to worship God in whatever manner each individual thought most appropriate occupied Penn's thoughts as he attempted to create a frame of government. In a 1680 draft of what he called the "fundamentall constitutions" of Pennsylvania, he decreed as the "first fundamentall of the Goverment of my Country, that every Person that does or shall reside therein shall have and enjoy the Free Profession of his or her faith and exersise of worsip towards God, in such way and manner As every Person shall in Conscience beleive [sic] is most acceptable to God." Penn's justification for his liberal grant of liberty of conscience reflects the concerns he had expressed in his polemical writings as well as his recognition that "this unpeopled Country can never be peopled if there be not due encouragement given to Sober people of all sorts to plant," for few would venture into the wilderness unless guaranteed that they and their posterity would not suffer for their beliefs.

Concerned that the "Christian Liberty" he granted might degenerate into "Licentiousness,"[99] Penn advocated enactment of laws that
would restrain Pennsylvanians' behavior, if not their ideas, within
certain boundaries. While he thought that religion in a generalized
form should be at the core of all societies, he recognized distinctions
between civil behavior and religious belief. Thus, laws were formulated to regulate marriage, forbid drunkenness and the drinking of
healths, ban dueling, prohibit "rude and riotous sports," and otherwise encourage what most would consider to be proper or acceptable
behavior. Other laws, such as the one requiring the use of numbers
instead of the common "Heathen" names (e.g., Eleventh Month for
January) for the reckoning of time, mixed Quaker religious beliefs
more closely with the state.[100]

Although in England Penn had advocated religious liberty and the
removal of governmental constraints on faith and practice, limitations
on complete freedom of belief appeared when colonial laws began to
be framed. According to the Laws Agreed Upon in England, only
individuals who believed "the one almighty and eternal God, to be
the creator, upholder and ruler of the world" and also held themselves
obliged in conscience "to live peaceably and justly in civil society"
would be protected in their religious observances and not compelled
to attend any particular form of worship.[101] Atheists were thus barred
from the colony. A further restriction was also placed upon conscience: "according to the good example of the primitive christians,
and for the ease of the creation, . . . people shall abstain from their
common daily labour" on the first day of the week.[102] This law could
be injurious to sabbatarians and Jews, both because of infringements
on their religious observances and the fines that could be imposed for
violating the law.[103] But the most significant constraint was the requirement that voters and members of the assembly and council "profess faith in Jesus Christ."[104] When this law was reenacted by the first
assembly, this generalization was defined to include the belief that He
is "the son of God, the Saviour of the world."[105] It should be noted,
however, that despite the limitation of the franchise to Christians,
Roman Catholics were entitled to political participation.

Additional restrictions on liberty of conscience were imposed during the two years in which the Crown governed the colony directly

only God?→
veto in B+V

through Governor Benjamin Fletcher, following the temporary abrogation of Penn's charter in 1692. The assembly petitioned Fletcher to reenact the laws concerning liberty of conscience and the qualifications of officeholders. Although he consented, he insisted that, under the terms of his royal commission, assemblymen must subscribe the declarations required of dissenters by the English Toleration Act of 1689. Officeholding would now be specifically limited to trinitarian Protestants, yet assemblymen objected not to the content of the tests nor to restrictions on officials' beliefs, but to Fletcher's insistence that subscription be made by oath rather than by affirmation.[106]

The frame of government William Markham promulgated for the colony in 1696 after its restoration to Penn retained the restriction on officeholding to those who could conform to the beliefs required by the Toleration Act, although electors were no longer explicitly required to be Christians. The primary purpose of Markham's frame of government was to reestablish proprietary government. Liberty of conscience and toleration were not mentioned; the only religious matter included was the formulation of affirmations to be taken by various officials who would not swear oaths.[107]

The first statute enacted upon Penn's return to the province defined and guaranteed liberty of conscience. Once again, inhabitants were required only to believe in God and consider themselves conscientiously obliged to live peaceably under civil government. Perhaps reflecting the religious disputes that had already occurred in the colony, this law stated that "if any person shall abuse or deride any other for his or her different persuasion and practice in matter of religion, such person shall be looked upon as a disturber of the peace and be punished accordingly."[108] The English attorney general, scandalized by a law that paid "no regard . . . to the Christian religion" and gave Quakers greater privileges than they were allowed in England, successfully recommended its disallowance.[109] The qualifications for political participation were also liberalized. Penn retained the provision of Markham's frame that did not explicitly require voters to profess Christianity, but, more importantly, extended this freedom to candidates for elective office.[110]

The 1701 frame of government, under which Pennsylvania would be governed until the Revolution, included a declaration of liberty of

Still 1701 re printed.
of freedom of Cons
All can hold off incl Calla.
Assembly more rest
Trinity
O T A N T
& No RC
h all

conscience to all who believed in God that was very similar to earlier
formulations. There was one significant restriction: for the first time,
the constitution explicitly stated that only Christians could serve in
the executive or legislative branches of the government. Nevertheless
all Christians, including Roman Catholics, were capable of holding
office, "notwithstanding their other perswasions and Practices in Point
of Conscience & Religion," for the only tests to be subscribed were
those of allegiance to the Crown and fidelity to the Proprietor.[111]
Slightly contradictory was the provision that the "Qualifications of
Electors & Elected, and all other matters and things Relating to Elections" remain as established by laws formulated in the previous session of the legislature.[112]

In the absence of Penn, and prior to repeal of the liberal statutes of
1700, the Pennsylvania assembly made its final statements on the extent of religious freedom acceptable in the colony. They represent a
more restricted sphere for liberty of conscience than one would expect
from Penn's earlier, more abstract writings on the subject. Unlike the
laws he helped to frame, they were permitted to remain in force.
Colonists not only had to believe in the Trinity, but were also to
"acknowledge the Holy Scriptures of the Old and New Testament to
be given by divine inspiration."[113] Officials were required to fulfill
the religious qualifications stated in the 1689 Toleration Act, although
affirmations could be substituted for oaths. Catholics were thereby
barred from public office.[114]

Legal restraints on conscience, however, seem to have applied only
to men who hoped to attain positions of profit or honor. The beliefs
of prospective settlers were not scrutinized; non-Christians were neither forbidden to settle in nor expelled from the colony. Although in
one tract advocating toleration Penn had argued that religious liberty
and the requirement that officials conform to certain beliefs were in-
congruent,[115] it appears that he was forced to acquiesce in the distinction between personal and political rights in his province.

Penn's role in the transformation of liberty of conscience into religious
tolerance is ambiguous. Despite his pleas for the rights of men and
women in many lands to worship in the way each thought most appropriate to the will of God, he seemed unable to understand that it

might be possible, in good conscience, not to believe in God. And while he knew that non-Christian societies could be stable and properly governed, he was unwilling to allow Pennsylvania to be such.

He did help to frame the Laws Agreed Upon in England, the statutes of 1682 and 1683, and the 1701 frame of government, all of which simultaneously proclaimed almost complete freedom of conscience and restricted officeholding. Only in 1700 were statutes enacted that did not require voters or candidates for office to be Christians. Nevertheless, under none of these laws was "Christian" further defined to eliminate adherents of certain tenets or to require specific beliefs. Those restrictions were enacted when Penn was not present in his colony and exerted little influence over legislation.

It is unclear why Penn did not object to the 1705/6 law establishing religious qualifications for both settlers and officials that, if enforced, could have severely circumscribed freedom of conscience. Perhaps he feared that he would again lose the colony if it did not conform in law to some of the boundaries of English toleration, especially concerning the rights of Roman Catholics. Yet although he disagreed with them on many points of doctrine and worship, he did extend a measure of toleration toward them.[116] And perhaps the frequent inclusion of Christianity as a qualification for enjoying certain rights and privileges was intended to answer the doubts some people still had at the end of the seventeenth century whether Quakers were Christians.[117]

Penn's idealism and devotion to the concept of religious freedom were, however, intertwined with his particular concern about the welfare of his coreligionists. Central to his thought was the idea that, in planting a colony, he was establishing a refuge for Quakers. Others were welcome, but when the conflicting demands of conscience required lines to be drawn, they would be in favor of Quaker tenets or to safeguard Quaker privileges. Penn's insistence upon the substitution of an affirmation for an oath is perhaps the clearest issue in which the consciences of Christians diverged; he supported the Quaker view. For why should they be, after all, "dissenters, & worse than that in our own Country."[118]

Despite ambiguities, blind spots, and occasional contradictions, Penn's thoughts concerning religious liberty played an important part in laying the foundation for an extremely heterogeneous society. His belief that conscience should not be restrained and that persecution was wrong led him to work for the relief of oppressed Christians, primarily but not exclusively Protestants, in England and abroad. Thus, when he needed colonists to people his territory, he turned to those persecuted for the sake of conscience but also advertised his province in more secular terms. Whatever the precise nature of the appeal to each individual who chose to emigrate to Pennsylvania, the province grew rapidly, adding greater variety to the pre-1681 settlers and soon overwhelming them.

Penn never seems to have considered how individuals of different faiths, languages, and nationalities could live together peacefully. He seems to have thought initially of establishing semi-autonomous "patroonships," but his plans were vague. And he does not seem to have thought beyond the formulation that good men would make good laws: "Though you are not of one Judgement in Religion, you are of one ffamily in Civilis, and should Aime at ye publick good," he once lectured the council.[119] He expected sects ready to persecute when they came to power in the European setting to live in harmony, or at least in restrained competition. Penn always seemed surprised that not all of the colonists shared his ideals, and that social, religious, and political harmony was often elusive.

CHAPTER 3

Penn's Province,
1681–1718

[handwritten marginalia: 1681–1718 / Little direct or indirect control → rapid growth / 1700 21000 / 1717 36,000]

The intertwining of ideas and reality is a dominant theme during the years between the founding of Pennsylvania in 1681 and William Penn's death in 1718. Because Penn spent very little time in his colony and exerted only indirect or ineffective control over it, and because he did not delineate the process by which his colonists could live together peacefully, the ramifications of his ideas became clear only when emigrants of various backgrounds began to settle in the province. Pennsylvanians themselves played the most decisive role in determining how the various components would coalesce into a society. If many shared Penn's ideas concerning toleration and pluralism, others did not. Contentiousness is evident as Pennsylvanians groped for a practical meaning for his ideology.

This period was one of rapid population growth. An estimated 21,000 people had settled in the colony by 1700; perhaps as many as 30,000 were living in the province by the time the migrations from northern Ireland and Germany began in 1717.[1] Immigrants added to the ethnic and religious diversity that characterized the colony before its grant to Penn. Yet despite the widening variety of national and linguistic groups present, people tended to identify both themselves and their neighbors in religious terms, a mode of categorization which remained

[handwritten marginalia at top: "Transf Crown to WP in Pa smooth / Act union of Del & Pa / immediately / 3 Co / colony"]

dominant throughout the colonial period. Conflicts in the first decades were primarily religious, and arose out of the need to accommodate attitudes and behavior to the novel situation of living in a colony dedicated to religious freedom and equal civil rights for all. There were divisions within various religious denominations as well as the more fundamental split between what might broadly be termed "church" and "sect." Quaker and Anglican elites, the principal antagonists, argued about a combination of religious and political issues within the political system. Some of the most crucial questions, including the qualifications of those who might legitimately exercise political power and the formulation of laws and policies when the conscientious beliefs of participants collided, may be traced to Penn's ideas about the nature of his colony. Resolution of these issues would determine the future course the colony would take.

I

The formal transfer of government from the Crown to William Penn was accomplished with ease. Local magistrates gave Penn ceremonial possession of the territory upon his arrival in New Castle in October 1682. Addressing the assembled people, Penn guaranteed their "Spiritual and Temporal Rights, Liberty of Conscience and Civil Freedoms"; he expected only "Sobriety and loving Neighbour-hood" in return.[2] He believed that "ye Union of two distinct People that are under one Governor is both most desireable in it self & beneficial to ye Public." Therefore one of the first acts of the assembly convened to ratify his proposed frame of government and the Laws Agreed Upon in England was an act of union between Pennsylvania and the Lower Counties, or Delaware, that made them "Equally Sharers in Benefits & Priviledges" under one set of laws.[3] The exact composition of this assembly is unknown, although it did include representatives from both the province and the territories.[4] Once the government was established, representation in the assembly, and in the council while it was an elective office, was by county, with each assigned an equal number. For the first few decades both Pennsylvania and Delaware were composed of three counties, thus creating a balance of power between the two sections of Penn's province.[5]

The political union proved unsatisfactory. One Pennsylvanian thought that the "unruly Spirited people of the Territories" were "diminishers of our just p'veledges and underminers of our happynesse and quiet"; the act of union had opened "Pandora's box" and "our innumerable miseries flew out."[6] Councillors from the Lower Counties resented accusations that they were "against friends" or "ringleaders of the rable" whenever they attempted to assert the rights and privileges granted by the constitution. They professed themselves satisfied with Penn's government and promised obedience "notwithstanding the many provocations we have had from them of the Province,"[7] but there were limits to their patience. In 1691, Delaware representatives boycotted the assembly in a dispute over the choice Penn had offered his colonists of lodging the executive part of the government in a single deputy governor or in a five-man commission of state. The assemblies reunited in 1692, but each section had a separate executive who controlled the appointment of officials and local matters. The act of union was not reenacted under Benjamin Fletcher's royal government, although the area was governed as one province. Because all laws not reenacted presumably became invalid as a result of the royal interlude, questions about the continuance of the original legislation arose following Penn's return to the colony. Representatives from both sections were reluctant to pass a new act of union without attaching conditions each thought would protect its own interests.[8] Finally, Penn appended to the 1701 frame of government a provision that "If the Representatives of the Province and Territories shall not hereafter agree to Joyn together in Legislation," they could each have a distinct assembly.[9] The two assemblies began to meet separately in 1704.[10]

The issues at stake were primarily political and economic. The rapid growth of the northern section would eventually require the creation of new counties, which would reduce the influence of the geographically restricted lower counties. Meanwhile, rivalry developed over control of the Delaware River. The exposed lower portion felt the need for defensive measures, while the pacifistic and more secure northern portion did not.[11] Religious and ethnic differences played a role, although their importance has been exaggerated.[12] Tensions between old and new settlers because of ethnic differences were rare,

[handwritten marginalia: Narrow Quaker vers. H / Territorio v. counties / all qualif of all faiths / No relig qualif]

while the contention between Quakers and non-Quakers occurred both within the province and territories as well as between them.

The problems that would emerge within Pennsylvania over political matters were foreshadowed in the first assembly. A Quaker was selected as speaker by a one-vote majority only because "Two of ye other side y^t were not Friends" were absent.[13] Yet while the people of the province were primarily English and Quaker and those of the territories were primarily non-English and non-Quaker, men of Swedish descent were selected to represent the province and Quakers were among those chosen by the territories.[14] Penn, although somewhat apprehensive about the precarious balance of power—for non-Quakers might hinder the creation of the type of society he envisioned—nevertheless insisted that qualified men of all backgrounds and faiths be elected or appointed to public office.[15]

The composition of the provincial government and the functions it was to serve reveal some of the ambiguities in Penn's thought. He rejected the notion that adherence to rigidly defined religious tenets was an essential consideration in the selection of officeholders, although he did agree with royal officials and his legislators that certain minimal beliefs were necessary. He emphasized repeatedly that one of his purposes was to guarantee to Quakers the religious, civil, and political rights denied to them in England. Because many Quakers had emigrated in order to live under statutes more congenial to their religious beliefs, they should participate in the enactment and enforcement of laws. At the same time, Penn was unwilling to hinder non-Quaker participation; his principles demanded unrestricted political privileges. He also justified impartiality on pragmatic grounds, for "this hath been often flung at us, (vizt) If you Quakers had ~~it in your~~ power, none should have a part in ye Governm^t but those of y^r own way."[16]

Penn did more than advocate equality. He appointed men of diverse backgrounds and persuasions to fill official positions, and also encouraged diversity in elective positions. Such policies would "Ballance factions, not . . . Irritate nor give Strength to them."[17] A "union in civils" would benefit the colony, especially in times of danger when

Anglican oppos. as loss of Eng privil dom

fear of loss of Quaker control

Friends' principles might be a hindrance to proper government and dangerous to the colony's continued existence.[18]

Colonists were ambivalent about the wisdom of Penn's grant of equal civil and religious privileges to all settlers. Attempts to exclude adherents of certain tenets from political positions contributed to the contentious politics of the period. According to some Quaker leaders, most of the earliest settlers had been Friends, who had endured the hazards of the wilderness "to be ffree of her (ye churches) power & out of her reach . . . not to make Colonys for her, but from her, for our Selves," and therefore enacted laws agreeable to their beliefs. Quakers took credit for the rapid development of the province, and thought their beliefs should be respected by others who came later for allegedly more worldly motives.[19] Many thought that Pennsylvania offered an opportunity to demonstrate to the world the propriety of Friends' government, and were reluctant to share power. Others, including the Philadelphia Monthly Meeting, feared that the persecution and oppression that Friends had experienced in both England and the New World would be extended to Pennsylvania if another religious group gained control.[20]

Nevertheless, not all Friends objected to sharing power. They agreed with Penn that "the Quakers desires no more priviledges, than they are willing they [Anglicans] should enjoy," although they resented attempts by those who did not understand this to wrest the government out of their hands.[21] Robert Turner, one of Penn's supporters, informed him of the "great discuntent" in the province occasioned by a failure to follow his advice to distribute power equitably: "our ffriends for this severull years—in ye province: I observe doe not put up or proposse—Either dutch—sweed. ffeene [Finn] or any other person not of our perswation: Baptist Endpendent-Presbitterian—or church of England man—(but what wee did force this Election) wch gives occation of mutteringe & discuntent—& workes a gainst our good & Quiet." He recommended, "lett us not strive for all. least we losse all[.]"[22]

Just as some Quakers objected to Penn's insistence that political power be shared, many Anglicans objected to a government dominated by "Dissenters and apostates." Resenting the loss of the exclusive political privileges they had in England and the extension of various rights and privileges to those unqualified by English standards, they tried to have laws favoring or accommodating "dissenters" repealed and attempted to convince the Crown to revoke Penn's charter. Their complaints in part reflected an extension of the virulent English anti-Quaker sentiment of the period. Active opposition increased following the 1695 organization of the first Anglican church in the colony, and was particularly strong between 1700 and 1705.[23] Although no colonial Anglican phrased his opinion as succinctly as Penn's second non-Quaker deputy governor, John Blackwell, who contended that Quakers held "Principles un-suitable to civill Governm' & polity,"[24] most would agree that they were unfit to govern. Complaints involved Quaker beliefs and practices with respect to oaths and affirmations, the operation of the judicial system, the assembly's refusal to establish a militia or to contribute to imperial defense, an alleged condoning of piracy and other illegal trading activities, and innovations in social, political, and religious affairs. Anglicans disparaged the civil and religious freedoms Penn guaranteed, and hoped for closer English supervision "that we may Injoy the liberties of English Subjects & be Governed by the laws of England."[25]

The extreme hostility in Anglican–Quaker relations gradually diminished in the early eighteenth century. While tensions never completely disappeared and could easily be brought to the surface, each party came to accept the other's right to participate in public life. Challenges to the concept that power did not inherently belong to one particular category of colonists decreased. As Pennsylvanians considered issues other than religion in forming coalitions, compromise became possible.[26] The growing factionalism of Quaker politics between proprietary and antiproprietary interests helped to break down the unity that the founders had hoped to achieve among religion, society, and government. By the early eighteenth century some Friends expressed reservations as to whether their principles were consistent with political participation.[27] Meanwhile, perhaps recognizing the futility of the project, Anglicans and others gradually abandoned their goal of ejecting Quakers from office. Accepting the permanence of pluralism, they began to unite with men who held similar political or secular ideals despite religious differences.[28]

In 1710 the Philadelphia Yearly Meeting became directly involved in provincial politics. Dissatisfied with the constant wrangling in the

Oaths refused = practice for N.T.
swearing perhaps → lying
God as witness = presumptions

42   "A MIXED MULTITUDE"

assembly, its failure to perform its functions, and the disruption that
resulted, it requested Isaac Norris to prepare an essay advocating the
election of a new set of assemblymen.[29] Shortly before the election,
the Yearly Meeting epistle advised that Friends eligible to vote "do it
for such of any p^{r}swation who come up nearess to those good Qualification[s]" desirable in officials. That is, they should select men who
feared and loved God, aimed at "righteousness truth & peace," and
were concerned about the interests of the community rather than their
own advancement.[30] This had been Penn's argument for years.

II

Isaac Norris shrewdly analyzed the inherent contradictions in Pennsylvania's political structure. Noting that "Wee are a Mixt people who
all claim aright to use their own way," he found that many Friends
had concluded, "Wee must Either be Independant & Intirely by ourselves, Or If mixt; partiall to our own Opinion & not allow ye liberty
to Others . . . we desire from y^m, Or be as thou [Penn] Us'd to
Express it Dissenters in our Own country."[31] The conflicting demands of conscience resulting from the heterogeneity of the Pennsylvania population provided the catalyst for severe tensions in both society and government during the province's early years. Examination
of some of the specific issues over which compromise was difficult to
achieve reveals the attitudes of churchmen and sectarians toward the
world and toward each other, and the slow development of accommodations among divergent interests.

One of the principal conflicts arising from Penn's guarantee of liberty
of conscience involved the use and validity of oaths and affirmations.
Although the debate was carried on primarily by Quakers and Anglicans, the issue had broader significance, for its resolution would affect
people of many denominations who settled in the province.
   The dilemma arose when Quakers, who could neither tender nor
subscribe oaths, took their places in the political and judicial systems.
Firm adherents of the New Testament prohibition on their use, Friends
believed that oaths originated in man's fall from righteousness. "We
dare not swear because we dare not Lye," while those whose con-

[handwritten margin notes: promise to tell truth / not oath & punish for perjing / promise of fidelity to Crown / Prop on who oath]

sciences did not forbid lying would have few qualms about forswear-
ing. Moreover, it was presumptuous to call God as a witness to man's
trivial affairs.[32]

Penn's instructions to the commissioners who preceded him to the
colony directed "That all Evidence or Engagements be without Oaths,
thus I. A. B. doe Promise in the Sight of God & them that heare me
to speake the Truth, the whole Truth and nothing but the whole
Truth A B."[33] Early laws stated that "in all courts all persons of all
persuasions may freely appear in their own way, and according to
their own manner," although the laws enacted to regulate the testimony of witnesses provided only for promises to speak the truth. Severe penalties were imposed for perjury.[34] Nevertheless oaths were
not forbidden, and "as early as in [16]83, when an Oath was desir'd
of such as could Swear, an Oath was given."[35] Few protested against
this deviation from English customs until after 1695, probably because the relatively small number of people who might demand an
oath lacked the wealth and prestige needed to challenge the Quaker-
dominated government.[36]

An English statute of 1696 prohibited affirmations in giving evidence in criminal cases, serving on juries, and qualifying for office.
Although it did not extend to the colonies,[37] Pennsylvanians hastened
to declare in the 1696 frame of government that all persons conscientiously opposed to swearing who would subscribe to the provisions of
the 1689 Toleration Act would be entitled to qualify by affirmation.[38]
Some colonists objected to Quaker practices that were contrary to the
English law,[39] while royal officials entered the contest after a provincial act in 1698 exempted nonswearers from provisions of the 1696
Navigation Act requiring oaths from certain officials.[40]

Passage of two affirmation laws in 1700 provided the catalyst for a
debate over oaths and affirmations that raged sporadically until 1725.
One act provided new forms of attestation that, with the promises of
fidelity to the Crown and the Proprietor required by provincial laws,
would fully qualify public officials and jurors. Magistrates unopposed
to oaths were expressly permitted to administer them to individuals
free to take them; such oaths were deemed the act of that magistrate
alone, although they were considered as valid as if done by the entire
court.[41] Thus magistrates who objected to swearing could remain on

the bench, a compromise not all Quaker officials proved willing to accept.[42] The other statute declared that witnesses appearing "to testify their knowledge . . . in any court or before any lawful authority" could "deliver in their evidence by solemnly promising to speak the truth." Penalties were provided for "willful falsehood."[43] Similar laws were enacted in 1705/6, 1710/11, 1715, 1718, and 1724.[44]

The first four affirmation laws generated the most controversy. Questions involving the qualifications of those who could legitimately exercise political and judicial power, infringements upon religious beliefs, security of liberty and property, and the purposes for which the colony had been founded came to the fore. The motives of each party were questioned; each thought its opponent was attempting to monopolize the government for its own ends. Added to the theoretical arguments over principles was the very practical problem of enforcing laws and securing justice.

Anglicans believed that affirmations were insufficient protection for their "lives liberties Or Estats." They also questioned the allegiance of unsworn officials to the Crown. Affirmation laws attempted to "establish Quakerism" in the province and to "destroy the present settlement, both ecclesiastical and civil." The phrasing of Pennsylvania's acts was also objectionable, for it did not conform to English usage. Churchmen argued that "the equity of the cause required the same liberty for men of other persuasions" to testify "according to their own way and profession." They recognized that Penn's appointment of non-Quakers to the bench was intended to provide witnesses with a choice in their manner of giving evidence and would enable prospective jurors to be sworn, but found Quakers "obstinate" in their refusal to remain on the bench while oaths were administered.[45]

On several occasions Anglicans obstructed the judicial system by refusing to act in their positions, forcing the courts to stand adjourned. Some refused to accept commissions as magistrates or to execute the dedimus used to qualify officials, while others refused to serve on juries. Hysterical reports of "the great deficiency of Quaker Government" reached England. Justice was delayed, prisons were full, and the courts "have Condemned People to Death by Judges that are Quakers, and by a Jury of Quakers, and neither Judges nor Jury under any Oath."[46]

Quakers interpreted Anglican efforts to repeal affirmation laws as a naked attempt to remove them from all official positions and to gain control of the colony for themselves. Churchmen had "no other End than to seduce us into Anarchy & trample upon ye Queen's Peaceable Subjects."[47] Friends questioned the qualifications of their opponents, believing that "such as have neither Morals nor Understanding sufficient to recomend them to the seats of Judicature must . . . be let in to keep up a show of Administring Justice." It was unfair that "those who have no ffreehold are made to pass on Juries Upon the Estates & Liberties of the people Whilst the ffreeholders & adventurers who made this a Country are layd aside[.]"[48] Their adversaries had "Sinister ends" and used the disputes over oaths as "Skreens to the most abominable Wickedness."[49]

Quakers also argued for the affirmation on pragmatic grounds. They accused their opponents of exaggerating their numbers and influence, for it was indeed difficult to find a sufficient number of men who could swear oaths, especially in Chester and Bucks Counties where Friends formed a majority in the early years. Crime might go unpunished if oaths were required and the only witnesses conscientiously opposed swearing.[50] If those who could not swear were excluded from juries, "they should almost wholly consist of Swedes & other foreigners in whom there would be a much less security."[51] Provincial Secretary James Logan anticipated that Quakers would be "reduced to a real Slavery for if in all p^{ts} of Such a Govm^t as this, none but Ch: men are to judge us."[52] Colonists reminded Penn and English Friends that Baptists and other settlers also had scruples about oaths, and reported that "the Affirmation is Lookt upon by ye Generallity of the People, who are not of our Perswasion, to be as binding as an Oath."[53]

Pennsylvania statutes that received royal approbation were similar to British laws, which had been gradually liberalized. A 1718 law to improve the administration of justice, which allowed Quakers to use the affirmation in criminal as well as civil proceedings, enacted the form of affirmation recently adopted by Parliament. Pennsylvania lawmakers and royal officials recognized that the presence of so many individuals opposed to oaths entailed hardships that required some type of accommodation. There was little protest against the law, and it was confirmed within a year of its passage.[54] A 1724 statute provided forms for declarations of fidelity, abjuration, and allegiance that were similar to English procedures. The preamble noted that Parliament had come to believe in the loyalty of Quakers, and that they had not abused the privileges previously extended to them.[55] The right of Friends to participate in the government was finally secure.

New British policies aided final ratification, while the lack of protest from Pennsylvania is indicative of the adjustments that had been made to life in a pluralistic society. By 1715 "tis allow'd by Every man here of note among other pSwasions" that it was "Impracticable" for the legal system to function without Quaker participation.[56] Assemblymen even requested councilmen to "join with some of the Vestry, or Members of the Church of *England*, in an Address to the King of the same Nature and Purport" of its petition for favorable action on the 1718 law.[57] Pennsylvanians were willing to make more compromises and to be more tolerant of different beliefs than they had been in the early years, when the memory of persecution was fresh and novelty appeared to pose a threat. Had this dispute not been resolved in this way, the tolerant policies advocated by William Penn might have been thwarted, for they were largely devised and developed by Quaker-dominated assemblies.[58]

Military affairs provided another forum in which the fundamental beliefs of churchmen and sectarians clashed. With the exception of pirates ravaging Delaware Bay, the problem of defense during this period was relatively abstract. But granting funds for imperial defense and establishing a colonial militia proved continuing sources of division and contention.

William Penn's charter empowered him or his deputy to "levy, muster and traine all sorts of men," to "make warr and pursue the enemies and Robbers" by land and by sea, "yea, even without the Limits of the said pvince," and to "doe all and every other Act and thing, which to the charge and office of a Captaine generall of any Army, belongeth or hath accustomed to belong."[59] Because the Quaker tenet of pacifism prevented Penn from exercising these powers himself, he usually selected a nonpacifist as his deputy governor. Penn could both adhere to his religious principles and fulfill his obligations to the Crown, for while Friends believed that warfare was sinful, they recognized the validity of other men's conscientious belief in its propriety.[60] Penn's

[handwritten margin note: Penn's charter abrogated in 1692 NY's Benjamin Fletcher → gov't for 2 yrs WP argued for col. rich h his ownership   Pa. v. Fletcher on def of NY]

attempted compromise soon unraveled. Once Quakers were in official policymaking positions, especially in the assembly which controlled financial matters, their principles created tensions within the sect and difficulties with imperial officials and nonpacifistic Pennsylvanians, a dilemma that was never quite resolved.

The alleged inadequacy of Pennsylvania's defensive measures was a primary reason for the abrogation of Penn's charter in 1692 and the two-year government of New York's Benjamin Fletcher.[61] Arguing for the restoration of his province, Penn declared that it was surrounded by other colonies and not vulnerable to French attack, as his enemies claimed. Objections to his government based on the notion that the inhabitants of the province were pacifists were specious. If the people were pacifists, "another Governor can do no more than He can do"; more to the point was the fact "y^t there is as many of other Persuasions, & seven times more than can be expected as their Quota."[62] He promised to "take care of the Government and Provide for the Safety and Security thereof" if it were restored, and to "carefully transmitt" all directions the monarchs might "think fitt to send, for the supplying such Quota of Men or the defraying their part of the charges . . . necessary for the safety and preservation" of the Empire.[63]

Convincing the Pennsylvania assembly to appropriate money for defense proved difficult. When Fletcher presented Queen Mary's letter ordering the colony to provide men or other assistance to defend New York, the assembly refused to pass a supply bill until some of its proposed laws were approved. The law it finally enacted did not comply with the governor's demands.[64] Fletcher concluded that assemblymen had "so much self conceit they will rather dye than resist with Carnall weapons," "nor will they dip their money in blood."[65] The following year he more tactfully acknowledged "your Principles, that you will not carry arms, nor levy Money to make War," and instead asked them to *"feed the Hungry, and clothe the Naked,"* that is, to provide supplies to the Indians in order to maintain their friendship with the English. Again the assembly declined.[66] Fletcher unsuccessfully demanded eighty men or the equivalent in 1695.[67] But when reminded of the Queen's demand, Penn's promises, and the plight of "the poor *Indians*, whose Corn and Provisions were destroyed by the

French," the assembly capitulated, appropriating £300 in 1696 to support the government and *"for relieving the distressed* Indians *inhabiting above Albany."*[68]

Disturbed by the assembly's reluctance to conform to royal commands, Penn feared that "Complaints" about its inaction "may over sett y[e] Goverm[t] again." Like many English Quakers, he believed that funds could be granted, "especially, since Money be given under the Style off Peace & Safety, or to defray the exegences of the Goverm[t]." Officials could handle it in such a way that Friends would aid the Indians but not contradict their testimony against war. Furthermore, "others there will give besides frds & others pay as well as frds, so it is a mixt thing, & for mixt services."[69]

Governor Charles Gookin, recognizing the difficulty of obtaining the 150 men demanded for a 1709 expedition against Canada in a "County where most of the Inhabitants are obliged, by their Principles, not to make use of Arms," suggested that the assembly raise £4000 instead.[70] It refused, claiming "the raising Money to hire Men to fight (or kill one another) is Matter of Conscience to us, and against our religious Principles."[71] The governor replied that Englishmen of "all Perswasions" paid their taxes, whereupon the assembly adjourned.[72]

Several Quaker councilmen, chastened by the example of their English counterparts who "pay all Taxes & never scruple even y[t] w[ch] is Expressly Declared to be for Carrying on a vigourous War ag[st] france," met with prominent assemblymen to attempt to persuade them to compromise. While they opposed war, they recognized an obligation to satisfy royal commands.[73] The assembly, however, refused to do more than vote additional money for the support of the government in addition to the £500 it had granted as a present to the Queen before its adjournment.[74] London Quakers subsequently questioned their Pennsylvania brethren's excessive scruples. If the expedition was intended to prevent an invasion of the colonies, they could not understand "how Ffriends could be wholly exempted from their proportion's of the Charge if layed upon them by publick Taxation (any more than We are here in England)." Although "by our Principles Wee canot bear Arms nor fight nor hire Men to fight for Us: Yett

Wee pay the Queen's taxes towards such a Defence of O^r Country, as
the Government judges meet."[75]

A mode of compromise was devised by 1711. When 240 men were
demanded for a new campaign, the assembly, with few arguments,
voted £2000 as "Tribute" and as an expression of its affection for and
loyalty to the Queen. It was appropriated "to ye Queen's Use," as
"wee did not See it Inconsistent wth our principles to give ye Queen
Mony notwithstanding any Use She might put it to, y^t not being our
part but hers[.]" This became the formula subsequently employed when
the assembly was faced with similar demands.[76]

These controversies over funding military campaigns primarily concerned Quaker assemblymen and the governing authorities in both
England and the colony. Few, if any, Pennsylvanians encouraged their
representatives to vote for increased taxes for any purpose. But if the
assembly's reluctance to raise taxes was not a matter of widespread
concern, its refusal to establish a militia, which many nonpacifists
believed essential if their lives and property were to be protected from
Indians, the French, or other possible threats, did arouse significant
protest.

When Governor Blackwell first proposed the organization of a permanent military force in 1689, most Quaker council members were of
the opinion that it was unnecessary. The only danger one member
saw came "from the Bears & wolves." They informed the governor
that he had the authority to create a militia, and left the matter to his
discretion. Although they "would not tye others' hands," they would
take no part in an action that violated their conscientious beliefs.[77]

The following year several prominent Pennsylvanians, "old settlers"
as well as Anglicans, petitioned the council to establish a militia. The
French had "barbarously murdered" many Englishmen in neighboring
colonies, "which hath struck no Small terrour in vs and our ffami-
lyes," they argued.[78] The council granted their request, but sanc-
tioned only a temporary and entirely voluntary militia. Members were
not to appear with weapons until there was definite information of an
impending invasion, were not to show any "hostility" toward any but
the declared enemies of England, were to behave decently at musters,

and were to disband at the "Cessation or discontinuance of this noised warr." Costs were to be defrayed entirely by the participants, who could not solicit contributions from other inhabitants.[79]

The disinclination to create a permanent militia initiated a dispute that could not be contained within the boundaries of the province. A petition sent to the King following the restoration of the colony to Penn argued that he "did Oblige himselfe that the Mallitia of this pvince Should be so Effectually Settled as to defend and Preserve his Maj[es] Subjects Against all Enemies." Yet Penn had placed the government in "y[e] hands of Quakers who Not Only refuse to Settell y[e] Malitia but give all the discurrigment they Can to So good A worke."[80] Pacifists argued, in a counter-petition, that "there is as much a Militia here now as ever even in Govern[r] Fletcher's time." While they admitted that there was no coercive militia law, they "know none that are deny'd to bear Arms that place there Security in them."[81] Anglicans who petitioned for a minister in the mid-1690s also mentioned their desire to "make use of our arms as a Militia to defend our estates from enemies." They had heard rumors of an impending French invasion, and were concerned about pirates as well. But they received little sympathy from Quaker officials.[82]

Following England's declaration of war against France and Spain in 1702, Anglican demands for a permanent militia increased.[83] Robert Quary, a royal official who believed that colonial defense in general was deficient, singled out Pennsylvania, where "there is neither Militia, arms nor ammunition, no not so much as a Military Commission," for censure. The Queen's subjects were "exposed to all the Miseries Imaginable both by Land and Sea," while Penn "Endeavours all he can to invite all foreign Indians known to be Villains, and some French lately come from Canada, to come and settle in his Countey."[84] An Anglican priest declared that Quakers were hypocrites "who pretend they can't fight," and left the province "very naked" and prey to attack.[85]

When the deputy governor issued a proclamation of war and, in compliance with royal commands, urged Pennsylvanians to put themselves in "a posture of Defence," few heeded the call to arms. Instead, members of what Quakers termed the "hott Church Party" of militantly anti-Penn Anglicans labored to discourage men from enlisting.

Only a few men of "a much meaner sort" than "expected" responded to the first call to arms. The second recruitment attempt produced even more meager results. An Anglican-inspired rumor that militiamen would be forced to "march toward Canady" dissuaded many of the "most ignorant" from joining, while wives of prospective militiamen were pressured to discourage their husbands from enlisting. These "ungentleman-like" practices by "those whoe to the scandall of their profession call themselves Churchmen" were part of their effort to convince English authorities to confiscate Penn's province again. Because many Anglicans thought that their most effective complaint against Penn was his failure to establish a militia and otherwise provide for provincial defense, to join a voluntary militia would be self-defeating.[86]

Penn carefully instructed John Evans, the new governor appointed in 1703, about forming a militia. Because so much "Pretence & Clamo'" had been made by a "disaffected Gange," Penn ordered that provisions be made for raising, training, and regulating a militia. However, Evans was to consent to no coercive law or to one that "may be penal, or affect ye persons & Estates of Our ffriends" who had emigrated to escape such burdens.[87] Evans formed "3 good Companies" in Philadelphia, but "because the Service was all voluntary and Many of the Soldiers begrutching their Time and labour without any manner of recompence," he proposed to exempt them from service on the town watch. This disturbed the Philadelphia Common Council, which was experiencing difficulty in forcing townsmen to serve on the watch. Then "the Ch: party Who desired to Discourage the Milita" refused to serve on the watch because "all would not," and a riot erupted between the militia and the watch.[88] Although Evans was pleased with his success, he suspected some Quakers disaffected from the government had tried to discourage men from enlisting. He obtained passage of a law in Delaware requiring all men between the ages of sixteen and sixty to form companies, with no exemption for Quakers despite their petition based upon the constitutional guarantee "that None Should be molested or Disturbed on Account of their Religious Persuasions."[89] Friends termed the law "Wicked" and suffered distraint rather than comply, while Penn was outraged that Evans had approved a law that persecuted Quakers in their own province.[90]

Despite the problems that Pennsylvania and Delaware experienced with pirates, especially between 1708 and 1712, few steps were taken to combat them. Privateering and piracy were widespread during the late seventeenth and early eighteenth centuries, especially after the outbreak of King William's War. The long coastline of Delaware Bay, with its numerous inlets and sparse population, offered a haven. Furthermore, pirates would not leave the wealthy province, "so able to supply them wth Provisions," undisturbed "when so small a force is capable of Mastering it, w[ch] they know as well as we[.]" The reluctance of the Quaker-dominated government to prevent these illegal activities roused the ire of the inhabitants of the Lower Counties, the usual victims; royal officials, who used it as another charge against the Penn government; and Pennsylvania residents who believed that a militia was necessary.[91] In an attempt to create a militia in 1706, Governor Evans participated in a scheme wherein Delaware officials appeared in Philadelphia with false reports that Lewes had been destroyed, New Castle briefly attacked, and six French vessels were headed toward the city. Chaos, but no militia, followed this effort to demonstrate the province's defenseless condition.[92]

As early as 1697, reports had reached England that Pennsylvanians "Embrace Pyrats, Ships & men," and that Governor William Markham was personally involved in their activities.[93] As the raids increased, worried colonists made "great Reflections on fr[ds]." Isaac Norris reported "they would as soon shoot us as a fr[ench] man." Yet although "Those of the church of England grew very uneasy and unneighbourly in their expressions because of the defenselessness of the place," they continued to "use all endeavours to prevent the designs of the Gov[r] to encourage and discipline such as were willing" to join a militia. "Nothing but a Coercive law will Sattisfie,"[94] which was impossible while Friends dominated the government.

Some Pennsylvania Quakers became concerned about their defenseless condition, and wondered whether their opponents were right when they argued that "a due Administration of Governm[t] (especially in a time of War) under an English Constitution, is irreconcilable with our Principles."[95] James Logan was among the most prominent Quaker dissidents. He noted "the absurdity of ptending to Govm[t] without supplying force . . . when necessary to defend the Subject in their

Lives & Property." To tell nonpacifists that "they are free to fight themselves if they please" was unreasonable and unfair, for they would be "at all the hazard & Expence in defending what others are at least as deeply concerned in." Those who could not personally serve in a militia should be required "to contribute a due Proportion to the Expence." Since one purpose of government was to protect life and property, there was little difference between using force against public and private wrongdoers. If the government could hang a murderer, why should it not proceed against an enemy who was attacking it?[96] This dilemma of governing in accordance with Quaker principles frequently provoked contention, but no longer would it simply pit Anglican against Friend. It would increasingly become a crisis within Pennsylvania Quakerism.

In addition to conflict over fundamental principles concerning oaths and war, the antagonism between church and sectarian groups led to disputes over minor issues. Even something as trivial as the governor's proclamation of a day of thanksgiving to celebrate the birth of the Prince of Wales aroused dissatisfaction.[97] In a colony in which a variety of beliefs were espoused, modifications of English laws or customs in order to meet the needs of provincial society were initially regarded as persecution or oppression.

Marriage practices were a source of friction. An act to prevent "clandestine" marriages required a couple to inform a justice of the peace of their intentions a month before the ceremony and to post the justice's certificate in a public place.[98] This new law provided an opportunity for Anglicans to attack the provincial government. Clergymen argued that because church canons required calling the banns three times in their congregations, any other form of announcement contravened the oaths to uphold Anglican practices that they had taken upon ordination. They dispatched a petition demanding repeal of the law to the Bishop of London, who presented the objections to the Board of Trade. He argued that this statute would make it "impossible for any but Quakers to live when that law should prevail."[99] Penn responded that in a colony where people attended different churches, the law merely protected parents' and masters' interests and prevented abuses. The law applied to everyone and was equally inconvenient.

Moreover, it was "ill Consequence to plead Conscience agst the Security of property."[100] Before this law could be disallowed the assembly replaced it with new regulations that permitted each denomination to announce upcoming marriages in its own manner as long as parents, guardians, or masters of the parties involved were informed a month before the ceremony.[101]

III

Attempts to transplant European religious institutions to Pennsylvania occurred simultaneously with the establishment of secular institutions. In the absence of a government that could or would provide order or structure, the organization of churches and meetings depended primarily upon the efforts of the colonists themselves. Tolerance for most varieties of belief forced individuals and the congregations they founded to accommodate themselves to the novel situation in which there was neither "establishment" nor "dissent." Each person was free to decide whether or not to become involved with a religious group, and could select the one most congenial to his or her particular views, create a new religious movement, or ignore spiritual matters.

The congregational government and roles for a lay ministry proved advantageous to sectarian groups, and gave them a disproportionate degree of influence in the early years of Pennsylvania's history. They could organize themselves more easily than church groups who required an educated clergy and were accustomed to hierarchies or other supervisory bodies that exerted authority over individual congregations. Often coming out of a state church tradition, church groups experienced difficulty forming congregations of like-minded believers and obtaining qualified clergymen.

Quakers, with an essentially congregational organizational structure, rapidly replicated the English pattern of preparative, monthly, quarterly, and yearly meetings. By 1685 this phase had been completed, although with some variations from English patterns. Meetinghouses were constructed, committees created to receive the certificates of new immigrants and to dispense charity, epistles written to guide Friends' behavior, and disciplinary procedures established. Meetings could easily

G. Keith Pro-discipl→
chr. Qvakers = schismatic grp

PENN'S PROVINCE, 1681–1718   55

be founded to meet the needs of the rapid influx of Quaker settlers, who dominated the religious life of the province during its first decade.[102] Although the religious composition of the colony gradually diversified—by the end of the century there were recognizable congregations of a variety of denominations—the first challenge to Quaker religious hegemony came not from adherents of other faiths but from within its own ranks. The career of George Keith, which had an impact on other Pennsylvania Christians as well as on Friends and helps to explain Anglican contentiousness during the early eighteenth century, reveals the limits of Friends' toleration in the face of apostasy. It was one thing to permit a variety of religious beliefs to be publicly expressed; it was quite another to tolerate dissent from within the Society of Friends.

George Keith, a Scottish Quaker originally educated for the Presbyterian ministry, settled in Philadelphia in 1689. One of the most highly educated Friends of the period, he had been a leader in the pamphlet warfare Quakers conducted against other sects. Disturbed by the ignorance of many of his fellow Quakers and concerned that they would be unable to properly train their children in their faith, in 1690 he proposed a creed for the sect and revisions in discipline that would bring structure to the spontaneity characteristic of Quakerism. His attempt to purify the errors he perceived led to lengthy discussions and disputes with more orthodox Friends. Disowned by the meeting, he and several followers organized the "Christian Quakers." The controversy soon became embroiled in provincial politics, for Keith expressed doubts about the consistency of Quaker principles with participation in government. He insisted that this was a religious question, but the council and magistrates interpreted it as a seditious attack on the government. The printer of his works had his type confiscated for printing unlicensed books, and Keith and a few associates were tried and convicted of defaming several magistrates. Only John Holmes, the sole Baptist magistrate in Philadelphia, objected to the proceedings. He considered the problem a religious dispute that had no place in the civil courts. Keith sailed for London in 1693 in an attempt to convince English Friends of the validity of his beliefs, but in vain. He was again disowned, and responded by embracing Anglicanism.[103]

Keith's followers scattered after his departure for England. Some returned to their old meetings, which were inclined to be conciliatory; others adopted Baptist principles; and some became involved with German millenarians. Some, particularly after Keith returned as an Anglican missionary, joined the Church of England. Still others drifted in confusion. Or, as the Philadelphia Yearly Meeting phrased it, they "are much divided among themselves, Some of their preachers having been dipt in the Delaware by a baptist preacher; and one of them having been at [New] York lately was there sprinkled by an episcopal priest; and Some turn to the Pietists."[104]

Orthodox Quakers responded angrily to Keith. Hugh Roberts "never" saw a man "in mor pasion & bitternes of spirit and more redy to carp & to discover the weakness of ffrds," and accused Keith of "endeavour[ing] to put many things to frds charge, when they are very clear." Keith allegedly called Friends "blood thyrsty hounts" and used "abundance of such bad language" that was unrepeatable.[105] A spirited pamphlet war continued into the early years of the eighteenth century. Keithians argued that Quakers were "persecutors," and accused leading Friends of all vices imaginable. Quakers, for their part, denounced their opponents as persecutors and charged Keith with attempting to convince English authorities to suppress Quaker books because of their "'pretended errors in doctrine.'"[106]

The Keithian schism also divided German Quakers. Six Germans signed the certificate of Keith's disownment, while at least five prominent Germans supported him.[107] English-speaking Keithians joined them in following the teachings of Thomas Rutter (a former Mennonite turned Quaker, then Keithian) and Heinrich Bernhard Köster, who attracted a variety of people to his Germantown services. Köster, using the Lutheran liturgy, baptized several Keithians but refused to become the group's pastor. In 1696 several Keithians disrupted the orthodox Yearly Meeting. Demanding to speak, they hoped to refute principles contained in the books of Robert Barclay and William Penn. London Yearly Meeting was informed that "the Chiefest of them was one of those called Pietists," Köster. Pennsylvanians believed that English Friends had assisted Köster's group during their journey, and thought them "very Ungrateful, and Forgetful of their Kindnesses."

Germans were also involved in the pamphlet war between Keithian and orthodox Quakers.[108]

Anglicans attempted to take advantage of the religious disturbances that followed the Keithian schism. In 1695 they organized a congregation and petitioned the Bishop of London for a priest.[109] Anglicans reported that, as a result of the "late great distractions and divisions amongst the Quakers" caused by the "many notorious wicked and damnable principles and doctrines discovered to be amongst the greatest part of them," many Pennsylvanians grew "very uneasy and inquisitive after truth and the sound doctrines of the Church of England."[110] Thus Thomas Clayton, the first priest assigned to the colony, attempted to convince Quakers (Keithian and orthodox) and Baptists to return to the Church of England. In his attempt to end "schism," Clayton seems to have been influenced by contemporary English efforts at comprehension, where modifications in doctrine, liturgy, and church government were proposed to encourage dissenting denominations to reunite with the established church.[111] His appeals were rejected. Baptists resented the accusation that they were schismatics, and questioned the scriptural warrant for the "constitution, orders, officers, worship and service" of the church.[112] Quakers thought that the church was "sound" in fundamental Christian doctrines, but considered some of the "modes and customs in her forms of worship" unscriptural and deplored its persecution of nonconformists.[113]

Energetic opposition to Quakerism and to religious toleration followed the organization of the Society for the Propagation of the Gospel in Foreign Parts in 1701. It dispatched the newly ordained Keith to investigate religious conditions in the North American colonies.[114] Immediately upon his arrival in Pennsylvania the zealous convert entered into arguments with adherents of various doctrines, especially Quakers and Anabaptists, with the intention of exposing their "errors."[115] Keith became "ye Talk & News of ye Town," but most Quakers refused to debate with him, and ridiculed his meetings as a "Jangleing boute."[116] During the sessions of the Yearly Meeting, Keith and Evan Evans, rector of the Philadelphia church, held daily services with sermons. Violence erupted when John Talbot, chaplain on the ship that had brought Keith to the colonies who subsequently decided to enter the service of the S.P.G., and Keith entered the Quaker meetinghouse and tried to speak.[117]

Keith's "Account of the State of the Church" presented many of the anti-Quaker sentiments held by Anglicans, especially by their clergy. He accused Friends of using charity to proselyte poor people. They constantly sent missionaries to preach everywhere they could gain access, and liberally supported them. George Fox's "Orders and Canons," but never the Bible, were read in their meetings. Inexpensive Quaker books prejudiced the minds of youths against the church by misrepresenting its doctrines. The refusal to swear and to fight, he claimed, induced many to join the sect merely to avoid these obligations. Scandals committed by ministers or churchpeople were publicized and used to defame the church, while "gross faults" committed by Quakers were concealed. Friends recorded sudden misfortunes that happened to their adversaries and termed them "Judgments of God" to terrify individuals who might try to leave the sect.[118] Keith's report concerning Pennsylvania's religious situation influenced the S.P.G. to establish six missions in Pennsylvania and Delaware between 1704 and 1708. It seems also to have contributed to the anti-Quaker combativeness that characterized many of the missionaries sent to the colony.[119]

In their pleas for ministers, Anglicans stressed the threats posed by liberty of conscience. Keith thought that if priests "come not timely; the whole Country will be overrunne with Presbyterians, Anabaptists, and Quakerism."[120] Talbot reported that "People in many places take the Liberty to Say there be three Gods, or no God, & nothing is done to them." He suggested that the English penal laws and Act of Toleration be enforced in the colony against Quakers. He was not surprised that the Roman Catholic Mass had been celebrated in Philadelphia. He "thought that the Quakers wou'd be the first to let it in, particularly Mr Penn, for if he has any religion tis that, but thus to tollerate all without controul is the way to have none at all."[121] George Ross, the missionary in Chester, reported that some who professed to be churchmen were "strangely Bewitch'd" by Quaker doctrines.[122]

In Anglican opinion, one of the most effective methods to combat "dissenters" would be establishing schools where young people could be converted to the true faith. One priest lamented that "the Heathens should have 3 Schools" in Philadelphia "& the Christians not one."[123] Oxford vestrymen complained that Anglicans had been forced to send their children to Quaker schools, where "they imbibe such principles as very often occasion them when they are grown to fall away into Heresie." They pleaded for a schoolmaster to relieve them from the choice of raising their children in "blind ignorance" or sending them to be educated by the "Enemies of our holy Religion."[124] Conversely, Chester churchmen believed that Quakers would send their children to a school conducted by an Anglican master rather than do without. There "they might imbibe such Principles as afterwards they could not easily forget."[125]

Pamphlets were also considered effective weapons against noncon- formists. Missionaries argued that Quaker books were "industriously spread abroad" to strengthen Quakers in their opinions, while a short- age of Anglican treatises left their parishioners unable to defend their beliefs.[126] Keith suggested that ministers preach against the "most er- roneous" Quaker tenets at least once every three months.[127]

Religious disorder in the colony and its variety of faiths and prac- tices caused some Anglican clergymen to press for a colonial bishop as the only way for their church to survive. While other religious groups could perpetuate a ministry, "the poor Church" had no one in the colonies to confirm children or to ordain ministers. Many young men who planned to enter the ministry lapsed "again into the Herd of the Dissenters" rather than risk the dangers and expense of a voy- age to England for ordination. Because there was no bishop to admin- ister confirmation, many had "fallen away into Heathenism, Quaker- ism & Atheism,"[128] although some ministers contravened the church rubric and admitted unconfirmed adults to communion. An authority who could discipline the clergy and laity was also required. Priests who depended upon the voluntary contributions of parishioners fre- quently discovered that attempts to reprove their "Profaness & imo- rality" resulted in financial loss.[129]

Anglican priests, like ministers of many denominations in later years, had little faith in the commitment of their coreligionists to their church. At first Anglican laymen assured English churchmen that many col- onists attended Quaker meetings "purely because there hath been no

other way of worship in this place since the settlement of this Country." Anglicans left without a minister "Stray'd away like Sheep having no Shepheard."[130] The Welsh were particularly prone to being
"unhappily perverted" to Quakerism when no priests who spoke their
language were stationed in the province.[131] By the end of the S.P.G.'s
first decade of work, however, priests were less optimistic about the
ease of their task, for the "seeds of Apostacy" had "taken deep Root"
in the Quaker province.[132] Nevertheless, they did report reclaiming
Quakers, Anabaptists, and others who had drifted away from the
church. One priest noticed that when Quakers "leave their own Way,
and become Christians," almost all of them joined the Church of England, even though it was heavily outnumbered by dissenting churches
and ministers. He thought "Tis really wonderfull to consider how the
Church prevails, even where it is most oppos'd."[133]

Anglicans brought with them their liturgy and pride in being part
of the established church, but they could not transfer its stable polity
and union of church and state to the province. If Anglicans had difficulty in colonies in which another church had legal preference and
social prestige, they at least understood the concepts of "establishment" and "dissent." It was psychologically more difficult to adjust to
life in a pluralistic, officially tolerant society, in which no church was
favored and all were, in effect, in competition. Furthermore, Anglicans brought their prejudices with them.[134] To Anglicans, Quakerism
was the established religion, while they were "stigmatized with the
grim and horrid titles of treacherous and perfidious fellows, dissenters
& Schismaticks from the Establish't Religion," or as "Intruders and
Invaders" in the province.[135] When James Logan reported that
churchmen claimed to be suffering "Persecution," he concluded this
meant "not allowing their Clergie here what they of right Claim in
England and not Suffering them to be ye Superiour."[136] Confronta-
tion and a refusal to accept the permanence of Pennsylvania's religious
and political situation was their first response.

Nevertheless, the clergy and laity of the Church of England gradually came to accept the diversity of provincial society and the principles on which it was founded. By 1715 negative statements about
both Quakerism and liberty of conscience appear less frequently in
missionary letters than during the earlier years of the eighteenth cen-

Quakers more tolerant
of other relig

tury. The violence of the response also moderated to some degree, as Anglicans began to decrease their open hostilities in favor of other tactics for gaining influence or converts, and also began to cooperate with other religious groups.[137]

Friends were more tolerant of the religious practices of Anglicans, and other non-Quakers, than churchmen were of them. Most Quaker hostility toward members of the Church of England was expressed through the political system, where religious beliefs partially determined political opinions. For the most part, they were willing to accept anyone who peacefully worshiped after his or her own fashion, even if they privately made scornful remarks about non-Quaker liturgical practices. The caveat was that others recognize the religious rights of Friends. For Anglicans "in the Pulpit" to "enveigh agst our principles" was indeed "very impertent & provoaking."[138]

Nevertheless, not all Quakers viewed the arrival of the Church of England with equanimity. Logan hesitated to enumerate the inhabitants of Philadelphia County, thinking it would create "jealousies and distrust" if it became known that Friends and others were "near upon a Ballance."[139] As the number of Anglican churches increased, he prayed, "God grant that a spirit of charity and kindness may be cultivated among us in place of hatred and persecution."[140] Hugh Durborough, "an honest Fr^d," was reluctant to have Anglicans as neighbors. He desired first refusal or at least an option to lease on a vacant lot between one he owned and one purchased by the vestry of Christ Church, "the others having an Eye upon it, & could they Obtain it his psn^t Dwelling would become So inconvenient he must be Obliged to leave it, which is their desire."[141] When Philadelphia Friends requested Penn to revise the charter they had for a school to allow them to erect a hospital for poor Quakers, they urged him to grant their request speedily. They feared that after he resigned the government, as he was attempting to do, "obstructions . . . may be Cast In the way by an angry Interested Church Party which here have been allwayes ready to doe any Ill Office agst ffriends."[142]

Penn, for his part, encouraged his influential friends to develop working relations with Anglicans. When the Reverend Evan Evans, described by Penn as "a man Sober and of a mild Disposition," was

Little evid
of other rely
in PA   Prsby + Bapt coop

62   "A MIXED MULTITUDE"

appointed to the Anglican church in Philadelphia in 1700, Penn requested its members who were "for Peace and a ffriendly Understanding" to "make Impressions on his mind for the best."[143] Although Evans "brought over printed books & broad sheets in great
quantities" in opposition to Quakerism, Penn believed that "what is
done is co[n]certed at home," for Evans himself was "pretty quiet."[144]
Penn developed a close relationship with Evans, eventually entrusting
him with political messages.[145] Remaining rather openminded about
the Anglican clergy, the Proprietor announced that another priest came
with "an absolute disposition to be friendly & Neighbourly, & to meet
us in Generall Dutys & virtues." He asked his friends to "pray be as
easy, as Truth will let you," toward the clergyman.[146] By 1705 Penn
noted that he had "ffriends of the Church-party" and admitted that
his "Enemies" included "as well false Quak[rs] as false Church-men."[147]

Little is known about the smaller religious groups present in Pennsylvania or their relationships with other groups during this period. There
were as yet few representatives of Scotch-Irish Presbyterianism or the
German Lutheran and Reformed churches, denominations that would
have a significant impact on the colony later in the eighteenth century.
Smaller sects, including Baptists of various nationalities and beliefs,
pietists of radically differing beliefs, Roman Catholics, and others were
present, but rarely left evidence of their relationships with outsiders
or their views concerning diversity or toleration.

There is testimony to cooperation between Presbyterians and Baptists in Philadelphia. Members of these two denominations met together in a storehouse for a few years in the early 1690s, and listened
to any Presbyterian or Baptist minister who happened to be in town.[148]
In 1695 John Watts, a Baptist teacher, arranged to preach on alternate
Sundays. Although "divers of the persons that came to that assembly
were presbyterians in judgment," neither party had "scruple[s] of
holding communion" with the other "in the public worship of God
and common duties of religion nor of admitting their ministers." But
when in 1697 the Presbyterians obtained the services of Jedidiah Andrews, a New England-trained minister, "there appeared some scruples on their side" about sharing a meetinghouse and pastors. The
Baptists proposed that each group accept "approved ministers who are

fitly qualified and sound in the faith and of holy lives to preach and pray" in common assemblies, and that each would "own, embrace and accept" the other as "fellowbrethren."[149] Before reaching an agreement the Presbyterians requested a conference, but when their representatives failed to appear at the appointed time the Baptists decided to meet separately, and concluded "this was what the presbyterians wanted in reality."[150] In 1707 the Keithians invited the Baptists, who had been meeting in a brewhouse, to use their meetinghouse.[151]

While Pennsylvania Anglicans singled out Quakers for special odium, they criticized other "dissenters" as well. The Reverend Thomas Clayton "upbraided" Andrews about the joint Presbyterian-Baptist services, warning him that he was "cherishing a schism against himself, as well as me."[152] Anglican clergymen also complained that Presbyterian ministers were allowed to perform marriages, a right they did not possess in England. They believed that this privilege enabled them to gain converts when one party was Presbyterian and the other was Anglican.[153] The Presbyterians, "very busye in sowing Fears and Preaching their damnable Doctrine of Predestination and Reprobation," caused some people to despair and others to turn to Quakerism. There was even apprehension some "will be forced to turn Papists."[154] Governor Markham's wife and daughter frequently attended Presbyterian services; one priest contemptuously remarked that this "shews neither good breeding, reason, nor religion."[155]

Anglicans also considered Anabaptists objectionable. Like the Society of Friends, they were deemed "pests"; tracts refuting their tenets were in demand.[156] Yet one priest noted that some Baptist parents accepted his offer to catechize their children, although they would not attend his church themselves. He thought this instruction might prove beneficial to the future growth of the church.[157] Another priest found that Anabaptist parents would attend his services and allow their children to be instructed, even though they had not yet overcome their objections to infant baptism.[158]

Early Pennsylvanians, for the most part, exhibited tolerance for, or at least indifference to, the beliefs and practices of other settlers. The diversity of the province's population played a role, as did Penn's promise of liberty of conscience. The initial lack of strong religious institutions was also a factor. The weakness of organized churches fostered cooperation among people of different backgrounds and faiths; broad similarities became more important than minor differences in doctrine or ritual. The influence of sectarians, many of whom shared Penn's commitment to liberty of conscience or had fled to Pennsylvania to avoid persecution and therefore insisted on the strict fulfillment of Penn's guarantees, contributed to the lack of friction between adherents of different tenets, especially in the early years. Although some groups proselytized, most were uninterested in imposing their views on others and simply wanted to enjoy their right to freedom of worship. Certainly early Anglicans, especially priests, were obstreperous and found much to dislike in Penn's province. But their opinion was a minority one, and its importance must not be exaggerated.

As early as 1684 Pennsylvanians were commenting unemotionally about the religious diversity of their province. Francis Daniel Pastorius once wrote that among his domestics were "such as hold with the Roman, the Lutheran, the Calvinistic, the Anabaptist and the Church of England, but only one Quaker." He compared the ship that brought him to the colony with Noah's Ark, a description that is applicable to Pennsylvania as well.[159] A Welshman described "our way of worship first the Church of England secondly the quakers 3[dly] the prespeterians 4[thly] the Babtists, 5[thly] the sabottarians." Only a few "Papists" resided in the province. Moreover, "we all agrees and are att peace with one another and Every one worships God in his own way."[160] A Quaker, looking back on the first years of Penn's experiment, described the "good Concord, & benevolent Disposition amongst People of all Denominations, Each delighting to be Reciprocally helpful & kind in Acts of Friendship for one another, & (as it's Said) there was no difference in form of Worship, for ye Quakers having built a Large Meeting house, about ye Center of ye City, all Came there."[161]

Religious differences remained a potential source of conflict, especially among newcomers who often took time to adjust to religious diversity and to show forbearance toward their neighbors. But most Pennsylvanians rapidly accommodated themselves to the situation and even viewed it as a positive asset. Joris Wertmuller included in his description of the colony's abundance and the opportunities it offered the additional inducement that "farmers here pay no tithes nor contributions. Whatever they have is free for them alone."[162] When Louis Michel, a Swiss gentleman who hoped to establish a "colony" in Pennsylvania, visited Philadelphia in 1704, he was "astonished" at its rapid growth and evident prosperity. He believed that the "strongest reason, why there is such an influx of people from other provinces is partly due to the liberty which all strangers enjoy in commerce, belief and settlement, as each one understands it."[163]

Daniel Falckner's *Curieuse Nachricht from Pennsylvania*, based upon questions about America, and in particular about Pennsylvania, posed by the Reverend August Hermann Francke in 1699,[164] clearly informed readers that there were many sects in the colony and that everyone was expected to live peacefully together. When queried "How to conduct oneself . . . circumspectly and inoffensively toward the divers sects," Falckner admitted that it was "almost impossible to answer, and still harder to observe." He suggested that settlers "show ourselves actually as devout as they demand, and yet be not proud," extend friendliness to everyone, and demonstrate "vital Christianity."[165] When asked "How to seek out persons imbued with a true Philadelphian spirit from among the Swedes, English, Germans, and religious persuasions who are there," he urged charity toward one another until "all sects and parties . . . abjure their birth marks and enter with one accord into a resolution of resigned brotherly love."[166] To a question about the settlement pattern, "if in every town there are divers sects and religions, or only one," Falckner replied that "The sects and religious parties live among one another."[167] Finally he advised that because "one cannot dispense with the daily intercourse and help of his neighbor, though he be of a different religion," people should "maintain a magnanimous silence" in religious matters.[168] He also noted, somewhat inaccurately, that Pennsylvania granted complete freedom to all but Jews and others who denied Christianity. Furthermore, "all sorts and conditions" were admitted to public office. He contrasted Pennsylvania with other, less liberal, colonies.[169]

By the time William Penn died, the first tentative steps toward recognition of the rights of individual conscience had been taken. His refusal to compromise religious liberty and his encouragement to share political power, combined with a British failure to seriously obstruct

Anal came to
accept rely tol of Quakers

wp ideal < No
colny church all allowd = holy expt

the colony's tolerant policies, fostered the development of more liberal attitudes among the colonists. The experience of living in a heterogeneous society encouraged people to understand the needs and rights of others. Thus, Anglicans were forced to accept the permanence of religious toleration, while Quakers came to understand that not all challenges to their ideas were precursors to persecution. Interests such as wealth, status, and political opinions also helped to foster interaction among members of different religious groups. As early as 1703, in the midst of the Quaker-Anglican political antagonism, "most of Note both of our ffriends and Church ffolks," including Robert Quary, attended the most lavish Quaker wedding held in the province to date.[170]

Penn's ideal of creating a province that would never have an established church and in which, insofar as possible, all religious groups would be treated impartially, was gradually accepted. If Anglicans and Quakers had not learned to love one another, they at least came to find mutual coexistence possible. If these denominations continued to be suspicious of each other, individual members of each found grounds for cooperation. Tensions between Anglicans and Quakers had threatened to destroy the province; that they did not is due to the relative harmony and mutual forbearance demonstrated by other participants in the "holy experiment."

IV

The emigration to Pennsylvania by people from several European states with a variety of languages and widely divergent worship practices resulted directly from William Penn's promotional activities. Yet although his recruitment campaign added significantly to the diversity of his province, he does not seem to have considered how these often antagonistic peoples might live together peacefully. Although Penn was interested in their welfare and implored his officials to assist immigrants, his influence was limited during the years he lived in England. Accommodations necessary for the creation of a new society reached by individuals already resident in the Delaware Valley and those who arrived prior to 1717 established basic patterns of provincial life. Pennsylvanians could have thwarted Penn's goals by making immigrants unwelcome or by passing restrictive laws, as they did in limiting officeholding to trinitarian Protestants. That they rarely responded unfavorably to newcomers indicates that many settlers shared Penn's principles, including the belief that numbers were a positive good in themselves as contributing to economic development, as long as there was little civil discord.

Perhaps in part because he followed the precedents of earlier possessors of the territory and confirmed local officials in their offices, Penn noted that the "ancient Inhabitants" received him with "much Kindness & respect."[171] Furthermore, the new, primarily English and Quaker immigrants evinced little prejudice against the non-English, non-Quaker people already resident in the colony. Many of these early English arrivals expressed interest in the previous settlement by, or presence of, Dutch, Swedish, and Finnish colonists, and described in more or less detail the improvements they had made in the colony. These reports often included the writer's estimation of the previous development of the country as well as its potential.[172]

Penn considered the Dutch and the Swedes "a plain, strong, industrious People," yet he noted that they "have made no great progress in Culture or propagation of fruit Trees." He believed this was because "they desired rather to have enough, than Plenty or Traffick," although he suspected that the easy trade with the Indians, for both provisions and profit, had caused them to grow lazy.[173] Francis Daniel Pastorius thought them "poor agriculturalists" who failed to labor with sufficient diligence on the excellent soil. He claimed that they "let their grain lie unthreshed for several years under the open sky," had no barns or stables, and allowed their livestock to run freely.[174] On the other hand, another settler reported that they "have lived much at ease, having great plenty of all sorts of provisions."[175] Although agricultural techniques might have been primitive and surpluses limited,[176] they were not "backward in friendly dealing with us [the colonists who immigrated after 1681] for wheat, rye or Indian corn as they could spare it," and sold livestock for both breeding purposes and provisions.[177] Nor did they take advantage of the needs of a rapidly expanding population by charging unfair prices; at the weekly markets, "ye ancient lowly Inhabitants come to sell their Produce to their Profit & our Accomodation."[178]

The new colonists were curious about the life and culture of the Dutch and Swedish inhabitants. Thomas Paschall was amazed that they used very little iron in their buildings. Using few tools other than axes, the Swedes were more efficient in cutting trees and making them into planks than men using saws. They were "but ordinarily Cloathd," even though "their Women make most of the Linnen cloath they wear, they Spinn and Weave it and make fine Linnen." The people "generally eate Rye bread," although he hastened to add that wheat grew very well.[179] Penn reported that the people were strong and healthy, with large families. There was one Dutch meetinghouse and three Swedish ones.[180] The only serious criticism was that the old settlers had corrupted the Indians. Europeans had introduced vice, deceit, and drunkenness, but had not made strenuous efforts to convert the natives to Christianity.[181]

Misunderstandings between some of the older inhabitants and Penn arose over property matters. The commissioners Penn had dispatched to the colony before his arrival arranged to purchase some land, most significantly the site of Philadelphia; some tracts along the Delaware River were also exchanged for land further back in the country.[182] Penn intended to confirm the holdings of the prior settlers. He ordered deeds and certificates of survey to be submitted to his property commissioners so that new grants could be made under his authority. These would give the owners a firmer title than the ones they had had under the Duke of York or earlier regimes. But officials concerned with property matters discovered that individuals often claimed more land than they actually held title to, for customarily swamp, marsh, and other waste land partially under water at high tide were not included in deeds, although used by the claimants as pastureland. Quit-rents were levied on all of the land an individual was granted; it appeared that Penn demanded higher ones than had been previously paid.[183]

In part, difficulties arose because the Swedes did not fully understand English procedures and Penn's policies. A group that petitioned Governor William Markham requested that the land policy "bee Layd out in a more plainer way," for they did not comprehend terms such as "Customara does." Although willing to pay Penn "all Such Rents as they formerly payd" as well as taxes necessary to support the government, they suggested that his rents were too high.[184] A few years later a Pennsylvania official complained that Swedes refused to pay quitrents for their "Meddows Marshes swamps & cripples" because they had not under the jurisdiction of the Duke of York. He suggested assigning these tracts to others if the claimants continued to refuse to pay the rents demanded.[185] This was a situation that could be easily exploited.

Discontent festered until 1709, when twenty-seven Swedes presented a list of grievances concerning property matters to the assembly. Urged to do so by Englishmen who had purchased some formerly Swedish-owned land, they complained that their old patents had been "fraudulently gotten" by proprietary agents and increased quitrents exacted. After examining the petition, unsympathetic councilmen declared that the quitrents were the same as under the Duke of York's government. When the Swedes threatened to petition the Swedish ambassador to England for relief, the council termed them "exceedingly Insolent" and the governor informed them that such a procedure would be improper. The only means of obtaining redress of their grievances would be applications to the Proprietor or the commissioners of property, or legal actions taken on an individual basis. Swedes were reminded that the Proprietor had generously confirmed their land titles. Although angered by the Swedes' complaints, councilmen understood that "what they had done was not of themselves, but at the instigation of some very ill disposed persons." The petitioners admitted that they were "altogether ignorant of the Laws & no masters of the Language," and that only lately had they "been made sensible that they had been abused, &c."[186] Appeals to the commissioners of property brought another reminder of Penn's generosity and of his sole right to dispose of land.[187] When they persisted and presented their case to the Swedish ambassador in London, and through him to the Swedish Crown, they were admonished to obey English laws and the Proprietor. They were threatened by a termination of missionary assistance if they did not.[188]

The length to which these few malcontents carried this dispute was exceptional. Swedish colonists attempted to establish a close relationship with the Proprietor and his government; for their part, Penn and his officials were usually willing to compromise over land questions and to assist their efforts to maintain religious services. The Proprietor helped to arrange for Swedish religious books to be shipped to them following his first return to Europe from the colony, and included as his own gift a small collection of English works. Translations of several of the letters the colonists wrote to Sweden requesting ministers and the replies they received were submitted to the deputy governor for his information and approbation.[189] The first ministers dispatched from Sweden visited Penn in London. He offered them his protection, gave them advice about the province, and recommended them to his deputy, who received them cordially when they presented their credentials.[190] The Swedes, noting that they "Live Peaceably both in Temporall & Spirituall," wrote to thank Penn for his "Loveing Kindnesses" in obtaining priests and books "In our Own Nattive Speech & Linguo," and promised to be dutiful and obedient subjects. They asked him to disbelieve "any false stories and Ill deserved Reports" that "illdisposed and Mallicious people" might spread against them.[191] They joined other Pennsylvanians in rejoicing at William Penn's return in 1699. Swedish books were once again entrusted to him; he assured the Swedish colonists that he would continue to show them "all possible favor."[192]

These colonists had been neglected by Swedish religious officials after the collapse of New Sweden. Although services were conducted by two ministers during the late seventeenth century, by the early 1690s one had died and the other was aged and blind. After letters sent to Sweden requesting ministers had remained unanswered, the Swedish congregations, with the aid of New York merchants who traded with Holland, appealed to the Lutheran Consistory in Amsterdam for a minister. They "know that in Amsterdam persons of various nations are to be found, and especially students of theology, who are waiting for appointments as clergymen." However, no assistance was forthcoming.[193] When a Dutch Reformed minister visited Pennsylvania in 1690, one congregation tried to persuade him to remain as its pastor. He declined on the grounds that they were Lutheran and he Reformed, but the congregation thought the differences insignificant. He preached for three weeks in another Swedish parish, and offered the sacrament of communion before returning to New York.[194] Swedish officials finally became interested in the colonists in 1692.

Responding to a letter of inquiry from John Thelin, postmaster at Gothenburg, the colonists asked for two well-educated ministers who "may be able To defend them [the Scriptures] and us against all false opposers who can or may oppose any of us, and also one that may defend ye True Lutheran faith." Bibles, religious books, and primers were also requested.[195]

The first priests, who arrived in 1697, found a chaotic situation. Although the country "overflows with every blessing" and the government was mild, the years of neglect had taken their toll. The people were "daily overrun" by Quakers; only with difficulty had a layreader held one congregation together. The colonists were unable to fulfill some of their promises about providing adequate support for the ministers, and the churches were in disrepair. The colonials were "quite irregular" in holding divine service, observing church ordinances, and instructing the youth. But the priests were optimistic, for although their people were dispersed among a variety of nationalities, they spoke pure Swedish and had taught their children to read.[196] The priests set to work building new churches and reestablishing Swedish customs that had lapsed, such as singing psalms during worship.[197]

Not unlike their Anglican counterparts, Swedish priests had doubts about their neighbors and the wisdom of the policy of religious liberty. One thought that "here there are fanatics almost without number. Because there is freedom of conscience, here they have gathered together, of every opinion and belief."[198] The variety was remarkable, as well as confusing; "even in the same family or house, 4 or 5 may be found [each] professing a different religion: . . . parents and children, owners and servants, yes even man and wife, may each have his religion."[199] Lutherans shared the Anglican contempt for sectarians. The sabbatarians "cause[d] a good deal of vexation" to one minister, who was "offend[ed] . . . very much to see them going with plow in hand" when he was on his way to church on Sunday mornings.[200] Sects, including "*Anabaptists, Calvinists, Presbyterians, Sabbatarians* and *Latitudinarians*" and a new German sect called the "*Newborn people— the family of the regenerate*," hindered the planting of the Swedish church because each "is diligent in propagating the teachings of their principles."[201]

As for the Quakers, they "do not celebrate the sacrament of the altar, they never sing, they never pray."[202] One Swede believed that the Quaker faith included only "what is pleasing to their minds." Their belief in the Inner Light was false, for Quaker preachers often disagreed, and "therefore it must be acknowledged that one or the other inner light has contradicted itself."[203] Andrew Hesselius thought the Quakers denied the possibility of the resurrection, "by which they are making themselves the most noxious vermin in America."[204] One Swedish pastor brought legal action against two Quakers who "made disturbance with me in the very act of the burial" of a parishioner. The men eventually appeared before the vestry and priest to acknowledge their fault and beg forgiveness.[205] Despite criticism of Quakerism, Andrew Rudman found a notable virtue among adherents of that sect. Their honesty in business and refusal to haggle over prices demonstrated an "uprightness and brotherly love" he prayed would soon become more characteristic of tradesmen in his homeland.[206] For the most part, the contact between the Swedes and sectarians appears to have been minimal; perhaps because they were beneficiaries of the policy of religious toleration, the Swedish priests did not share the combativeness of their Anglican counterparts.[207]

Ironically, the very diversity of Pennsylvania's religious life helped to foster cordial relationships between Swedish Lutheran and Anglican priests. Despite differences in language and doctrine, the two national churches had more in common with each other than with the other religious groups in the colony. In the eighteenth century both tended toward latitudinarianism, possessed a hierarchical, episcopal order, and shared similar liturgical customs. European superiors, who saw the necessity of a unity of interests if "orthodoxy" were to be maintained in the midst of a wide variety of sects, encouraged cooperation.[208] Swedish pastors were "counseled and instructed from Sweden to maintain friendship and unity with the English, so that we and the English Church shall not reckon each other as dissenters like the Presbyterians, Anabaptists, Quakers, &c., but as sister Churches."[209] English clergymen were directed to receive Swedish missionaries "with all brotherly friendship and charity, and to cultivate the best understanding you can with them, and to assist with any direc[t]ions they may stand in need of."[210]

Shortages of ministers also encouraged Anglican-Lutheran cooperation. Dispersed settlement patterns required the creation of large parishes, within which were churches of other communions. Itinerant ministers serving isolated churches were welcomed, regardless of their affiliation or native language. Because Swedish pastors usually learned English rapidly, they were in demand throughout the colony. Often they arranged to preach regularly in vacant Anglican congregations. Ministers of the two denominations united to consecrate new church buildings, and Swedish pastors were invited to attend conferences held by Anglican missionaries.[211] One Swedish pastor accompanied several Anglican priests who went to hear George Keith expound on the errors of sabbatarians and other "heretics," and was later invited to hear another Anglican debate with a sabbatarian.[212] Recognizing the services performed by Swedish ministers, the Anglican Society for the Propagation of the Gospel frequently provided funds to assist them in returning to Sweden, and invited several Swedish bishops to become honorary members.[213]

In contrast to the close relationships that Swedish and Anglican priests and congregations had with each other, German Lutherans remained somewhat isolated. German Lutheran services were first conducted by Heinrich Bernhard Köster, a Lutheran with leanings toward millenarian pietism, who immigrated in 1694 and returned to Germany in 1701. It is uncertain how long he continued to hold orthodox services, for he also preached in English and became involved with Keithians and other sectarians.[214]

By the early eighteenth century, "church" Germans were experiencing serious difficulties. Writing in 1701, Justus Falckner, a Lutheran pietist who had studied theology in Germany and had briefly lived as a hermit in Pennsylvania, concluded that the condition of the churches "in this spiritual and corporeal wilderness" was "still pretty bad." Germans, "destitute of altar and priest," were in "a deplorable condition indeed." Falckner and his brother Daniel, also a pietist, attended a Swedish church and persuaded other Germans to attend even though they could not understand the language. As a result, they were "gradually being redeemed from barbarism, and becoming accustomed to an orderly outward service." One Swedish priest, Andrew Rudman, offered to learn German so that he could occasionally preach for them until they were able to obtain German ministers. By 1702 he had "made some attainments" in the language. Some German Reformed colonists also accepted the sacraments offered by Swedish Lutheran pastors, and raised no objections to differences in doctrine or form.[215] If individual Germans attached themselves to Swedish churches, there was little effort to maintain ties based on their common faith until German Lutherans began to receive missionaries in the 1740s.

Religious diversity characterized the Continental emigrants from the beginning. German- and Dutch-speaking settlers prior to 1717 seem to have been primarily sectarians who sought liberty of conscience; only sectarians established meetings during the colony's first decade.[216] The Lutherans and Reformed lacked organized worship until the 1690s, and for several decades thereafter it remained inadequate. Thus, many who had belonged to European "state" churches turned seemingly at random to English or German sects, preferring to "select one than none at all" when no regular forms of worship were available. Despite his own experience as an anchorite in the wilderness, Justus Falckner complained that Europeans were "divided into almost innumerable sects, which pre-eminently may be called sects and hordes." They seemed to take as their creed, "Do away with all good order, and live for yourself as it pleases you!" The "spirit of errors and sects has here erected for itself an asylum," a situation which should be remedied "since the Germans are now increasing rapidly."[217] His brother complained of the "visible zeal in proselyting" exhibited by sectarians who "spread themselves and their followers like unsown weeds in the flower garden."[218] Ministers were urgently needed.

Relationships among the various ethnic, linguistic, and most religious groups in the colony prior to 1717 were relatively harmonious. Unlike the seriously divisive religious differences between Anglicans and Quakers, differences in national origins seem to have been of little importance. Some people brought their prejudices with them, but there were only random expressions of antipathies or stereotypes.[219]

The only category of "foreigners" consistently regarded with suspicion were Frenchmen involved in the Indian trade. In 1694 the council received a petition from several Philadelphians indicating their "Jealousies relating to the French in generll amongst them, and more speciallie referring to those trading in remote & obscure places with the nativs." The petitioners thought that the Frenchmen should be required to obtain permission to trade and to provide security that would bind them to acquaint the government with information relating to the "natives and enemies of the Countrie."[220] One of the assembly's grievances against Governor John Evans was that he "allows several *Frenchmen* (who are *Papists*, and have been at *Canada*), to trade with, and reside amongst, the Indians of this Country."[221] Not all traders were suspect, however; when Peter Bezalion twice had imported goods seized by customs commissioner Robert Quary, James Logan and others were outraged because "he is useful & accounted very honest by those that trade with him."[222]

More significant was the positive reception given to immigrants. Penn's interest in recruiting settlers was shared by others. The council aided in redressing grievances and in procuring naturalization,[223] while the commissioners of property helped to arrange the sale of or settlement on land.[224] One Welshman was "glad to hear that many Germans are about buying great tracts of Land," and "heartily wish[ed] they may come forward with their designe."[225] London Friends helped to arrange transportation to Pennsylvania for a group of Palatines in 1709, and requested their Philadelphia brethren to exert "care and Charity" so that the new colonists might have the "comfort of a friendly succor in a Strange Land."[226] When Germantown Quakers issued a protest against the extension of slavery to the province, they argued that it might discourage potential immigrants from the Continent. They said it "mackes an ill report in all those Countries of Europe, . . . that ye Quackers doe here handel men licke they handel their ye Cattel."[227]

Several letter writers mentioned the diverse origins of Pennsylvanians. Perhaps they thought potential emigrants would be encouraged if they knew that settlers of their own language, background, or faith were already in the colony. Non-English colonists unfortunately seldom revealed their attitudes toward pluralism or Penn's tolerant policies. Their writings do, however, strongly imply that spiritual or secular benefits—or both—might result from emigration. Furthermore, they indicate that all immigrants were welcome, and would have to learn to live with their neighbors.[228]

One early Continental emigrant reported that "Many men are coming here from many parts of the world, so that it will be overflowed with the nations."[229] Louis Michel had been encouraged by the "many good reports" about the colony. "Many Germans and Hollanders live there and many other advantages were related to me" while he was sojourning in Virginia.[230] Pastorius mentioned that among "these newly-engrafted foreigners, . . . sundry High Germans are found, who have already been settled in this country for twenty years, and thus have, as it were, naturalized themselves, namely: Silesians, Brandenburgers, Holsteiners, Switzers, etc. Also a Nurenberger."[231]

Readers of tracts intended to promote emigration also became aware of its heterogeneous nature. In a 1685 portrayal of his colony, Penn wrote that "The People are a Collection of divers Nations in Europe: As, French, Dutch, Germans, Sweeds, Danes, Finns, Scotch, Irish and English; and of the last equal to all the rest: . . . But as they are of one kind, and in one Place and under One Allegiance, so they live like People of One Country, which Civil Union has had a considerable influence towards the prosperity of that place."[232] The diversity that characterized the province was also evident in one of the first poems that described the fruits of Penn's venture.[233]

Some Europeans remained interested in group migration. Michel emphasized the idea of Pennsylvania as a sanctuary for the oppressed or persecuted. Because he believed that the Frankfort Company's purchase was intended to establish a "certain and secure dwelling place" in case their people "should be compelled through war, religion, or other accidents" to leave their homes, he argued that the government of Berne as well as private citizens should follow the example of Holland, Sweden, Finland, Germany, and other nations in sending people to the colony to establish a potential refuge for their countrypeople.[234] Daniel Falckner noted that the Germans in Pennsylvania "as yet do not live together as a distinct colony,"[235] but several of his answers to Francke's questions indicate that this was possible. Responding to a question whether "when new Colonies come over" they must join with older ones or build new settlements, he replied that individuals could choose where to settle. He suggested that newcomers could benefit from the experiences of older settlers, and recommended that older people remain in settled areas but that younger ones move toward the frontier.[236] A small group of Swiss Mennonites migrated to the Pequea Valley in 1710, and founded the first settlement in what would become Lancaster County.[237] Amish settlers in particular wished to be isolated from their neighbors. In a protest sent to the governing authorities, they argued that they had migrated in order to escape persecution but had found that civil demands were being made on them with which they could not comply. Their religious principles precluded participation in elections, holding office, or using the legal system; they desired the freedom to live peacefully under their own customs. Probably as a result, the sheriffs of Lancaster and Chester Counties were directed to exempt the Amish from jury service.[238]

The Welsh Quakers who had negotiated with Penn about establishing an exclusive settlement where their language and culture could be maintained failed to achieve their goal. This caused some harsh feelings toward Penn, but there seems to have been little antagonism in general between Welshmen and Englishmen. Not all of the Welsh were unacquainted with the English language; the letters between Penn and the Welsh leaders were in English, and some emigrants used the voyage to learn the language.[239] Nor did Welsh immediately become obsolete, despite the inability to remain isolated. Welsh Quakers remained within the same Quarterly Meeting even after new county lines that would have divided them were drawn.[240] Although the business of the Yearly Meeting was conducted in English and predominantly Welsh meetings kept their minutes in English, testimony in their meetings was often spoken in Welsh.[241]

Not all Welsh immigrants were Quakers; many were Baptists or Anglicans. Some continued to use their native language in worship, even when they joined with their English speaking coreligionists. Several Welsh Baptists who settled near a mixed congregation of English, Irish, and Welsh Baptists near Pennypack in 1701 initially united with them. Following a dispute over a minor point of doctrine, they moved to the "Welsh Tract" near New Castle in 1703. Although this group kept its records in Welsh until 1722, the linguistic difference does not seem to have been an issue in the quarrel.[242] Other Welshmen rapidly adopted English; as early as 1712 a Welsh Baptist minister "fear[ed] but few are likely to keep up the true Protestant religion or their language. The English is swallowing up their language, though assisted by religion."[243]

Welsh settlers posed a special challenge to the S.P.G.'s missionary work. Although many had been members of the Anglican communion in Wales, in Pennsylvania they had a tendency to attach themselves to other religious societies. This resulted primarily from a shortage of Welsh-speaking Anglican priests, especially in the early years when many Welshmen were still unfamiliar with the English language. Appeals were frequently directed to the S.P.G. by missionaries and Welsh laymen for ministers who could preach in Welsh and for devotional books in that language. Emphasis was placed on the "ignorance" of the Welsh and their drift out of the church. The S.P.G., however, experienced considerable difficulty recruiting ministers who could meet this need. Because the Welsh lived in dispersed settlements, priests were itinerants who preached to small congregations less frequently than they or their parishioners found desirable. Yet the S.P.G. and the Pennsylvania Welsh community found it financially impossible to maintain more than one Welsh-speaking missionary at a time. Some Welshmen were content to employ a layreader when a minister was not available, but others would go to hear Welsh sermons preached by ministers of other denominations on Sundays when their Anglican priest was officiating at a distant church.[244]

There was little prejudice against settlers who could not speak English, and little pressure was placed upon them to adopt the language. The presence of aliens was rarely mentioned. Only once did officials express fear of non-English residents. In 1715, responding to a threat of war in the Baltic in which France might ally with Sweden against England, the council noted that the "Old Inhabitants" had an "intimate acquaintance" with the Indians that might prove dangerous. Councilmen also noted that the Swedish government had been sending missionaries to the colony, and that Swedes continued to use their native language. They thought the Swedes "have too much kept up the Distinction of their nation from us" and questioned, momentarily, their loyalty to the English regime.[245] They forgot that Swedish ministers usually learned English rapidly and associated with Anglicans and that several men of Swedish descent had held positions in Penn's government.

Welsh and Swedish leaders might have preferred that their countrypeople preserve their native language, but made no strident efforts to discourage the adoption of English and the slow drift toward bilingualism. German leaders encouraged full participation in provincial life. Pastorius reminded his children that, even though they were of German parentage, their father had been naturalized and they were native-born English subjects. "Therefore, it would be a shame for you if you should be ignorant of the English Tongue, the Tongue of your Countrymen."[246] Germans who learned English often participated with Englishmen in religious services, both as members and as teachers.[247] On several occasions Daniel Falckner referred to the English legal system established in the colony, and recommended that his readers learn and follow English customs and procedures. He also encouraged aliens to be naturalized so that they could participate in international or intercolonial trade.[248]

Penn's dream of establishing a refuge where people of all nationalities and faiths could live with minimal infringements upon their religious inclinations and exercise what he considered the fundamental rights of English subjects was difficult to achieve. In their attempt to create a framework for civil society, Pennsylvanians learned that the demands of conscience could be diametrically opposed. Initially, there was little inclination to compromise; cries of "persecution" were frequently heard.

Yet prior to William Penn's death in 1718, the relationships among Pennsylvania's diverse religious groups stabilized into relative toleration. Many people seemed indifferent to organized religion, while others, faced by a lack of formal worship in the modes to which they were accustomed, became more interested in the similarities among sects than in the differences. Although many held strong religious beliefs and considered those holding different views to be in error, proselytization was limited, and only Anglicans hoped to diminish freedom of worship. Individual colonists and ministers alike reached a form of accommodation to Pennsylvania's religious situation similar to that advocated by Johannes Kelpius, a German mystic. Although he resented charges that he was a Quaker or a Roman Catholic, he pointed out that he "love[d] them from my inmost soul, even as I do all other sects that approach and call themselves Christ's." Rather than concern themselves with fine points of doctrine, it was important that brotherly love remain on a firm foundation and that individuals not be narrowminded.[249]

Not all colonists agreed, and religious strife characterized the colony's existence for several years. At the same time, though, tensions among ethnic and linguistic groups were minimal. Perhaps this was due to the clear dominance of the English-speaking portion of the population, with only relatively small admixtures of other groups. Pennsylvanians knew that their colony was heterogeneous, yet pluralism did not pose a threat. Perhaps the low population density of the 30,000 colonists present in 1717 limited their perception of the colony's variety. Many writers mentioned that all colonists lived in peace; others simply noted the diversity and discussed other matters, primarily economic or religious, in more detail.

Writing to a Welsh Quaker in 1717, Francis Daniel Pastorius commented on the meanings of friendship and Christian fellowship. Christian fellowship seeks at all times and places the good of our fellow mortals; the primary commandment is "to love one another." But, he continued,

Of the Old Romans we read, they had their 1st 2d & 3d rate friends, admitting some only into the Court-yard or hall, others into the Antichamber, or parlour; but their privados into their Closets, & bed rooms. So me thinks we may do the same with a blameless partiality. The Welsh & Dutch &c. may endear those of their own Nation more than either French or Danes like as the Apostle was deeplier affected with his Countrymen.[250]

By 1717 most of the ethnic and religious groups in Penn's province had come to accept one another as at least third-rate friends. It was a fragile arrangement, however, that could be eroded by the pressures of new events unless Penn's heirs and Pennsylvanians accepted the charge to maintain his ideals through the coming decades.

CHAPTER 4

Immigration,

1717–1740

Pennsylvania experienced the first of several waves of migrants from northern Ireland and the German-speaking states bordering on the Rhine and extending into Switzerland in 1717. Throughout the remainder of the colonial era it was the favored destination for thousands of emigrants from these areas, for it offered both economic opportunity and freedom of conscience.[1] The magnitude of this migration increased the colony's population and prosperity, while the variety of its sources significantly enhanced the province's cultural, linguistic, and religious diversity. The implications of William Penn's decision to create a refuge for oppressed people became clearer as Pennsylvanians were forced to devise methods of adjusting to the unusual and rapidly developing complexity of their province.

The initial responses of provincial leaders to the sudden and unexpected arrival of German and Scotch-Irish immigrants foreshadowed themes that would become prominent as immigration continued. Out of their uncertainty and confusion would evolve generalized patterns that constantly shifted as conditions altered. It soon became evident that immigration raised practical questions about land policy, the relationships of immigrants with the Indians, naturalization (or other

immig nd wh prejudice
Scots fr Ireland

assurances of allegiance to the English and proprietary regimes), public health, and ultimately the nature of the "Quaker" colony itself.

Prejudice was not unknown. Some stereotypes developed that distinguished the "Palatines" from the "Irish." Occasionally and for brief
periods the colonial elite expressed nativist fears and prejudices and a
desire to limit immigration or to deflect it to other colonies. More
frequently, and more consistently, they rejoiced at the industry of
newcomers and the prosperity they brought or might bring to the
province.

                                      I

The eighteenth-century emigration of Protestants from Ireland originated in England's seventeenth-century efforts to control and colonize
that island. Impelled by poverty at home and low rents in Ireland,
many lowland Scots emigrated to Ireland, especially to Ulster, where
large tracts of land had been confiscated by the Crown. Others followed as soldiers sent to crush the Irish sequel to the Revolution of
1688, and as colonists recruited to settle on lands that came under
English ownership following the Williamite Settlement.

For many, Ireland was only a temporary home. Beginning in 1717
and at intervals thereafter, leases granted on favorable terms to encourage Protestant colonists began to expire. Landlords, primarily
English absentees interested only in deriving profits from their estates,
refused to renew leases except at higher rates that were difficult to
meet, especially on marginal land. Furthermore, tenants faced competition from the native Irish Roman Catholic population. The Scots
complained that the Irish would accept a lower living standard and
that landlords leased farms to whoever would pay the highest rent,
regardless of nationality or religion. Frequent crop failures, partly due
to poor agricultural techniques, and the resulting threat of starvation
provided further motives for emigration. New regulations on the export of agricultural products and on the woolen and linen industries
reduced employment prospects. In addition, the regional right of tenants to sell their interest in farms if they were unable to pay the rent
or desired to give them up also stimulated emigration from Ulster. At

Palatinate immigr
motives?
    30 yrs war
    Louis XIV

least in theory, these tenants were more mobile than those elsewhere in Ireland.

Religious motives added a further incentive for emigration. With the consolidation of English control in Ireland, the predominantly Presbyterian Scots, who had formed the established church in Scotland, found themselves classed as "dissenters" barred after 1704 from holding civil and military commissions. Subsequent laws impinged upon their educational institutions and on the functions their ministers were permitted to perform. A further source of discontent was the rigorous collection of tithes, which increased proportionately with rents.[2]

Unlike the emigration from Ireland or the 1709 emigration from the Palatinate, which was triggered by war, severe weather, and crop failure, there were no precise causes for the beginnings of widespread emigration from Europe in 1717. Instead, the sources of emigration from Switzerland and the German states of the Palatinate are found in generalized conditions and in pressures on individuals living in different areas.

The Thirty Years War (1618–1648) had resulted in widespread destruction of farmland, livestock, and property, as well as a severe reduction of the population. Subsequent raids by French armies into the Palatinate during the wars of Louis XIV again brought desolation to the region. Crop failure and famine often followed military activities or harsh weather. Remnants of feudalism increased the poverty and misery of the Germanic peoples, for petty nobles exacted heavy taxes in order to imitate the luxury of the French court. Religious factors contributed to the economic incentives for emigration. Sectarianism flourished in the turmoil of the age, but rarely did secular or religious authorities tolerate dissent from the established order. Harassment, persecution, and banishment occurred, driving sectarians to consider migration, while the tolerant policies of an occasional ruler who offered sanctuary to the oppressed were often reversed upon his death or with a change in political conditions and alliances. Most emigrants, however, were adherents of the Lutheran and Reformed faiths that, with Roman Catholicism, had obtained a measure of toleration following the settlement of the Thirty Years War. Although some experienced hardships because of their beliefs, the primary motives for emigration were economic.[3]

To individuals living under adverse economic or religious conditions, Pennsylvania offered inexpensive land, low taxes, an opportunity to improve one's economic status, and almost complete freedom from restrictions on religious beliefs or forms of worship. The reputation that Pennsylvania had acquired as a haven for immigrants of all backgrounds, in contrast to the chilly reception the Scotch-Irish met in Massachusetts[4] and the unfortunate circumstances in which the Palatine emigrants of 1709 found themselves in New York,[5] influenced the choice of European emigrants' destinations.

The intensive promotional activities conducted by William Penn and his allies were not continued by his heirs following his death in 1718, although Penn's writings and other promotional literature continued to circulate. Merchants and their agents, who profited by transporting passengers to the colonies, played a greater role in arousing interest in migration and in helping to direct the flow to Pennsylvania. Private letters from colonists describing provincial conditions played a significant part in directing later emigrants to that colony and in convincing family members and friends to join recent arrivals in the colony. In 1755 the German printer Christopher Sauer claimed that his earlier letters had been "printed and reprinted, and provoked many a thousand people to come to this province."[6]

One aspect of life in the province that many writers emphasized, both positively and negatively, was freedom. In a letter written shortly after his arrival, Sauer praised the liberality of a country where all inhabitants were free to live "quietly and piously" and where "everybody may believe what he chooses."[7] He expanded on this theme in a letter written the following year. It was "a good and free country" where each inhabitant could live "according to his will and knowledge." Sauer realized that there were drawbacks to liberty, for Pennsylvania had become a "gathering place" for all sorts of "restless and eccentric people." He also believed that the ease with which prosperity could be attained posed the threat of "great spiritual danger." Nevertheless, the "children of God" could find asylum "secure from outward persecution."[8]

More negatively, another German who wrote a few years later observed that "Socinianism, Naturalism, and Atheism" were "expanding greatly" in the province.[9] Esther Werndtlin, whose letter was publicized by Swiss officials in order to discourage emigration, criticized conditions in Pennsylvania: "here are religions and nationalities without number; this land is an asylum for banished sects, a sanctuary for all evil-doers from Europe, a confused Babel, a receptacle for all unclean spirits, an abode of the devil, a first world, a Sodom, which is deplorable."[10] But Durs Thommen, also from Switzerland, noted that "one has excellent liberties in this country in all sorts of things." The "great variety of sects" notwithstanding, "all nationalities are friendly and serviceable toward one another."[11]

Except to sectarians, Pennsylvania's primary appeal lay in its promises of opportunity. While many believed that individuals should not emigrate solely for economic reasons and without divine direction, conditions were attractive. Artisans were in demand, well paid for their labors, and the authorities imposed neither guilds nor other burdens. Anyone willing to work could readily find employment. Land was excellent, affordable, and highly productive. Wildlife was abundant, and food was inexpensive. Prospective immigrants were advised not to indenture themselves to the captain of the vessel on which they traveled. They should promise to pay the fare upon arrival and invest in a stock of goods that could be sold in the colony. They could then pay for the voyage out of the proceeds, for imported goods were expensive and some items were scarce. Robert Parke advised his friends to bring three or four servants with them and agree to pay for their passage upon arrival. Two could be sold to pay the expenses of all of them, and the transporter would be guaranteed a source of labor for a few years if he retained the other servants. If, however, young people chose to come as servants, they would serve only for a few years while being decently clothed and well fed.[12]

Pennsylvanians were surprised at the unusually large number of ships, transporting German and Irish passengers, that were arriving in Philadelphia in the summer and autumn of 1717. Initial reactions varied. Jonathan Dickinson, a Quaker merchant, recalled that about five years earlier, a number of "Laborious Industrious" Palatines had purchased land along the frontier and had "made Very Considerable Improvements" in the colony. He expected the same from these newcomers. In addition to "our Common supply from Wales & other parts of great Brittain," immigrants from Ireland were expected. Most of the colonists, he reported, were "ffree passengers" rather than indentured servants.[13] Quaker leader Isaac Norris, on the other hand, wrote that "thinking people here are a little Shockt to See such great numb[r] of forreign[rs] Come in" to settle in the province. He "could be more pleas'd to See fewer," and thought they should "mix in y[r] Settlem[ts] as other people do" rather than settle in compact groups "between our Indians and us."[14] Proprietary functionary James Logan declared that "the Number of these Strangers has given some uneasiness" to Pennsylvanians, which he was apprehensive would increase if immigrants continued "their Swarms." He was amazed that such large numbers who did not understand English and possessed no "Credentials" could be "exported" to a single English plantation "without y[e] least notice taken of it" by royal officials or the proprietors.[15]

By November Dickinson, too, had begun to worry about the colony's future. Estimating that "above 2200 [immigrants had landed] in aboute four months," he predicted that "we Shall have a great mixt multitude." Like others, he began to wonder "how to Deal" with those who are "Strang[rs] to our Laws & Customes & we to their Language" who arrived with no official status except the shipmaster's report on the number of passengers who had embarked. Proposals had been made to follow the precedents of other colonies to levy duties of £5 and £10 on different types of immigrants.[16] Logan advised a correspondent that Palatines who came in 1718 should expect to pay £10 per head, for "we are resolved to receive no more of them."[17]

Despite the consternation of governor, council, and assembly at the sudden population increase, no steps were taken at this time to restrict immigration.[18] Governor William Keith informed his council that "great numbers of fforeigners from Germany, strangers to our Language & Constitutions," had arrived in the colony. Without producing any information indicating "from whence they came or what they were"— indeed "without making the least application to himself or to any of the magistrates"—they "dispersed themselves" immediately after they landed. Such practices were dangerous, for aliens "from any nation whatever, as well Enemys as friends" might "throw themselves" upon the province. The council concurred, ordering shipmasters to provide lists of the number and "Characters" of passengers they had transported. Incoming vessels would not be entered until this information was produced. Immigrants who had recently debarked, and those who subsequently arrived, were ordered to appear before a magistrate to subscribe declarations "of their being well affected to his Majesty and his Government."[19] When the assembly convened a month later for a brief organizational session, Keith advised it "not to lose any Time" in securing the colony from the "Inconveniencies" that might arise from the "unlimited Number of Foreigners that, without any Licence from the King, or Leave of this Government, have been transported" to the province.[20] The assembly recommended forming a joint committee with the council to "concert proper Methods for removing the Jealousies already raised in the Minds of the Inhabitants" concerning aliens. Steps should be taken to prevent "their Settlement in one Place, or promiscuously amongst the Indians."[21] Nevertheless, Keith decided to postpone action until he received the advice he expected from England.[22]

Although late in 1717 James Logan declared that "Our Countrey People are inflamed ag^st" the emigrants from the Palatinate and "we are to sell them no more Land,"[23] several German residents petitioned the surveyors and commissioners of property for land grants adjacent to their settlements that would be set apart for newcomers. They assured the commissioners that their "Relations, ffriends or acquaintances" were "Honest, Conscientious People." The commissioners pointed out that aliens could not sell their property nor could their children inherit it, but the petitioners replied that they had known the regulations before they had emigrated. Despite the risks, they were "willing to purchase Lands for their own Dwelling." After suggesting that the petitioners apply to the assembly for a naturalization act that would guarantee their property rights, the commissioners issued the warrants.[24]

Immigrants, regardless of nationality, hoped to obtain new homes and land to farm, while the Penn family, colonial officials, and private landholders wanted to sell or lease land and obtain orderly settlement patterns. Unfortunately a dispute in the Penn family between 1718 and 1732 over the terms of William Penn's will made it difficult, if not impossible, for land titles to be issued; the land office was closed for several years. An unresolved dispute with the Calvert family over the boundary between Maryland and Pennsylvania also added to the insecurity of settlers.[25] Isaac Norris believed that the Penn family dispute encouraged "this Pyraticall Insolence & disregard to propertie," or squatting.[26] Logan told Hannah Penn that most immigrants "resolutely sitt down and improve, without any manner of Right or Pretence to it." He urged "a final and absolute Settlem'" of the family dispute, and then "the Presence of the Proprietary himself to direct how his Lands Shall be disposed of."[27]

These problems that precluded land sales and the preservation of order fostered negative views of immigrants, who were denounced for their unwillingness to delay settlement until they could legally purchase land. Little distinction was made among the origins of settlers who, "prest by their necessity," moved toward the frontier.[28] "Impudent Voluntary Settlers" encroached upon lands belonging to the proprietors, absentee landlords, speculators, and Indians alike. Defending their actions, they argued that "they are come into a new Country to Settle it & must have Land."[29] It was becoming a "Custom" to settle on remote lands. Living like "Hermites," squatters could inflict great damage on property before anyone "Can, does, or will, Informe."[30]

A visible increase in the number of vessels carrying Irish and German passengers in 1727 aroused more definite concerns about immigration and the quality of life in the province. Officials, dismayed at the number of "Strangers," became increasingly interested in devising methods to regulate or restrict immigration. The council's 1717 order that lists of passengers be provided before they were permitted to land had frequently been ignored.[31] Thus, when Governor Patrick Gordon informed the council in September 1727 that a ship carrying four hundred Palatines had recently arrived and that several additional ships were expected, it was prepared to consider more effective action. Gordon echoed Keith's earlier concerns: immigrants "design[ed] to settle in the back parts of this province" and took up land without the knowledge or consent of the proprietors or the commissioners of property. Provincial peace and security were endangered by the "Strangers . . .

who being ignorant of our Language & Laws, & settling in a body together, make, as it were, a distinct people from his Majesties Subjects."

Councillors noted that because "these People pretended at first that they fly hither on the Score of their religious Liberties, and come under the Protection of His Majesty," it was appropriate that they declare allegiance to the King and fidelity to the proprietors, and promise to obey provincial laws. They decided to require lists of the names, occupations, places of origin, and reasons for emigration, and to formulate a declaration of loyalty for each immigrant to sign. A week later the first group of immigrants was brought before the council to sign the statement of allegiance after the shipmaster had provided vague information about them.[32]

In December 1727 several Philadelphians petitioned the government about the situation. Having observed that five ships from Rotterdam carrying more than 1300 people had arrived during one month, and having heard rumors that 5000 to 6000 emigrants would arrive the following year, they expressed concern about the colony's future. They traced the origin of this movement to the Swiss Mennonites who had arrived in 1710, purchased inexpensive land, and reported their favorable reception to friends and relatives, whom they encouraged to follow them to the colony. Other accounts of the province had subsequently excited "the same Inclination to remove," with the result that immigration "considerably encreased . . . one Ship-Load after another of all professions." But in contrast to the Mennonites, "All these men" were "generally very well armed" and appeared "inured" to war or other hardships. Palatines "retire commonly back into the woods," sometimes purchasing land but more often settling on vacant tracts "without asking questions, Menacing those afterwards who offer to disturb them in their possessions." Few requested naturalization, supposing themselves, as the petitioners thought, "secure in their Numbers from all Danger of Escheats." Nor did they attempt to learn the English language or customs. A further danger was that the immigrants, many of whom allegedly spoke French, settled along the frontier near territory claimed by France. It was assumed that they would support that nation as willingly as they would England if war broke out. The petitioners also believed that "many" immigrants were "Papists," who thus posed another threat to the colony. They suggested enactment of a law that would ban immigration by Europeans who had not been naturalized in England or who did not hold a pass from one of the secretaries of state.[33]

Other Pennsylvanians shared these sentiments. Logan feared that if Parliament did not regulate immigration, "these Colonies will in time be lost to ye Crown."[34] Governor Gordon informed the Duke of Newcastle of the dangers posed by the "vast number of armed fforeigners crowding in upon us," and suggested that Parliament consider regulatory methods. He argued that, since British interests in the plantations were carefully guarded in other respects, this new issue of alien immigration merited due consideration.[35] Logan believed that the situation had been ignored because Pennsylvania was a proprietary colony and therefore not directly under royal oversight.[36]

When the assembly convened in January 1727/8, it appointed a committee to study the magnitude of German immigration, their disorderly settlement practices that were to the "great Prejudice and Disquiet" of other inhabitants, and the refusal of "many" of them to "yield Obedience" to the government.[37] It reported that "considerable Numbers" of the Germans were "very sober and honest People, both in their religious and civil Duties," who had purchased and paid for land, shown a proper respect for the government, and paid their taxes. Nevertheless, "sundry" Palatines were squatters who refused to obey the authorities. The rumor that Pennsylvania could expect "great Numbers" of German immigrants the following summer was confirmed. On the strength of this ambivalent report, the assembly carried in the affirmative a motion that "the great Importation of Foreigners into this Province . . . who are Subjects of a foreign Prince, and who keep up amongst themselves a different Language, may, in Time, prove of dangerous Consequence to the Peace" of the colony.[38]

Addressing the governor on this issue, the assembly substantially repeated the committee's report and added, "forasmuch as the Inhabitants of this Province, in general, are a People whose religious Principle is against bearing of Arms, or making of War," continued immigration "might be of dangerous Consequence to the Peace and Safety of the Province."[39] Following another summer during which "The Palatines crowd[ed] in upon us and the Irish yet faster,"[40] Governor

Gordon declared that he had "positive Orders" from England to enact a law against the "Crowds of Forreigners" who yearly inundated the province. The need for regulations arose not from "any Dislike to the People themselves," many of whom were "peaceable, industrious, & well affected," but "to prevent an English Plantation from being turned into a Colony of Aliens." Germans were not the sole problem; measures were required "to prevent the Importation of Irish Papists & Convicts," several of the "most notorious" of whom, Gordon asserted, had recently arrived in the colony.[41] Expressing gratitude that British officials had recognized the wisdom of regulating alien immigration, the assembly promised to give its attention to the problem. Furthermore, "no Endeavors . . . shall be wanting" to prevent the "Importation of Irish Papists and Convicts." Such immigrants were "so pernicious an Evil" that they threatened the "Religious and Civil Rights" of Pennsylvanians.[42]

Despite these concerns, not until 1729, and "with great Difficulty," according to Gordon,[43] was a law enacted imposing a duty of twenty shillings on all Irish servants and redemptioners and one of forty shillings on all aliens who entered the province. Male aliens over the age of sixteen were to subscribe declarations of allegiance, supremacy, and abjuration within forty-eight hours of their arrival. To prevent the landing of Pennsylvania-bound passengers in adjacent colonies, all aliens and Irish servants discovered in the province within a year of their arrival were liable for the tax, and any person responsible for fraudulently landing them could be fined £20 per individual. The purpose of the law was frankly stated: "to discourage the great importation . . . of foreigners and of lewd, idle and ill-affected persons" who disturbed the "quiet and safety of the peaceable people" of the province or who were burdensome because of their "age, impotency or idleness."[44]

Although the assembly rejected appeals to mitigate the unexpected tax,[45] almost immediately after the new assembly convened in October 1729 a motion was made to repeal "certain Clauses" of this act.[46] Without recording discussion, the assembly voted on 16 January 1729/30 to repeal it completely. It was replaced by a duty of £5 on all "persons convicted of heinous crimes." To prevent the importation of "poor and impotent" persons, the shipmaster or merchant who transported

Quaker meeting

them was required to return them to their place of origin or to "in-
demnify the province" for any charges that might result from their
settlement. In addition, a registry of servants was to be maintained.[47]
Gordon reported that the original law had proved "very inconvenient
& like to produce a general Dissatisfaction amongst the Irish, who in
this Country are very numerous, and likewise amongst the Germans
all of whom have hitherto been very averse to factious Principles."
They had apparently united in petitions to the council and assembly
for repeal of the law.[48]

   The anomalous character of the earlier vote is highlighted by the
assembly's simultaneous consideration of several requests for naturalization from established German residents. Mennonite petitioners were
allowed to subscribe the declarations of allegiance in their own fashion, while other Protestants swore the required oaths.[49] The governor, after "strict Enquiry" into the petitioners' "Characters," recommended favorable action. Because many of them had emigrated under
a "particular Agreement" with William Penn, had "regularly" taken
up lands and had proven their "Honesty & Industry," they deserved
the "Esteem of this Government, & a Mark of its Regard for them."[50]
Anticipating a later concern, he suggested a year later that naturaliz-
ing wealthier Germans or "honest Tenants" might "make a considerable Addition to our [the proprietary] Interest at Elections."[51] The act
that naturalized 113 men recognized the contributions they had made
to the prosperity of the colony and their religious and obedient behavior.[52]

Pennsylvania officials demonstrated concern about the implications of
immigration for the province's future most consistently between 1727
and 1740. Immigrants presented problems, irrespective of their origins.
During this period they seem to have been poorer than earlier immigrants; a greater proportion came as indentured servants or redemptioners.[53] They were often considered to have undesirable traits. When
the Yearly Meeting exhorted Friends to live according to the tenets of
the sect and to avoid vice and immorality, it took notice of the "many"
among the "great increase of People" who "appear regardless of religion, Probity, and Vertue" and "Rush into Immoralities and tumultuous Practices."[54] When some immigrants mentioned promotional

materials or William Penn's invitations as a motive for migrating to the colony, officials contemptuously remarked that "In y[e] year 1681 now 46 years agoe he invited many honest People, to come & settle under him, but y[e] acco[t] we have of y[e] Conduct, of too many of these folks, they doe not appear, to be the men intended."[55]

The quality of provincial life, some Quakers believed, had seriously deteriorated as a result of unrestricted immigration. Begun and "for a Considerable time Improved by a Sober Industrious people," the colony had attracted undesirables through its reputation for "Ease & plenty." "[K]idnappers or procurors of Servants" had exploited its reputation for "kind Usage" of them to "Crowd us without Choice or Care." In addition, Pennsylvania was a victim of British laws for the transportation of felons. These laws might be "human and mercifull," but in consequence "Roberies, housebrakeing Rapes & other crimes are become Common." Although many "honest ffr[ds] And Other Sober Valluable People" still lived in the colony, the problem, Isaac Norris believed, was the "Disproportionate Encrease of Others" that presaged a "Melancholly Prospect" for the province.[56] James Logan found it surprising that, despite a variety of problems, "especially . . . y[e] Concourse of foreigners," the colony was in "no worse a Condition." He concluded that the "most indulgent Eye of Providence" had been watching over Pennsylvania.[57]

During the first extended period of immigration the articulate elite often indicated that the colony was experiencing an unprecedented and unending stream of "Idle worthless people."[58] Almost hysterically, provincial leaders reported that vacant lands were "invaded by those Shoals of foreigners the Palatines & Strangers from the North of Irel[d] that crowd in upon us"[59] and that the backcountry was "fill'd" by the "vast numbers of Strangers and foreigners settling in it without order or method."[60] Pennsylvanians no longer needed colonists to "fill our Wilderness Country," which had allowed earlier immigrants to be "Mostly Swallowed Up" in the country.[61]

Immigrants were accused of taking up land by irregular methods. Both the Germans and Scotch-Irish "sitt frequently down on any spott of vacant Land they can find," asserted Logan.[62] The "Custom of Setting down upon back lands w[th]out leave or paying anything" had become "So generall" that it was termed "Oppression" to hinder such

settlements or to demand rent.[63] Squatters not only disturbed property owners and the proprietors, but also caused "ye further dissatisfaction of the Indians" by crossing the Susquehanna River into their
territory.[64] By the late 1730s, as a result of the desire of new immigrants to acquire property, one official in the land office claimed that
"it is now difficult to finde a Tract of one Thousand Acres of Tolerable Land in one Spot."[65]

Immigrants allegedly could not, or would not, pay for their land.
The Germans and Scotch-Irish "pretend they would buy, but not one
in twenty has anything to pay with."[66] Because the Penn family owned
most of the land, "people think or are told that they may make free
Under pretence of paying for it" when the land office reopened after
the family dispute among Penn's heirs was resolved. Furthermore,
they utterly disregarded the claims of private owners; when questioned about the justice of their actions, they replied, "What must
poor men do."[67] Others said it was "against the Laws of God & Nature that so much Land should lie idle, while so many Christians
wanted it to labour on and raise their Bread."[68] A new and dangerous
innovation was that some who had never paid for land had "No Scruple" against selling their "Improvements as they call it" and relocating
on a more pleasing site.[69] Some individuals went about "Marking Unsetled places And then keeping Em for a Market and Selling them to
Newcomers or Strangers" or reserved tracts for their friends or children, even if they had not "payd a penny" for their land.[70]

In dealing with these issues, Pennsylvania officials initially had difficulty recognizing leaders or spokesmen for the German community,
but occasionally attempted to use Presbyterian ministers as intermediaries in dealing with the Scotch-Irish. Although there was some
question about the "Interest or Influence"[71] ministers had, officials
hoped that the clergy would bring their auditors to a greater regard
for the principle of justice. Ministers were requested to persuade
squatters to move before legal action became necessary.[72] One clergyman was asked to remind a parishioner that his "Duty as a Profess'd
Christian" required him to forbear cutting timber on another man's
property.[73] Logan once questioned the minister of a Scotch-Irish congregation at Donegal, "Pray how have these people been taught?" if

they failed to comprehend what "the Glory of God, Justice or Honesty had to do with their Agreem^t" with the proprietors.[74]

With the beginnings of immigration from new sources, Pennsylvanians confronted the problem of ethnic pluralism. New attitudes toward life in a pluralistic society were expressed; these ideas would be further defined, clarified, and modified as migration continued. It was in the period after 1717 that residents first became fully aware that their province would differ from England not only in its religious diversity and tolerant policies, but in its ethnic composition as well.

As immigration continued, stereotypes of the newcomers became more clearly defined. Provincial leaders could find very little to say in favor of colonists from Ireland, except that the "prodigeous Numbers" of them "alone are enough to keep up the price of our Commodity^s[.]"[75] One thought that the "Great Numbers of ye Ordinary and profligate" who had arrived from that island were, for the "great part," the "very Scum of Mankind."[76] The immigrants were "mostly poor beggarly Idle people" who might "Trouble" other inhabitants.[77] Another admitted that "'tho' there are some truly honest," many of them were "capable of the highest villainies." New laws were needed to "curb their insolencies."[78] Governor Gordon confessed to a "Dislike" of the "Irish," whom he thought had "little Honesty and less Sense." Irish servants, he believed, "have mostly been gathered from Goals [sic]."[79] Emigrants from Ireland were "tricking and contentious." Logan's experiences in the land office convinced him that "the settlement of 5 families from Ireland" gave "more trouble than fifty of any other people."[80] A "disorderly People" who made "Audacious Attack[s]" on property, they "threatned to hold it by force of arms"[81] and could be removed only with difficulty. They were, in brief, "Idle trash."[82]

The Scotch-Irish also were perceived as a threat to the peaceful relations the provincial government hoped to maintain with the Indians. When an Indian "Disturbance" threatened in the 1720s, Logan directed "a considerable Number of good Sober People" from Ireland to the frontier. He thought it "prudent to plant a Settlem^t of such men as those who formerly had so bravely defended Derry & Inniskillen" to secure the territory.[83] But large numbers of immigrants were difficult to regulate, for they disregarded Indian claims. It was difficult to pacify Indians whose lands were "invaded by Swarms of Strangers that they have an Aversion to, for the Irish are generally rough to them." When three Indians were found murdered, Civility, their leader, was "of opinion that ye Irish" had committed the crime.[84]

German immigrants did not evoke such frequent and contemptuous comments. Despite the initial concern voiced over the "strangers to our Language & Constitutions"[85] and occasional comments favoring means to discourage their immigration, little was actively done toward this end.[86] Palatines were described as "a surley people," and it was said that the men were "generally well arm'd." There were "divers Papists" allegedly among them.[87] They were "S^d to be Sowre & Ill-natur'd fellowes."[88] Some complained that, like the Scotch-Irish, the Germans encroached on land belonging to the proprietors and others.[89]

Such comments were nevertheless balanced by a recognition of positive attributes most German and Swiss settlers were thought to have. Some Germans were skilled in producing copper and iron, industries certain Pennsylvanians hoped to develop.[90] There appears to have been a greater assumption that they were honest and would pay rent or purchase land once proper grants could be made.[91] Many believed that the Palatines had brought money with them and hoped to sell land easily to them.[92] Mennonites were singled out as an "Industerious and Laborius people" who had brought considerable wealth with them.[93] The Penn family continued to negotiate with individuals from Switzerland and Germany interested in purchasing large tracts of land and recruiting colonists from among their countrypeople.[94] By 1732/3 John Penn, who believed that the prosperity of a country depended on the number of its inhabitants, concluded that "we ought by no Mean's to Debarr their Coming over," for impoverished German emigrants would settle on "advanced rent." Once settled, all would come to consider themselves Pennsylvanians, "& from the first Law of Nature (self Preservation) always Joyn in acting for the good of the Country."[95]

It took time, however, for these views to predominate, especially toward Germans whose skill with arms allegedly matched their proficiency with the plow. Some of the prevailing attitudes toward immigrants from the Palatinate and the problems that they might cause are illuminated by the reception accorded a group of Germans who arrived in 1723. Invited to settle in Pennsylvania by Governor William Keith while he was attending an Indian conference in Albany in 1722, they were part of the 1709 contingent sent to New York. Dissatisfied with conditions there, sixty families accepted Keith's offer and decided to migrate to Pennsylvania. The first group arrived in 1723, with others following in 1728. Keith directed them toward the Tulpehocken region, where they settled on land not yet clear of Indian claims and on privately owned land.[96] Keith was accused of settling "a Parcel of imprudent necessitous Foreigners" and "An unruly Sort of Palatines" on some of the best land in the province.[97] Furthermore, Indians complained that they "had their Corn destroyed by those Peoples Creatures."[98] Logan finally suggested that these people, "too numerous and resolute" to be removed and who had settled on these lands "by what they accounted an authority," be allowed to remain. By 1727 he thought they would be willing to pay rent or a reasonable purchase price for their land.[99]

Because Keith had been attempting to gain autonomy from the proprietary family, it is not surprising that his opponents accused him of trying to curry favor with the Germans in order to increase his power.[100] One thought his goal was to "gain them as his Janizaries upon occasion," for the Germans "have generally ben Soldiers."[101] Another believed it would not be "Unreasonable" to conclude that the Tulpehocken settlers might be used as an "Oblig'd & Engaged Army of Mirmydons for purposes Yet in ye shell."[102]

When Keith introduced a bill to naturalize almost 400 aliens, including some of the Tulpehocken residents, in March 1724/5,[103] colonial politicians resisted. Some thought that Keith would be paid by the aliens to obtain passage of the bill. Since almost all of the foreigners were "unknown" to the assembly, with few of the "better sort" of immigrants included in the proposed bill, this procedure "Alarm'd Every body, Who have any thing like Estates" in the province.[104] After a lengthy debate, the assembly demanded that the aliens fulfill conditions it had previously required, including proof that they had made declarations of allegiance and fidelity to the Crown and proprietors and would make a profession of their Christian belief according to parliamentary statutes, before the bill would be considered further. Information from a justice of the peace concerning their "Characters, Belief and Behaviour" was also required.[105] Although Keith objected that it was contrary to "natural and equal Justice" and "a most dangerous Precedent" to inquire into "private Conversation and Faith" as well as to "pry into the Circumstances of their private Estates,"[106] the assembly remained obstinate.[107] By August it was inclined to require only that the aliens qualify themselves "as the Law in those Cases directs,"[108] and in November it accepted the petition of a few Germans who had so qualified for permission to submit a naturalization bill. Finally, in March 1725/6, it enacted a bill that naturalized seven Germans.[109]

The assembly's objections to the original bill seem to have arisen more from a suspicion of Keith's motives, the number of individuals included, and its presentation by the governor rather than by the personal appearance or petition of the men involved than from their attitudes toward alien immigration. Germans were caught in the middle of political disputes involving issues other than naturalization.[110] The assembly's concern about the estates of these aliens was probably intended as a delaying tactic, for poverty alone did not preclude naturalization. In fact, the men naturalized in 1725/6 later petitioned for, and were granted, a rebate on part of the costs incurred in obtaining the bill's passage on the grounds of their impecunity.[111]

The Scotch-Irish and the Germans were not always more open to each other than the English sometimes were to either. In 1727 Donegal inhabitants requested the commissioners of property to forbid the "Dutch" to settle between their settlement and Swatara Creek.[112] A few years later there were complaints that Germans were interested in purchasing farms originally owned by Scotch-Irish emigrants. The Donegal settlers had intended to form a relatively compact community where they could support a Presbyterian minister, but "unstay'd" people had begun to consider their private interests and to sell their farms to the "best Bidders," usually Germans. James Logan confirmed that there had been no alterations in the stipulation that newcomers could not be admitted without the "Consent" of the community. Although the "Improvem^ts" made on a tract could be sold, the right to purchase the land was restricted. It would be safer, Logan concluded, for Germans or others to "forbear."[113]

Immigrants were only occasionally viewed in political terms, and only rarely was the diversity of the colony perceived to threaten the established governmental order. Although Keith was suspected of attempting to form German colonists into a personal faction and Gordon suggested that naturalized Pennsylvanians might express their appreciation by supporting proprietary interests, these were only hints of a theme that would become prominent in provincial politics after 1740. One Pennsylvanian noted the influence Welshmen in Chester County had with their sheriff. Because they were "the Greatest Votarys for Election," they elected "Such men . . . as shall screen them." Some officials feared "they should be in danger of their Life" if they tried to enforce laws within the Welsh community.[114] In one election, it was rumored that a potential candidate favored "charging foreigners wth a Duty on their Trade," but Logan, who believed that this man was highly qualified for the assembly, "boldly" and "freely" gave his word that the candidate "will attempt nothing of the kind."[115] Only a broadside objecting to proposed changes in the court of chancery used the argument that "in a Colony numerous of Foreigners of divers Nations," the proposed scheme might be dangerous to the administration of justice "when possibly these Foreigners may be advanced to those Seats." The anonymous author was concerned primarily, however, that "artful Men" might manipulate credulous electors and thereby pervert justice.[116]

One example presaging the future politicization of ethnicity involved the Swedes. In 1721/2 several men of Swedish descent petitioned the assembly to confirm land titles granted under the government of the Duke of York, for "designing Persons" had given them "Uneasiness" by questioning the validity of their titles.[117] Investigation by the commissioners of property revealed that none of the petitioners had tenuous titles. The Swedes, they concluded, "have certainly the least reason to complain of hard Usage," and reviewed Penn's benevolences to them in property matters. Remarking that this was not the first time that Swedes had been used by the government's opponents, the commissioners noted that "of themselves, & when not misled by others," the Swedes were "quiet honest Men." But they suggested that the governor consider "how far it is consistent with the Peace, Honour, or Security of an English Governm^t, that they who, by their Birth are really English" subjects "Should upon occasion be thus nationally distinguished."[118]

Swedes came under suspicion for apparently minor reasons. In 1726 Logan noted that "they are generally managed here by every disaffected Party," although a "quiet People, when left to y^{m}selves." But English authorities should be aware that a Swedish geography book termed the country "New Sweden reckoning it among ye Swedish Dominions," and that a Swedish-Indian catechism published between 1690 and 1700 included a map in which the Delaware Valley was labelled "Suecia Nova." Logan recommended that Swedish missionaries, whom he termed "by far ye best of ye Cloth y^t come amongst us," preach and conduct their services in English. Since these priests obtained a "competent Skill" in English "in a short time" and "frequently" preached in Anglican churches, adoption of the English form of worship would be no "hardship."[119]

The following year the Philadelphians who petitioned for limitations on German immigration pointed to the Swedes as a warning. With four churches and priests regularly sent to the colony on temporary missions, religious services and instruction were carried on in the Swedish language. Swedes rarely intermarried with other Pennsylvanians, but "carefully keep up a national Distinction." They, too, noted that the region was termed "Suecia Nova" in Swedish books and maps. Because there were no restrictions on alien immigration, Swedes could transport themselves to the colony as easily as Palatines, and, consequently, "'tis evident with how much Ease they might in fact make Good their Title."[120]

Few immigrants commented directly on the attitudes Pennsylvanians expressed toward them, the reception accorded them, or their own views of pluralism and tolerance. Their letters focused instead on the general conditions prevailing in the colony. During the 1730s the portrait they drew of Pennsylvania shifted somewhat from the rather uncritical descriptions of earlier years, yet discouraging reports appear to have had little influence. Although in 1724 Sauer had thought the colony "pretty well settled" by 100,000 inhabitants from France, Wales, Sweden, Holland, and Germany, nevertheless "Here may one select a piece [of land] where one desires, near or far."[121] By 1732 the promises of unlimited opportunity had begun to fade. Caspar Wistar indicated that "Some years ago," when Pennsylvania had been "but sparsely inhabited" and labor scarce, immigrants were "cordially welcomed" and "very easily" earned enough money to purchase land. But since then thousands of colonists had arrived, and "filled all parts of the country"; now those who wished to purchase a farm "must go far into the wilderness" and pay higher prices for land.[122] A Schwenkfelder immigrant noted in 1734 that "Farm land is not so easy to secure as one thought." Although there was "plenty" of it, "money is needed for its purchase as very little can be had cheap."[123] An anonymous 1738 letter indirectly advised Germans to cease migrating to the colony in large numbers. Because "there is not very much more land for sale," many people were leaving Pennsylvania for Maryland and Virginia, where "great unoccupied districts and better soil" were available.[124]

In November 1738 several men of German and Huguenot background, disturbed by the high mortality rates on ships that had arrived in Philadelphia the previous summer, wrote an open letter that revealed conditions during the voyage and in the colony. Its authors hoped to discourage unthinking emigration, but ironically echoed some of the views of the English elite. Pennsylvania, established through "an especially beneficial providence of God" as a refuge for the oppressed and persecuted, offered opportunities for those willing to work industriously. Early settlers had shared an "unpartisan mutual friendship toward all nationalities," but this had been diminished by later immigrants who had only worldly motives for coming to the colony. As people sought the "promised land," it became crowded and land prices rose. The voyage to the colony had become a horror. Enticed by "Newlanders," or emigrant agents, passengers were "packed in almost like herring" and given scanty rations. If the voyage were longer than anticipated, passengers might starve. Goods were carelessly handled and often damaged. Illness and epidemics frequently resulted from filth, crowding, and poor food and water. Mortality was high, especially among children. Upon arrival, families were separated as they were sold to pay for their passage; only young, healthy people easily found positions. Although the government had rented some houses outside of the city to care for sick passengers, "in reality. . . . The burden rests mostly on those Germans who still have some love for their countrymen."[125]

Although these men did not pressure the government to improve facilities for distressed immigrants, the authorities recognized that measures were necessary. In 1700 a law had been enacted to prohibit "Sickly Vessels" from coming nearer than one mile to towns or ports in the province without providing certificates of health. Passengers and freight could not be landed without the permission of the governor and council in Philadelphia or two justices of the peace in other towns. If passengers were allowed on shore, "suitable provision" was to be made for their care.[126]

Following the arrival of several unhealthy ships in 1738, Governor George Thomas berated the assembly for its failure to erect a "Pest-House" or hospital. He stated that he had strictly enforced the law and employed a physician to visit the ships. Sick passengers had been taken, at their own expense, to "Houses in the Country convenient for their Reception." Urging the assembly to enact measures to safeguard public health if similar circumstances recurred, he pointed out that the colony's "present flourishing condition" was "in a great measure owing to the Industry" of "distressed Protestants" from Germany.[127] The assembly partially disagreed, admitting that prosperity was "in part owing to the Importation of Germans and other Forreigners," but stressing that it was "chiefly to be ascribed to the Lenity of our Government, and to the Sobriety and Industry of the first Settlers of this Country, and of the other British Subjects inhabiting the same."[128] The matter dropped until the following summer, when Thomas recommended to the assembly the petition of Dr. Thomas Graeme, who had visited incoming vessels for the past twenty years without receiving a salary. He was paid £100 for his services.[129] Although John Penn advised both his brother Thomas, then in the colony, and the governor to try to obtain passage of a law that limited the number of passengers who could be transported in each vessel,[130] nothing was done until the next crisis.

The responses of Pennsylvania's leaders as they confronted the issues raised by immigration during these years were mixed. Combined with apprehension about the purported characteristics of some emigrants was a welcome for the positive attributes some of them were thought to possess. Throughout the colonial period Pennsylvania leaders panicked at a sudden arrival of a large number of immigrant vessels, briefly discussed limiting immigration or voiced concern about the characteristics of immigrants, and then lost interest in the subject.

Expressions of hostility directed toward immigrants were rarely absolute or categorical statements. In most cases exceptions were made, often in the same letter, for those who were considered desirable colonists. There were clear statements that national or religious distinctions could not be universally applied. One writer noted that "all ages and all nations produce Witts and Blockheads, Brave men and Cowards, and the same as to virtue and vice." But he recognized that it required "some greatness of mind, some nobility in the Soul," to "preserve Generous Sentiments" toward one's neighbors.[131]

II

Immigrants added not only to the ethnic pluralism of the province but also to its religious diversity. Adherents of many faiths, they brought new varieties of religious expression to the colony and increased the strength of many of the denominations already present. German religious groups remained in some disorder as sects proliferated and proselytized, while the Lutherans and Reformed began to take tentative steps toward organizing congregations, obtaining ministers, and developing ties with their European counterparts. Presbyterian immigrants from Ireland were somewhat more successful in reestablishing their church structure, for several ministers emigrated and used the denominational institutions already present in the colony to meet the needs of immigrants. Contacts among people of roughly sim-

Roman Catholics
could voted hard oltho
1730s Catholic chapel in Phil!

104   "A MIXED MULTITUDE"

ilar beliefs continued to cross national, linguistic, and sectarian
boundaries. Despite some religious tensions, due largely to the di-
chotomy between church and sect or to schisms within sects, mutual
toleration and acceptance of religious pluralism continued to characterize Pennsylvania. Brief episodes of intolerance surfaced, but, considering the variety of beliefs and practices in the colony, were only
of minor significance.

Relative toleration even extended to Roman Catholics, a suspicious
group to most eighteenth-century Protestants. In contrast to their legal status in England and in other colonies, they could vote and, at
least initially, be elected to office; however, the qualifications officeholders were to subscribe after 1705/6 limited positions to trinitarian
Protestants. According to Thomas Penn there were "but one or two
[Catholic] ffamilies that are tolerably genteel in the Place" in 1740,
which further accounted for their absence from official positions.[132]

Although Pennsylvania's statute governing the purchase of land for
churches, schools, and cemeteries extended only to Protestant religious societies,[133] in the early 1730s a Roman Catholic chapel and
priest's residence were constructed in Philadelphia.[134] In July 1734
Governor Gordon informed the council that he was "under no small
Concern" to learn that a "House" had been "lately built" that was
"sett apart for the Exercise of the Roman Catholick Religion." It was
"commonly" termed "the Romish Chappel," where "several" people
"hear Mass openly celebrated by a Popish Priest." Gordon believed
that such practices contravened English laws enacted under William
III, while Catholics were under the impression that Penn's charter of
privileges permitted the free exercise of their religion.[135] After examining the English statute and various Pennsylvania charters and laws,
the council was unable to reach any conclusion about the extension of
the English law to the colonies or the applicability of an unrepealed
provincial law for liberty of conscience dating from the reign of Queen
Anne. Indifferent to the issue, the council "left [it] to the Governor,
if he thinks fitt, to represent the matter" to English authorities.[136] The
problem was not referred to again. Even members of the Society for
the Propagation of the Gospel in Foreign Parts, who had been disturbed by the early celebrations of Mass and had expressed fears con-

cerning the spread of Catholicism in the tolerant colony, made no objection to the organization of a permanent Catholic congregation.[137]

Anglican attitudes toward Pennsylvania's pluralistic society began to moderate during this period. Although some penned eloquent statements of the need for missionaries, schoolteachers, and religious books and emphasized the dangers of living in the midst of "dissenters," many accommodated themselves to a situation in which their church was not established, and accepted the reality that it would not be. Complaints about nonconformists are balanced by success in gaining converts and declarations that the negligence of the S.P.G. in filling vacancies was responsible for some of the problems. Several ministers devised creative means of reaching non-Anglicans instead of continuing the combativeness typical of the first few decades. For the first time, Anglicans commented about peaceful relations with their neighbors of different faiths.

Anglicans occasionally expressed displeasure with a situation in which the government was in the hands of "dissenters" and the Quakers had the greater measure of wealth and prestige. As late as 1728 one missionary questioned Penn's motives for granting freedom of conscience in his colony. Penn acted "not so much, . . . for the ease of consciences that were or are truly scrupulous, and the general benefit of mankind with respect to the undisturbed freedom and enjoyment of their Civil privileges and Religious liberties," but rather "for the laying a foundation for the furtherance and advancement of a Particular Interest and Faction."[138]

Economic factors played a role in this discontent. Ministers resented their dependence on the S.P.G. and relatively poor congregations for their salaries.[139] Assistance from the S.P.G. in the form of schoolmasters or subsidies for teachers was also requested. A Philadelphia teacher stated that he would probably leave his post if the royal bounty that augmented his salary were not restored. Churchmen could not by themselves provide an adequate salary, while the "richer" inhabitants, the Quakers, supported several teachers. He had discovered, however, that since his arrival some of them who "pretended to teach Gramar" had "deserted ye place," which "occasioned several of ye more thinking" among the Friends to "trust" him with the education of their children. Even though he gave some "hints" to the children that might "make them better Christians than their Progenitors," he could not zealously propagate Anglican ideas if he depended upon Quakers for his income.[140] Chester Anglicans argued that the £6 annual supplement to their schoolmaster's salary, given with the stipulation that a number of poor youths be educated, had been beneficial, for children of the congregation "became more Riveted to the fundamentals" of their faith. They blamed Quakers for discouraging potential Anglican teachers and feared that, as a result, children might be more easily "Seduced to Heretical oppinions."[141]

Anglican clergymen argued that because they were "Surrounded on all Sides with so many dangerous Sectaries," missionaries were required to "prevent ye ruin of many poor Souls" who were "in danger of being Seduced" by the "Cuñing Craftiness" of those who only waited for opportunities to "deceive" them.[142] One S.P.G. priest believed that the "Carelessness" of the Burlington missionaries who failed to cross the Delaware River to serve the Bristol congregation had "dispersed the people Some to Presbyterians most to Quakers."[143] Another believed that "meerly for want of a Missionary" Anglicans "lost even the Sence of all religion, Neither do they join wth any Society at all."[144]

But not all Anglican leaders in the colony blamed sectarian preaching or inadequate S.P.G. support for the problems they encountered; they simply tried to find new ways to resolve them. Richard Backhouse requested Anglican treatises, for "The best Arguments in ye world" availed little when expounded in person by a man "agst whom the Dissenters have Entertain'd a dislike," while they would pay attention to an author's "good Reasonings." Books were more influential than an orator's "most moving discourses on ye Same Subject" delivered from the pulpit, and might convince individuals "Ignorant off, or prejudiced agst ye principles & Ceremonies of our Church" of their truth. They would also combat the written propaganda of the church's opponents, although Backhouse was as much concerned about books written by men of "loose principles" falling into the hands of the "common People" as he was about Quaker tracts.[145]

Griffith Hughes' parishioners had been "Neglected in their Education, & Ignorant of the very fundamentalls of Religion"; the "princi-

ples" of some of them were "very Much vitiated with false doctrines."
He began to visit the homes of his parishioners to instruct them in
Anglican tenets and to correct their erroneous ideas.[146] Another minister visited his "Common hearers" twice each year, and also called on
"many Dissenters of all Denominations."[147] George Ross gladly accepted an invitation to preach to a distant settlement of newcomers
from Ireland in order to prevent the Anglicans among them from lapsing from their faith. He found a large and attentive congregation, a
"mixed multitude" that included many Presbyterians. The second time
he visited these settlers he preached without notes. Ross "very often"
did this in country congregations to show "Dissenters" that "we Can
do as well as Others, And to gain them in their own while Innocent
Way[.]" He hoped his superiors would approve the use of a "Method
Suitable to their taste" to "reconcile prejudiced persons to Our Sound,
but misrepresented Communion[.]"[148] Alexander Howie reported that
several individuals who had been "lost in the wilderness . . . Informed themselves of the principles of Christianity," and was pleased
by the "daily coming over of Roman Catholicks, Anabaptists and
Quakers" to the Church of England.[149]

Perhaps the success of indirect methods in bringing dissenters and
wayward Anglicans into a closer connection with the Church of England encouraged missionaries to live peacefully with their neighbors.
One minister noted the "General disposition" of Pennsylvanians "to
hear the glad tidings of Salvation notwithstanding the Prejudices that
they had been brought up in."[150] Backhouse discovered that "tho' we
are Beset on all Sides with Sectaries and men of Loose principles,"
recently "the Number of those that Devoutly approach the Altar" had
"much Increased."[151] He had been "much Discourag'd" by the lax-
ness of Anglicans when he arrived at his mission, but now his churches
were in a "Flourishing Condition."[152] Although most of the people in
his parish were Presbyterians and Quakers, he asserted "I live as quiet
among both these kinds of Dissenters as any clergyman of our Co-
munion Can Expect to do." He tried to give them a "good opinion"
of his church "by fair means & in as Easy & perswasive a way as I
possibly could, without moving their Choler," and had a "very good
Effect" on some of them.[153] William Lindsay felt that his situation
among so many non-Anglicans "require[d] great Watchfullness & Care

to manage Evenly & Discreetly." Yet he discovered that "Dissenters Comes very often" to his services and seemed "Very Moderate."[154] As to Quakerism, priests were "generally of Opinion, That let it alone, & it will die of its self. We study to be quiet & to mind our own Business."[155]

The mutual friendship and association of Anglican and Swedish missionaries continued to deepen and became formalized. A Swedish priest arranged to supply a vacant English church regularly,[156] while an Anglican minister preached occasionally to a rural Swedish congregation. He believed that the Swedes "Should be Encouraged," for they had demonstrated "good will and friendship" to the Church of England.[157] Late in 1720 the Anglican clergy commented on the assistance they had received from two Swedish missionaries who "preach fluently" and "with good Success" in English in vacant Anglican churches. Because "their provision here is very mean & unadequate to their worth," the clergy requested the S.P.G. to show "some marks of your favour" to encourage the Swedes' "Pious Labours."[158] The S.P.G. decided to give each of these ministers £10 in recognition of his services, and to offer £10 a year to Swedish priests who preached in English in unsupplied Anglican churches twenty times a year. Believing themselves engaged in the "same Comon Cause," and "Sensible how nearly we are allied in the purity of Doctrine & worship," the Swedish pastors gratefully accepted the S.P.G.'s bonus and proposal.[159]

One Swedish priest, Samuel Hesselius, cooperated with Anglicans farther than some of his parishioners thought proper. Reporting Hesselius' "neglect" of his assigned parish to his Swedish superiors, they accused him of deserting his church to preach in English ones, of failing to catechize or instruct his parishioners, of neglecting to visit the sick, and of selling church property for his private gain. To clear himself of these charges and to prevent his suspension from the ministry, Hesselius requested Governor Gordon to conduct a formal inquiry into the charges so that evidence from both sides might be obtained. In his defense, Hesselius cited the old custom of Swedish missionaries who preached among the English as well as his bishop's direction to continue the practice. He admitted that he preached only one sermon in his church on Sundays instead of conducting both morning and afternoon services, but argued that if his superiors knew of the "desolate state" of nearby Anglican churches, he would not be criticized for his "readiness to do good amongst my distressed neighbors" by preaching to them in the afternoon. Anglican ministers and members of the Chester church wrote to the Bishop of Skara in support of Hesselius. The magistrates, thinking it "uncharitable" to accuse him of neglecting his parish "because he was assistant to those who had no teacher," cleared him of the charges.[160]

Welsh-speaking Pennsylvanians continued to challenge Anglican efforts to keep them firmly within the church. After a Welsh-speaking missionary was appointed permanently to the Oxford parish, he appealed for a resident priest for the Radnor congregation that he had left. Radnor needed a man "well Conversant in the Welsh Tongue, to Reside amongst them and to visit them from house to house as well as to preach" to them. Two years later the request was reiterated, with an offer of an annual £40 salary. Competency in Welsh was essential, for "a Considerable number" among them were "Strang^{rs} to ye English [language]."[161] Anglican religious books were in demand. One Welsh congregation testified that "for the want of Good Books in their own Language," forty Anglican families "at Last Yielded to the generall Cor̄uption of Quakerisme" despite monthly services conducted by an itinerant minister.[162]

Other Welshmen were Presbyterians, who by 1714 had formed at least two distinct congregations. The minister of one of them, David Evans, had begun to preach while still a layman. In 1710 this came to the attention of the Presbytery of Philadelphia, which disapproved but, recognizing his talents, ordered him to spend a year studying theology. In 1711 he was licensed to preach, and in 1714, following his graduation from Yale College, he was ordained.[163] In 1740, after having received permission to preach to English-speaking Presbyterians near his Tredyffrin congregation, Evans became embroiled in a dispute with his congregation over several issues, including their request that he "might be prevailed with to preach more to y^m in ye welch Language, considering ye Inability of several of the People to

understand English." Evans, however, thought the problems were too
severe to be resolved and requested permission to resign this position.[164]

Most Presbyterians were Scotch-Irish. This denomination grew slowly
until the beginning of massive emigration from Ireland. A presbytery
was formed in 1706, and by 1716 there was a sufficient number of
ministers and congregations scattered over a wide area to form a synod,
centered in Philadelphia.[165] Despite the beginnings of an organizational structure, European assistance was requested as early as 1716.
One minister requested a general collection in Scotland to benefit provincial congregations. Ministers must be settled in places "where the
Gospel has never at all been preached" and "where there are wicked
prophane debauched carelesse creatures of the bishop of London."
Although objections might be raised due to the "jealousie" of the Church
of England, he argued that the Church of Scotland was also an established church in Great Britain. Furthermore, since Pennsylvania lacked
an established church, the Scottish church could send missionaries or
funds to support ministers.[166] A subsequent plea for pastors recommended the Swedish policy of sending talented men to the colony on
a temporary mission, and then placing them in good positions upon
their recall. This plan attracted men of "bright qualifications" who
promoted the interests of religion.[167]

   The Presbyterian church benefited from the emigration of ministers
from both Scotland and Ireland. During the 1720s the church kept
pace with the movements of immigrants, but by the 1730s it could
bridge the gap only by sending younger ministers on strenuous itinerant journeys throughout the backcountry.[168] Perhaps because Presbyterians were concentrated in frontier or rural areas, they appear to
have had little contact with other religious or national groups. While
they published a few tracts to refute Anglican doctrines,[169] Presbyterian ministers were preoccupied with organizing congregations and
gathering their scattered flocks, work more crucial than involvement
with other Pennsylvanians.

As individuals and as a denomination, Presbyterians had some contact
with Dutch Reformed churches in Bucks County, some of which were

reorganized as Presbyterian churches, and with German Reformed churches, since all derived their tenets from the Calvinist tradition.[170] In 1730 the Presbyterian minister in Philadelphia noted that among the German immigrants were many "Presbyt'n, or, as they call themselves, Reformed." Many came to him for the baptism of their children, and some joined with the English congregation for communion rites. He was impressed by the qualifications of John Peter Miller, who applied to the Presbytery of Philadelphia for ordination, for the candidate spoke Latin "as readily as we do our vernacular tongue" and was soundly grounded in theology.[171] Miller was ordained and began preaching to rural German congregations, but within a few years resigned his ministry and eventually joined the monastic community at Ephrata.[172]

The Dutch Reformed church, which began to take an interest in the German Reformed residents of Pennsylvania during the 1730s, expressed interest in uniting with provincial Presbyterian churches. It requested information from the Dutch Reformed church of New York about the Reformed in Pennsylvania, including "whether there are not English churches, either Presbyterian or even Episcopal, with whom many unite themselves."[173] It thought that "If there were" Presbyterian churches, the Germans "might join themselves to these, if they could get along with the English language."[174]

The German Reformed who wrote to Europe for assistance emphasized the dangers of living "among all sorts of errorists." "Indeed," several congregations averred in 1728, "we do not know of any blasphemous opinion which has not its defenders among one class or other of those among whom we are dispersed."[175] One early Reformed pastor asserted that "most" of the colony's multinational population was Reformed, "but the other people are of all imaginable sects, Atheists, Anabaptists, Quakers, Arians, Enthusiasts, Nestorians, Pietists, Mennonites, Waldensians, etc., etc., more than a hundred types, for there is complete freedom of conscience in this land."[176] After detailing the "blasphemies" of a new sect, one minister questioned "whether it is not the all too great freedom which causes such audacity, by which this pernicious sect has led astray such an appalling number of people."[177]

Quakers and William Penn's tolerant policies were viewed inconsistently by the Reformed. They gave Penn credit for opening his colony to the "oppressed inhabitants of Germany," but because immigrants were unable to obtain ministers, some had been "attracted by the good morals and blameless conduct of the Quakers, [and] joined themselves to them, preferring their worship to none."[178] Reformed church officials in the Netherlands feared that Quakers might proselytize successfully among the Germans, "especially when temporal advantage also may serve besides as a powerful motive."[179] Such fears were confirmed by a minister who asserted that many among the Reformed "have already been enticed away by the destroying wolves of the artful Quakers, who in the sheep's clothing of external modesty know how so insidiously to creep into the hearts of the ignorant and those less exercised in the fundamentals of the faith."

Yet this same minister informed the Classis of Amsterdam that neither colonial officials nor the Bishop of London need be consulted about religious affairs. Everything was left to the "free choice" of individuals or congregations; for example, churches could be built without the government taking any notice. The real need was for "orthodox and rightly conditioned" pastors.[180] Dutch clergymen did suggest that the colony might provide a "safe refuge" where "the Church in Europe, persecuted and driven out by the Anti-Christ, may resort and find her safe abode" if ministers were sent.[181] A Philadelphian, although under the mistaken impression that the "Romish are not permitted to hold services," praised religious freedom. "The government consists of all sects, chosen for that end by the Governor and other Councillors," while the Quakers "by their conduct and polite reception invite many strangers."[182]

Members of the German Reformed and Lutheran churches, unable to compete or even to carry on theological arguments with their opponents, had more to fear from the activities of German sectarians than from Quakers or other English-speaking groups. Sects proselytized actively, exploiting the failure of church groups to make adequate provisions for their people and sowing confusion.[183] With only four German Reformed ministers to serve twenty-six congregations and three Lutheran ministers for twenty-seven congregations in 1740,[184] the drift of church people into sects or indifference is not surprising. Peter

Miller's desertion of the Reformed church allegedly convinced three hundred others to accept the "errors" of the Seventh Day Baptists.[185] One Reformed pastor criticized those who labored on Sunday "without shame!" But the worst group of heretics, from the Reformed point of view, were the "Neugebohrene," or Newborn, who believed they were without sin.[186]

German sectarians, still a visible component of Pennsylvania society, played a major role in the development of tolerance, for many of them, such as the Brethren, Mennonites, and Schwenkfelders, emigrated in search of religious freedom, valued liberty of conscience, and insisted that the government adhere to Penn's guarantees.[187] But for certain groups freedom spawned only endless controversy as arguments over minor points of doctrine and form of worship led to schism and separation. In 1738 an anonymous writer lamented that "the spiritual struggle between the smaller Protestant groups continues strong. One group seeks to overcome the other and to aggrandize itself."[188]

Debates and controversies carried out by German Baptists over the form of baptism and strictness of adherence to certain customs added to the turmoil of German religious life, but did not attract the attention of other colonists. The precise nature of the disputes is unclear; their importance is that they caused certain groups to clarify their beliefs and to become more aware of the need to propagate, defend, or explain them in some way. For example, the Mennonites published a pamphlet in both German and English that explained their central beliefs, while others published controversial tracts that examined sabbath observance or points in dispute with other sects.[189] The disarray among the smaller German religious groups became more important later, as they began to organize more permanently and as polemical literature increased with the advent of Lutheran and Reformed clergymen ready to battle the sects.

In the mid-1730s a few members of the Unitas Fratrum, or Moravian Brethren, arrived in Pennsylvania. This sect became a significant element in the confusion that characterized provincial religious life after the arrival of Nicholas von Zinzendorf and a number of his followers in 1741. The zealous evangelism of the Moravians, directed toward bringing their version of Christianity to both the Indians and white Pennsylvanians, regardless of their language or denomination, aroused fierce controversy. More interested in converting people to a Christianity that transcended narrow denominational distinctions than in obtaining recruits to their society, Moravians searched for the operation of the Holy Spirit in the sects present in the colony.

The first Moravians accompanied the Schwenkfelder emigrants, who arrived in 1734. For several years these sectarians lived in harmony.[190] In contrast to their later experience, the early Moravians generated little animosity.[191] The first report of their activities pleased James Logan, who was glad to hear of their promotion of "Virtue and truth." He commended their lack of interest in "gaining over of Proselytes to their own peculiar way," although he disapproved of an unspecified "Singularity."[192] After hearing of the work of Augustus Spangenberg among rural Germans, he described the Moravians as "a Sober & most religious sort of People," who "truly deny the world, live, feed & are Cloathed meanly, [and] Seek not to distinguish themselves otherwise y^n in their communcation with each other." He praised their consideration of "exteriour appearances in language Speech or Dress as matters indifferent"; they "are ever modest and humble," signs of true Christianity from which Friends were lapsing.[193] Logan became "intimate" with Spangenberg, who "Sincerely zealous joyns with those whom he finds So in placing religion in the interior worship whatever their outw^d profession may be."[194]

Moravians visited members of various sects to discern the "awakened." Spangenberg reported that "With many other souls, whatever their name might be, we find warm reception."[195] Initial contacts with the Brethren, who invited Moravians to attend love feasts and other ceremonies, were cordial. The Moravians slowly began to question whether the Brethren were lapsing from strict regulations on who might receive the sacraments, and becoming loose in discipline, emphasizing outward rather than inward matters. As divisions occurred within the anabaptist sects over sabbath observance and strictness of discipline, Spangenberg commended those who hoped to revive spirituality and to reestablish purity of life, for he thought some of their leaders were governed by the spirit of the world. Initially Moravians approved the emphasis placed upon poverty and chastity by Johann Conrad Beissel and his followers, but as divisions among the Brethren became more

Baphsls worshipped
on Saturday but no
labor on Sunday either

severe, Spangenberg expressed concern about the formation of a "new religion and sectarian business."[196]

The confusion and consternation resulting from the myriad sects was primarily of interest to provincial Germans; only occasionally was there interaction with English-speaking Pennsylvanians. One issue of broad concern involved the observance of a day of rest and worship. Beissel, the founder of a monastery at Ephrata, was influenced by English and Welsh Baptists, some of them former Keithians, who lived in western Chester County. When he adopted their views and publicized them, he ran afoul of colonial laws. While English-speaking Baptists conducted their religious services on Saturday, they abstained from labor on Sunday as well. Beissel, however, cited the biblical injunction to labor on six days of the week, and broke the law requiring labor to cease on Sunday. Several of his followers were arrested, imprisoned, and fined by zealous magistrates in Lancaster County. Persecution only strengthened their convictions. Eventually, the nonresistance of some sabbatarians and the willingness of others to pay the fines mitigated the officials' severity, and they began to overlook violations of the law.[197] On another occasion, the monastic community itself divided over payment of the head tax imposed on single men. Some were willing to pay, but others argued that early monastics had been exempted from taxes in recognition of the contributions they made to the poor. The sheriff, unwilling to accept such an argument, jailed six men until a friend provided security for their appearance at a trial. A compromise was reached whereby the assets of the community would be assessed as if they were all members of one family.[198] It is ironic that as early as 1736 this community of monks and nuns, considered suspicious because of their communal way of life and advocacy of celibacy, began to attract visitors, among the earliest the governor himself.[199]

Within the English-speaking community, religio/political questions continued to arise, although without the severity of the earlier years. Compromises could be reached on some issues, while on others customs differed widely enough that several religious groups were unhappy with the solutions. If representatives of various denominations expressed discontent, they did not usually complain of persecution.

Marriage customs continued to pose problems. A law enacted in 1729/30 to prevent clandestine marriages levied a £50 fine on justices and ministers who violated the act, which strengthened earlier provisions requiring both the permission of parents or masters if the parties were under age or servants as well as publication of the announcement. It did not extend to individuals married within their own congregations or by license, provided parents and masters were notified.[200] Anglican priests objected that this "Odious and Tyranical" law contravened church rubrics. It attempted to "exterpate the Doctrine and Discipline of the Church of England" out of the province and ought to be repealed.[201] Backhouse added that "notwithstanding the Quakers' liberal indulgencies," the government had not remained "contented only with taking away our Properties and Perquisites and giving them to others," but "Struck even at the Constitut^n" of the church by requiring a particular form of publishing intentions of marriage and imposing a fine for noncompliance.[202] Another minister complained that Governor Gordon "Granted marriage Licenses promiscuously to Us, & the Presbyterian Ministers," something that he claimed had not been common until Governor Keith's final year in office, when "he was willing by any means to raise Money." He requested the Bishop of London to intercede with Gordon to "bring him to our Interest," which would help to augment their salaries.[203]

A few years later Presbyterians objected to the form of marriage licenses. The Synod of Philadelphia ordered ministers to cease performing ceremonies by license until alterations were made that "hath no peculiar respect to the ministers of the Church of England, nor oblige us to use any of the forms and ceremonies peculiar to that church." Within a year this regulation was found to have been too restrictive. It was altered to permit each presbytery to make its own determination whether ministers could conduct marriages by license, but to limit severely the circumstances under which members of Presbyterian congregations could marry by license.[204] At about the same time the Philadelphia Yearly Meeting concluded that it was "inconsistent with our Principles, and not any Part of their Duty as Magistrates" for Friends who were justices of the peace to marry couples by license.[205]

Difficulties over oaths and affirmations recurred, but without the virulence of the early years. In 1724 a bill was enacted that extended to Pennsylvania Quakers the privileges Parliament had granted to English Friends in 1722.[206] While the provincial act was being considered in England, several Quaker delegations met with the governor to request that they be permitted to appear in court after their own fashion, for the law stipulated that it would not go into effect until royal approbation had been received.[207] In Philadelphia only "ye begotted people of other pswasions seem[ed] much disturb'd" with the final passage of the bill.[208]

Quaker scruples against magistrates remaining on the bench while oaths were administered emerged once again in 1732,[209] and in 1740 Chester County magistrates set aside a juror because he would not make an affirmation, while they could not tender an oath. Disturbed by this "Illegality" in their proceedings, Provincial Secretary Richard Peters, who was also an Anglican priest, warned "they will hurt the Reputation of the whole Body & exasperate many good & well inclin'd People gainst them" if such actions continued. He added, "No man wishes the Quakers better than I do nor wou'd be better pleas'd to see them well respected by other Religious Society's & particularly by the Government,"[210] a remark earlier Anglicans faced with this situation would not have made. The Penn family, "Concern'd" and "Much Surprised" to hear of the dispute, ordered new commissions of the peace issued so that a majority in each county were such as could administer oaths.[211]

Others also expressed concern about oaths. In 1739 the Donegal presbytery began to agitate for alterations in the form of oaths required in the colony, and a month later Presbyterian ministers and laymen from Lancaster County petitioned the assembly about the matter. They stated that because Presbyterians "cannot, without wronging their Consciences, swear in Judgment, according to the common Form of kissing the Book (a Ceremony in their Opinion contrary to the Word of God, and not free from Superstition)," their beliefs prevented them from holding office or giving evidence in court.[212] The assembly speedily enacted a law that validated the "oath commonly administered and taken in Scotland" as well as the English form used in the colony, "the ceremony of the book excepted." Since promises of liberty of conscience had attracted Protestants of various beliefs to the colony and Quakers had been relieved of burdensome oaths, it was just to relieve others who were "obliged to bear their share of the burden of the government and to serve their country in common with the rest of the inhabitants."[213] The Board of Trade, however, objected to giving a "Scotch Presbiterian" a "greater Privilege" than he had in England, and the law was repealed.[214]

By the 1730s, most Pennsylvanians, clergy and laity alike, accepted the diversity that characterized the colony and concentrated on strengthening their own denomination. Efforts to proselytize were, for the most part, directed at the unchurched, especially those living on the frontier, while members of organized churches remained undisturbed and attempted to live harmoniously with their neighbors who professed different beliefs.

Pennsylvanians and outsiders began to recognize that the liberty of conscience granted by William Penn and maintained by his successors and colonists was a major factor in the rapid development of the province. A merchant who had resided in America, concerned with demonstrating Britain's need for its colonies, pointed out that the primary reason for Pennsylvania's "Increase of People and the Improvement of the Country, is the wholesome Laws of that Province, by which all Men, without distinction, are protected from Injury and Persecution, on Account of any religious Opinions."[215] One recently arrived German settler declared that "Liberty of conscience" was the "chief virtue of this land and on this score I do not repent my immigration." Then he added, "But for this freedom, I think this country would not improve so rapidly."[216]

During this period, some Pennsylvanians began to publicly advocate toleration. A writer in the *Pennsylvania Gazette* in 1736 condemned prejudicial opinions and stereotypes. He denounced those who "endeavour to support the thorny dire Enclosures of National Prejudice," and was disappointed that some Pennsylvanians were "of Opinion, that *Yorkshire* men are naturally enclined to Horse-stealing, that most *Irishmen* deserve hanging, that the *New Englanders* are generally Hypocrites, and Cheats under the Masque of Religion, and that the *Westindians* are a People abominably vile, wicked and profane, for whom nothing can be expected but general Damnation." Religious prejudices were the worst, and he believed that with "Knowledge and Good Sense" prejudices would lessen, and supposed "there may be therefore as little Partiality of this kind in *Pennsylvania*, as any where in the King's Dominions."[217]

An assemblyman extolled the virtues of the "perfect Freedom as to Religion" in a speech to his colleagues. Experience demonstrated that "an Equality among Religious Societies, without distinguishing any one Sect with greater Privileges than another, is the most effectual Method to discourage Hypocrisy, promote the Practice of the moral Virtues, and prevent the Plagues and Mischiefs that always attend religious Squabbling."[218] An essayist, opposing clerical authority, urged his readers to "shake off all manner of Prejudice" and learn to think "*freely, fairly*, and *honestly*." He believed that "Ignorance and Error, Bigotry, Enthusiasm and Superstition, more or less," increased with submission to the "Impositions of Priests" of all denominations. He urged Pennsylvanians to "endeavour to preserve and maintain Truth, Common Sense, universal Charity, and brotherly Love, Peace and Tranquility, as recommended in the Gospel of Jesus, in this our infant and growing Nation."[219] Such an ideal could be difficult to attain or maintain; Pennsylvanians soon discovered that religious harmony could be fragile.

CHAPTER 5

Religious Awakening
in the 1740s

1740s end to toleration
evangelists v. lutheran + Gov Ref

The tentative mutual forbearance evident in the relationships among Pennsylvania's varied religious groups during the first period of large-scale immigration was challenged during the early 1740s by the arrival of evangelists and missionaries professing newly assertive creeds. Attempts to organize congregations, to restore denominational consciousness, and to proselytize among Pennsylvanians of all persuasions threatened the pragmatic toleration that had in part resulted from the weakness of most groups. The denominationalism espoused by some ministers, especially the early representatives of the German Reformed and Lutheran churches, conflicted with the evangelical and ecumenical ideas of revivalists, particularly George Whitefield and his associates and the Moravians. Lay Pennsylvanians, accustomed to ignoring religious differences and relatively indifferent to precisely formulated religious beliefs, resisted both denominationalism and proselytization.

This decade of religious upheaval had an impact on most religious groups in the province, although the experiences of German- and English-speaking colonists reveal distinctive patterns. Within the English community, the central event was the explosion of revivals known as the Great Awakening.[1] In other colonies this revivalistic movement may have resulted in the formation of new sects, placed pressure on church-state relations, and indirectly fostered toleration, but in Pennsylvania the primary institutional consequence was a schism within the Presbyterian church that weakened that denomination for several years. More surprisingly, while the Awakening may have had a permanent impact on the beliefs or behavior of individuals, it did not significantly alter the dimensions of provincial religious life. German colonists were more peripherally involved in the revivalistic surge. Their ministers concentrated on problems peculiar to Continental emigrants, and directed their most important efforts toward establishing churches and halting the drift toward sectarianism or indifference. The aspect of the religious awakening that crossed ethnic and linguistic lines involved the ecumenical Moravians, who propagated their ideas among colonists of all faiths and nationalities. Inevitably, English and German, "church" and "sect," reacted with hostility.

This decade of disorder and strife challenged Pennsylvanians to reach a deeper understanding of the meaning of religious toleration and pluralism. As they had in the past few decades faced the implications of William Penn's policies for the ethnic composition of the colony, they now had to consider the implications of religious liberty in the midst of strong, competing churches and aggressive evangelism. If colonists benefited from stronger religious institutions and an increased opportunity to worship in the manner they preferred, they also influenced their spiritual leaders to adopt more tolerant attitudes toward outsiders and to cease active proselytization and unnecessary disputes with those whose religious views differed.

I

George Whitefield's arrival in Philadelphia in November 1739 initiated a brief period of religious ferment that attracted the attention of many of his contemporaries. An Anglican priest, Whitefield adopted some unorthodox ideas and used unusual means in his effort to foster a revival of experiential Christianity. Directing his appeal to all active Protestants as well as to the unchurched, he demonstrated a catholicity of spirit that recognized at least implicitly that the fundamental truths of Christianity could exist simultaneously with a variety of practices in less important matters. Nevertheless, despite his prayers for a day when "bigotry and prejudice were banished from the Christian world,"[2] Whitefield's doctrines and style became the focus of religious controversy.[3]

Whitefield was initially welcomed among people of his own denomination, if hesitantly on the part of some clergymen. Upon his arrival in Philadelphia he was invited to participate in the regular Anglican services and to dine with the minister and churchwardens. He was permitted to read prayers and preach in the church daily, although Archibald Cummings, the rector, reported some pressure from his parishioners to allow Whitefield to use the church. Whitefield drew large crowds to the building, and also preached outdoors to "vast multitudes of all sects."[4]

Cordial relations between Anglican priests and Whitefield deteriorated rapidly, for within a week of his arrival the evangelist began to criticize his brethren openly. Driven to bear "testimony against the unchristian principles and practices of our clergy," he warned listeners that "the generality of their teachers do not preach or live up to the truth as it is in Jesus." Although "Three of my reverend brethren were present," he was perhaps naïvely uncertain "whether they were offended," for he "endeavoured to speak with meekness as well as zeal."[5] Two weeks later Richard Peters, an Anglican priest then employed as the provincial secretary, rose at the end of Whitefield's sermon to dispute his doctrines. Whitefield answered briefly, and returned to the disputed points in more detail during his afternoon sermon.[6] He left Philadelphia shortly after this exchange, temporarily quieting dissension. At the close of this missionary tour, Whitefield concluded that the Church of England in Pennsylvania, especially in Philadelphia, was "at a low ebb," but remained confident that people could be awakened to the message of Christianity. He was more impressed by the spiritual vitality he found in the Presbyterian and Baptist churches in the colony.[7]

Whitefield found Anglican priests united in their opposition to him when he returned to Pennsylvania in 1740. They refused to allow him to preach in their churches, in part because of his continuing attacks on local clergymen and his criticism of Richard Allestree's *The Whole Duty of Man*, a popular devotional book, and the writings of the ven-

Whitefield used Edwards
to attack Bishop Tillotson
Pro-Predest v. Anglicans

erated Archbishop John Tillotson. Undaunted, Whitefield continued
to mock the clergy and to use the arguments of "dissenters," particularly Jonathan Edwards, to buttress his case against Tillotson.[8] Furthermore Whitefield, influenced by Calvinistic doctrines through his
associations with the Presbyterian Tennent family, placed an emphasis on predestination that most Anglicans considered objectionable.[9]
The evangelist continued to attend Anglican services, drawing inspiration from the sermons he heard for topics on which he could preach
in refutation. Terming his clerical opponents "enemies," Whitefield
believed that if they realized how beneficial their sermons were to his
cause they would cease their vocal opposition "out of spite."[10]

Anglican missionaries, concerned about the possible consequences
of Whitefield's unorthodox but popular preaching, reported varying
reactions to what one priest termed "That Great Enthusiast (to say no
worse of him)." While the minister in Chester boasted that his congregation remained unmoved by the "Religious Freaks & Antick Tricks
the Whitefieldians Are Acting up & Down the Country,"[11] the Radnor missionary believed that the "strolling preacher" had raised "a
confusion" in the province and had "made a very great rent in all" of
the Anglican congregations. He accused Whitefield of endeavoring "to
rob us of our characters & then of our hearers."[12] The Oxford missionary blamed the "Pernicious doctrine and Printed Libels of M^r
Whitfield against the whole body of the clergy" for a decrease in the
number of communicants in his church. Whitefield "undoubtedly will
ruin the Missions" unless "special authority" in England intervened.[13]
Other ministers complained that Whitefield's activities had encouraged some of their parishioners to become careless about contributing
toward their salaries.[14]

Nevertheless, the disruption in Anglican congregations proved
transitory.[15] By 1741 the Radnor missionary declared that "All the
people in my Congregations who were Smitten wth Whitefield" had
returned to orthodox Anglicanism. The number of communicants in
one parish increased, while two communicants "who were Dissenters"
joined another following Whitefield's departure from the colony.[16]
Richard Backhouse found that members of his Pequea congregation
who had "of late Grown Giddy-Brain'd with Whitefields preaching"
were willing to return to the church after he had "Convers'd" with

Clergy vacancy w/ Whitefield crit
saw him as Antinomian
Whitefield Pro-Presby & Anabapt

124   "A MIXED MULTITUDE"

them. They promised "Not to be Drawn Aside or Deluded Any Longer by those Bold & Ranting Enthusiasts."[17] Another priest "undeceived" wayward Anglicans through public statements and private meetings in which he countered Whitefield's false "notions."[18] According to William Currie, the evangelist's condemnation of *The Whole Duty of Man* unintentionally stimulated interest in the book, even among people previously unacquainted with it. He gave away several copies to his "unsettled hearers."[19] Ministers continued to mention "Whitefieldians" or "New Lights" throughout the decade, but by 1741 the crisis had passed.[20]

Despite their grudging acquiescence in Pennsylvania's religiously pluralistic society, Anglican ministers remained uncertain of their church's ability to thrive in a colony where it was not established. They therefore felt threatened by Whitefield's criticism of Anglican clergymen, his friendship with "dissenting" ministers, and his doctrines. His argument, Cummings thought, "turns mostly on the antinomian scheme" and was little more than "railing against the regular clergy."[21] Whitefield, "like a true fanatic," decried the ministers and hierarchy of the Anglican church "as no Preachers of Jesus Christ, but as Sorcerers, Simon Magnus's, with a great deal more of the same stuff"; even worse, he "warmly admonished" his followers to attend Presbyterian and Anabaptist services in his absence.[22] Another priest complained that Whitefield "pretends to be the only true minister" of the Anglican church in America. He had a "criminal regard" for the "avowed enemies" of the church, the Presbyterians, and urged Anglicans to "cleave" to Gilbert Tennent and other revivalistic Presbyterians. Although "discreeter" Presbyterians had long viewed Tennent "as a kind of mad man," Whitefield's recommendation had enabled him to gain a considerable following. As a result, this "mad enthusiast's" emphasis on predestination had caused several people to go "raving mad."[23]

Whitefield's most significant support in Pennsylvania came from Presbyterians, whom he continued to refer to as "Dissenters" despite his close personal and intellectual connections with them. However, convinced that ministers of other faiths could effectively awaken people in their denominations, he was more interested in revitalizing the religious experience than in converting "dissenters" into Anglicans.[24]

Quakers unaff by whitefield & Grt Awakening
Quaker shift to enthusiasm
& quietism

While dissension within the Presbyterian church over revivalistic practices and the qualifications of ministers antedated Whitefield's arrival, his activities helped to crystallize the different views, resulting in a schism that lasted from 1741 to 1758.[25] Whitefield commented that William Tennent and his sons were "secretly despised by the generality of the Synod," but he believed that they would be able to accomplish great things. He was impressed by the academy Tennent founded to train "gracious youths" for the ministry.[26] Nonrevivalistic Presbyterian ministers, on the other hand, objected to Whitefield and the activities of his friends. They were particularly disturbed by accusations that ministers were "graceless" or "unconverted," and by the intrusion of itinerant evangelists into their churches or parishes. Opposition centered around the frontier Donegal presbytery, where ministers were still trying to organize congregations. They found the individualism engendered by frontier conditions difficult enough to counteract—the individualism fostered by an emphasis on a personal conversion experience only added to their difficulties.[27] Orthodox ministers, who retained control of the Synod of Philadelphia, believed that the revivalists were attempting to *rend the Church of Christ to Pieces.* When a minister confessed his "Error and Sin" in joining with the revivalists, "Old Side" leaders inserted his recantation in a Philadelphia newspaper.[28]

Quakers, for the most part, were unaffected by both Whitefield and the Great Awakening. Although Quaker tenets emphasized a personal relationship with God, and early proponents of the sect had acted in ways similar to the awakeners, by the mid-eighteenth century the emphasis of Quaker practice had shifted from "enthusiasm" to "quietism."[29] Whitefield, however, was interested in the sect and did not condemn it outright as some Anglicans were wont to do. He twice lent his cabin to a Quaker minister when crossing the Atlantic in 1739, although after hearing him Whitefield concluded that the man's testimony was improperly grounded.[30] In Pennsylvania he attended Quaker meetings and met privately with a few members of the sect. Invited to attend the funeral of a Quaker child, Whitefield thought it proper to "give a word of exhortation" when no Quaker spoke. He hoped this might encourage Friends to attend his sermons, including those "preached within church walls."[31] Whitefield admired the Quakers' simplicity of dress and manners, regularity of life, and diligence in attending meetings, and gave them credit for founding a colony where "all are permitted to worship God [in] their own way, without being branded as schismatics, dissenters, or disturbers of the established constitution." However, he believed that their preeminence in the colony had led to a decline in genuine spirituality. He feared that the majority of Quakers could provide no other reason for their adherence to the sect "than that their fathers were so before them,"[32] and remained hopeful that he could convince Quakers of the truth of his message.[33]

Quakers were uncertain how to respond to Whitefield's overtures and to the religious enthusiasm inspired by his evangelistic tours. Some Friends, especially "curious Youth of rash judgment," attended his meetings.[34] While most Quakers were unmoved by the orator, one Friend considered him "an Inspired Man" because he emphasized the "Spiritual part of Religion."[35] Some Quakers perceived a reformation in the manners of Philadelphians as a result of the mission of "that Shining Light," George Whitefield. Religion had become the primary "Topick of Conversation." Whitefield's piety and plain language were assets in converting those with "no true Sense of Religion" and in "endeavouring to reclaim a wicked Vicious and Sinfull Age."[36]

Other Friends expressed doubts. James Logan initially thought Whitefield's "preaching has a good Effect in Reclaiming many dissolute people," but was concerned about his "Countenancing so very much the most hot headed Presbyterians," men the "more Sober" of that denomination dismissed as "little more than Madmen." Logan feared the revival would end only in "Confusion to the great prejudice of the Cause of Vertue and Solid Religion."[37] Commenting on newspaper reports of the revival in New England, one Quaker expressed his belief that it "proceeded more from the Terrifyg Expressions of Some of their Teachers there, than any real Sense of a true hearty religion."[38] Judah Foulke, a Quaker who initially held a favorable opinion of Whitefield, soon decided that the man's "Seel" carried him to extremes. "Pulling Down the Writings of them who are Dead and not here to Vindicate their own Cawes" demonstrated too much pride and "bigatry."[39]

Although the intensity of the religious enthusiasm engendered by

New church for Whitefield
Vandaliz 1745
Whitefield little impact
on Gov Pa

RELIGIOUS AWAKENING IN THE 1740S   127

the Whitefieldian revivals could not be sustained, his activities and those of his associates generated an outburst of publicity. Printers rapidly published Whitefield's letters and journals, while Philadelphia newspapers provided ample information about his travels throughout the colonies and promotion of an orphanage in Georgia.[40] After the colony's Anglican churches were closed to the evangelist, several of his followers proposed constructing a large church in which he and other revivalists could preach unhindered. Despite some reluctance, lest it lead to bigotry or the formation of a sect,[41] his supporters from several denominations went ahead with the project. Construction began even before clear title to the land had been obtained, and within six months work had progressed far enough that Whitefield could preach in it.[42] This building subsequently became embroiled in a conflict between competing religious interests, and early in 1745 some "ill minded Person or Persons" vandalized the building, damaged the pulpit, broke one of the benches, and "committed sundry other mischievous Irregularities."[43]

Probably because of language differences, Whitefield had limited contact with German-speaking Pennsylvanians. He once preached in Germantown to a large audience, and received a favorable response. Germans, Whitefield asserted, were interested in translating and publishing his writings. In Germantown, he spoke with several Germans and a Swiss minister who had been exiled for "preaching Christ." Impressed by the number of denominations in the town that emphasized vital Christianity, Whitefield concluded that many Germans had been driven from their homes because of their religious beliefs. He also visited Conrad Matthai, an aged hermit, with whose beliefs he found himself in fundamental accord.[44] During a subsequent visit to the colony, Whitefield preached to a largely German audience in a "very wilderness part of the country." Peter Böhler, a sympathetic Moravian, followed Whitefield's sermon with one in German. Whitefield also preached at a Moravian's farm and spent the evening in religious conversation with several of the "German Brethren."[45]

Whitefield's primary contacts among German-speaking people were with the Moravians, with whom he had first become acquainted in London during the 1730s. Due to their shared evangelicalism and ec-

umenism, relationships were initially cordial, and were strengthened
by Moravian interest in Whitefield's charitable projects in Georgia.[46]
In April 1740 Böhler requested "a couple of well grounded brethren"
to assist the English missionary, whom he admired as a man who
"awakens many souls" and "works powerfully on the sects."[47] Whitefield played a significant, yet largely unintentional, role in the settlement of Moravians in Pennsylvania. In the spring of 1740 he purchased 5000 acres "on the forks of the Delaware" approximately sixty
miles north of Philadelphia, where he planned to settle some of his
English friends and to establish a charitable institution for blacks. When
the financial arrangements for this project were disrupted after the
murder of Whitefield's agent, it was thought prudent to sell the land,
and the Moravians purchased the tract.[48]

Despite the earlier mutual interest in each other's projects, as the
Whitefieldians and Moravians became more familiar with each other's
ideas they began to move toward vocal opposition. This was due in
part to differences in doctrine, especially Whitefield's growing attachment to Calvinistic principles, and in part to different emphases on
fundamental beliefs. In Pennsylvania the development of active hostility was sparked by the arrival of Count Nicholas von Zinzendorf
late in 1741, which led to a reconsideration of the sect by leaders of
the revival movement.[49]

Gilbert Tennent, who was to spearhead the opposition to the Moravians in the colony, first met Zinzendorf in New Brunswick when
the Moravian leader was traveling to Pennsylvania from New York.
Almost immediately he began to denounce the sect, which he considered "very Dangerous," if only because its members "artfully Conceal
their principals." Nevertheless, he managed to compile a list of twenty
erroneous ideas, primarily concerning sin and salvation, following the
interview with Zinzendorf. Because Tennent found "their principals
as Strangely as Madly of Confusion as ever My eyes Saw," he could
understand why "they try to hide them as much as they Can."[50] He
urged the warring factions of Pennsylvania Presbyterianism to heal
the schism in order to present a united front against the "Enthusias-
tical *Moravians* and *Long Beards* or *Pietists*."[51] His foes reminded him,
however, that the Moravians had been Whitefield's "most eminent

Christians in *Georgia* and *Delaware*-Forks," and that Tennent's friend had been the "chief Tool to lead them in Swarms" to the province.[52]

A few Presbyterian ministers wanted to learn more about Moravian doctrines before judging them or engaging in controversy. Thus in December 1742 Samuel Finley arranged to meet with several Moravians. He questioned them especially about whether Christians could sin. When one asserted that he "had never been overcome by any Sin, Since he knew Christ," Finley wondered "whether he knew him at all." The debate continued fruitlessly as both sides quoted texts to support their beliefs.[53] He later wrote that their doctrine "Secures them effectually from noticing the inward Corruption of their hearts," even though their outward lives were inoffensive. Moravians were "deluded," for "they speak much of X^t but horridly corrup & pervert his word," especially the "doctrine of his distinguishing Grace."[54]

Meanwhile, Tennent informed Whitefield about Moravian attempts to alter the articles governing the use of the nondenominational "New Building" in Philadelphia so that they could preach there. Tennent declared that Moravian teachings conflicted with the Gospels. They were "deceivers" or *"Wolves . . . in Sheeps Clothing"* who were *"adoing the Devils Work* in Debauching & Corrupting the Professors of Religion."[55] Whitefield immediately wrote to Christopher Prylaeus, the Moravian minister in Philadelphia, requesting him not to preach in the church "built for Me, & for the preaching of the Calvinistics Scheme." He hoped to avoid an open breach with the Moravians, and argued that it would be "most for the Glory of God to let such preach there, & the Moravians preach elsewhere." The two groups followed this procedure in London, "& yet continue friendly."[56] He also wrote to the trustees of the New Building requesting them to forbid Moravian preaching there. If they insisted and *"thrust themselves* into *other Mens labours,"* it would be a "Notorious proof that they are Enimies to the Doctrines of the protest reformed Churches."[57] Nevertheless, Whitefield thought that "Where the Spirit of God is in any great degree, there will be union of Heart" despite differences in specific doctrines.[58] To Tennent he urged a "Cath. Spirit" that would accept the contributions the Moravians made toward bringing people to Christianity, and advised his friend "not [to] fall out with them."[59]

Presbyl attack
Moravian poch
whitefield cond some Moravian prad idolators!

130   "A MIXED MULTITUDE"

Despite Whitefield's exertions, by 1743 peaceful coexistence had become impossible. Böhler informed Zinzendorf that "The Presbyterians in Philadelphia are talking about the people who go to hear us, as though it were a sin against the holy spirit."[60] A few years later a Moravian mentioned that a frontier woman who had heard Moravians preach several times was favorably disposed toward them, "But this she dare not tell the Presbyterians."[61]

Several Presbyterian ministers penned lengthy tracts to refute Moravian doctrines.[62] Moravian leaders, claiming to have been misrepresented and misunderstood, published a warning against unauthorized translations of essays concerning their religious society.[63] A fresh assault on the sect began after publication of a letter from Zinzendorf giving his "Opinion" of the "different States among which the Christian People are now dispersed," followed a few weeks later by a series of questions and answers dating from 1742. Tennent wrote a lengthy rebuttal to each of the Count's statements.[64]

Following this exchange, public disputes between Moravians and their English-speaking opponents diminished. Not until 1753, when an "Expostulatory Letter" from Whitefield to Zinzendorf was publicized in both England and Pennsylvania, did the sect again attract wide public attention. Whitefield queried whether "the first Christians" engaged in practices such as "walking round the Graves of their deceased Friends on Easter-Day, attended with Hautboys, Trumpets, French-Horns, Violins, and other Kinds of musical Instruments?" He deemed the display of illuminated pictures of individuals in celebrating birthdays and the use of incense to greet prominent people at love feasts idolatrous. He found greed in the authority Moravians exerted over the estates of converts.[65] These attacks were not without effect on John Penn II, grandson of the colony's founder, who became convinced that the Moravians were "a very bad people."[66] Thomas Penn, however, thought Whitefield had "gone rather too far" in his anti-Moravian pamphlet and urged his nephew to visit the Moravian settlements in the colony.[67]

Not all English-speaking Pennsylvanians were as hostile to the Moravians as the men who were attempting to foster a religious revival along primarily Calvinistic lines. Conflict between the two sets of revivalists was perhaps inevitable, and increased by Moravian efforts to propagate their ideas outside of their expected German-speaking constituency. But they had some success in bringing their message to English-speaking Pennsylvanians, many of whom were at least curious about the new sect.

Because of settlement patterns, most English-Moravian contacts occurred in or near Philadelphia and during the missionary journeys the Moravians conducted throughout the colony.[68] The first ship transporting a large number of Moravian colonists arrived in the city during the summer of 1742. A few days later these immigrants separated; most of the Germans went to Bethlehem, where the Moravians had established a small settlement, while the English remained in Philadelphia.[69] English worship services were held weekly in Bethlehem for the benefit of the "English neighbors and the Irish" and of the Moravians who understood English or wished to learn it.[70]

A "terrific desire" among English people in the city for a resumption of Moravian meetings was reported to Zinzendorf very shortly after these immigrants landed.[71] An anonymous Philadelphian requested that a minister fluent in English be sent to the city for the "Deliverance" of many people out of "Presbyterian Slavery." Because earlier Moravian ministers spoke the language poorly, they had been of little benefit to interested seekers.[72] By late 1743 Böhler asked Zinzendorf to send more "English speakers" to the Pennsylvania mission.[73] In 1746 a Scottish Moravian compiled a list of places in the colony where English services had been conducted; he noted that English, Irish, and Welsh people attended. Even those who were formally Anglican or Presbyterian were eager for services to be continued.[74] Because many English Pennsylvanians visited the settlement at Bethlehem, the congregation formulated regulations for the conduct of "fremde Leute," or "strangers," and for the community's contacts with visitors.[75]

Moravian itinerants frequently encountered Quakers during their journeys. One missionary met several Friends who were so "wonderfully Civil" that they "Constrain'd" him to remain for dinner.[76] In Darby, a "cold & indifferent" Quaker asked many questions, the answers to which he offered no objections. This town, the missionary believed, could profit from regular visits by Moravians.[77] When he visited the town again, he was directed to the home of a Quaker "who lov'd us much." Although the head of the household was absent, the Moravian missionary had a profitable discussion with the wife, who "has no Enmity ag^t the Breth^{nn}" and invited him to return. Again he recommended occasional visits by Moravians, for "there are severall Souls a seeking."[78] Christian Henry Rauch met a Quaker "who had a great desire to debate with me" about the sacraments and various Moravian religious practices. He refused to argue, but reported that his negative response to the Quaker's final question, "whether we preach for money. . . . pleased him very much."[79]

One Moravian found that if he asked for directions, people would frequently invite him into their homes. This was a good opening, and he often found "freedom" to converse with them about religious matters.[80] Some itinerants fell into conversation with other travelers. One met an Englishman interested in visiting Bethlehem. Because the missionary "could not freely speak with him," he gave the inquirer a few tracts.[81] A Baptist who attended Moravian services aroused the displeasure of his church and caused an "uproar"; Moravians concluded, however, that further visits among Baptists might be valuable, for there were many "awakend" souls among them.[82] Official opposition to Moravians notwithstanding, one was pleased to find that one of "M^r W—f—ld's People" was "quite free from Dispute, or bitterness." Both men agreed that "the Lamb's grace on our Hearts" was more important than denominational labels.[83] Another man who had been "awaken'd" by Whitefield but had returned to his sinful ways was encouraged to strengthen his faith and was given a tract the Moravian thought might be helpful.[84]

The Pennsylvania elite, although interested in the new sect, were wary. The magistrates before whom the first group of immigrants was brought to take the oaths of allegiance were confused when the colonists declared that "our Church do not swear," but allowed them to promise fidelity.[85] Curiosity led at least one Pennsylvanian to request the German-born Indian interpreter, Conrad Weiser, to translate anti-Moravian tracts into English.[86] Weiser also provided information about European objections to the "upstart modern Sect of ignorant Fanaticks" who "artfully" misappropriated the ancient and respectable name of the Moravian Brethren. Provincial Secretary Richard Peters considered their tenets "nonsensical." Their hierarchy demanded absolute obedience, their marriage practices were "foul," and their members would undoubtedly become the "Pests of Society." He claimed to have "no prejudices" against the sect, yet he questioned the wisdom of allowing members of a pacifistic sect to settle "in Large numbers at a distance from the Seat of Government."[87]

Although James Logan had been impressed by the Moravian vanguard in the colony, his attitude changed after Zinzendorf's arrival, seemingly due in part to the Count's rudeness. After expressing interest in meeting and dining with Logan, he made only brief visits and without apology failed to honor an invitation to dine.[88] Zinzendorf also declined to meet with several Friends who traveled to Germantown for discussions they had been told he desired. His conduct, it appears, "lost him all credit" among the non-Moravian elite. One bizarre incident involved Zinzendorf's request that Logan translate into English his Latin renunciation of several hereditary titles. Logan thought the document written in a very "odd" style, "in Some parts, carrying a Shew of Elegance but very little Propriety, in other parts meer balderdash, in Some places plain enough, in others pfectly unintelligible." Zinzendorf had the original version printed and held a meeting with several gentlemen who understood Latin to discuss it, but then, "to ye no Small astonishm^t" of his guests, decided to proceed no further. Not surprisingly, they "generally concluded him crack'd as all men of Sober Judgm^t . . . must."[89]

Although the compact settlement of Moravians near the frontier gave colonial officials cause for concern, the proprietary family was interested in disposing of land, especially in large tracts. Lengthy negotiations were carried out between the Moravians and Penn and his colonial representatives to reach satisfactory agreements on property matters.[90]

Moravian interest in the Indians aroused suspicion.[91] Shortly after Zinzendorf's arrival, Governor George Thomas admitted that, while he held a "high Opinion" of the Count's "Integrity & Religious Zeal" and would be "very well pleased" if the Moravians could convert the Indians into good Christians, he was extremely doubtful about the project. He believed that "the common sort of People amongst Christians are worse than the Indians, who are left to the Law of Nature, that is their own natural Reason, to guide them," and feared that Christianized Indians might turn out to be worse than they were in their heathen state. Thomas was reluctant to allow the Moravians to entertain Indian messengers, fearing that they might be denied the customary refreshments and report that the province "failed in Civility to save Expense."[92] On the other hand, Logan approved Zinzendorf's plan to send a few young men to live with the Indians in order to learn their language. Moravians "utterly dislike ye fopperies of ye Romish Service," and held no views inconsistent with British interests. He was impressed by the refusal of Indian converts to Moravianism to drink anything but water even when their German companions accepted Logan's offer of wine.[93]

At first some considered Zinzendorf's influence on the Indians baneful, for a few who had been converted—or "pretend[ed]" to be— wrote to the governor requesting permission to remain on land that had been sold by a treaty. They did not wish to be forced to "remove to live wth Heathens tho' of their own Nation" since they were now "of ye same Religion wth ye white People." They even had the "Impudence" to subscribe themselves "Your Honour's Brethren in ye Lord Jesus."[94] Yet by 1750 Thomas Penn suggested that, since Weiser was reluctant to train one of his sons or relations as an interpreter, a Moravian appeared to be the logical alternative to receive provincial support to live among the Indians and learn their language.[95] Nevertheless, the provincial council hesitated a few years later when several Moravians requested a passport that would permit them to travel among the Indians, leave a few men in their villages to "improve themselves in their Language," and bring a few Indians to their settlement at Gnadenhütten. The council feared that the Indians would resent the intrusion and that the Moravians might "meddle with the Affairs of Government." The matter dropped when the Moravians failed to renew their request.[96]

Moravians became involved with the authorities over a few minor issues. Perhaps because of qualms about the desirability of a Moravian settlement, a constable was twice dispatched to find out the number of inhabitants in Bethlehem.[97] Once Zinzendorf, his daughter, and a

companion were accused of breaking the Sabbath and brought before
a justice of the peace. They were fined six shillings each for their
crime of having "written and done a little copying, namely, of several
hymns, composed by Bro. Ludwig [Zinzendorf]."[98] Shortly thereafter the Bethlehem congregation decided it was essential for the community to become acquainted with the *"constitution of the land"* and
provincial *"rights and laws."* It purchased a copy of the Pennsylvania
statutes and assigned a brother the responsibility of familiarizing himself with it, so that in all circumstances Moravians might know "what
is customary here and how far one may or dare go."[99] The congregation also decided to formulate its own regulations to which anyone
who wished to settle on Moravian-owned property would have to conform, for it was "impossible under our church regulations to concede
to them the Pennsylvania liberties, which are so readily abused."[100]

Zinzendorf's purpose in coming to Pennsylvania was neither to establish a Moravian settlement nor to organize the Moravian church as a
distinct sect, but to bring order out of the chaotic religious situation
of the Pennsylvania Germans. During the 1730s Moravians had informed him of the neglected condition of the Germans and of the need
for evangelical and educational work among them, although encouraging signs of a religious revival had been discerned. Zinzendorf hoped
to create an ecumenical "Congregation of God in the Spirit," a fellowship of experiential Christians that transcended sectarian lines, yet left
adherents within their original congregations where they could ex-
emplify the meaning of vital religion. Pennsylvania's multiplicity of
sects and lack of an established church that might hinder his mission
influenced his choice of a site for his experiment in Christian unity.

The Zinzendorfian fellowship was based upon the assumption that
the essential beliefs constituting the fundamental Christian message
were unitary. Denominations—especially national churches—were of
divine origin, intended to provide different approaches to grace for
people of different temperaments or "national" characteristics. The
real barrier to Christian unity was not the institutional divisiveness of
the visible church, but the disjunction between true believers and
nominal members. Believers could unite despite differences in out-

ward forms, for they were at one in their experience of God. Zinzendorf saw no contradiction between being both a Moravian and a member of another church, for the "Moravian" was merely attempting to unify Christians through the denominational structure. Thus the sect refused to define itself as such or to develop a creed. The vagueness of the ideal of a "Congregation of God in the Spirit" and active evangelism only added to the divisions, tensions, and confusions within provincial religious life.[101]

One precursor to Zinzendorf's scheme, and an example to him of interfaith cooperation in Pennsylvania, was the Associated Brethren of Skippack, a group of devout laymen of diverse religious beliefs who gathered monthly between 1736 and 1740 to concert their efforts to improve German religious life and for mutual edification. Included along with several separatists were Henry Antes, a lay teacher of the Reformed faith, Christopher Wiegner, a Schwenkfelder on whose farm the future Moravian bishop Augustus Spangenberg lived for a period in the late 1730s, and George Böhnisch, a Moravian who accompanied the Schwenkfelders to the colony.[102] Antes issued a circular invitation in December 1741 requesting members of all sects and denominations to attend a conference in Germantown. Participants would discuss the fundamentals of Christianity and try to reach an agreement on beliefs that did not affect salvation. This meeting inaugurated the "Pennsylvania Synods," seven conferences held between January and June of 1742 in which Zinzendorf labored to organize his Congregation of God in the Spirit, although after the third conference most representatives of other groups withdrew, leaving the subsequent meetings as essentially Moravian gatherings.[103]

The Moravians' irresolvable problem was that a doctrine or practice outsiders might consider unimportant was often deemed essential and zealously defended by a sect. Zinzendorf indirectly recognized this dilemma when, in a summary of "religion in general" in Pennsylvania, he concluded that it "consists of placing little or no emphasis on the main point but rather of selecting *one* of a hundred nonessentials and making it the main point."[104] Moravians were not unwilling to make concessions to the beliefs of others, although they, too, favored distinctive doctrines and rituals. For instance, at the first meeting of the

2 days of rest for Moravians susp of Zinzendorf

Bethlehem congregation, convened after the conferences had ended, it was proposed to make both Saturday and Sunday days of rest. Appropriate precedents for Sabbath observance were cited, and it was specifically mentioned that the Ephrata cloister was "quite right on that score," although according to the Moravians that community went to extremes by calling Sunday a "whores' day" and working on that day "just to annoy" people of other persuasions.[105]

Moreover, many people questioned Zinzendorf's motives and goals, and resented his involvement in the affairs of other religious groups. Proselytization and attempts at union appeared to threaten the freedom of belief and practice that colonists enjoyed. One sectarian suspected that the Count "wanted to be the head of the Separatists, Brethren, Sabbatarians, Mennonites, Schwenkfelders, Quakers, Reformed, and Lutherans."[106] After attending the third conference, one of the Brethren who had listened to "queer and wonderfull things" concluded that the conferences were "snares, for the purpose of bringing simple-minded and inexperienced converts back to infant baptism and churchgoing and of erecting the old Babel again."[107] Schwenkfelders, many of whom had lived on Zinzendorf's estate in Germany, suspected that "he has *pretensions* on us."[108]

Although outside of the conferences some Moravians and sectarians established friendly contacts, Zinzendorf lacked the breadth of vision to succeed in his ecumenical mission. In answering a question posed by members of the Church of the Brethren, usually referred to as the Dunkers, about the form of baptism, he declared that they do not "baptize after the ordinances of Christ" even though he admitted that they "live according to the ordinances of Christ." One synod, after criticizing the Dunkers for failing to prove that they were not related to the Anabaptists condemned in the Augsburg Confession, recommended that they reach an agreement with the Mennonites on a form of baptism, which would "make one sect less in the country."[109] When Zinzendorf twice baptized Indians using a form unacceptable to the Brethren after promising that he would not, "conscientious people" said that they "could accuse him of lies to his face."[110] Another synod condemned the Ephratans, an offshoot of the Dunkers, as nothing but a "schismatic pack" who attempted to "steal their baptism and calling" from the Brethren. Their chief innovation was "imprisoned cloister-virgins" who suffered greatly. The synod concluded, "May the Lamb crush this satan to death soon!"[111] Not surprisingly, the Ephratans "wrote an entire book" against the Moravians. Many participants at the conference were offended by the harsh judgments levied against the monastics.[112]

Such denunciations were probably unexpected, for the Moravians had been especially interested in the monastics. During Spangenberg's visit to the colony in the late 1730s, relations between the two sects had been cordial. He initially thought that Johann Conrad Beissel and his followers had instigated a reform movement to purify the Church of the Brethren, and that "in those matters in which they oppose them [the Brethren] they are in the right." He commended their practices of poverty, chastity, and rigorous discipline. A lengthy discussion between Moravians and monastics about their religious views was "not without blessing."[113] But as Spangenberg became more familiar with the beliefs of the Ephrata community, he questioned whether it was "necessary and profitable to seek a union between the Moravians and the Sabbatarians?" Although Moravian ecumenism and his belief that the monastics were "very sincere and the Lord is with them" made it difficult to "separate" from them,[114] he could not help noticing that the outward practices of the Ephratans had become very "peculiar," for they dressed like monks, refused to sleep in beds or on straw, refused to eat pork, did not engage in commercial transactions, and diligently kept vigils. For a time Spangenberg kept "quiet" about their differences, even though he feared they sought grace through works. At last he refused to have anything to do with them, seeing "quite clearly that false powers and not the Spirit of Christ are ruling the congregation."[115]

Differences between the two sects before Zinzendorf's visit to the colony were not serious. Moravians were welcomed to the cloister and invited to participate in love feasts. But once Zinzendorf arrived cordiality deteriorated; arguments centered upon marriage, justification, and, perhaps as significantly, the personalities of two strongminded leaders. At the first conference representatives from Ephrata were given a favored status. Nevertheless, when Zinzendorf planned to hold the second conference at the cloister, Beissel refused.[116] Controversies led to the publication of pamphlets on both sides,[117] with the acrimonious situation exacerbated by the refusal of Christopher Sauer to publish anything against the Ephrata community.[118]

The most significant contacts, and conflicts, Moravians had with provincial Germans were with members of the Lutheran and Reformed churches. The crucial issue was whether ministers sympathetic to the Moravians could at the same time be orthodox Lutheran or Reformed pastors. Several congregations were disrupted by this problem; suspicion, riots, lawsuits, and further religious chaos ensued. The arrival of Henry Melchior Muhlenberg in Philadelphia in December 1742 was the catalyst. Of pietistic leanings and already opposed to the Moravians, he had been sent to the colony in part as a response to the threat the sect posed to the survival of the Lutheran church in the colony.[119]

A year before Muhlenberg's arrival, the Lutheran portion of a Lutheran-Reformed "union church" that met in a Philadelphia warehouse requested Zinzendorf, an ordained Lutheran minister, to preach to their congregation. John Philip Boehm, the Reformed pastor, was asked for his consent. Declining any authority over the Lutherans, he advised the Reformed to have nothing to do with Zinzendorf. When in January 1741/2 Zinzendorf received a call to serve the congregation, Boehm's consent was again solicited, with the same result. Zinzendorf served the congregation until summer, and then appointed Christopher Pyrlaeus as minister while he went on a mission to the Indians. At this point the tensions in the congregation that had been festering over Zinzendorf's Moravian Lutheranism caused one of the orthodox Lutheran deacons to affix a lock to the door and one faction of the congregation to forbid Pyrlaeus from preaching in the building. When the door was broken open and Pyrlaeus entered the pulpit a "tumult" occurred, and the Moravian faction initiated a lawsuit.[120] Several members of the anti-Moravian faction issued a broadside in English explaining the dispute and insisting that they were peaceable men, while the Moravians published their version in the *Pennsylvania Gazette*.[121] Although Richard Peters and others tried to reconcile the dispute outside of the judicial system, the parties were too impassioned to compromise.[122]

When Muhlenberg arrived in the colony he found that, by winning over certain deacons to their cause, the Moravians had gained possession of the church record book and chalice. Muhlenberg first asked Zinzendorf to return the items, and then appealed to the mayor to bring legal action to force their restoration. Although Zinzendorf promised to return the book, he later denied any knowledge of it. The mayor threatened to arrest the Count, but Muhlenberg was content with exposing his mendacity. After the orthodox Lutherans were acquitted of charges of riot and given possession of the meetinghouse, Muhlenberg decided to forget about the contested property, for "if they are capable of retaining possession of something illegally, then they are acting contrary to the Seventh Commandment and will have to answer for it."[123]

Philadelphia was not the only place where Moravians became entangled in disputes with both Lutheran and Reformed congregations. Early in the 1740s German Lutherans in Lancaster, who had occasionally been served by Swedish ministers, petitioned church authorities in Sweden for a pastor.[124] The arrival of Lawrence Thorstensen Nyberg in Advent 1744 brought a lengthy dispute with the Moravians that involved both Swedish and German ministers and seriously disrupted the congregation. The crux of the problem was that Nyberg was sympathetic to Moravian teachings, although at his ordination he had promised to uphold orthodox Lutheranism. While visiting London on his journey to the colony, he had allegedly sought out the Moravians and become a member of their community, which was kept secret so that he might be accepted in Lancaster "without suspicion." Indeed, he was joyfully welcomed "as an angel from God."[125] But soon Nyberg began to criticize other Lutheran pastors as "pietists" and to establish cordial relations with the Moravians. Lutherans held an acrimonious conference during which Nyberg denied that he was a Moravian, but argued that in any case there was nothing objectionable in their confession of faith. Other ministers disagreed.[126]

Tensions increased when Nyberg married a Moravian woman, and exploded when he openly espoused the Moravian cause by attending one of the conferences they held in Lancaster. When Nyberg subsequently tried to preach in his church, a large crowd prevented his entrance and a riot nearly occurred. The dissidents argued that "'Since

Neuberg is in agreement with the *Moravians*, he cannot be a genuine Lutheran,'" while Nyberg countered that "'A man can be a genuine Lutheran teacher according to the Augsburg Confession and the symbolical books even if he does maintain a connection with the Moravian Brethren.'" The dispute continued with further violence, a lawsuit, and appeals to local justices, the governor, and the assembly.[127] The proceedings were extensively reported and debated in the Germantown newspaper.[128] The legal wrangling was resolved in favor of the orthodox party, but finally, with the assistance of many of the wealthiest Lancastrians, the Moravian-minded erected their own church in which both German and English services were conducted. Tensions gradually subsided after a German Lutheran pastor was appointed to serve the orthodox congregation regularly.[129]

The German Reformed also experienced problems with the Moravians. Warned by Dutch church officials to be on their guard against the sect, Reformed ministers tried to prevent inroads into the congregations they had organized. Boehm received a book cautioning against the "heretical teachings" of the sect,[130] from which he extracted many of the major arguments, added new information specifically relating to their activities in Pennsylvania, and published as a *Getreuer Warnungs Briefe* to combat the "soul-corrupting and conscience-destroying teachings" of the sect. A year later he published a shorter essay to alert people about Moravians posing as Reformed ministers.[131] Nevertheless, the Moravians, who came "in sheep's clothing and with smooth, hypocritical words offer their services to instruct all men without cost," gained many converts.[132]

Moravians secured a foothold in the Reformed churches of Germantown and Lancaster through the efforts of Bartholomew Rieger, a minister who "had very much intercourse with all sorts of people and all sorts of sects." He encouraged John Bechtel, one of the "worst proselytizers" among the Moravians, to take charge of the Germantown church. Bechtel promised to adhere to the Reformed faith, but soon began to take exception to certain tenets. The church divided and dismissed him after his one-year contract expired, but in order to regain possession of the church the orthodox party was forced to pay for costly improvements the Moravians had made to the building. Rieger was in Lancaster long enough to install Pyrlacus in the church, cause

a disturbance in the congregation, and instigate a legal battle.[133] In
1745 and 1746 the Moravians were still sufficiently strong in Lancaster to inspire Reformed pastor Caspar Schnorr to preach against them.
His special target was Jacob Lischy, an itinerant Moravian Reformed
minister, whom he termed a "sorcerer." However, Schnorr's zeal
backfired. Because his discourses were little more than "scolding," he
"unwittingly secured to Br. Lischy very much influence," and even
many of Lischy's "enemies" went to hear him.[134]

By the late 1740s both the Lutherans and the Reformed were experiencing fewer difficulties with the Moravians, largely because of
Zinzendorf's recognition of the failure of his ecumenical project and
his willingness to organize the Moravians as a distinct sect. There also
appears to have been a decrease in proselytization among white inhabitants, especially among those already affiliated with a religious society. Furthermore, once regular sources of orthodox ministers from
Europe were established, Moravian teachers were in less demand, and
churches experienced less disruption and dissension over the meaning
of orthodoxy.[135]

II

The 1740s, in addition to the religious disorder caused by evangelicalism, saw the beginnings of stabilization in the religious life of Germans who professed the Lutheran and Reformed faiths. After many
years of indifference to the colonists' frequent requests to church officials in Germany, Holland, Sweden, and England for pastors, missionaries were finally dispatched. Although no ecclesiastical body had
responsibility for the emigrants, the pietistic Lutheran institution at
Halle and the Dutch Reformed Classis of Amsterdam slowly recognized the magnitude of the mission field, and especially the threat
posed by Moravian activities, and began to take an active interest in
the province. Although colonists never received sufficient assistance
to meet their religious needs, ministers strove to organize congregations and restore denominational consciousness. Hostility toward sectarians characterized early ministers, yet paradoxically their writings
reveal the practical toleration characteristic of lay Pennsylvanians.[136]

Henry Melchior Muhlenberg had a rude introduction to colonial

conditions. When he stopped at an inn, the Englishmen there immediately asked him "whether I was a *Moravian*, a *Lutherien*, a *Calvinist*,
or a *Churchman*." Unaccustomed to such a welcome, he "gave them a
reprimand and said they must learn better manners and not welcome
strangers with such questions."[137] He soon discovered the diversity
that made such curiosity understandable. In Philadelphia he noticed
that the English, Swedes, Quakers, Moravians, Catholics, and others
had churches or meetinghouses; only the Germans did not. He wrote
to a friend that "there is not a sect in the world that is not sheltered
here. Here one finds people from all countries in the world. Everything that is not tolerated in Europe finds a place here."[138]

The primary difficulties confronting Lutheran ministers included
the poverty of their parishioners, their settlement among a multiplicity of sects, and the years of neglect that had caused people to yield
to sectarian proselytization or to become confused about their beliefs
or indifferent to religion. Muhlenberg declared that "People here cannot be stimulated to diligent attendance on the exercise of divine worship by honor, respect, and material advantage; rather, on the one
side they often take upon themselves contempt and insults, and on
the other side must overcome the enticements of other parties."[139]
Preliminary steps for building a church, necessary because of the small
size of the warehouse shared by the Lutherans and the Reformed and
its involvement in the Moravian controversy, were undertaken with
difficulty. According to Muhlenberg, congregational officials had trouble
finding a site in the city, for most of the land was owned by Quakers
who refused even to lease it for ground rent when they heard a church
was to be erected on it.[140] He was under the curious misapprehension
that Lutherans had been granted special permission to build a church;
he believed that "According to English and provincial laws, no sect or
denomination is permitted to construct a church except for the Anglicans, and besides them, the Lutherans."[141]

Muhlenberg observed that, because Englishmen and German sectarians had been among the first arrivals in the province, they had
been able to purchase large tracts of land and become prosperous.[142]
Because the wealthiest and most influential Pennsylvanians were sectarians, those who wished to improve their status "find no better opportunity than to betake themselves to those sects."[143] Furthermore,

as long as "church people" remained "unenlightened and unconverted," sectarians could argue, "'You have so many worthless and
dead members. Your preaching and your churchgoing do no good.'"
He accused sectarians of attempting to lure people who were "improving" in their faith into their "sectarian net."[144] After several years
of labor in the Pennsylvania mission combatting the appeal of sectarianism, Muhlenberg pessimistically concluded, "Experience teaches me
that it is easier to convert people to a sect in which boundaries are
established that natural temperaments can attain through their own
powers."[145]

The variety of competing faiths engendered confusion among religiously inclined Pennsylvanians. The father of one young man who
came to him for baptism, asked by Muhlenberg why his son had not
been baptized as an infant, replied, "because there were so many sects
in this country he had not known which was the best. When he made
inquiries of the teachers of each party, every one of them would say,
'Here is Christ; we have the best medicine and the nearest road to
heaven.'" He had, however, taught his children to read the Bible so
that they could judge for themselves which sect was in the closest
harmony with it.[146]

Lutheran pastors considered all types of sectarianism objectionable,
but Quakers were the targets of particular criticism. One reason was
the Friends had "control, wealth, and worldly prestige," but did not
believe in baptism; their example had caused many Germans to become content with their neglected condition and to grow "slothful" in
their religious duties.[147] Muhlenberg considered Quakers "quite capable of blaspheming against God's Word and Sacraments, but at the
same time they are very blind in spiritual things."[148] Other problems
stemming from sectarianism were more specific to the German community—in particular the anticlerical stance of Christopher Sauer, the
influential separatist printer. Sauer published unsubstantiated accusations against innocent ministers and reported in detail scandals caused
by purported ministers. He also publicized internal disputes within
churches.[149]

Despite these hindrances, the writings of the Halle pastors reveal
that people of all nationalities and faiths were willing, often eager, to
avail themselves of the spiritual assistance offered by them. Weddings

cross overs in
relig — Baptism
confirmation
diff laws.

and funerals frequently brought diverse people together; ministers used these occasions to speak simply but effectively about the fundamentals of Christianity rather than about narrow denominational ideas. At funerals one minister always preached a sermon so that his auditors would know "that we insist upon a genuine Christianity," for sectarians or nonbelievers often thought that "the churchpeople . . . place their salvation in church-going."[150] When Muhlenberg buried a woman in the Mennonite cemetery near her home, he intended to preach under a tree, but because of the "great heat," the three Mennonite teachers in attendance insisted that he preach in the meetinghouse. Although they requested that Muhlenberg "use no strange ceremonics," following the sermon the Mennonites expressed their agreement with its contents, for Muhlenberg spoke only of "repentance, faith, and godliness" and ignored doctrinal issues on which the two denominations differed.[151] At the funeral of a Reformed man who had previously asked Muhlenberg to bury him, the English-speaking neighbors in attendance requested "a lesson in their language."[152] When another Lutheran minister married members of the Reformed and Mennonite churches, he reported that the guests were pleased with what he had said. At another marriage attended by people "of all sorts of sects," the guests listened attentively to the address, "in particular several elderly, respectable Quakers and Mennonites, who, contrary to their custom, kept their hats off."[153]

Pennsylvanians sometimes went to great lengths to attend church services or to receive instruction and the sacraments. Often indiscriminate about the affiliation of the minister, they seemed unclear about the theological differences that in Europe seriously divided Christians. Prior to the arrival of German ministers, one man learned Swedish so that he could attend Lutheran services conducted in that language. A German Lutheran purchased an English New Testament for his "heathen" Quaker wife, who eventually joined a Lutheran congregation. An Irishman of the Reformed faith who understood German regularly attended Lutheran services.[154] On several occasions parents of different faiths and nationalities asked Lutheran ministers to baptize their children, even occasionally when neither of the parents was Lutheran. Frequently the adult offspring of non-Lutheran parents came to these pastors for baptism, instruction, or confirmation.[155] Others, dissatisfied with sects or desirous of regular preaching that emphasized the fundamentals of the faith rather than minute doctrinal tenets, attended Lutheran services, sought out ministers for conversation, and encouraged them to visit places destitute of formal worship. Ministers, who were frequently requested to preach in Dutch or English, often noted how mixed their congregations were.[156]

Concern for the religious needs of servants, many of them recent immigrants from Germany, crossed ethnic and denominational lines. Masters sometimes pressured servants to adopt their faith; other servants lapsed from religious observances while serving masters who held different beliefs.[157] Lutheran ministers were concerned that parents who apprenticed their children "among those of strange religious connections and sects" take steps to make certain that they were properly instructed in religious matters.[158] However, in 1745 an English colonist asked Peter Brunnholtz, a Lutheran pastor, to preach to a large number of servants, and offered him the use of an Anglican church. This service was the first German one held in Chester in six years. Brunnholtz encouraged those in attendance to meet weekly in a private house, and promised to send them a volume of German sermons to read there.[159] An English justice of the peace living near Lancaster requested Muhlenberg to preach to servants in his neighborhood, most of whom did not understand English. With the consent of the priest, they would be permitted to meet in the Anglican church provided a sermon would also be preached in English.[160]

Ministers of the German Reformed church faced many of the same problems encountered by the Lutherans. One minister, complaining of his low salary, blamed it on the "numerous wicked sects, especially the Moravians." Sectarians, he believed, would easily lead "simple souls" astray if a fixed salary were demanded.[161] Ministers disparaged the colony as "a land of great liberties" where "The people are not well restricted therein."[162] Inroads into the Reformed faith also occurred through intermarriage, the lack of teachers to instruct children in their native language and religion, and vicissitudes that could place Reformed redemptioners with sectarian masters.[163]

Organization of the Reformed church and the development of effective congregational structures and ministerial associations were hindered more by serious, internal problems than by external pressures. The situation was worsened by reports in Sauer's *Pensylvanische Berichte* of disputes between ministers and their elders and of the immoral behavior of ministers.[164] But the Reformed also publicized their disputes, paying for advertisements or providing information that was reported as news. A lengthy dispute within the Reformed church in Philadelphia, involving financial questions and a division within the congregation over which of two contenders should be the pastor, received attention in newspapers of both languages and was discussed by Pennsylvanians of various nationalities and beliefs. In an attempt to resolve the problem, a group of arbiters, mostly English Quakers, was selected; their decision was reported in both English and German newspapers.[165]

The seemingly infinite variety of sects among the German-speaking colonists and their propensity to make their religious disputes public contributed to the development of an attitude among English Pennsylvanians of amusement mixed with contempt. An Anglican minister plainly stated that "The Dutch have Several Odd sects of Religion," and described some of them, although not completely accurately.[166] James Logan was of the opinion that "there is Scarce any notion too wild" regarding religion "for a German to entertain."[167] Governor Thomas concurred: "The Germans imported with them all the religious Whimsies of their Country, and, I beleive [sic], had subdivided since their arrival there; for of the names of some of them I never heard in any other Country."[168]

As the emotional fervor of the Great Awakening and Moravian revival dissipated, Pennsylvanians drifted toward unity within diversity. There was increasing cooperation among religious groups, yet paradoxically a growing sense of denominational consciousness. The gradual increase of German pastors enhanced opportunities for contact with colleagues of other faiths, and permitted a growing number of laypeople of diverse beliefs to gather in worship. Another factor leading to cooperation or efforts toward union with a fairly similar group came from perceptions of a common threat, such as those posed by the Moravians or by the ramifications of the Great Awakening. The un-

dogmatic views of lay Pennsylvanians helped to persuade many ministers to adopt more tolerant views, and fostered positive interaction
among pastors representing different churches.

The Halle missionaries rapidly established cordial relations with
ministers of the Anglican, Swedish Lutheran, and German Reformed
churches. Despite differences in doctrine and language, these churches
had more in common with each other than any of them did with the
assorted sectarians living in the colony. Upon his arrival in Philadelphia, Muhlenberg visited the Anglican priest in the city, who expressed the hope that "very friendly relations" would develop between
them, as they had with the Swedes.[169] When the German Lutheran
church in Philadelphia was consecrated in 1748, Anglican, Swedish,
and German Reformed ministers were invited to participate in the
ceremonies.[170] In addition, German pastors shared in the responsibility for a rural Swedish-English congregation.[171] Muhlenberg was welcomed to Philadelphia by several officers of the Swedish church, who
invited him to preach in their building. Because the German meetinghouse was involved in the dispute with the Moravians and because
the Swedish church temporarily lacked a pastor, this invitation was
accepted on several occasions.[172]

Disruptions attributable to the Moravians led to an abortive effort
to unite the two Lutheran bodies. In 1745 Peter Kock and Henry
Sleydorn, two laymen, convened a conference of German and Swedish ministers and church officials in an attempt to coordinate their
common interests in furthering Lutheranism and opposing Moravianism. Differences between the churches, including language, ceremon-
ials, organization of the national churches, and missionaries' responsibilities to their superiors in Germany and Sweden, prevented the
plans from succeeding.[173] Nevertheless, the two groups did cooperate
to oppose the Moravians, for instance, by sharing information about
them from European religious leaders.[174] Swedish clergymen were also
advised to work with German ministers to advance the faith; these
instructions were similar to those that guided relations with Anglican
clergymen.[175]

The closest relationships German Lutherans maintained with members of another faith were with their countrypeople, the Reformed.

They often shared churches on a formal or informal basis, and members of both faiths were encouraged to assist one another in building churches. Fearing that disputes might arise, Muhlenberg attempted, without much success, to discourage the construction of "union churches."[176] Shortly after Michael Schlatter arrived to investigate conditions among the Reformed for the Classis of Amsterdam, he visited Muhlenberg in part "because it is very necessary to preserve friendly relations with the Lutherans, in as much as there are many mixed marriages and the people live almost everywhere together." Cordial relations were immediately established between the two ministers.[177]

During the 1740s the Dutch Reformed church and the colonial Presbyterian church expressed an interest in union. The Dutch synodical deputies, after being informed of the existence of a "Scotch-Presbyterian Coetus" in the colony, suggested that the Reformed either unite with it or establish another form of church organization in order to preserve order and maintain the faith.[178] One minister discussed the Dutch Reformed church's proposal with the Synod of Philadelphia,[179] but most Reformed ministers and their lay officers were unenthusiastic about union. They argued that few Germans understood English. Furthermore, the foundation of their faith was the Heidelberg Catechism and their church order was based upon the decrees of the Synods of Dort, while the Presbyterian church was founded upon the somewhat different Westminster Confession. They also objected that Presbyterians used no liturgies for baptism, communion, weddings, or other special occasions, and that to depart from the formularies of the Reformed church would be interpreted by people as "an apostasy from our true religion."[180] Nevertheless the Synod of Philadelphia, concerned about the "deplorable state of religion" among the Reformed churches and the losses suffered to Moravians and the sects, voted to view Reformed pastors as members of the same communion and to work with them to achieve union, or, if that proved impossible, to assist them in forming their own ecclesiastical organization. It also requested Dutch financial assistance in promoting a school to train young men for the ministry, and pointed out the benefits in which the Reformed could participate. A few years later the Presbyterians again expressed interest in union. Stating that the fundamental beliefs of the two churches were similar, they refuted accusations that some Presbyterians held errors associated with Mystics, Arminians, or Pelagians.[181]

The Presbyterians might have viewed union with the Reformed as a means of strengthening the conservative or "Old Side" branch against the awakeners. The schism, however, seems to have turned the Presbyterian church inward, and partially isolated it from other religious groups. With the exception of the German Reformed, it had little contact with people other than the local Scotch-Irish or Calvinists in other colonies. Instead, both factions competed in organizing missions to the neglected Scotch-Irish immigrants on the frontier, initiating missions to the Indians, and founding educational institutions.[182]

Pennsylvanians of most persuasions were concerned about schools, but held different views about the type of education their children needed and the religious beliefs of the teacher. Many were convinced that religious education was essential if children were to develop a firm attachment to the faith of their parents. Anglicans were concerned that teachers share their beliefs. The Chester congregation exhibited the most consistent interest in obtaining a schoolmaster from the Society for the Propagation of the Gospel, which was also requested to supplement his salary. On several occasions they accused their Quaker neighbors of using "all their power & Ill Offices" to drive qualified teachers away and to substitute a "Native Irish Bigotted Papist."[183] The Reformed complained of losses to their religion and language that occurred from the lack of educational facilities. Most teachers, one minister claimed, were "escaped papish Irishmen" or only slightly better educated Quakers.[184]

Other parents were concerned more with educating their children than with indoctrinating them. When Mennonites living near Quitopehilla who planned to begin a school had difficulty finding a qualified teacher, they asked the Moravians "to take charge and educate their children."[185] The "Better Sort" among Chester Anglicans, according to their priest, sent their children "to the Conventiclers" for their education.[186] In the backcountry, schools were attended by a wide variety of children. One Lutheran school had English, Irish, and Reformed children, even though the town contained both English and

Reformed schools. Some Lutheran schools became so overcrowded that the non-Lutherans were asked to leave. At another Lutheran school, children of sectarians were given religious instruction along with the Lutherans, with no objections from their parents.[187] While some town promoters reserved lots for schools and some teachers were purchased as redemptioners,[188] the educational needs of colonists could not be adequately fulfilled. As a result, many parents appear to have utilized any instruction available.

Coincidental with the increased tensions within various segments of the Protestant community during the 1740s and the general concern about religion was a greater interest in the province's non-Protestants. Perhaps because of their increasing (although still quite small) numbers, Roman Catholic colonists attracted more attention than when the first congregations and missions were established.

One early Jesuit missionary noted that "We have at present all liberty imaginable in the exercise of our business." Missionaries of his faith were "not only esteemed, but reverenced, as I may say, by the better sort of people."[189] Not all of the "better sort," however, approved of Catholics. Quaker Richard Hockley, apprehensively reporting to Thomas Penn that Roman Catholicism was increasing in the province, wondered "whether or not 'tis true Policy to suffer these People to go on and flourish in the manner they do if it coud be prevented," for they had become "a great bugbear" to the colonists. Informed that "they grew a little Insolent at their Chappel," Hockley decided to visit a service to see how they behaved. All he could report was the growth of the congregation and its ability to furnish the church handsomely.[190]

Penn, apparently impressed by this letter, told Hockley he would approve "legal Restraints" on Catholics if the assembly saw fit to enact them.[191] He requested Governor George Thomas, if he were on good terms with the assembly, to consider "some Law for restraining them, by making it very penal for any Priest to exercise his Function in Pennsylvania." But Penn subsequently realized that such a move would be unpopular, and informed the governor that what he had written about restricting Catholics was "from my apprehending the Assembly were desirous such a Bill should pass"; he advised Thomas not to press the issue.[192] Penn thought that Thomas and his friends had encouraged Catholics, thereby giving the assembly an excuse to alarm the populace.[193]

There was concern about selling or giving property to Roman Catholics to be used as sites for churches. When new towns were laid out, lots were often reserved for churches of various denominations in order to encourage settlement. This had been the policy of James Hamilton, proprietor of the first speculative town, Lancaster, who gave land to Roman Catholics as well as to Protestants.[194] Penn commended Thomas Cookson for granting lots to the Lutherans and the Reformed in York, but he "desire[d] no ground may be granted to any Roman Catholicks," even for private dwellings, as Catholics "hold Tenets destructive of all others," and ought to be discouraged.[195]

A few Protestant ministers were disturbed by the growing number of Catholics in the province. In 1740 one Anglican priest noted with alarm that living in his parish were "a great many more Papists than I formerly imagined"—ten families.[196] Robert Janney thought that Philadelphia, unlike New York, was "very much infested with Popery."[197] One Anglican priest reported that many of the Germans living in rural areas were "reputed Papists."[198] A German Reformed minister who expressed concern about the "very unstable" people in the province, proof of which was the increased number of sects, included "The Jesuits [who] are also coming into the foreground in Pennsylvania."[199] Yet when one Lutheran minister met a Catholic priest while waiting for a ferry, he noted that "his conversation was modest and sincere."[200]

Pennsylvania newspapers occasionally reprinted articles from English or provincial sources about Roman Catholicism. Many of them criticized customs such as indulgences or the use of "Crosses, and other religious Trumpery" at burials. The implied message was the superiority of Protestants and the "Bigotry," intolerance, or tyranny of Roman Catholics.[201] Only one piece was of local origin—an advertisement in which a man requested a copy of the Jesuits' reply to his "protest against popery" so that he could "rejoin to any sophistical fallacies, or sarcastical falsehoods" he had heard raised in their defense. Addressed to Jesuits in Maryland and Pennsylvania, it was signed by a man from Bohemia, Maryland.[202]

In comparison to their qualms about Catholicism, most Pennsylvanians were indifferent to the extremely small number of Jewish residents. In 1747 the Anglican priest in Lancaster noted laconically that "here are ten families of Jews."[203] There were approximately twenty-five Jewish families in Philadelphia by the mid-1760s, while a few lived in other towns. They appear to have been accepted by their neighbors, for leading Jewish Philadelphians joined social clubs and intermarried with Christians. Merchants and traders for the most part, they established commercial relations with their counterparts among both Jews and Christians,[204] although one Quaker merchant commented unfavorably that "the Jews are always quicker with their Intelligence than other people."[205] Only one anti-Jewish incident occurred in Pennsylvania during this period. A decade after land had been granted for a Jewish cemetery, "unthinking people" used the fence surrounding it for target practice. A reward was offered for the conviction of these "sportsmen."[206]

Most encounters with Jews occurred by chance, and were considered noteworthy simply because of the novelty. Shortly after his arrival, Muhlenberg overheard an altercation about cabinetmaking between a Jew and a member of his congregation. He managed to reconcile the parties, but when he "admonished" the Jew for his "offensive language" during the argument, the man "took it in bad part and made a joke of it, saying that I did not yet know the manners of the country."[207] When a member of Muhlenberg's congregation tried to give "German–Jewish writings" to a prominent Philadelphia Jew, the latter replied that he would not read essays intended to convert Jews to Christianity, and in what Muhlenberg probably considered a reasonable statement, declared that "'The foremost *gentlemen* in the city with whom I associate, men who are called Christians, say themselves that their Messiah was an *impostor*. Give the books to them.'"[208] One Lutheran pastor was surprised to learn that five Jewish women had been present at a baptism, for "outwardly they showed themselves to be very orderly and devout."[209]

Lay Pennsylvanians during the 1740s and early 1750s demonstrated significant interest in religious matters that went beyond participation in revivals led by ministers. There was an upsurge in the level of curiosity Pennsylvanians displayed about the beliefs and practices of their neighbors.

The Moravian settlement at Bethlehem attracted some attention, but far fewer visitors than after it was more fully developed and the hostility toward the sect had dissipated. In this period Ephrata was the focus of visitors and newspaper coverage. In 1736 Governor Thomas visited the cloister while he was in Lancaster negotiating an Indian treaty.[210] In 1744, again during Indian negotiations, Thomas and a group of thirty-four delegates from Maryland and Virginia visited Ephrata, where "They were pleased on all sides, and departed with much information."[211] A group of Friends visited the monastery at about the same time. Shown "every thing Curious. but the house in wch the women live," they were impressed by the workmanship and manufactories of the brotherhood. The visitors concluded that "they differ very little from frds Except in baptism. bread & wine (wch they won't allow to be Call'd sacrament) & Singing." When asked if Quakers could pay a religious visit, the monks said they would not object if a Friend spoke after their service.[212] The younger John Penn, visiting the colony a decade later, "went to visit the Duncars, whom I could Make nothing of," except that "they seem'd to be a very stupid Crew."[213]

Ministers often commented on the spiritual wanderings exhibited by many Pennsylvanians and on the diversity of their audience. They frequently noted that their congregations listened politely to their message. A Quaker who held meetings in the backcountry noted that many Presbyterians, Baptists, and Germans attended, while in Philadelphia "Abundance of other Societies mostly flock" to Quaker meetings.[214] Like the Lutheran and Reformed ministers, Anglican priests continued to report that "Dissenters" crowded their churches.[215] One minister declared that he "found no Maltreatment from any Denomination hitherto, Nothing but Civility so far as I have been conversant with any of y^m."[216] Converts were made, and duly reported to the S.P.G., although mere attendance was more typical. But Anglican ministers also had to consider the possibility that their parishioners might stray. One priest noted that "Many of my Congregation" visited newly instituted Moravian services near a church he served periodically, but "I hope (& Believe) more thro' Curiosity, than Any thing else, Because they show me the Same Respect they ever did, And Carefully Attend the Church, as formerly, when it is my Turn to be there."[217] George Craig, analyzing the weakness of the Anglican church, concluded "The first Settlers who came in well principled are decaying, & many quite extinct; And their Children take to dissenting Teachers of one kind or another . . . thinking it their Duty to hear A Sermon on Sunday, be ye preacher who will."[218] Another minister commented that "The People of our Province are this and that, here and there, of no Steddy Principles, Sometimes any thing or nothing, just as the Humour takes them, or the Spirit of Giddiness moves them."[219]

Newspapers and printing presses were utilized to foster interest in religion as well as to set forth particular viewpoints. Publication of religious material that might be termed educational increased during the 1740s. Although several factions issued polemical literature attacking their opponents, more representative publications were those directed toward advancing Christianity in general, strengthening the adherents of a particular creed, or making specific beliefs more widely known.

Early in the 1740s, probably in consequence of the interest in religion aroused by the revivals, Christopher Sauer decided to publish a German edition of the Bible. The project was intended primarily for the benefit of poor Germans who were unable to afford the costly imported ones. Sauer appealed to English colonists for contributions so that "the Books may be afforded cheaper to real poor Persons whether Servants or others," and promised to give a public account of all donations. He may have received assistance from several of the Ephrata monks who were more experienced in printing. This project became the focus of a controversy over the translation he would use, for the Lutheran (Halle) and sectarian (Berleburg) versions of the Bible differed. Sauer's solution, to reprint the Halle translation with an optional appendix to the Apocrypha from the Berleburg version, pleased neither churchpeople nor sectarians.[220] Several Lutheran and Reformed ministers, suspicious that Sauer might alter the text or interpolate sectarian interpretations, warned their parishioners against purchasing the Bible. Denunciations of the Bible by Caspar Schnorr, the fame of which spread to German communities as distant as Virginia, elicited an especially lengthy and vituperative ripost by Sauer.[221]

In 1742 Pennsylvania Mennonites, fearing that as nonresistants they and their children might find their beliefs challenged if war erupted, wrote to their Dutch brethren requesting a German translation of Dielman Jans van Braght's *Martyr's Mirror*, a compilation of the sufferings of Anabaptists. They repeated the request in 1745, and emphasized the difficulty of finding a competent translator and the poor quality of the paper available to Sauer for his Bible. After receiving no reply, they reached an agreement with the Ephrata monks, who would translate the work and print it on special paper made at their mill. Once completed, a committee would inspect the volume and, if acceptable, would establish a reasonable price for it and encourage other Mennonites to purchase it. This three-year project, undertaken in a spirit of mutual trust, proved satisfactory to both parties.[222]

While Mennonites were concerned about providing edifying literature for their children, Quakers began to disseminate their principal tenets among foreigners in the province. The impetus came largely from English Friends, although Philadelphians were in some sympathy with the idea. When the London Yearly Meeting sent several German copies of Robert Barclay's *Apology for the True Christian Divinity* and Willem Sewel's *History of Quakerism* to Philadelphia in 1750, a committee was appointed to distribute them to "such Persons as will be most likely to make them useful."[223] The Philadelphia Yearly Meeting responded that "many of those people are well disposed toward us and desirous of being more acquainted with our Principles," and sent a contribution to defray part of the cost of translating and printing the books. A year later a small Quaker tract was given to Sauer to translate and print.[224]

Newspapers printed several articles expressing relatively uncontroversial religious ideas and sometimes advocating toleration. For instance, one issue of the *Pennsylvania Gazette* included an essay on "The Folly and Absurdity of Atheism," reprinted from the *American Magazine*, and an anonymous essay on "The Right of Private Judgment." The latter essayist argued that it was one of the "*sacred* and *original*

Rights of human Nature," and encouraged his readers to take full advantage of this "inestimable Priviledge," for

if they proceeded in all their religious Inquiries with Candour and Impartiality, and were neither corrupted by irregular Passions, nor prevented by Prejudice, nor enslaved by Education, nor controuled and awed by the Restraints and Terrors of human Authority, whether Civil or Ecclesiastical; such an *Openness* and *Ingenuity* of Mind, such a *cool, disinterested* and *free* Examination of the Grounds of Religion, and the Principles it contains, must be attended with eminent Advantages to themselves, to Christianity, and Mankind in general.[225]

Religious disturbances in Upper Austria elicited comments that "Dissenters from the established Religion of any State cannot reasonably expect to be favoured in *all* Respects equally with Conformists; but they have a Right to Liberty of Conscience." It was hoped that the British ambassador in Vienna would become an advocate for the persecuted Protestants.[226]

Because of his anticlerical bias, Christopher Sauer published numerous articles intended to promote vital Christianity. He penned a long essay, "Of Conversion and God's Word," in which he argued that "Conversion is nothing other than turning from evil to good, from falsehood to truth."[227] Another article, "Of Religion," simply argued, "The sincere worshiper worships the Father in spirit and in truth. That is sincere worship. That is religion." Ministers, the author added, must live as if they have been reborn and not merely preach about redemption. They must be an example to others.[228] One essayist argued that everyone had a right to formulate and defend his own beliefs, and was capable of doing so because "the Holy Bible is very clear, plain, and easy to understand, and will be understood by those who with an unbiased heart and disposition diligently read and reflect upon it."[229] Another essay emphasized the blessings of the complete freedom of conscience granted by William Penn. Noting that "there is no land known in the whole world where the people may so completely and without hindrance live in accordance with God's will," the author concluded that "Freedom is excellent."[230]

A broadside issued in 1740, "The Sum of Religion," provides an apt statement of what was emerging as the dominant attitude of religious Pennsylvanians. In very simple form it stated the fundamental concepts of Christianity, and declared that everyone who accepted them, "whether he be an *Episcopal*, or a *Presbyterian*, or *Independent*, or an *Anabaptist*; . . . hath the LIFE of RELIGION in him; . . . notwithstanding his Practice or Non-practice of things indifferent." But "If a Man *fears* not the eternal God," no matter how scrupulously he adheres to or opposes particular customs, "he wants the LIFE of RELIGION."[231]

Throughout the vicissitudes of the decade resulting from revivalism and attempts to organize churches, and despite the failure of ecumenical schemes, the practical toleration and openmindedness commended in this essay characterized Pennsylvania. When a Reformed minister who died suddenly in 1749 was buried by a Mennonite teacher, the only suitable person available to conduct the funeral, Christopher Sauer pointed to the moral of the episode. "When such things become customary and common without being compelled by necessity, then all party and antagonism between parties will come to an end. How beautiful will it be when there is only one shepherd and only one flock?" Pessimistically concluding "Until then patience,"[232] he failed to realize how close Pennsylvanians had come to achieving this ideal.

CHAPTER 6

Religious and
Ethnic Politics, 1739–1755

war & rumors of war
challenged Quaker dom

A variety of social and political issues required consideration amidst the religious ferment that occupied the attention of many Pennsylvanians of all classes, creeds, and nationalities during the 1740s and 1750s. Many problems originated in the nature of the colony's population; others arose from external factors but were exacerbated by the pluralism of provincial society. With continued immigration and a further extension of settlement into the backcountry, the problem of disorderly land practices reemerged. The government's ability to meet the legal and administrative needs of frontier settlers was strained, while the creation of new counties and the selection of officials to fill positions in them presented difficulties. Immigrants often endangered public health, especially in Philadelphia, yet efforts to regulate shipboard conditions and to assist sick passengers became entangled in lengthy disputes between governors and assemblies that usually centered upon other issues. Germans became increasingly involved in efforts to pressure the authorities to ameliorate the conditions endured by their countrypeople during their journey.

For the first time, ethnic diversity was viewed in political terms. As wars and rumors of war challenged the Quakers' political power and their dominance of the assembly, pacifists and nonpacifists alike began to search for new sources of support. German politicization after 1740 was stimulated by a new law simplifying the naturalization process, encouragement by printer Christopher Sauer to participate fully in provincial affairs, growing familiarity with colonial customs, and the advent of new issues. Although many leaders feared that Germans might threaten English control of the province, both factions turned to German-speaking colonists for support. Tensions among ethnic groups were thereby added to the smoldering, and more significant, tensions among adherents of differing religious beliefs.

I

Passage of a general naturalization act by Parliament in June 1740 facilitated the absorption of aliens into provincial society. Although the assembly had previously enacted several laws conferring the rights of British subjects upon aliens, relatively few immigrants had availed themselves of their privilege to petition for such private acts.[1] The new law recognized that "the Increase of People is a Means of advancing the Wealth and Strength" of a nation, and that "Foreigners and Strangers" might be encouraged to settle in the colonies if they could enjoy the "Advantages and Privileges" of natural-born subjects. It permitted aliens who had resided in any British colony for seven years, without being absent from the British domain for more than two consecutive months, to appear before a colonial court to take oaths of allegiance to the Crown and to subscribe declarations of their Christian belief. They were required to produce a certificate that they had received communion in a Protestant church within three months of their application for naturalization. Quakers and Jews were exempted from the sacramental requirement, and the oaths were modified to accommodate their beliefs. The fee for this simple process was minimal, only two shillings.[2]

In May 1742 the Pennsylvania assembly, arguing that the British law was too restrictive, drafted a bill that would enable non-Quaker aliens conscientiously opposed to oaths to affirm their allegiance to the Crown. It would also protect the estates of aliens who died prior to naturalization and guarantee aliens the right to purchase, sell, and inherit land.[3] Proprietary officials did not object to the affirmation portion of the bill, but believed that the property clauses were "calculated to curry favour with the Germans against the next Election, & to divest" the proprietors of their "Rights." Although it was proprietary policy to allow the heirs of deceased aliens to inherit properly purchased land, to enact such a guarantee infringed upon their legitimate privileges.[4] Thomas Penn did not object to an extension of the affirmation, as long as it was not linked to property rights.[5]

Probably recognizing that a law combining the two issues would be vetoed by the governor or disallowed by the Crown, a new assembly separated the issues in two bills. Both were speedily passed and sent to Governor George Thomas for approval,[6] but he refused to consider the law pertaining to aliens' property rights until he received instructions from the proprietors. Hesitant about the affirmation bill, he cited as a precedent the disallowance of a previous law altering the form of oaths and declarations of allegiance and abjuration so that Presbyterians could in good conscience subscribe them. He suggested that a new bill be drafted specifying the religious societies whose members would be exempted from oaths, which might be more readily approved by the Crown. He also recommended the expedient of provincial naturalization for those who could not swear.[7] The assembly then pointed out that other British laws extended a general indulgence to nonswearers, and expressed the opinion that a general law was most suitable for provincial conditions. If, however, the governor insisted that this would be the best method to prevent disallowance, it was willing to designate the religious groups that would benefit from the statute.[8] The governor, still believing a specific bill less liable to British objections, decided to accede to a general one rather than postpone action until he could be informed of the sects to which it would be applicable.[9] The law, enacted in February 1742/3, granted the privilege of naturalization to all persons scrupulous of oaths who fulfilled the conditions required of alien Quakers in the 1740 statute.[10]

Initially the Board of Trade objected to granting this indulgence to German Protestants, the primary beneficiaries, but the Penns had "interest enough" to prevent its repeal.[11] The Board decided that since the analogous declarations required of Quakers sufficiently ensured their loyalty, and the provincial Germans had been "represented to us as a quiet and industrious people . . . who conscientiously refuse the

taking of an oath," it was reasonable to confirm the law.[12] In 1747
Parliament followed Pennsylvania's example and extended the exemption from oaths in naturalization to members of all religious societies
opposed to swearing oaths.[13]

Copies of the naturalization oaths were given to a Reformed minister "in order to explain it to the people of Protestant faith." In April
1741 more than two hundred people appeared at a supreme court session to be naturalized, but most were rejected because they had not
brought certificates of fulfillment of the sacramental requirement.[14]
The *Pensylvanische Geschicht-Schreiber* of February 1741/2 informed readers
that a list of Germans naturalized under this act had recently been
published. A translation of the declarations was included for the benefit of those who might wish to be naturalized.[15] The following year
the *Pennsylvania Gazette* reported that 304 Germans had been naturalized at a recent supreme court session.[16]

Christopher Sauer, in his newspaper, provided detailed information
about the naturalization process, printed summaries of the residency
and religious requirements, and announced the dates of upcoming court
sessions at which aliens could be naturalized. He emphasized the benefits of naturalization. "[F]irst, one has all the freedoms of a native-
born Englishman to trade, purchase, and sell"; land titles became more
secure; and "moreover, one is permitted to vote."[17] He encouraged
Germans to take advantage of their newly acquired rights as British
subjects, and educated them about their privileges and responsibilities. In 1743, in response to repeated requests, he began to publish
the provincial charter and various laws in translation, "so that the
Germans may see what freedoms the king of England granted to Penn,
and that Penn granted to his colony[.]" Copies were given to subscri-
bers to his newspaper, and sold inexpensively to others.[18] A few years
later he was requested to publish a translation of "the entire English
[Pennsylvania] law book," but refused on the grounds that there were
too many laws and that the most important of them had already been
made available to German-speaking colonists. He promised to print
laws of general interest, such as those relating to freedom of conscience, property, and schools and churches.[19] Sauer urged his countrymen to vote, sometimes but not always recommending the incumbents or members of the Quaker faction. Only if German

Pennsylvanians were active could they expect to retain the liberties they found in their new land.[20]

For both aliens and native-born settlers, the crucial issue involved in naturalization was property rights. Transactions in which aliens were involved could be challenged by the Crown or the proprietors, and the land of aliens technically escheated to the governing authorities upon death, although there is no evidence that the Penns ever exercised this prerogative.[21]

To what extent could naturalized subjects participate in politics? Thomas Penn wondered if they could sit in the assembly, a privilege denied to all but the native-born in England.[22] The 1740 act forbade individuals naturalized under its provisions from becoming a member of the Privy Council, sitting in Parliament, or enjoying any "Office or Place of Trust" in Great Britain or Ireland, but did not explicitly mention the colonies.[23] Provincial Secretary Richard Peters once lamented that "It is a great pity" there was no law "to incapacitate every person from sitting in Assembly who cannot speak English and read it so well as to understand our Laws, forms of Justice & Court Proceedings."[24] But his concern was abstract; Germans proved reluctant to stand as candidates for high offices.

Voting was of more immediate significance. Although many immigrants failed to take advantage of the naturalization act, colonial leaders perceived a sudden increase in political participation, and sometimes a threat to the established order.[25] In 1755 the governor pointed out the "Danger" of giving the assembly extensive powers, especially "one annually chosen by a People, a great part, if not a Majority of whom are Foreigners, unattached to an English Government, either by Birth or Education."[26] This issue—greater access to participation in provincial life rather than the simplification and systematization of naturalization—intensified the struggles within the colony, especially during the early 1740s and subsequent years of crisis.

During the 1720s and 1730s individual Quakers and the Quaker-dominated assembly had gradually formed an informal coalition with German settlers. They had helped immigrants obtain land, while Quaker merchants were enriched by trade with the immigrants and the export of German agricultural products. The assembly occasionally granted naturalization. Moreover, religious interests, at least among

sectarians, were similar. Although Germans lacked a tradition of political activity and were often unfamiliar with the English language
and laws, the alliance could be developed when an important issue
arose. However, with the commencement of a European war in 1739,
proprietary officials thought they might be able to develop an effective
opposition party to the Quakers, based on the question of defense.
The prospect of an increased number of voters, not yet firmly committed to either faction, stimulated the development of a two-party
system.[27]

II

During the quarter-century of relative peace that followed the Treaty
of Utrecht (1713), the question of governmental participation by pacifists was submerged, only to reemerge as rumors of war spread in the
late 1730s and became a reality in 1739 with the War of Jenkins' Ear
and the ensuing War of the Austrian Succession.[28] Quaker principles
and policies were challenged not only by a governor intent upon performing his obligations to the Crown but also by Pennsylvanians of
various religious persuasions. Unlike the earlier disputes over a militia
and other military activities—quarrels that were essentially fought by
Anglicans and Quakers—colonists of many beliefs were involved in
these arguments. Dissension within the Quaker fellowship exacerbated the difficulties faced by the ruling elite. Defense was discussed
primarily in religious terms, but was complicated by the struggle to
gain the support of nonpacifistic Germans, who were thought to have
enough strength to play a decisive role in the outcome of elections and
help to determine the course the province would take.

When in 1739 John Penn advised Governor Thomas to attempt to
form a militia, he expected "great Difficultys" might arise because "A
Number of the People are principled against fighting" and would argue that any law that would "oblige them to Carry Arms, would be
persecuting them." Anticipating that the assembly would not enact a
militia law, he suggested an alternative: the governor could issue commissions to "Gentlemen" who would raise a volunteer force, a precedent dating from the time of Governor John Evans, nearly thirty years
earlier. "The Least" the assembly should do would be to purchase

weapons for the use of this voluntary militia. In a letter to his brother Thomas, then in the colony, Penn added that the volunteers should be given a small stipend each time they attended military exercises.[29]

At the brief organizational session of the assembly elected in October 1739, Governor Thomas, after painting a gloomy picture of the prospect of a war with Spain and its possible consequences, "earnestly recommend[ed]" that the members consider the colony's "Defenceless State" and take steps to put it into a condition worthy of "loyal Subjects" of the Crown. The European situation "gives me Reason hourly to expect his Majesty's Commands" for defensive measures. Already "neighbouring Provinces" were "vigorously pursuing these laudable Ends."[30] The assembly, although "conceiving it in its Nature a Matter of very great Importance," chose to defer the issue on the grounds that little business was traditionally transacted at the October session.[31] Thomas responded that he was aware of the custom, but believed the assembly should "wave a Rule" in order to provide for provincial security.[32]

Proprietary supporters, disappointed with a Quaker-dominated assembly that "will do nothing but Trust in the Lord," had neglected to mount an opposition at the election because "many hot Headed People" among the inhabitants "were for chooseing none but People of that Perswasion."[33] Thomas, however, thought that, because of the assembly's inaction, "People of all other Perswasions" even at this early stage of the war appeared determined to oppose Quakers in the 1740 elections. A petition in favor of defense was being circulated. Proposals were made to organize a voluntary militia, but Thomas preferred to postpone action until it was definite that the assembly would not enact a militia law that exempted Friends. He believed there was "very little sincerity" in the Quakers' policies, for "They who profess Conscience, will not allow others to act agreable to theirs."[34]

When the assembly reconvened in January 1739/40, members acknowledged their duties as "loyal Subjects and Lovers of our Religion and Liberties," but entreated the governor's "Charity" toward "our different Sentiments." They reminded Thomas that promises of freedom of conscience had attracted many immigrants, especially Quakers, to the colony. Although the population had diversified since its early years and numerous inhabitants, "disciplined in the Art of War," thought it their "Duty to fight" in defense of their country, families, and estates, "great Numbers" opposed warfare. The assembly recognized that it was caught in a dilemma, but refused to enact any law pertaining to military matters. To compel people to bear arms would violate the constitutional guarantee of liberty of conscience and "commence Persecution," yet to exempt Quakers and other pacifists "would be an Inconsistency with themselves, and partial with respect to others." It suggested that the governor use the military powers granted to the executive in the provincial charter.[35] It ignored petitions in favor of defense, since the "Sentiments of the House" on that subject had been fully stated in its address to Thomas.[36]

Thomas replied that he had addressed the assembly as representatives of the people and as Protestants, not as Quakers. Denying any interest in circumscribing religious liberty, he remarked that "no Sett of religious Principles, will protect us from an Enemy." He reminded the assembly that money had previously been granted to the Crown for defense, and urged the members to adopt measures to protect the colony.[37] The assembly then insisted that the colony was in little danger of attack. It distinguished between using force for military and civil purposes, which the governor had linked. That English Friends paid taxes used for warlike purposes and that the assembly had previously voted "tribute" to the Crown were irrelevant to the militia question. Assemblymen declared that they were loyal subjects who loved their country, "but if any Thing inconsistent" with their religious beliefs "be required of us, we hold it our Duty to obey God rather then Man."[38] After another exchange of messages repeating essentially the same arguments, the assembly adjourned.[39]

During the assembly's recess, Thomas issued a proclamation in April 1740 encouraging men to enlist for an expedition against the Spanish colonies in the West Indies. He promised recruits plunder and an opportunity to remain anonymous. Although Pennsylvania was expected to supply only 400 men, more than 700 volunteered and were enlisted.[40] The assembly wrangled over the issue and considered petitions regarding the enlistment of servants when it met briefly in May.[41]

Tensions caused by this voluntary force exploded during the July session. The governor presented royal orders to provide transportation, food, and other supplies for the provincial troops raised for the expedition. Noting that other colonies had offered bounties to recruits, Thomas stated that if Pennsylvania had done so it might have prevented the enlistment of servants. Freemen, he declared, would not volunteer without a bounty; servants who had enlisted would be sent on the expedition because of the need for men.[42] The assembly flatly refused to comply with the governor's demands. Although it acknowledged its *"Duty to pay Tribute to* Caesar," members *"cannot preserve our good Consciences, and come into the Levying of Money, and appropriating it to the Uses recommended to us in the Governor's Speech, because it is repugnant to the religious Principles professed by the greater Number of the present Assembly, who are of the People called* Quakers."[43] After further prompting the assembly began to consider an appropriations bill,[44] but then shifted the debate from religious principles to the economic problems raised by the enlistment of indentured servants, many of whom were recent German and Scotch-Irish immigrants.

According to the assembly, an adequate quota for the province was three companies of soldiers, while the governor had overzealously enlisted seven. It blamed Thomas for encouraging servants to enlist and directing their names to be *"concealed."* The loss of the servants' labor was a *"Calamity"* that *"the Crown never intended to befal any of its Dominions."* Because the Crown had on several occasions encouraged the *"Importation"* of white servants and had vetoed laws regulating immigration, allowing them to desert their masters would discourage the servant trade and thus work at cross-purposes. If masters' interests in the labor of their servants could be so *"unjustly invaded,"* the assembly wondered if any property were safe. After describing the *"very melancholly Prospect"* facing masters and the province as a whole, it refused to grant funds for the expedition until the grievances were redressed.[45] Thomas denied that he had encouraged servants to enlist, and claimed that he had ordered the release of servants whose masters applied to him for a discharge "if they can be persuaded to return to their Masters, and it can be done consistent with the Service." Names of recruits had been concealed for "justifiable Reasons; and, amongst others, to prevent their being arrested and confined for trifling Sums."[46] Eventually the assembly resolved to grant £3000 "for the Use of our present Sovereign," on the condition that servants be returned to their masters and that none be enlisted in the future.[47]

Meanwhile, proprietary supporters blamed the "perverse Assembly" for what appeared to be an inadequate number of volunteers. They thought its behavior would plainly demonstrate to British authorities "that a Quaker Governm^t is not only useless but in time of War may prove exceeding dangerous." Richard Peters, disgusted by the "unaccountable behaviour" of the assembly, thought "it looks as if people were tired wth Liberty Riches and plenty & wanted to get rid of them as fast as they can."[48] A Quaker, however, thought that Thomas "took Delight in Vexing the People" by enlisting servants "Contrary to the Practice of all Other Governors." John Reynell also suspected Thomas of trying to get the government "Intirely out of the hands of Fr^{ds}" through any means possible.[49] For his part, Thomas concluded that the whole affair had been "a tryal both of my Constitution & Temper." He wondered why he had ever "risqued my Character amongst such a low, sordid & hypocritical sett of People."[50]

Defense, support of the war, and enlistment of servants "so generally provoked the People" that they became election issues in 1740.[51] But notwithstanding the "great Pains" taken by the "Governours friends" to represent Quakers as "unfitt" to be involved in government, "People of all Perswasions" reelected most of the incumbents.[52] Governor Thomas complained that "by the arts of the same people and the positive directions of their yearly meeting," which "have taken upon them to direct the civil affairs of the government," the assembly contained only three non-Quakers. This was achieved by "deceiving" the Germans "into a belief that a militia will bring them under as severe a bondage to governors as they were formerly under their princes in Germany"; that the expense would impoverish them; and that if new assemblymen were selected they would be "dragged down from their farms and obliged to build forts as a tribute for their being admitted to settle in the province."[53]

One Quaker reported that the election attracted "ye greatest appearance of People that Ever was known in this Province,"[54] a statement with which the disappointed leader of the proprietary faction, William Allen, concurred. Although his party had received "200 more [votes] than ever lost it before," its opponents, "by their dextrous knack of lying," had "brought down upon us about 400 Germans who hardly ever came to elections formerly, perhaps never 40 of them having voted at any other election." By hiding politics "under a cloak of religion," Quakers took advantage of "ignorant country people." The "Dutch," Allen asserted, "are a sordid people and very loth to part with any money," while it had been impossible to convince people in the hinterland of their duty to help defend the capital.[55]

Complaints reached London that at the Philadelphia Yearly Meeting, held shortly before the provincial elections, Quakers focused upon "State afares" rather than "Settling the Church afares."[56] Anticipating "a probability of a Complaint being made to the King against the Principles of Friends in regard to Government," the Yearly Meeting appointed a committee to marshall the support of the London Meeting for Sufferings.[57] Indeed, shortly after the election Governor Thomas wrote a "Violent Letter" to the Board of Trade complaining of the Quakers' "obstinacy."[58] He had hoped that Friends would withdraw from the assembly in 1740, but instead they openly campaigned for reelection. "Such," he concluded, "is the effect of power, even on a people who in most other governments are contented with a bare toleration in religious affairs." Because the previous year had been spent in "fruitless disputes," little of the King's or the province's business had been accomplished. Quaker principles were clearly unsuitable for governing a colony. He threatened to resign, deeming it "impossible" to serve the Crown because of the "narrow, bigotted views of the governing sect here."[59] Nevertheless, Thomas tried again to obtain funds for military purposes from this assembly, but without success. It spent considerable time instead reimbursing masters for the loss of their servants.[60]

The 1740–1741 assembly received a petition signed by eighty-five merchants and other Philadelphians advocating defense. Colonists were obligated to contribute toward *"their own Safety at least"* when the King was involved in what the petitioners deemed a *"just and necessary War."* More immediately, Spanish privateers allegedly threatened commerce, the source of the province's prosperity. Because many people were willing to support defensive measures and there was sufficient money in the treasury to pay for them, assemblymen were asked to make *"some publick Provision"* to protect trade and the colonists. The remonstrance closed with a threat to petition the King if these requests were ignored.[61] The assembly responded that the "Representation itself is extraordinary," and "insinuate[d] Facts which are in themselves untrue." Because it was a "high Insult and Menace" to the assembly and had a "Tendency destructive of their Freedom and Constitution," it was "rejected."[62]

A petition subsequently dispatched to the King described not only the colony's flourishing condition but also its vulnerability by land and sea. It lacked fortifications, was "Destitute of Arms & Amunition," and the people were "under No obligation of Military Duty." Blame was placed squarely on Quakers "(a few prudent and Moderate Men of that Society Excepted)." Friends retained control of the assembly by appealing to the religious beliefs of some voters and "by Allarme of Expence and Danger to Libertie from Ev'ry thing Melitary" to others. The petitioners suggested that the province would be lost if the King failed to insist that it organize a militia and provide for defense. They hinted that Quakers should be forbidden to sit in the assembly when their religious beliefs prevented fulfillment of their obligations.[63] Thomas Penn urged his brothers to "procure an Instruction" from the King "to recommend to the Assembly the making some preparations"; he thought it might be most effective if such orders arrived before the October elections.[64]

Tensions mounted in 1741 as both factions made determined efforts to gain the support of German voters. A few weeks before the election "Some ill minded ~~People~~ Tools," attempting to discourage country-people from coming to the city to vote, spread "monstrous Lies" that a serious disease was raging in Philadelphia.[65] A Lancaster County leader, hoping to acquire German support for the proprietary cause, requested Indian interpreter Conrad Weiser to use his influence among his countrymen. He informed Weiser that the Quaker faction prevailed with the Germans by telling them that if the opposition were victorious, "They will be Assessed at a High rate & Obliged to Labour at erecting Forts &c & then putting them in mind of the Tyranny" of German princes. Such "monstrously Absurd" ideas were intended to "presume altogether on yᵉ Ignorance" of the Germans.[66]

Weiser, in conjunction with Quaker proprietary supporter James

Logan, *"cook'd up"* and published "Serious and Seasonable Advice to our Countreymen yᵉ Germans in Pennsylvania." He emphasized the advantages Germans had found in the colony and their responsibilities to it. Noting that most Germans had "retired into this Country for Peace & Safetys Sake & to get Our living Easier than in Germany," he reminded his readers that they had been "well received and protected" by the government. Because the recent naturalization act had "invested us protestants upon Very Easy terms with so many Priviledges & Libertys," Germans should be moved to an "Actual thankfulness." Continued opposition to the British government by reelecting Quakers might "draw a particular displeasure upon us." It was time to end the strife between the governor and the assembly, especially in view of the strength of the French in Canada and the west, which posed serious threats to the colony. Attempting to dispel apprehensions that Germans would be subjected to "Slavery" if Quakers were not reelected, he argued that "whomsoever you shall Chuse by much the Greater part will be Englishmen, there is no Nation in the World more Jealous & Carefull of their Liberties that the English & therefore You may fully trust them."[67]

Two days before the election an anonymous German reply to Weiser's letter, often attributed to Christopher Sauer, was published. The author declared that Weiser failed to give "honest and well intentioned Advice," and that "his Intent is rather to cheat and deceive you." Weiser, recently commissioned as a justice of the peace, disseminated falsehoods in an effort to retain the governor's favor. This essayist denied that the assembly had refused to appropriate money for defense; it was the disposition of the money that was in question. He, too, emphasized the blessings of the province, and attributed them to the leniency of the Quakers. He praised them especially for the extension of liberty of conscience to all and the substitution of affirmations for oaths in most cases. The threat of war was simply dismissed. German voters were warned that "One single Mistake" in an election "is perhaps never to be set to rights." Because members of the assembly had "carefully and diligently watched for our Good," they deserved to be reelected.[68]

Despite the appeals of the opposition, "yᵉ Old Assembly is Chose without Interruption" by an alliance of Germans and others in favor of the Quaker faction.[69] Proprietary officials were incensed at the reply to Weiser's essay. It was "carefully distributed & every Dutchman furnish'd with it"; consequently they came to the polls with "so much Zeal for ye old Assembly that all ye Arguments in the world wou'd have had no Effect upon them."[70] The election was brought to the attention of English officials as part of the agitation against Quaker participation in the government. Proprietary supporters stated that "great Endeavours" had been used to secure a Quaker victory, "particularly" by the publication of a German "Book" for that purpose. The witness, nevertheless, confessed that he did not understand German and conceded that there had been no bribery involved in the election and that it had been "fair."[71]

A new element had been introduced into this tense situation when Quakers found their beliefs and policies in the assembly challenged from within their own ranks. James Logan took the extraordinary step of writing a pamphlet advocating defensive measures. In this essay, delivered to the September 1741 Yearly Meeting, Logan firmly stated his belief that offensive war was wrong, but emphasized the "Lawfulness of Self-Defence." He argued that "where-ever there is private Property, and Measures taken to increase it," there will be a temptation to "invade" it. Thus, "it has always appeared to me, to be full as justifiable to use Means to defend it when got, as to acquire it." Because "all Civil Government, as well as Military, is founded on Force," Friends who strictly adhered to their religious tenets should not participate in either aspect of government. He reminded Friends that Pennsylvania was a subordinate government and obliged to obey the sovereign's commands. As recipients of the privileges inherent in being a part of the British Empire, and in particular the toleration granted to Quakers in both England and Pennsylvania, Quakers should act responsibly if they wished to retain them. Logan concluded by recommending that Friends who could not support defense refuse elective office.[72]

Although one Quaker believed that the pamphlet "contain[ed] several things that were intended for the good of the Society at these fickle & precarious times,"[73] Logan's views were poorly received. Friends appointed to consider whether it should be read publicly concluded that it "related to the Civil and Military Affairs of the Government," and was therefore "unfitt" to be read.[74] Thus "his good Design was eluded," the more so because Logan had been dissuaded from distributing among Quaker leaders the thirty copies of his address that he had printed.[75] Logan also tried to influence the election by "pressing" William Allen to persuade his allies "to make an opposition" to the people who had been "so mischeivous [sic] to the peace of the Government." But Allen's associates preferred to await the outcome of their petition to the King rather than actively campaign against the Quakers.[76] John Fothergill, an influential English Friend who received a copy of Logan's essay, was disturbed by the "publick declaration of differing sentiments," which might provide "a basis for your enemies to build a good deal of mischief upon." This address, he believed, allowed the petitioners to the King to label some Quakers *prudent men.* Probably expressing the view of most Friends, he objected to Logan's argument that all government was based on force without making distinctions in the way its powers were used.[77]

Following their success in the 1741 elections, Quakers turned their attention to the petition Philadelphia merchants had sent to the King. They noted that "scarce 200" out of more than 1100 mostly non-Quaker voters in the "most remote county of this Province" had cast their ballots for the opposition, a "plain proof" of their satisfaction with the conduct of the incumbents. They then requested London Meeting for Sufferings to use its influence to prevent alterations in the constitution, which was "particularly adapted" to the "Disposition" of Friends and other "Religious Inhabitants" who opposed bearing arms.[78] Meanwhile the London Meeting for Sufferings had presented a statement to the Board of Trade defending Pennsylvania Friends. It argued that the colonists' "Carracter" had been "unfairly aspersed and the Libertys & priviledges they enjoy were unjustly attacked." A similar petition was prepared for presentation to the King.[79] Delays in consideration of the merchants' petition encouraged Pennsylvania Quakers about the efficacy of their English counterparts' activities. The English petition, they learned, had "lessen'd a prejudice" against the colonists, while personal meetings with officials helped to convince them that some of the "allegations were extremely unjust." To exclude "any set of men" without the "free voice of the People" could only be "productive of numerous calamities &c."[80]

At one hearing before the Board of Trade the Quakers attempted to diffuse the demands of the militaristic petitioners that Friends be forbidden to sit in the assembly into a request that the King give definite orders to place the province in a "proper posture of Defence." Quaker solicitors emphasized that, since there had never been an attempt to invade the geographically secure province, its constitution should not be altered unless the colonists failed to respond to an actual attack. Furthermore, they argued that the charter obligated the proprietor to provide for defense. Since he was "absolute Lord of the Soile" and demanded quitrents in recognition of his position, he ought to pay for defense.[81] The Board of Trade disagreed. Pennsylvanians, it believed, ought not to be exempted from the customary obligations of other colonists. Liberty of conscience related "Intirely to matters of Religion, and not to Affairs of Government." The Board advised the King to order the province to initiate defensive measures, but made no recommendations for constitutional change.[82]

Contention over the unresolved issues of defense, religion, and politics climaxed in the 1742 election. Both sides, bidding for what each perceived as the crucial support of the Germans, began to prepare their tickets early. The proprietary faction again sought Conrad Weiser's influence, this time requesting him to delay a visit to the Indians as interpreter for Nicholas von Zinzendorf in order to help "prepare" his countrymen for the election.[83] Proprietary supporters also met with "yᵉ Heads of yᵉ Dutch" at Germantown in an effort to gain support for a ticket that included some new candidates. Germans agreed to support four new candidates, or half of the Philadelphia County delegation, if the governor would promise not to organize a militia unless war with France broke out; if war occurred, Germans who conscientiously opposed military service would receive the same exemptions as Quakers. Proprietary officials were optimistic about the outcome of the election, for the city of Philadelphia "was 9 to 2 in favour of a change of halfe" of the delegates, and "if yᵉ Dutch cou'd be divided that yᵉ Country might be pretty near on a par." But their hopes were dashed when Christopher Sauer cast doubts on the governor's attitude toward the agreement. Influential Germans allied with the Quaker faction spread rumors about the oppression resulting from the militia law in the Lower Counties that had been approved by the man who also served as Pennsylvania's governor, and hinted that "ye Prop^{rs} intended to make use of ye Militia to eject such as coud not pay of their Possessions." Attempts to form new coalition tickets were made in other counties as well.[84]

Expiration of a 1739 law regulating the selection of inspectors to determine the qualifications of prospective voters exacerbated the struggle. Under this law, inspectors were chosen by township or ward a week before the provincial elections, and then by lot on election day. With its expiration, the colony reverted to the older, potentially turbulent practice of selecting inspectors by gathering around candidates, which sometimes permitted unqualified persons to participate in an environment conducive to mob intimidation once voting began. There were attempts to reach an agreement, before the election, on the choice of inspectors representing the interests of both factions, but to no avail.[85]

As election day approached, Philadelphians heard rumors that many unnaturalized Germans, some armed with clubs, intended to be in the city on election day. Violence was feared, as was the possibility that they would attempt to vote themselves or affect the outcome through intimidation. Supporters of both factions tried to dissuade the unnaturalized from attempting to vote or gathering in the vicinity of the polls. When a group of sailors appeared at the polling place on election day they refused to disperse, claiming that they had as much right to be present as unnaturalized and therefore unqualified Germans. A riot ensued, with the sailors "crying out down with the plain Coats & broad Brims" and a ship captain telling his mate to *"go and knock those* Dutch *Sons of Bitches off the Steps."* The Germans routed the sailors, and the Quakers' victory was complete. Investigation of the incident by an assembly composed almost entirely of Quakers, for they had won most of the seats from the other counties without violence, placed the blame squarely on William Allen and several city officials.[86]

The riot, commonly thought to have been instigated by proprietary officials, discredited the party, which for several years thereafter received scant support. The decisive defeat of the proprietary supporters, and the anticipation that the merchants' petition would "cost more mony & time" than they had expected, inspired confidence among many Quaker leaders.[87] Finally the Privy Council decided merely to advise the King to solicit information about "what he apprehends necessary for ye Security" of the colony from the governor. Nothing was done about the "capital point, of intermeddling with the constituents of a free people."[88]

When Governor Thomas issued a declaration of war against France in July 1744, the stage was set for renewed struggle. The Mayor and Common Council of Philadelphia, a body in which the balance of power had recently shifted from Quakers to non-Quakers, sent a new petition to the King describing the wealth of their city and the dangers it faced. Easily accessible to vessels of war but lacking fortifications or a "Legal Obligation" for its inhabitants to defend it, the province was "Daily Under an Apprehension of an Invasion," for the French were well aware of their situation. Even a few privateers could inflict heavy damages. Because the proprietors, governors, and inhabitants who favored military preparations had been rebuffed by an assembly that emphasized "religious Principles," there was no recourse but to petition the King for relief from their "Deplorable Condition."[89]

Quakers immediately prepared a counter-petition, arguing that the petitioners were not representatives of the citizens, for new council members were selected by those already in office. They complained that the petition, already drafted, had been presented to a meeting "kept secret from those that were of different Sentiments (of which there is a considerable Number) and as tho' they feared that by proceeding with the usual Deliberation in Matters of this Consequence they should not be able to succeed in their Intention." Quakers suspected that the petitioners intended to "revive Disputes between the Branches of our Legislature," something "very disagreeable" not only to Friends but also to members of other religious societies who had freely chosen them as representatives. They did not address the substance of the petition, but merely remarked that "we have lately had the Satisfaction of a publick Acknowledgment even from our Governor that he thinks our present Situation rendered by several late Circumstances more secure than formerly."[90]

Indeed, the early war years were marked by relatively benign relations between the governor and the assembly, as both sides strove to find modes of accommodation following the 1742 election.[91] When Thomas informed the assembly that during its adjournment he had declared war on France, he also told it that he had issued a proclamation requiring all residents "able to bear Arms, forthwith to provide themselves with them" in order to defend the province. He was compiling lists of the most qualified men in each county to organize the troops, and expected to issue commissions shortly. He asked the assembly to provide "a Magazine of Arms and Ammunition" and to enact a militia law.[92] The assembly, declaring its satisfaction with the governor's actions, cited the precedents of former governors who had raised militias simply by granting commissions, and hoped to be *"excuse[d] . . . from preparing a Bill to this end."*[93] The governor chose not to press the issue.

The following year Thomas requested funds to help support an attack New Englanders were organizing against Canada. He argued that all of the English colonies had a common interest in destroying the French base at Louisbourg in order to protect their trading vessels. The assembly remarked that if New Englanders wanted aid they should have consulted other colonies in advance, and for various reasons, including the lack of royal sanction for the expedition, declined to render assistance.[94] A few months later the governor presented proof of royal approbation of the plan, but the assembly responded only indirectly. Reminding the governor of its "peaceable Principles" but recognizing its "Duty to render Tribute to Caesar," it appropriated £4000 to be expended on "Bread, Beef, Pork, Flour, Wheat or other Grain" intended for "the King's Use."[95] When men and provisions were requested the following year for another expedition, the assembly complained that it had recently granted a large sum of money "which the Governor was pleased to apply to the Use of the Garrison" at Cape Breton,[96] but after five months of discussions, the assembly resolved to give another £5000 to the King.[97]

While war was distant, the governor and assembly presented their divergent ideas simply and dispassionately, while colonists did not complain about their policies. But as a perception that Pennsylvania might be in danger developed in late 1746, and became more acute during the next two years, the familiar arguments arose. Colonists again had to consider the implications of life in a pluralistic society in which adherents of many faiths could participate in government. Conflicting demands of conscience came to the fore in the effort to resolve pressing military questions.

In July 1747 French privateers landed in Delaware Bay and plundered a few plantations. News was brought to Philadelphia that one hundred men had landed at Blackbird Creek, robbed inhabitants of their slaves and anything else they could carry off, shot a woman, and taken her husband prisoner. Reportedly, "Even the Quakers faith failed them" at this news.[98] Although some "doubted the Truth" of the reports, many people were "much frightned" and the council was convened to discuss the situation.[99] But when on the following day the goriest details were discounted, one Quaker gloated that "the many hard Speeches made against the poor Quakers for their harmless principles, serve only to show the malice of those who made them[.]"[100]

That autumn, perhaps in part because the colony was temporarily without a governor who could issue military commissions,[101] Benjamin Franklin published *Plain Truth*, a pamphlet that challenged Pennsylvanians to organize a militia. He reminded colonists of their vulnerability along the frontier from Indians acting in the French interest and by sea. Citing the recent grants to assist New Englanders and the British in carrying out military maneuvers, Franklin queried why Pennsylvanians should aid comparative "Strangers" and yet refuse to help themselves. Defense was economically sound. Although it might appear expensive to construct a warship and to man it, the money would be spent within the colony and thus provide employment. Furthermore, money expended in defense would be minimal compared to losses that might be sustained if the colony were attacked. He argued that protection was a governmental obligation, and suggested that Quakers either resign from their positions or appropriate money for the King's use and leave its disposition to others. He denounced the men of wealth and influence who could have organized a militia had not their "ENVY," "*Rage*," and "Hatred" prevented them from doing so. Quakers could justifiably plead conscience in refusing to support military measures, but conscience required nonpacifists to defend their country. Franklin appealed to the characteristics of the English, Scotch-Irish, and German inhabitants that suited them for warlike actions, and informed readers that a plan for a defensive association would soon be published.[102]

Within a few weeks of the publication of *Plain Truth* two meetings were held in Philadelphia to organize a voluntary association to defend the province. Following the second meeting, "upwards of Five Hundred Men of all Ranks" subscribed the agreement, and more were expected to do so. A lottery was proposed to pay for the militia's equipment.[103] People of various beliefs, including several Quakers, signed a petition to the assembly requesting financial support for the association.[104]

Clerical support was also forthcoming. The rector of the Anglican church in Philadelphia preached an "excellent Sermon on the Lawfulness of Self-Defence, and of Associating for that Purpose" to a large congregation.[105] The most controversial contribution, though, came from Gilbert Tennent, who published a lengthy sermon entitled *The Late Association for Defence, encourag'd, Or The lawfulness of a Defensive War.* His purposes were "to shew my Approbation" of a voluntary association "as well as to essay the Encouragement of it, by attempting to remove the Scruples of such, who by their *Religious Principles,* are hindered from joining in the ASSOCIATION."[106]

John Smith, a Quaker "moved at the deceit and Quirks" of Tennent's sermon, responded with *The Doctrine of Christianity, As held by the People called Quakers, Vindicated,* a direct refutation of Tennent's arguments written with the approbation of several leading Friends.[107] He arranged to have one thousand copies of the essay printed, half of which were to be given away.[108] Tennent in response composed another essay, considerably less moderate than the first, specifically intended to refute Smith's tract. He defended himself from the insinuation that his real purpose had been to attack Friends, and reminded Smith that other, non-Quaker, pacifists resided in the colony. After countering several of Smith's arguments, Tennent concluded that the Quaker was not only wrong but also uncharitable.[109]

In an effort to attract German recruits, *Plain Truth* was translated into their language. But Christopher Sauer advised his newspaper readers to ignore the pamphlet if they hoped to avoid spiritual dangers. They should instead read a Quaker pamphlet, *Verschiedene Christliche Wahrheiten, und kurtz Betrachtung über ein kützlich heraus gegebenes Büchlein, geñant Lautere Warheit.* Sauer cautioned against Gilbert Tennent's sermon in defense of war, but believed that as long as this "true masterpiece of the old serpent" remained untranslated, it would not "harm" the Germans.[110] Sauer printed a translation of the articles that regulated the defensive association, but appended a lengthy essay opposing it on religious grounds.[111] Very few Germans enlisted in the militia. Credit, or blame, was given to Sauer, who "tho' he is no Quaker he discourages his countrey Men from bearing of Arms on any Acot[.]"[112]

The need for a defensive association was temporary, for by the summer of 1748 there were rumors of a truce between the warring European powers. One Pennsylvanian believed that peace might help to relieve the conflicts within the colony.[113] A colonial Quaker, perhaps in an attempt to demonstrate Friends' loyalty to the Crown and interest in peace, submitted a letter from English Quakers congratulating the negotiators of the Peace of Aix-la-Chapelle on their successful conclusion of the war to the *Pennsylvania Gazette.*[114]

The proclamation of peace in late August 1748,[115] shortly before the provincial elections, diffused defense and the association as potential campaign issues. According to one Quaker, the election was particularly "quiet," and with little opposition most of the incumbents were reelected. Men "turned out" were those "the country thought were too much inclined to favor those who have been for laying unnecessary burdens on the province."[116] But Henry Melchior Muhlenberg commented on the "violent newspaper war" conducted by pacifists and nonpacifists over defense during the election campaign. The Lutheran *"collegium"* had been carefully watched to discover where they would lend their influence, but both sides were disappointed. Ministers were in the colony solely for religious purposes, "and hence we could not mix in political affairs unless we had express orders from our highest or provincial government; accordingly we remained silent."[117]

III

Germans began to participate more actively in political affairs toward the end of the 1740s. Not only were increasing numbers voting, but their concentrated settlement in the backcountry provided opportunities for election or appointment to public office. English-speaking politicians, regardless of their religious views and attitudes toward the proprietary regime, now had to grapple with ethnic pluralism in the political sphere.

In 1749 two German Lutherans were elected burgesses in Lancaster, and others were selected for lesser offices. Their pastor was pleased with the outcome, and especially with the way the election had been carried out: "nearly all of our Lutherans, after my hearty entreaty and remonstrance on the Sunday before, avoided all of the otherwise usual disorders at elections, while previously none were more complained about than the Lutherans."[118] But the countywide elections a few weeks later did not proceed with such good order. Complaints were brought to the assembly that no lists of voters had been kept, proxies had been allowed, many men had cast multiple ballots, underage boys had been permitted to vote, and the inspectors had been illegally chosen or had failed to fulfill their obligations to ensure a fair election. In contrast to the fears expressed earlier in the decade, the possibility that unnaturalized Germans in this heavily German county had voted was not mentioned. The assembly, after several hearings on the matter, decided to accept the candidates who had received the largest number of votes. It then issued a lengthy admonition to the sheriff and inspectors of Lancaster County spelling out their responsibilities. The assembly subsequently ordered this statement printed in the Philadelphia newspapers.[119] Sauer published the charge in August 1750 so that German voters and officials would know how to conduct themselves properly. He commented, "if everyone diligently comes to the election, it will be obvious whether it has been honestly and impartially conducted."[120]

Voters in York County failed to heed the advice, and several disturbances occurred. Evidence, although incomplete, suggests conflict between the Scotch-Irish and German residents of the county. Instead of submitting a return to the assembly, the sheriff presented a statement about the election. He declared that he had opened it regularly, and that it had proceeded "quietly for some Time, until a Multitude of People, chiefly *Germans*, armed with Sticks and Billets of Wood, excited and encouraged by *Nicholas Ryland* the Coroner, began to beat and drive away all the People from the Court-House," whereupon a riot ensued and the officials were driven out of the building. The coroner then reopened the election, refused the sheriff readmittance, and, "supported by the outrageous Multitude," kept possession of the ballot box.[121]

The assembly accepted the irregular returns, but warned the sheriff to "take all the Care in his Power for the future to prevent any further Complaint of tumultuous Elections; that he be particularly careful to quiet the Minds of the People, by observing a discrete Conduct towards all Parties at his Return Home."[122] A few months later several county residents presented their version of the events. After the sheriff had delayed the opening of the election, the "*Marsh-Creek* People," largely Scotch-Irish, gathered around the courthouse and "would not suffer the *Dutch* People and other Friends" to approach. They "did what they could to keep them off with Clubs, so that the *Dutch* were obliged to do the best they could, or else go Home without voting; and being the most in Number, they drove the *Marsh-Creek* People from the House," and then came in a "peaceable Manner" to cast their ballots. But "when the Sheriff saw that his Party was mastered," he closed the election, "which made the *Dutch* People angry," whereupon they insisted that it be reopened. When he refused, the coroner continued it.[123] One inspector described three disturbances at the election, but apportioned the blame relatively equally among all parties.[124]

At least in part because this tumultuous election was "aduced as an Instance" of the "disposition and manners" of the Germans, some Pennsylvanians began to consider the ethnic composition of existing and proposed counties. They suspected that continuing immigration by Germans, whose industriousness allowed them to meet the property qualifications for the franchise, would result in their political dominance. One proprietary supporter therefore suggested that two new counties be created out of Philadelphia and Bucks Counties which, if the lines were carefully drawn, would include a majority of the province's Germans. If each county were assigned two assembly representatives, as had been the case with the most recently established counties, heavily German York and predominantly Scotch-Irish Cumberland, the political influence of the Germans would be effectively circumscribed. At most, German voters could control only ten out of thirty-eight seats.[125]

The actual apportionment was even more draconic. When the assembly created Berks and Northampton Counties in March 1751/2, each was assigned only one delegate. Residents, who were probably more interested in the greater convenience of courts and other offices, did not initially realize the implications of the minimal representation.[126] But as the 1752 elections approached, a Schwenkfelder leader protested the inequitable representation. People in Berks County had been pleased by the "conduct and good manners" of their assemblymen in "troublesome times," but now found themselves "deprived on ⅞ths of their former right to elect capable men" to represent them. This boded ill for the province, for residents "may be forced to accept such matters which are against their conscience and against their present valuable privileges." He pleaded for equitable representation.[127]

The attempt to segregate the Germans had at least one negative side effect, for it was sometimes difficult to find qualified men to serve in county offices and as justices of the peace. Governor James Hamilton complained that the new counties were "filld with such an exceeding barbarous kind of people" who were "impossible" to maintain "in any sort of order." With "three fourths" of the residents of each of them "Foreigners that understand neither our Language nor Constitution," it would be difficult to select officials. Moreover, duties such as jury service might become burdensome to the few English inhabitants, who were themselves "but very poorly qualified" for such responsibilities.[128] Thomas Penn was not so pessimistic. Since the "Lower part[s]" of the new counties had been settled for years, there should be enough men acquainted with colonial customs to carry out governmental functions until the Germans became sufficiently anglicized. They would gradually "Loose their attachment to their Language" and "become

English," and once they began to acquire property they would become "good Subjects." Germans would not "overturn" a constitution that granted them so much "Liberty."[129]

For several years the religious background of political appointees had been considered.[130] Because the governor controlled judicial and other appointments while the assembly was in the hands of his opponents, it was thought that "these two different Bodys will always be using their Influence one ag^t the other."[131] Thomas Penn agreed with Governor Hamilton that Quakers were "generally better qualified" for commissions of the peace than "the people of other Persuasions at a distance from the Town,"[132] but cautioned, "we would always shew the Society a regard but not so much as to set them above others."[133] A few years later Hamilton complained that several assemblymen, presumably Quakers or their supporters, were refusing to accept positions as magistrates because they feared that an identification with the proprietors would result in their defeat as assemblymen.[134] Yet even in the midst of the problems of 1741 Logan recommended the appointment of additional Quakers to the governor's council. Despite their refusal to support defense, "all parties must confess on occasions they are very useful men."[135] When a Presbyterian minister was requested to advise the government about possible men to serve as justices in his neighborhood, he recommended a Presbyterian and a Quaker. It was important, he thought, to select wise men who would discharge their duties properly. "If we have such," he concluded, "I care not what party they belong to."[136]

Not all appointments Philadelphia officials made for backcountry positions proved acceptable to the people they were to serve. Proprietary supporter Conrad Weiser, recognized by that faction as a German leader, was appointed a magistrate and given various responsibilities, but soundly defeated in a bid to represent Lancaster County in the assembly.[137] When William Parsons was appointed county clerk in Northampton, one proprietary supporter commented that he was "particularly acceptable to the Dutch."[138] But Parsons, who had married a German woman and separated from her when she became a Moravian, had little respect for either Germans or Moravians.[139] When he ran for the Northampton County assembly seat in 1754, Parsons was decisively defeated by a Moravian. He complained bitterly of the campaign tactics of his rival. Several Moravians, he claimed, qualified as inspectors by affirmation without presenting the certificates required by act of Parliament. One inspector admitted that he had not been naturalized, while another did not reside in the township he was supposed to represent. Furthermore, Parsons' opponent had declared "that all those were naturalized who had taken the Oath of Alegiance"—that is, the provincial declarations required of alien immigrants. Notwithstanding such irregularities, "their Votes were all viewed that were Offered." Parsons' only consolation was that "If Sodom and Gomorrah were spared for the Sake of 10 righteous Persons. Surely Northampton may have some Hopes of being spared for the Sake of 99" who voted for him.[140]

Apprehension among the proprietary elite about the increasing number of pro-Quaker Germans in the colony by mid-century played a significant role in the perversion of a project initiated by the German Reformed to educate their children into a scheme to anglicize the German colonists. Reformed ministers were greatly concerned about the lack of educational facilities in the colony, while members of their congregations feared that their children would grow up in ignorance of letters and God's commands. Thus when the Reverend Michael Schlatter returned to Holland after a five-year mission devoted to investigating conditions in Pennsylvania for the Classis of Amsterdam, he was prepared to argue that ministers and teachers were urgently needed. But attempts to solicit funds to assist the colonists intersected with English and provincial fears of "foreigners" and questions about their loyalty to the Crown. The results were entirely different from what were intended.

The report Schlatter penned for the Classis, and the copy of his journal that he included with it, influenced church officials to petition the Dutch government to conduct a fundraising campaign throughout the country to support ministers and teachers in Pennsylvania. The states of Holland and West Friesland granted two thousand guilders per year for five years, while substantial donations were collected in Amsterdam.[141] In May 1751 a minister of the German Reformed church at The Hague informed Thomas Penn of the religious needs of the Pennsylvania Germans and of the Dutch plans to assist them by establishing a fund to support ministers. He asked Penn to oversee any money collected in England for this purpose and put it out at interest in the colony.[142] A month later Schlatter forwarded a gloomy report on the condition of Pennsylvania Germans. Their morals had degenerated and they were "becoming bad Men." They would eventually "become also very bad and troublesome subjects." The "introduction of an orderly discipline and ministry" might allow "many [to be] made good subjects, who at present can scarcely be called Men[.]"[143]

Thomas Penn declined to become involved. Although he approved the "pious intentions" of the Reformed and "heartily" wished them "success," he cited his father's guarantee of liberty of conscience to justify his refusal to support the plan. The only way to "preserve that equality and independency" of each sect was for the government "not to interfere" in any manner in church affairs.[144] Schlatter and his associates professed themselves "convinc'd" by Penn's arguments about the impropriety of becoming involved in religious matters, but sent him a more complete summary of their plans to provide schoolmasters and books for children and support ministers.[145]

Contributions were solicited from churches in the Reformed tradition. Swiss churches flatly refused, "considering the most of those who emigrate as too lazy to work, who only go to Pennsylvania in the hope of finding fortunate islands (insulas fortunatas) there."[146] The Church of Scotland was more responsive after delegates to a church convention learned that German Reformed colonists were "almost entirely destitute" of Bibles and other religious books in German, and also needed teachers. The colonists might "degenerate into the darkness and idolatry of the Indian nations" or "fall prey to the superstitions and idolatries of Popery." Because it was in the British interest to promote an attachment to civil and religious principles among its subjects, a collection was ordered to be made throughout the country.[147] Ministers of the Dutch churches in London published a letter briefly summarizing the deplorable religious situation of Pennsylvania Germans and requested a charitable collection in England for their benefit.[148]

As contacts developed with Presbyterians, Anglicans, and influential Englishmen the innocent plan of the Reformed to provide pastors and teachers for their Pennsylvania brethren began to go awry. When

Schlatter's "Appeal" was translated into English, the disparaging remarks he made about the barbarity of the colonial Germans and their doubtful loyalty to the English government resulted in the formulation of a plan to "place Schoolmasters among the Dutch to teach the Children the English Language."[149] Englishmen expressed concern about "Sixty thousand foreigners continually increasing by new emigrations from Germany, speaking a different language from the English colony, without knowledge of our laws and customs, open to the seductions of the Papists, encompassed with Indians, without schoolmasters and schools, with but few ministers to instruct them or their children in religion and virtue." Supporters declared that there was "nothing of party in view nor any other design" involved in the plan "but the peace of his Majesty's government, the interest of the Protestant religion and the welfare of the Pennsylvania and other colonies."[150]

By February 1753 a London society to manage a charity for the Protestants in Pennsylvania, "in order to make them more so by their learning the British language," had been organized.[151] Its goals were to establish schools to teach German children both the English and German languages and to provide an education in the fundamentals of religious and secular subjects. Children would be taught "any *Catechism* of sound *Doctrine*, which is approved of and used by their own Parents and Ministers," and religious works in both German and English would be distributed. The "benevolent Design" of the Society for the Propagating of Christian Knowledge among the Germans in Pennsylvania was "to qualify the *Germans* for all the Advantages of native *English Subjects*," something that required a knowledge of English. The project initially received considerable support in England, including donations from the King and royal family and several members of the Penn family.[152] In contrast to his earlier coldness to Schlatter's project, Thomas Penn urged several colonial officials to assist the "Scheme."[153]

William Smith, a Scottish Anglican priest who had only recently settled in Philadelphia but who embraced all of the worst prejudices occasionally expressed about the Germans, played a major role in the final shape the society and its project would take. He professed himself entirely in sympathy with its goals, which were, in his words, "to keep a vast multitude of fellow Protestants from falling into deeper ignorance, being seduced by the enemy, living in a separate body, turning trade out of its proper channels, and at last giving us their laws and language." He proposed encouraging both German and English children to attend free schools, "for there they will form acquaintances and connections, learn the common language, like manners, and the meaning of liberty, a common weal, and a common country. Intermarriage will follow," thereby further unifying the colony. Teachers should be bilingual Pennsylvanians, trained at the College of Philadelphia. Local trustees would visit the schools monthly, and trustees-general would oversee all of the schools and visit each one annually to bestow prizes on students who mastered English or gave the best responses to queries about religious and civic duties.[154]

Smith journeyed to London, where he was "Ardent in promoting English Schools for teaching the Germans."[155] One of his purposes was "to have the management of this important Trust devolved upon Men of the first rank of Pennsylvania, and not upon Clergy who depend on Dutch Synods." He "hope[d] to see all such dependence entirely shaken off once we can supply the Germans with ministers from the Academy" of Philadelphia. It was important to maintain control of the funds in order to keep the German clergy "under proper awe." According to Smith, Schlatter's main "Fault" was "his too great Attachment to foreign Synods and clergy who would counterwork our design."[156]

Provincial trustees-general were formally appointed in March 1754, and Michael Schlatter was appointed superintendent of the schools. The purposes of the charity were declared to be the instruction of German youth "in the English Language & the Knowledge of the common principles of the Christian Religion & Morality," so that they "may become better Subjects to the British Government, & more useful to the Colonies where Providence has now fixt their habitation."[157] All of the trustees were proprietary supporters except Benjamin Franklin, who concurred in their anxiety about the growing number of Germans living in the province and the presumed threat they posed to the English culture. Even the only German trustee, Conrad Weiser, shared many of their suspicions of his countrypeople.[158]

By the time the trustees met for the first time, apprehension about the colonial Germans was mounting, due to the threat of war with France. Trustees feared that, "as the Generality of these Germans, place all Happiness in a large Farm, they will greedily accept the easy Settlements wch the French will be enabled to offer them. Thus vast numbers will be induced to go over to the Enemy." Because Germans born in the colony did not share their parents' first-hand experience of French tyranny, they must be taught the differences between French and British principles of government. Knowledge of English would be one method of securing their allegiance.[159]

In order to make the schools "more catholic & unexceptionable," the local trustees selected to oversee the schools in their communities were to be "Calvinist, part Lutheran Germans, & part Englishmen of any Protestant Persuasion whatever."[160] But they were carefully chosen in regard to their religious and political principles. Thomas Penn had suggested to the London managers that Benjamin Shoemaker be appointed a trustee-general, but then withdrew the recommendation, for Shoemaker was a Quaker.[161] A proposed trustee, who appeared "in all his Conduct to have the most prudence & best natural understanding of Men in Easton, whether English or Dutch," was nevertheless deemed unsatisfactory. He was a Roman Catholic, which was "an insuperable Objection to him." At least one trustee considered Moravians "to be as exceptionable as the open and professed Roman Catholicks are."[162]

Reaction to the "benevolence" of the Charity School Society was mixed. Opposition came most strongly and most consistently from Christopher Sauer, who had little use for higher education or for the professions that required advanced training, particularly the ministry.[163] His first information about the work of the Charity School Society was its plan to educate German youths at the academy. He reported that "ambition, greed, and lust" had resulted in a plan to make lawyers, physicians, and ministers out of "the Germans who do not want to work or to follow an honorable trade."[164] He subsequently learned that the plan involved the establishment of six free English schools, and that "German ministers should exercise themselves in English, so that gradually the Germans and the English would become one people and have the same ministers." It was "laudable" for the Charity School Society to "so liberally and kindly" offer to teach the Germans a new language without cost. However, he then informed readers that "this was done out of fear, so that the multitude of Germans do not make themselves into a separate people and in a war with France join with them to the damage of the English nation." Furthermore, "if Schlatter has accused the Germans to such a degree, and represented them as a nation of roguish and mischievous disposition, who would probably join with the French in time of war and villainously espouse their cause, then he has acted with great imprudence, and cast disgrace upon the King as well as himself." Accusations of disaffection were nonsense. And, he noted, Irish, Welsh, and Swedish Pennsylvanians "retain their own language, and are not looked upon as a disloyal people."[165]

Sauer also feared the repercussions of the project on the souls of the recipients. Many Germans of his acquaintance believed they would be "forced" to listen to English preachers, and, "being ignorant in that Language they would be obliged to set in their Meetings like Geese and hold their Tongues like Sheep." Under the "Pretext" of a "Charitable Scheme" to promote "Godliness," the schools "might turn into an English Carnal and devilish confused Learning instead of Godly." Others wanted their children to understand only German as a means of shielding them from "all Lawyers and Court Business."[166] In a letter to Weiser, Sauer questioned whether the local supporters of the schools "care in the least for the real conversion of the ignorant Germans" in the province. He wondered "whether the institution of Free Schools is rather supposed to be the foundation for the subjection of this country, since everybody will pursue his own selfish ends by means of this scheme." The sponsors, he asserted, "care very little either for religion or for the cultivation of the Germans; they rather want the Germans to stick out their necks by serving in the militia in order to protect the property of these gentlemen."[167]

Lutheran and Reformed pastors supported the project with varying degrees of enthusiasm. Ministers agreed to send their own children to the schools, on condition that each student be instructed in the "particular Catechism of his own faith."[168] But the clergy, echoing one of Sauer's objections, condemned Schlatter's insinuations that Germans were disloyal.[169]

The Reformed were annoyed at the turn their original project had

Prop schools?
Gov → good citizen?
1755 4 schools

RELIGIOUS AND ETHNIC POLITICS, 1739–1755   191

taken. Their Coetus believed that the schools "will not be of much public or private service to our Church," for the "only object" of the schools was the "introduction of the English language among the Germans," which was a "purely political matter." They also objected to some of the local trustees. In Lancaster, they said, "Moravians, Quakers, Separatists, perchance even Deists," but no members of the Reformed church were selected. Furthermore, the Reformed resented the fact that money was dispensed by the English trustees, who could therefore exercise supervision over the ministers who served as catechists.[170]

Among the Lutherans, Henry Melchior Muhlenberg praised the project as an extension of earlier, unfulfilled proprietary attempts to establish schools in selected towns. He concluded "that the high patrons are intent on making the Germans faithful subjects and good church members, which is most reasonable."[171] Muhlenberg provided the trustees with translations of some of Sauer's newspaper articles and suggested that a printing press be established in order to counteract them. The trustees "unanimously resolved" to accept this suggestion. A printer was hired on the recommendation of Franklin, who helped to make arrangements for purchasing a press and other equipment and served as the formal director of this aspect of the project.[172]

German colonists displayed mixed reactions to the charitable enterprise. Many recognized the value of education, regardless of the political motives or nativist fears at the root of the project. People in several towns, who emphasized their Protestant beliefs and lack of ministers and teachers, petitioned the Charity School Society for schools. Some volunteered money, supplies, or labor toward the construction of suitable buildings; others stated that they were extremely poor and needed assistance in both building schools and paying teachers.[173] By April 1755 four schools had opened, six more were expected to begin shortly, and the trustees had received petitions for fifteen additional ones. That summer, seven schools attended by three or four hundred children were in operation, while plans continued to establish a total of fourteen for boys and three or four for girls.[174]

Other Germans joined Sauer in opposition. Some felt uneasy about accepting charity while they had the means to pay for education, even though they could not otherwise find teachers. Others objected that their children might adopt bad habits from other children, and preferred to teach them at home. Still others thought that after learning English and associating with English people, children would want to ape their fashions. Some could not take advantage of the schools because they lacked the means to clothe their offspring properly, while still others found the distances to them too far for daily travel but could not afford boarding charges. The benefits therefore went disproportionately to the wealthy.[175] Most support for the schools came from members of the Lutheran and Reformed churches, while sectarians were generally opposed.[176]

Not all provincial leaders were enthusiastic about the schools or their prospects for success. William Parsons was frankly pessimistic. Germans were "so perverse and quarelsome" in all their affairs that the project would inevitably generate so much "Rancor" that in the end, neither side would allow its children to attend the school if the other did. He wondered "whether it be Men or Beasts that the generous Benefactors are about to civilize." Efforts to compromise differences among Germans were "like attempting to wash a Blackamore white." Nevertheless, Parsons had one practical suggestion about anglicization: educate girls as well as boys. They should be taught to read and write "(if Writing shall be thought necessary for Girls)," and needlework. He argued that because mothers had the primary care of their children, they would speak her language even if the father spoke English. He added, "I need not mention how industrious young Men generally are to appear in the Habit & to speak the Language which is most agreable to the Female world, in low as well as in high Life."[177]

Despite the political ideas entangled in this project, Thomas Penn urged the trustees to be cautious. He was confident that "Germans dislike the French as much as the English do, even the Catholicks do not like them." Since English "Fears" of the Germans and "declarations of those fears" might "give them a distaste to us, which ought with the most care to be avoided,"[178] trustees should not "sour" the Germans "by any general reflections, or make them uneasy by Laying them under any restraints they were not subject to, when they came from their native Country."[179]

Funding for the project was shaky, and its continuation was in doubt almost from the beginning. Early in 1755 Thomas Penn suggested that Governor Hamilton propose to the assembly the allocation of a few hundred pounds to support German schoolmasters. If the request were "worded in a tender kind manner with regard to the Germans, it must draw either some assistance from them, which I do not expect, or an answer that may be made a very good use of."[180] The project struggled on into the early 1760s, but finally collapsed because of a shortage of money and concern with more pressing issues, notably the war with France; more significantly, fears of the Germans subsided as they proved their loyalty to the British cause.[181]

During the 1740s and 1750s interest revived in the conditions under which immigrants were transported to the colony. But humanitarian concern became entangled in power struggles between governors and assemblies and with conflicting interpretations of the contributions immigrants made to the colony. The Germans' plight was frequently overlooked, resulting in delays and frustration for all parties.

A "most malign Distemper" had been brought to the colony in the spring of 1741 by ships from Ireland. At first it only "crept along the Wharfs affecting Strangers comon Sailors and the low & poor part of the People," but during the heat of summer it spread to the "better Sort of the Inhabitants" and consequently came to the attention of the authorities.[182] As concern mounted, the assembly granted £10 to Dr. Thomas Graeme, who had been employed by the governor for several years to visit incoming vessels and had in 1739 been paid for twenty years' service, in recognition of the "dangerous Consequences" of allowing "unhealthy Vessels" to dock. It then resolved to appoint Dr. Lloyd Zachary to visit the ships "as often as Occasion shall require," and when directed to do so by the governor and council or two city magistrates.[183] During its consideration of this resolution, the council revealed more facts about the situation and initiated a lengthy dispute with the assembly over the powers of each branch of government. Because Graeme had not been paid for his services in 1740, he had refused to visit any more ships, and other physicians had been unwilling to assume the responsibility. In consequence, many persons "afflicted with mortal and contagious Disease" had landed in the city, and infections had spread. The council blamed the assembly for this situation, for it had "in Effect, discharged" Dr. Graeme by refusing to pay him adequately. Its new appointment was *"unprecedented, illegal,* and *unwarrantable,"* for the authority to make appointments belonged to the governor. Nor had it any right to transfer responsibility over incoming ships from the executive to the magistrates; only the governor, as *"supreme Magistrate,"* could authorize visits by physicians.[184]

When the assembly reconvened in January 1741/2, Governor Thomas recommended constructing a hospital for sick immigrants. Several of the "most substantial Germans" had petitioned him about the hardships and needless deaths that resulted from the sick being confined to the ships. The assembly, "as Christians and indeed as Men," had an obligation to "make a Charitable Provision for the sick Stranger." Although "some look with jealous Eyes upon the yearly concourse of Germans to this Province," he declared that "every industrious Labourer from Europe is a real addition to the wealth of this Province, and that the Labour of every foreigner in particular is almost so much clear Gain to our Mother Country."[185] The assembly recognized the potential value of a hospital, but thought the "Malignant & Dangerous Distempers" brought to the colony by immigrants from Ireland and Germany might not have spread had there been a "due Execution" of the public health laws. While the colony's financial situation had not improved since a similar hospital proposal had been rejected in 1738, assemblymen promised to investigate the costs and to seek the advice of their constituents about the plan. Professing ignorance of those who looked with "jealous Eyes" on the Germans, it stressed its willingness to naturalize aliens prior to 1740 as evidence of its good will toward them.[186] From that point the discussion spiraled downward into mutual recriminations, defenses of past actions, and constitutional arguments.[187]

Several unhealthy vessels arrived during the summer of 1742. One ship, on which the captain and several passengers had died of "a Dangerous fever now Commonly known here by the Name of the Dutch Distemper," was ordered downstream until the passengers could be landed safely and the vessel cleansed.[188] When the assembly reconvened in August the governor urged it to action, and stated that "Enough has been said of your Apprehensions from the great and frequent Importation of Foreigners."[189] The assembly, although "of the same opinion," could not resist commenting that if he were really concerned about immigrants he would have approved the law confirming the land titles of deceased unnaturalized residents and extending the affirmation to allow non-Quakers to be naturalized.[190]

Following the 1742 election a committee was appointed to draft a bill for the construction of a hospital for "sick and impotent Persons" on Province Island.[191] There was only brief debate on the bill before it was passed and sent to the governor. In contrast to the disputes of the previous years in which the plight of immigrants was lost in the ensuing power struggles, the executive and legislature easily reached agreement on amendments.[192] In February 1742/3 a law was enacted to establish a hospital for the better care of sick passengers and the prevention of infectious diseases. Trustees were appointed to oversee the buildings already standing on Province Island, accept all individuals ordered there by the governor or two magistrates, and provide everything required for their recovery. Passengers were to pay for their maintenance; if necessary, the ship's master or servant's importer could be forced to give bond for the payment of hospital expenses. Pennsylvanians were forbidden to "receive" or "entertain" any passengers ordered to the island or anyone who did not have a proper certificate of discharge from it.[193]

This inadequate law provoked several responses. The author of an election broadside complained that the assembly had "sunk *Seventeen Hundred Pounds* in the Purchase of a Tide-Swamp to finish the Misery of Foreigners[.]" He was indignant that it would "bring a considerable annual Charge to keep it above Water . . . it being the first Instance that was ever heard of in any part of the World, that a Marsh is a proper Place to erect an Hospital!"[194] Several Philadelphians petitioned the assembly in 1743 to regulate the conditions under which immigrants were transported. They thought overcrowding was the source of the diseases that were afflicting immigrants and the reason why they "increase, spread, and become infectious," causing the "lamentable Death of great Numbers" of passengers and Pennsylvanians alike.[195] Christopher Sauer continued to report the wretched conditions that immigrants endured. He focused on the death rates, the failure of merchants to fulfill the conditions of the contracts they made with passengers, and the extortionate rates at which provisions were sold. He complained that it was virtually impossible for immigrants to obtain justice or redress of their grievances.[196] In fact, most responsibility for ill passengers rested with merchants, in whose interests it was to speed the recovery of redemptioners so that their labor could be sold to pay for their passage. One firm, for example, reported that one hundred people on a vessel had died and that many others were "very Sickly" in consequence of a "long & tedious Passage." Thus, "We have been Obligd to get pretty many of 'em on shore, & put 'em to Nurse, but with as little Expence as Possible."[197]

The assembly could easily ignore immigrants and their problems during the war years, for fewer than one thousand Germans arrived annually during the mid-1740s. But the peaceful interlude between 1749 and 1755 brought a resumption of the passenger and servant trade and, not coincidentally, an increased interest in regulating it.[198] The first hint of a problem came in September 1749, when a ship suspected of carrying an infectious disease arrived in Philadelphia. But the physicians and trustees of the hospital reported that "the Place was in great Disorder, & that for want of room, Household Furniture, & suitable Apartments, the Sick cou'd be but indifferently" relieved. Nevertheless, they promised to do their best for the passengers, and Sauer reported that they were taken to the hospital.[199]

In November several Philadelphians petitioned the assembly about negligence in caring for sick passengers. Merchants, "for the sake of Lucre," were overcrowding their vessels, which resulted in high mortality rates. Many passengers were forced to defray the transportation charges of deceased relatives, while other "poor Strangers" were "obliged to leave their Chests, Clothes and other Furniture behind them," which often resulted in their "entire Loss." Condemning merchants' "iniquitous and infamous Practice[s]," they asked the government to adopt measures to relieve "*Germans* and other Foreigners."[200] The assembly hastily formulated a law to limit the number of passengers traveling on a ship. Although the governor disliked several of its provisions, he feared that the next summer would "prove sickly" and agreed to sign it.[201]

The new legislation required that a space six feet long and one foot, six inches wide be allocated to each person over the age of fourteen, or to two youngsters under that age. All passengers were to be supplied with "good and wholesome meat, drink, room and other necessaries" during the voyage. An official would visit each incoming vessel to determine whether immigrants had been properly treated; violation of the law incurred a £10 fine for each passenger whose rights had been infringed. Inventories of the effects of all deceased travelers were demanded. After transportation costs were deducted, the remaining goods would be given to the survivors. A £100 fine was levied for failure to render a proper inventory.[202]

Negative responses to this law indicate approbation of continued immigration, at least for economic reasons. Richard Peters thought it had been enacted in "too great haste" and would have "ill consequences." Even though its purpose was to protect "poor ignorant Country people," he believed the regulations would only deflect the servant trade to other colonies.[203] Thomas Penn thought the act was so poorly written that it would be almost impossible to enforce. It might encourage Germans to migrate to Nova Scotia, for it made it "difficult" for people to settle in Pennsylvania. One ship captain was "much alarm'd" by the statute. He declared that passengers were aware of the amount of space and the provisions they would have during the journey before they agreed for transportation. To give them anything more than was customary would require an increase in the fare.[204]

Governor Hamilton, however, emphasized the humanitarian purposes of the law and the fact that Germans had pressed for its enactment. Mortality rates had been very high. Because "It is well known that they are an ignorant sordid People, and for the sake of saving a pistole would deny themselves any conveniency, thô ever so necessary for their health," Germans must be "restraind from throwing away their lives so ignorantly and foolishly as they were used to do." Merchants were not concerned about the welfare of passengers. Hamilton had been informed that the space allotted to passengers was "as little as ought to be allowed to any human Creature, and leaves Profit enough with the Merchants to make it a very beneficial Trade."[205] To prevent the "pernicious practice" of overcrowding, the Board of Trade recommended royal confirmation, which was granted.[206]

Sauer published the provisions of this act in a supplement to his

newspaper, prefacing it with a description of the appalling conditions
that had resulted in the deaths of more than two thousand emigrants
the previous year and a summary of the information the petitioners
had presented to the assembly. But he recognized the law's deficiencies, and advised passengers to negotiate the terms of transportation
carefully. They should make sure that they had enough room to sit
up in their berths. More importantly, they should obtain a written
contract that spelled out the captain's responsibility to bring them and
their goods to a specified destination, and have the agreement notar-
ized. Passengers who paid part or all of their fare in advance should
obtain and keep receipts.[207] A few years later Sauer complained of
violations of the law. Newlanders told immigrants shortly before arrival that when inspectors asked if their provisions had been adequate,
they must reply in the affirmative. Otherwise they would not be allowed to land for four weeks while the complaints were investigated.
Since passengers wanted to leave the ship, abuses went undetected,
for complaining about them after landing was futile. Captains found
it cheaper to pay a newlander a handsome fee than to comply with
the regulations or to pay the fines.[208]

Despite opposition from several disparate interests, consideration of
amendments to the 1749 statute was delayed until 1754, when an assembly committee appointed to examine the provincial laws concluded that several of them relating to immigrants were inadequate.
The law intended to prevent overcrowding failed to specify the dimensions in height to which passengers were entitled, and "poor
Strangers" had complained of other "Abuses."[209]

The legislature was spurred into action that autumn, following the
arrival of several unhealthy vessels and an outbreak of disease in Philadelphia. Many sick passengers were being cared for in private houses,
and those in two dwellings posed such a threat to public health that
they were ordered removed to the country. Doctors who visited the
ships reported that some of the sick had been "Wickedly Concealed
from us." They traced the cause of the fevers to overcrowding and
other shipboard conditions. The council was also informed that more
than 250 immigrants had been interred in the "Stranger's Burying
Ground" within two months.[210] Since the present regulations were
obviously inadequate, Governor Robert Hunter Morris commended

the subject to the assembly's attention.[211] An assembly leader estimated that a thousand immigrants, and many of the captains, nurses, and attendants who had contact with them, had died during this year. Convinced that people contracted the "Jail distemper" from the general "nastiness at sea," he advocated measures to improve cleanliness during the voyage.[212]

Germans actively attempted to obtain new regulations for the benefit of their countrypeople. In one petition they expressed apprehension that the "Sick Houses" had inadequate supplies of food, fuel, and clothing. But their primary concern was with the general conditions faced by poor immigrants. People who could not be easily placed as servants were often released on their own security; some were forced to beg in order to survive because merchants abdicated their responsibilities. Merchants often retained immigrants' chests containing tools and clothing as security for payment, while a number of passengers were bound "interchangeably" as servants to pay the fares of others.[213] Other petitioners expressed concern about the spread of disease and the "Hardships and Grievances" that immigrants "suffered."[214] Sauer publicized the large number of passengers who arrived on crowded vessels during 1754 and the mortality rate accompanying them. He translated and published some of the messages exchanged by the governor and the assembly on the problem, appended a lengthy commentary complaining of the impossibility of obtaining justice for passengers who had been exploited, and expressed the hope that an effective and enforceable law would be passed. He suggested that a few "honest visitors" investigate conditions on incoming ships to determine whether the regulations had been followed.[215]

The assembly and governor failed to frame a satisfactory law. Morris believed that the draft of a new bill "militated against the Principles of Humanity," and gave magistrates too extensive powers in some instances and infringed upon their inherent functions in others. It "amounted to an absolute prohibition of Importation of Germans."[216] Both the council and assembly proposed numerous amendments that would help to safeguard the city's health and protect immigrants from abuses, but the matter was dropped when sufficient compromises could not be reached and other, more pressing, matters had to be considered.[217]

Nevertheless, pressure to enact a satisfactory law continued. Thomas Penn advocated passage of a bill to regulate the transportation of Germans; he believed it should contain a provision requiring the installation of a ventilation system on all ships carrying a large number of passengers.[218] Christopher Sauer advised the governor to take effective steps to regulate abuses. He described shipboard conditions, and blamed the greed of merchants who "lodge[d] the poor passengers like herring" and carried insufficient provisions. Passengers often agreed to one fare in Europe, but when a higher rate was demanded upon arrival, merchants made them "pay what they please." It was useless for an individual to appeal to the judicial system for redress.[219] In an appeal to Governor William Denny after the assembly had adjourned without enacting a law to protect immigrants, Sauer emphasized the frequent abuses involved in transporting necessities owned by passengers. Often their chests were left behind so that merchants' goods could be shipped. If chests did arrive in Pennsylvania, they would usually have been plundered. Because passengers received no bills of lading that indicated the contents of their baggage, they had no recourse to law. Sauer reminded the governor of the Germans' industry and loyalty, and asked him to use his influence to preserve the "lives and property" of prospective immigrants.[220]

IV

Notwithstanding the concern about the possible political or cultural consequences of a heterogeneous population, Pennsylvanians tended to view immigration favorably. The Scotch-Irish still had a more negative image than the Germans, especially in regard to property matters and the wealth they might generate for the province. In 1741 an Englishman was discouraged from speculating in Pennsylvania land that he hoped to rent on long leases, because impoverished "Freebooters from Ireland" invaded the "rough Woodland" of the province and "have made a vast and shameless havock of the Timber erecting only poor Cabbins."[221] Later, the Penns were urged to purchase land from the Indians in order to reserve manors before it was "seized" by the Scotch-Irish. There was also concern that for "trifling Annual Considerations" the Indians would allow squatters to remain on their land without regular grants.[222] It was said that because "most of the Irish live high and fall into debt, and the Dutch buy them out at any rate," the Scotch-Irish were forced to move to backcountry Virginia or Carolina to obtain land. If the colony were to retain its "English" inhabitants, an Indian purchase was essential.[223]

Some Pennsylvanians considered German settlers "a jealous & boisterous people" and preferred not to have them as tenants.[224] One man, who believed that Germans had unfairly obtained warrants for land he desired, declared that "the Earth with the Fullness thereof belongs to the Dutch; at least they think so."[225] Some people believed that the nature of German emigration by mid-century had changed for the worse, for "Those who came over for many years were religious sober industrious People; But of Late the Deserters from the Armies and the very scum of Germany throng into the Country," comments reminiscent of those made during the first period of large-scale migration.[226] There were also complaints that Germans had introduced the "pernicious Custom of shooting Guns" to celebrate the New Year. The assembly was asked to prohibit the practice and the obvious dangers that attended it.[227]

Despite such reservations, Germans continued to be considered desirable colonists. Merchants were especially interested in recruiting them, for the sale of their services was lucrative.[228] One man hoped to persuade an unsatisfactory tenant to "take ye worth of his Improvements from Some Industrious Dutchman who will be able to pay his Rent duly & lay up Money into ye Bargain"; the "Varlots" ought to be "turned off & Some honest Dutch families put on their Places" in order to increase profits for landlords.[229] John Pemberton noted that "the Numbers of Foreigners that went over last year [1749] has given the Proprietors of Land great expectations" of selling it at inflated prices,[230] while others argued that land must be purchased from the Indians to accommodate newcomers.[231] Furthermore, Germans were "the most laborious, and by much the best improvers in this Country, and particularly of Towns, by having so great a number of Tradesmen among them, who are the only People to draw Wealth to any places[.]" Hamilton doubted whether Carlisle, the Cumberland County seat, would "flourish under the management of the Irish," and thought its prospects would improve if the "Dutch" got a footing there.[232] But

Easton, which had settlers of both nationalities, presented problems to William Parsons, its manager. He had "much difficulty from the Impudence of the Irish and the Majority which the Dutch have in that County."[233] Perhaps this was because "The Dutch & Irish hate one another," although it was hoped "they will unite and form a good Society together."[234]

Economic success could blunt prejudice, but not always eradicate it. Some Englishmen thought that borough status should not be granted to York "whilst the Body of the People Consists of ye Lowest Sort of Germans unacquainted with Our Constitution & Laws," for elections might be as turbulent as those of Lancaster.[235] Yet a few years later this town, "chiefly inhabited with Germans," was flourishing to such an extent that fixed market days were necessary, if for no other reason than to "Stop the Germans from their beloved Practice of buying & selling on Sundays."[236]

The advantages that accrued to Pennsylvania through the immigration of "foreign Protestants" inspired other colonies to begin to compete for them, for the province's tolerant policies were beneficial. In 1742 some New Englanders became interested in recruiting Germans to settle in Maine. The Governor of Massachusetts, in a speech to the General Court intended to encourage the settlement of *"foreign Protestants"* on *"our Waste and uncultivated Lands,"* pointed to the example of Pennsylvania, which had *"by this Method within a few Years, most surprizingly increased and flourished beyond all other of his Majesty's Colonies in North-America."*[237] Later in the decade another Massachusetts governor suggested that laws which required "security to be given" by those who brought laborers to the colony might have "discouraged and prevented" the immigration of *"protestant foreigners,"* whom he considered necessary to improve the colony's economy.[238] A Massachusetts land speculator requested a Pennsylvania Quaker to inform immigrants that his colony had established four new towns where foreigners would be offered favorable terms of settlement.[239] Virginia also tried to recruit Pennsylvania Germans, and in 1754 advertised the quality of its unsettled frontier lands and the favorable terms on which they would be granted in the *Pennsylvania Gazette*. Germans would be "allowed all the indulgences of the act of toleration here."[240] The British government demonstrated considerable interest in settling

Germans in Nova Scotia, especially during the years between the War of the Austrian Succession and the Seven Years War.[241]

Visitors to the colony noted the value of aliens and the benefits of toleration. A French officer stated that the "flourishing Settlement" was the "Work of a single Person, by Religion a Quaker; a single Instance of what a private Person is capable of achieving, when seconded by the Government."[242] A traveler declared that the "Province has Increased more in its Inhabitants than Any of its Neighbours, Owing to the Number of German & Irish Passengers who Annually come here and Settle." Many "are now become People of extensive fortunes," he noted.[243] An early historian believed that "by importation of foreigners and other strangers in very great numbers" the colony "grows prodigiously," although he feared that "by their superior industry and frugality [they] may in time out the British people from the colony."[244]

The political and military difficulties Pennsylvanians faced between 1739 and 1755 illuminated the colony's latent ethnic and religious tensions. Although the period appears to have been one of continual strife among different segments of the population, there were two distinct periods, both times of crisis, in which the central concerns were different. The first period, 1739–1742, involved an essentially religious struggle over military activities, into which was interjected a sudden concern about German entrance into provincial politics. Both proprietary and Quaker factions expressed fears of unnaturalized voters and their ignorance or gullibility simultaneously with an intensive campaign to win the support of a previously inactive segment of the population. With the decisive Quaker victory in 1742, concern about Germans declined, only to be revived, principally by proprietary supporters, during the period of high immigration, 1749–1755. This time, members of the Philadelphia elite were concerned with the obvious numbers of newcomers and the possible loss of the "English" character of the colony.

Notwithstanding apprehensions about the potential power of the Germans, there were no serious efforts to limit immigration or to deflect it to other colonies. Instead, officials attempted to extend naturalization and property rights to aliens and took hesitant steps to improve the conditions under which they came to the province. If some Germans were attracted to other colonies, large numbers considered their reception in Pennsylvania and conditions there satisfactory. Despite occasional anti-German rhetoric, they continued to immigrate.

Except in brief moments of near hysteria stimulated by external circumstances such as war or a sudden flood of immigrants, most Pennsylvanians would probably have agreed with the assessments of two men who served as governor during this period. George Thomas, looking back on his decade in the colony, pointed to the "Industry & Frugality" of the Germans as "the principal Instruments of raising it to its present flourishing Condition, beyond any of His Majesty's Colonys in North America." He was unconcerned about any threat they might pose. They all took oaths of allegiance, and he thought they "are like to continue as true to His Majesty & as useful to the British Nation as any of His Majesty's Natural born Subjects. They fled from oppression, and after having tasted the sweets of a British Constitution it does not seem probable to me, that they will ever look back to their old Masters."[245] Pennsylvania-born James Hamilton, a less detached observer, once complained about "that unhappy Act of Parliament which invested them [Germans] with the rights of Englishmen before they knew how to use them." But he "acknowledge[d] them to be a most useful people in the settlements of a new Country, and I know there are good and bad of all Nations."[246]

CHAPTER 7

Wartime Disruption,
1755–1765

A decade of war between France and England stimulated frequent, sometimes severe, political discord among members of Pennsylvania's varied ethnic and religious groups. Tensions evident during earlier wars culminated in the crises brought about by Indian depredations on frontierspeople during the first sustained period of warfare in the colony's history, when the issue of self-defense lost its abstract character. Settlement patterns that concentrated Scotch-Irish Presbyterians and German "church" people along the frontier while pacifists concentrated in the more secure eastern portions of the province that had disproportionate representation in the assembly, added ethnic and religious factors to sectional and military problems. A fundamental alteration in the structure of political power occurred during this decade, while attempts to change the province's constitutional basis failed. Ethnic and religious considerations were taken into account both by those wishing to bring about change and by those hoping to preserve the status quo.

The political and military struggles demonstrate some of the problems that could arise due to disparate views of the propriety of warfare, yet this strife must not be exaggerated. Controversy was expressed primarily through the political system, and may not have affected the ordinary colonist to any great extent. Furthermore, conflict was episodic in nature rather than sustained, and tended to dissipate rapidly. Despite intermittent concern about "outsiders" of various sorts, there were few efforts to alter the policies that had resulted in the creation of a heterogeneous society. Pennsylvanians resolved their disputes largely within the framework of their society's unique nature. Colonists of disparate backgrounds and beliefs reached out to others with similar religious, social, or political views; unwilling to permit political and military problems to tear their province apart, they worked to unify factions to further common interests.

I

By 1753, there were indications that war would soon erupt in the region west of Pennsylvania as England and France resumed their rivalry over North America.[1] Although the 1753–1754 assembly was reluctant to appropriate money for military purposes or to raise troops for this still-undeclared war, assemblymen did not argue on the basis of religious principles, as had so often been the case, nor did Governor James Hamilton raise this issue. Rather, they focused on the phrasing of the letter from Whitehall warning of possible Indian threats and directing colonists to "repel Force by Force" if necessary, but cautioning that it was the King's "Determination not to be the Aggressor." The assembly discussed granting money for the King's use and to purchase the Indians' friendship at length, but the terms on which it insisted, funding the grant through the issuance of bills of credit, were unacceptable to the governor.[2]

The failure to grant money was not an issue about which most Pennsylvanians were concerned. Even proprietor Thomas Penn understood that colonists might be reluctant to assist in removing French settlements that lay beyond the boundaries of their province, or to pay for the defense of land granted to Virginia. While the "greatest People" in England thought that colonists "should contribute jointly towards their Defence, and not Let the whole lye on the Mother Country," Penn realized that "there are so many calls for Publick Money, that it is difficult to get any appropriated" for such purposes.[3]

Pennsylvanians were nevertheless concerned about organizing a mi-

litia and devising measures for local defense. The governor recommended providing weapons and ammunition to westerners willing to
defend themselves. The assembly also received a few petitions from
frontierspeople emphasizing their defenseless condition and requesting
a law to obligate all men able to defend themselves to do so. Pacifists
should be required to "contribute" in some way to the efforts of those
who were not. The assembly ignored these requests.[4]

With the outbreak of the French and Indian War, defense became a
primary issue in provincial politics. Because Quakers formed a majority in the assembly, proprietary supporters and imperial officials blamed
the sect for the colony's apparent lack of support for the war. Yet it
was not Friends who raised the religious issue; it was their opponents.
If Quakers used tactics and arguments that might have delayed military preparation, they were much more willing to defend the province
than they had been during earlier wars. By mid-century most assemblymen had reached a position similar to that of their English coreligionists, and at times expressed concern about Friends who held the
rigid scruples characteristic of the early years of Pennsylvania's history. Although determined to protect the interests of pacifists, assemblymen more clearly recognized the concerns of nonpacifists and their
right to act according to their own consciences. Some historians have
accepted the opposition argument that Quakers deliberately attempted
to subvert the war effort or to aggrandize power at the expense of
provincial security.[5] On the contrary, they were willing to act, although not always in the manner that men favoring defense preferred.
   During the 1754 election campaign, several essayists wrote newspaper articles debating the assembly's conduct during its previous session. One writer stressed the danger the French posed to the civil and
religious liberties of British subjects, and reminded readers of the persecution practiced by the Roman Catholic church. Because the French
were still relatively weak and had not yet completely alienated the
Indians from the British interest, the time to act was at hand.[6] An
advertisement that announced a public meeting to nominate a new
slate of candidates to represent Philadelphia City and County raised
the religious issue more directly. Asserting that "many" current delegates were "bound, from their religious Scruples, not to afford the

necessary Supplies this important and critical Conjuncture requires"
for defeating the colony's "inveterate Enemies," the advertiser hoped
that they could be replaced by men who would act to preserve "our
Country, Fortunes and Families."[7] But a rejoinder declared that the
assembly had indeed voted to appropriate money. The source of the
problem was the governor, who refused his assent to the bill.[8] Another writer "publickly declare[d]" that he was not *"for electing Men
whom we judge would be for passing a military Law,"* yet he clearly wanted
to see men *"who are not, by their Principles, against Defence"* elected.
Accusations that the opposition's goal was to establish a militia were
false, and intended simply as a *"Bugbear to intimidate the industrious*
Germans, *who have been oppress'd"* by military laws in their homelands.[9] Presbyterian ministers preached anti-Quaker sermons, but failed
to achieve effective political union because of its "Several Sects mostly
Dislikeing, if not hateing one another," a legacy of the Great Awakening schism.[10]

Despite the literary efforts expended in this campaign, most incumbents were reelected in what was described as a "quiet & orderly"
election.[11] A disappointed proprietary supporter claimed that "they
had all the Dutch to a Man occasioned by false insinuations," and
"even turn'd others of diff[t] denominations who thought a Change absolutely necessary."[12] Quakers were pleased with their continued
popular support, for despite "a vigorous Opposition" their adversaries
"fail[ed] to get in one single member" into the assembly.[13] The Philadelphia Quarterly Meeting considered it "remarkable" that during
"Time of Warr" pacifists were repeatedly elected by the nonpacifistic
majority. It attributed this to the Quaker assemblymen's "sincere &
ready Disposition to provide for the Exigencies of the Government"
in a manner "least burthensome to the industrious Poor, & most consistent with our religious & civil Rights & Liberties."[14] Contrary to
what proprietary supporters might think, assembly speaker Isaac Norris
remained confident that the assembly would "Generously" meet royal
demands if the precedents that allowed Friends to remain uninvolved
in the disposition of the funds were followed.[15]

A new governor, Robert Hunter Morris, arrived in the colony shortly
after the elections. Reiterating Hamilton's demand for financial support of military actions against the French, he urged assemblymen to

"exert yourselves at this critical Juncture" to defend the province.[16] While the assembly admitted that it shared his concern about potential danger, it declared that no royal instructions indicating "how to conduct ourselves on this important Occasion" had been received, and requested permission to adjourn until its "usual Time" for transacting business.[17] By the time the assembly reconvened in December, "express Commands" for defense had arrived.[18] Although "A Majority of the House being of our [Quaker] Society they could not (as they never at any time have) litterally compli'd with such a Demand, however as we are always willing to demonstrate our Allegiance to our King by a ready Compliance with his Instructions as far as they do not affect our religious Principles,"[19] the assembly promptly resolved to grant him £20,000. Bills of credit would be issued, and the sum defrayed by an extension of the excise tax for ten years.[20] These, however, were the same terms that had been offered to Hamilton, and once again were unacceptable. After a lengthy discussion, the assembly blamed proprietary instructions to the governor for the irresolvable deadlock. Members declared that "we shall cheerfully continue to grant such further Sums of Money for the King's Use, as the Circumstances of the Country may bear, and in a Manner we judge least burthensome to the Inhabitants of this Province,"[21] but added that "whatever ill Consequences ensue, from Supplies not having been granted at this critical Juncture, must lie at his [the governor's] Door."[22]

Morris called the assembly into a special session in March 1755, and demanded "Men, Provisions and Money" to support General Edward Braddock's expedition against the French. The assembly complied, appropriating £25,000 to the King's use, again in paper money.[23] When Morris refused his assent to the bill, the assembly granted £15,000 to purchase provisions and other supplies for Braddock and a Massachusetts expedition against Canada. Funds would be raised through the loan office.[24] Although Morris opposed the bills of credit "now circulating in this Province, without the Approbation of the Government," this expedient indicates the assembly's willingness to accede to royal commands.[25] When the assembly was reconvened to appropriate additional money for Braddock's campaign, delays recurred, again because of difficulties over the method of granting money. Morris finally accepted a grant funded through bills of credit. Religious scruples were not an issue in the assembly debates,[26] although the question of granting money for war under this pretext did arise at the September Yearly Meeting of Friends.[27]

The governor convened another special assembly session after news of Braddock's defeat reached Philadelphia in July, and demanded additional funds to support the British war effort. The assembly immediately began to discuss raising £50,000 by a general property tax. Assemblymen declared that the special session was "agreeable to us, as it impowers us to exert ourselves yet farther in the Service of our Country," but Morris categorically refused to accept the terms of the proposal, for proprietary estates would be taxed. Despite efforts to reach an accommodation on this point, the assembly's term expired before an agreement could be reached.[28] Morris blamed the "quaker preachers and other political Engines" for the design of the bill; "that it might not pass they put in a clause for taxing the unprofitable lands belonging to the proprietors[.]"[29]

Support for expeditions against the French during 1754–1755 lacked the immediacy of local defense. As the war intensified, backcountry settlers began, for the first time in the colony's history, to suffer attacks by hostile Indians. To them, if not to assemblymen safely ensconced in Philadelphia—representing, for the most part, people equally immune from danger—a militia was essential. Several petitions requesting arms, ammunition, or other means of protecting frontier inhabitants were dispatched to the assembly.[30] The most pressing demands came from Morris,[31] who also proposed that a bounty of land, free from quitrents for fifteen years, be given to volunteers for a British expedition against the French.[32] The assembly declared that it was willing to provide "Arms and Stores of War" and to build "Magazines," but remarked that the requisite money for these things had been blocked by the governor's refusal to enact the appropriation bill.[33]

Defense once again became an election issue because of the failure to devise satisfactory arrangements concerning taxation and a militia, as well as the "very great surprize & fears among many people" occasioned by Braddock's defeat.[34] Morris believed that the assembly's actions and "very long abusive Messages highly reflecting on the proprietarys" were "plainly Calculated to render them Odious" to Pennsylvanians.[35] In a message to the assembly shortly before the election, he accused it of taking "great Pains *to infuse into the Minds of the People, particularly the* Germans, that the Government have designs to abridge them of their Privileges, and to reduce them to a State of Slavery." Such intimations might cause the "Foreigners" to favor the French cause and become indifferent to English success.[36] The assembly indignantly denied these allegations, and distinguished between loyalty to the Crown and approbation of the proprietors and deputy governor. It was the latter from whom, for good reasons, the people were disaffected.[37] A Quaker declared that "the Inhabitants are almost Universally" in agreement with the assembly that, if a tax were necessary, the Penn family "ought to be liable to the same."[38]

The election debates were bitter. Defending Quakers as guardians of the colonists' civil and religious liberties, "Philadelphus" offered evidence of their willingness to raise money for the King's use when necessary. Other colonies had refused to grant money when their governors tried to dictate the terms; the Pennsylvania assembly was merely safeguarding a "fundamental Privilege" of Englishmen. Quaker representatives would fulfill the legitimate demands for security without destroying liberty or allowing the people to be "burthen'd with Military Laws."[39] A broadside warned Germans that defeat of the incumbents might lead to a severe reduction in their liberties. It implied that proprietary supporters sought to abolish the secret ballot and empower the governor to select sheriffs and coroners, dissolve the assembly, and organize a militia with officers of his own choice. Such a force could be used against the people rather than against their enemies. Proprietary supporters were accused of believing that "It is illogical and unreasonable to see a horde of ignorant, proud, stubborn, German boors have the right and sanction" to elect assemblymen.[40] Christopher Sauer, emphasizing their Protestant religious beliefs and love of the English regime, indignantly defended the Germans against charges of disaffection in a lengthy essay in his *Pensylvanische Berichte.* He advised Germans to select Quaker representatives, for they acted for the general welfare.[41]

Election results demonstrated that popular dissatisfaction with the previous assembly was minimal, for most incumbents were reelected. Lancaster County, "Composed of all Sorts of Presbyterians & Independents, of all Sorts of Germans, & Some Church of England Electors" with "Scarcely One Hundred" Friends in the county, selected four Quakers as representatives "without the least Solicitation" on the part of the candidates.[42] If Quakers returned to their positions "with some Reluctance,"[43] their mandate was clear. One Friend believed that "So long as the majority of the People were willing to choose us to represent them, our Refusal might be interpreted as being ashamed to Confess our Testimony before men & we should in some degree be answerable for the Inconveniences consequent thereon with respect to our Religious or Civil Liberties."[44]

Proprietary supporters were disturbed by their inability to convince the non-Quaker majority that Quaker assemblymen must be replaced. They accused Quakers of neglecting to provide for defense by raising specious disputes about "Money & privilege to evade the Question" and to "amuse" the colonists. Not only were they unable to participate in military measures, they were "determined never to suffer" them in the province. According to one hostile source, "some" Quakers "would sooner see the Enemy in the Heart of the Country" than provide for defense.[45] One Pennsylvanian attributed the Quaker victory to the support of "the Poor deluded Dutch & Welsh,"[46] while another blamed the "wicked Insinuation" that Germans might be "obliged sometime to plough the Lord Proprietor's Manors" if the incumbents were not reelected.[47]

As the hostilities of the French and the Indians against backcountry settlers increased in autumn 1755, one proprietary official expressed his fear that if effective measures were not taken, "all the people over Susquehannah, . . . chiefly Scotch-Irish, will be driven from their Habitations, & when they come down among the Germans & Quakers there will be next to a Civil War among them."[48] Backcountry leaders threatened that "If we are not *immediately* supported, we must not be sacrificed and therefore are determined to go down with those that will follow us to Philad[a] and quarter ourselves on it's Inhabitants, and wait our Fate with them."[49]

The new assembly managed to avert such threats. It considered several petitions for weapons, ammunition, or other supplies, and for the construction of forts and the formation of a militia. Most appeals simply stated the need, although one from relatively safe Chester County begged assemblymen to "not keep up unnecessary Disputes with the Governor, nor, by Reason of their religious Scruples, longer neglect the Defence of the Province."[50] The assembly initially declared that it had "taken every Step" in its power "consistent with the just Rights of the Freemen" of the colony to relieve the distressed inhabitants. "Those who would give up essential Liberty, to purchase a little temporary Safety, deserve neither Liberty nor Safety." It noted that money granted to the King had been used to provide weapons and ammunition for those willing to defend themselves but unable to purchase supplies. The assembly also reminded Morris that the royal charter granted him authority to raise troops; if he would enact the proposed bill to raise £60,000 he would have a sufficient fund to defray the expenses involved.[51]

Nevertheless, when assemblyman Benjamin Franklin presented the draft of a militia bill, it was approved with alacrity and only four dissenting votes. The law recognized that the first settlers and most assemblymen were Quakers. To compel inhabitants to bear arms would violate the "charter of privileges" and subject Friends to "persecution," while to exempt Quakers would be "inconsistent and partial." But, the assembly observed, the "general toleration and equity of our laws" had induced people of "other religious denominations" who "conscientiously think it their duty to fight in defense" of their country and families to settle in the colony. Since nonpacifists had "an equal right to liberty of conscience with others," Pennsylvania created a voluntary militia that anyone but indentured servants and apprentices could join, but compelled no one to enlist. Volunteers were given the privilege of selecting their own officers, who would then be commissioned by the governor. Military discipline was based on English laws pertaining to mutiny and desertion.[52]

Franklin composed a dialogue intended to generate support for the militia and to counteract possible objections to its structure. He reminded readers of the 1747 association, in which men had voluntarily joined together and selected their officers. It would not be difficult to do so again; this time the body would be legal. A more serious issue was that "Quakers are neither compelled to muster, nor to pay a Fine if they don't." Franklin responded with a lengthy appeal to the provincial charter to silence that argument. Furthermore, wealthy Quakers and Mennonites would pay a large proportion of the taxes to finance the war. To the objection that nonpacifists could refuse to join the militia, Franklin's mouthpiece replied that "Cowards" were undesirable. Troops would be more effective if only those who wished to serve enlisted. When a participant in the conversation declared "For my Part, I am no Coward; but hang me if I'll fight to save the Quakers," he was silenced by the rejoinder "That is to say, you won't pump Ship, because 'twill save the Rats, as well as yourself." The essay concluded with a plea to forget party differences and to unite in service to the King.[53]

Proprietary supporters considered the law unsatisfactory. William Allen complained about the election of officers and the extension of British military discipline. The structure of Pennsylvania society made such provisions dangerous, for "the greatest number of the back Inhabitants are neither acquainted with our Laws, or Even Language, what work will they make, when one of those Boors has it in his Power to Punish Mellancholly indeed is our Situation."[54] In dispatching a copy of the militia act to the Penn family, Morris described it as "a most curious" as well as useless law.[55] Because British officials objected that the statute was not compulsory and did not require those conscientiously opposed to bearing arms to either find a substitute or contribute a monetary equivalent, it was repealed.[56]

At this same assembly session debates over a grant of money for military purposes recurred. An appropriation of £60,000 to the King was voted, but to be raised by a tax on all real and personal estates, including proprietary lands. The governor again found the proposal unacceptable, and lengthy arguments on constitutional grounds reached an impasse.[57] However, a letter from the Penn family offering a gift of £5000 provided grounds for compromise. The assembly accepted this as its share of the property tax, and agreed to exempt proprietary land.[58] A further inducement to accommodation was the arrival of several irate Germans who demanded protection. They brought with them "three Bodies Scalped, & other ways barbarously, & inhumanly treated" in order to "convince our Obstinate & Cruel Quakers" that the province was in danger.[59] According to one proprietary supporter, "About 300 Dutch having come to Town the Day after the Gift was made public went away to a Man on your Side, & made the Assembly promise them Relief."[60]

[handwritten margin note: 1754 rumors — Brit will force Pa to meet def. requirements loss charter?]

While the Quaker-dominated assembly struggled to fulfill demands for funds and to organize a militia on terms it believed constitutional, equitable, and acceptable to colonists professing a variety of religious beliefs, forces in England and within a small circle of provincial proprietary supporters were taking steps to remove Quakers from positions of power. In the analysis of John Fothergill, a London Friend, "There are two sets of people" who opposed the Pennsylvanians' choice of representatives. One was composed of "some very active and powerful people near the head of plantation affairs, who would be very glad to crush every appearance of liberty abroad; and are pleased that in a country like yours, so favourable a pretext is offering it self to make you an example." Presbyterians made up the other faction. "No disagreeable circumstance happens, but it is immediately sent to the party here," who used it as a means to "irritate those in power here, as to induce them to exclude us altogether from legislation."[61] Despite the mixed success of the opposition, it must be emphasized that Quakers never lost the favor of the electorate. However obstructionist their actions might have appeared to outsiders, Pennsylvanians remained satisfied with their leadership and policies, and consistently reelected Friends willing to serve in the assembly.

In June 1754 Thomas Penn hinted to Governor Hamilton that he thought it "not possible people possessed of the principles the major part of the Assembly profess, will long be permitted to sit in the House."[62] By the end of the year, rumors circulated that British authorities were preparing to force Pennsylvanians into compliance with the defensive needs of the Empire. Governor Morris believed that Quakers should be excluded from the assembly by act of Parliament,[63] while former Governor George Thomas agreed that "A Quaker Government was never calculated to resist Invasions." He feared the colony's situation would become "desperate" before "Power will be taken out of their hands," by which time it would be too late to preserve the colony.[64] Friends, who feared the "Destruction of that Charter" which guaranteed their rights, marshalled the support of the London Meeting for Sufferings, while the assembly urged its London agents to vindicate its behavior.[65]

The catalyst for serious thought about restricting participation in provincial affairs appears to have been the *Brief State of the Province of*

Pennsylvania, an anti-Quaker, anti-German diatribe penned by William Smith in 1754 and published in London early in 1755. Smith admitted that in the early years of the colony's history, Quakers, who formed the majority and therefore deserved to rule, had conducted official affairs with "Mildness and Prudence." They had not "as yet conceived any Thoughts of turning *Religion* into a *Political Scheme for Power.*" But their successors, "quite a different Sort of Men from the Founders of this Province," did everything in their power to maintain themselves in office. They entered into "Cabals" at their Yearly Meeting in order to mask political intrigues under the cloak of religion. Despite the colony's defenseless condition, which he described at some length, Quakers absolutely refused to provide for its security. The minority imposed its views on the province by threatening Germans that the opposition faction designed to enslave them and would exact heavy taxes. Through printer Christopher Sauer, they had alienated the affections of the Germans from the British government. Furthermore, the "insolent, sullen, and turbulent" Germans cared only for property, and would support the French if promised land. The "evil Genius of the *Quakers*" perverted them; if they could be so "misled by the Arts of a *Quaker* Preacher," they might also be influenced by "a lurking *French* Priest." In any case, *"Papists"* were given "extraordinary Indulgence and Privileges" in the colony. Smith's solutions were to severely restrict the use of the German language, forbid men unfamiliar with the English language and provincial constitution from voting, and, most significantly, require assemblymen to take an oath of allegiance and perhaps to swear that they would defend the country. He concluded by imploring English intervention into provincial affairs, as there was no possibility that reform could come from within the colony itself.[66]

Thomas Penn considered the contents of the pamphlet "proper enough," but thought its "Language" was "too violent." Although Morris had sent him a copy of the essay in late 1754, he denied any involvement in its publication, for "there are things in it especially relating to the Germans that I apprehend not fact, and I am sure whatever People may think of their dispositions in general, it is the greatest folly in the world to give just cause of offence to so great a body of People, and indeed I think they are very ill treated in it."[67]

English Friends believed that the tract had been all too effective. Henton Brown declared that the "Scandalous pamphlet" had "poison'd the minds of many" and so successfully "rais'd a general outcry" against the province that "A parliamentary enquiry must ensue." Although Brown had managed to "remove the prejudices" in the minds of some members of Parliament "& to Cause a Suspension of their Judgment till farther Light Appear'd," Pennsylvanians ought to send a delegation to London, or at least frame a reply, in an issue as important as their "Constitution."[68]

Pennsylvania Friends were disturbed by the tract, although they underestimated its influence in England and failed to draft a response,[69] perhaps because the assembly's agent reported that "the Resentment by people of the first Rank here against you does now pretty much subside[.]"[70] Isaac Norris considered it "truly Amazeing how Unanimously the falsehoods, the misrepresentations, and the whole tenor of that Notable Performance, is Abhorred here, by all Ranks of People, but it was not designed for this Climate." The colony had a "large Voluntary Militia," the type of force the colonists preferred, while other colonies lacked fortifications and only grudgingly appropriated funds for military campaigns.[71] Another Quaker reported that it "justly alarmed" many people to "find we have some among us so desperately bent on depriving us of our Liberties." Most of the material in the pamphlet was "absolutely false or basely misrepresented"; he thought it tended to "Unite instead of dividing" the colonists.[72]

Proprietary supporters, unable to muster an effective opposition to Quaker politicians at the polls, sent a barrage of inflammatory letters to England and to royal officials in other colonies intended to convince readers that Quakers ought not to sit in the assembly during war. One official feared that the French, "finding that our Quakers will not defend the Country seem to be about to take possession of this province, which they will inevitably do" if aid from England were not forthcoming.[73] The assembly did everything possible to render the English administration "odious" and "to set the great Body of Germans in this Province against the Government under which they live," which would make them receptive to French enticements.[74] Others argued that Quakers took "uncommon pains" to "disuade" people from taking up arms.[75] Thomas Willing cynically described appeals to "our hard hearted

Assembly, but all the return is *Trust in the Lord* who will most certainly Damn them for the Blood they have spilt, by keeping the province in so defenceless a state."[76]

Following the 1755 elections, proprietary supporters drafted a petition to the King for relief from the "Mislead Tyrants" who governed them. The "naked & defenceless State" of the province, and its precarious military situation in consequence of the "continual Inroads of a merciless Enemy," were emphasized.[77] A letter to the colony's London agent argued that Parliament should "restrain our Quakers & Germans from sitting in the House of Assembly, & the latter from even voting, till they know our Language and are better acquainted with our Constitution[.]" Germans were "so poysoned" by "false Stories" propagated by Quakers that there was little hope that they would ever support defense. The petitioners were confident that "can the parliam^t hear of our miserys and see the Risque the Province is in . . . they must disquallifie any man from Legislation who is principled against Defence."[78] Penn noted that English Friends did not "approve of the behaviour of their brethren in the Assembly," but desired the issue to be settled "amicably." Nevertheless, "the petitions must be heard, and I shal never agree to an accommodation but on propper conditions."[79]

Despite the probability that news of the assembly's actions on taxation and a militia had been received, by early 1756 support was growing in England for intervention. Thomas Penn informed a correspondent that he was "using my best endeavours to procure the assistance requested by the petitioners to the King," as were his agent and Samuel Chandler, an influential Presbyterian cleric. Once the petitions had been presented, he reported wide sympathy to the anti-Quaker cause.[80] Henton Brown believed that earlier passage of the militia act might have prevented the "great mischief" he feared would lead to a "parliamentary enquiry." The "temper and spirit which appears at present to prevail in general against us gives reason to apprehend it will conclude in an alteration of your present constitution by fixing some test which will exclude our friends from the Assembly &c,"[81] precisely what proprietary supporters intended.

The Board of Trade held a lengthy meeting with solicitors for both factions in February 1756; the following month it "made a strong Report against the Quakers sitting in the Assembly," and began to consider "some Test" to "prevent" them from doing so.[82] The Board believed that the provincial charter required the colony to defend itself. Measures taken by the assembly, at this time and in the past, were plainly inadequate. Moreover, members concluded that there was "no Reason" to believe that "proper or effectual Measures" would be taken while the majority of the assemblymen were pacifists. Furthermore, "contrary to the Principles, the Policy and the Practice of the Mother Country, [Quakers were] admitted to hold Offices of Trust and Profit, and sit in the Assembly, without their Allegiance being secured to the Government by the Sanction of an Oath."[83]

The Board was dissuaded from pressing for an oath of allegiance, but only because English Quakers promised that their Pennsylvania brethren would refuse to stand as candidates in the next election. Thomas Penn opposed this arrangement, thinking it "improbable, that the present Members, and the greatest politicians among the Quakers, will regard the injuction" of the London Friends.[84] A bill was drafted to exclude Quakers from the assembly, but the Earl of Halifax temporarily prevented its introduction. However, if Pennsylvanians refused to abide by the agreement made by London Friends, it would be proposed in Parliament the following year.[85]

London Quakers stressed that accounts sent by the opposition, never effectually "denied or refuted" by the assembly, were a significant factor in the actions taken by English officials. The assembly and the Society of Friends had been, inaccurately, equated. Only "a very few moderate persons," including, fortunately, "some of them in very high stations," were willing to effect a compromise. Although Londoners did not think it a "matter of so much importance" that Quakers sit in the assembly as long as their religious and civil liberties were protected, it was important that the "pretext" of their inability to fulfill one function not be used to obscure their valuable services in other aspects of government such as the magistracy. In an effort to prevent "some signal marks of disapprobation, and rivetting upon us as it were by act of Parliament the calumnys w[ch] your and our adversarys have broached," English Friends "stand bound for your good behaviour," that is, a refusal of reelection so that non-Quakers would compose a majority in the assembly.[86] An epistle to Philadelphia Friends informed them of the agreement, while a delegation was sent to exercise more direct persuasion.[87]

When news of the agreement reached the colony, six Quaker assemblymen promptly resigned their seats.[88] Yet many of their opponents were dissatisfied with any solution short of expulsion or outright exclusion, and the assembly's speaker, a Quaker who did not resign, was forced to issue writs for a new election because of the provincial secretary's "Neglect or Refusal" to do so. He queried, "is it not Strange Conduct that our Govr Should So Violently endeavour to dispossess ye Quakers of their Seats in Assembly & yet refuse his Assent to their Voluntary Resignation." He concluded that because their opponents had stressed the tenacious hold Quakers had on power and the "Strategem[s]" they used to gain it, "Such Resignations, must Confute with great force" their arguments.[89] Richard Peters thought that the replacements "will be just such as the Quakers & Mr Franklin please to recommend," a prospect he blamed on the strange reluctance of William Allen and other proprietary leaders to intervene in the special election. He hoped that Allen could be "perswaded to try for ye Election of moderate & reputable Members."[90]

Individuals not immediately involved in the dispute reacted with equanimity to the alteration in the assembly's membership. One merchant was pleased by the resignations and by the decisions of some magistrates to resign their commissions. A "happy Presage" of "better Times & management for the future," it was "a good Sign of better Conduct" of provincial affairs "for the future."[91] A Quaker commented that withdrawal from public office was widely approved within the Society, and that "to be active in choosing Others or in any Manner of expressing our Approbation of the measures lately pursu'd by our Brethren" would "directly contradict the Judgment of the most weighty experienc'd Friends amongst us."[92]

While the *Pennsylvania Gazette* laconically announced the resignation of the six members in June,[93] the *Pennsylvania Journal* printed a long essay publicizing some of the details of the English agreement. The writer was "sorry to acquaint you, that the Honest endeavours of the present Assembly to preserve the Liberties of their Countrymen have been so basely represented at Home, by a Set of Men whose principal

Aim seems to me to be nothing less than engrossing the sole Power of our Properties and Persons."[94] The *Pensylvanische Berichte* editorialized, "They know that they are only a hindrance in the house, when during this time of war they must undertake or legislate things that are contrary to their consciences; they should and will leave it to those who are capable of serving during wartime." Voters were given advice very similar to that previously given advocating the election of Quakers: "the wise will consider and recognize such men in the city, and will vote for none who do not know, or do not wish to know, what it is to be a needy, poor countryman when he pays heavy taxes and bears heavy burdens."[95]

By September, Peters noted that neither Quakers nor the proprietary party planned to be involved in the election, leaving the "Anti Proprietary party" under Franklin to "reign sole Arbiters" of a contest that he assumed would result in a new assembly composed of the "hot headed of all Denominations."[96] Some proprietary officials, uncertain about the Quaker response to the upcoming elections, delayed settling their ticket until the outcome of the Yearly Meeting was known.[97] Quakers allegedly worked for the election of "moderate Churchmen," in Peters' judgment "to shew the Ministry that it is not the Society of Quakers but the Proprietary Instructions yᵗ obstruct the King's Business."[98] Governor Morris thought Quaker activity contrary to the agreement made by English Friends.[99] In any case, the *Pennsylvania Gazette* announced that *"there are Sixteen of the People called Quakers, and that the Remainder are of the Church of England, and other Denominations"* in the new assembly.[100] English Friends who arrived immediately after the election persuaded four of the newly elected Quaker delegates to refuse to take their seats.[101] After these seats were filled by a new election, the assembly no longer had a Quaker majority.

The success of the English Quakers generally met with approval, although some Pennsylvanians wished that their passage had been speedier. At least one Quaker believed that the inconsistent behavior of Friends, many choosing not to run while others were candidates or were otherwise active in the campaigns, resulted from incomplete guidance from London. The emissaries could have been of greater service had they arrived prior to the election.[102]

II

Despite the compromise, for some time after 1756 the Pennsylvania assembly was perceived as being "Quaker," and political controversy often focused on the disparate views of Friends—and their supporters—and other components of provincial society. Friends were accused of using the "most unweened artfull endeavours" to be elected or to secure the election of men "under their immediate influence."[103] A London newspaper reported that in the new, 1756–1757 assembly, "there sits fourteen Quakers, and four Fifths of the rest their avowed Creatures" who would continue to obstruct military measures.[104] Early in 1758 William Allen complained that "Our Assembly is still chiefly composed of Quakers, and some low people, chosen by their Influence."[105] Another Presbyterian was convinced that Quakers formed a "disciplined regim'" able to secure the election of antiproprietary, pacifistic men. Potentially powerful segments of the population were too divided among themselves to effectively oppose them.[106] Indeed, as wartime demands diminished in the early 1760s, Quakers took a more active role in politics, while colonists indicated their approbation of Quaker policies by selecting them as representatives. To the dismay of some prominent Quakers, Friends composed majorities in 1761 and 1762, and formed a large contingent in 1763.[107]

The belief that Quakers had made only a show of relinquishing power was based primarily on their continuing pressure on the assembly on two issues of religious concern, the formation of a militia and taxation to support warfare. At the 1755 Yearly Meeting the question of war taxes had been raised, but only briefly discussed. In some confusion, one Friend wrote to another asking for a clearer distinction in the principles involved. William Foster thought that there had been war at the time that Christ told His followers that tribute should be rendered to Caesar. He did not understand the difference between paying taxes to Caesar and to the King, or why Friends should object to fulfilling the obligations required of all members of society.[108] When the assembly disregarded a Quaker petition opposing a grant of money to the King in November 1755, some Friends decided to disobey the law it enacted. They would suffer distraint rather than voluntarily pay the tax. Despite divided opinion, a circular letter was written to

Friends on the general subject of war and taxation. Although few Pennsylvanians supported the decision to refuse to pay taxes, this action disturbed the proprietors, British officials, and London Friends, who believed their brethren were taking an unwise, unjustified step.[109]

Following the repeal of the 1755 militia law and the more acute need for defense, the question of creating a provincial militia again arose. Quakers were singled out as obstructionists to the framing of a proper statute. While laws authorizing the governor to raise, regulate, and pay troops were enacted in most years between 1756 and 1764, the assembly consistently refused to enact compulsory laws or statutes requiring a compensatory payment from nonparticipants, although it once briefly considered imposing fines on them. Nor would it define precisely who might be exempt from service. It also insisted on allowing the men to select their own officers.[110]

Governor Morris' declaration of war against the Indians in April 1756 set the stage for active Quaker involvement in Indian affairs.[111] Their unofficial work through a private society, the Friendly Association for Regaining and Preserving Peace with the Indians by Pacific Measures, was widely regarded as meddling in governmental affairs in an attempt to retain influence or power. Furthermore, many suspected that Quakers were more concerned about the Indians than about their white victims.

The Friendly Association appealed to non-Quakers as contributors and members, although each trustee was to be "a Member in Unity" with the Society of Friends.[112] Outside support came primarily from Schwenkfelders, who shared with Quakers a desire to defend themselves against charges that they were unwilling to "bear their due share of the common burdens" and therefore dedicated themselves to restoring peace with the Indians.[113] Because Christopher Sauer, who offered to publicize the plan among the Germans, considered Mennonites the "most able and willing to contribute to such a purpose," the Friendly Association subsequently appealed to Mennonite leaders.[114] Charles Thomson, a Presbyterian who taught at a Quaker school in Philadelphia, was also involved in the Association's affairs and Indian negotiations.[115]

Morris was "highly displeased" by the Indians' willingness to discuss their grievances with Friends who appeared at a conference in Easton in July 1756. When one Indian referred Morris to Israel Pemberton for "some particulars," the governor ordered him to inform Pemberton, and through him the other Quakers, that he would consider them the King's enemies if they discussed official matters with the Indians. Quakers were indignant that Moravians were "allowed to entertain such Indians as they please, and to have full Liberty of conversing with them, tho' the Quakers in this Arbitrary Manner are forbid at the Time the Governor knew they came solely to promote and assist in the restoring Peace[.]"[116]

Despite their anger, Friends generously combined their gifts for the Indians with the "shamefully small" provincial ones. Peters assured Penn that if the Quakers had not cooperated by adding their "large Present" to the assembly's gift, "We shoud have been ruined, the Indians woud have gone away dissatisfied, and the matters made infinitely worse."[117] Nevertheless, he subsequently complained that the Friendly Association "are mighty fond of the Word Mediation and say they never meddle with Govern^t nor Govern^t matters, but whatever is necessary to give a weight to their Mediation they will do, and let me add, . . . they publickly declare the[y] cannot trust the Propriet^r nor their Officers who to their knowledge have abused the Indians." He thought they would "mould, fashion, turn twist and manage matters at the ensuing Treaty as they please."[118] One Pennsylvanian commented that "Our broad brim's Politicians have made a sort of Peace with the Indians at Easton, a part of whom are now & were during the Treaty Scalping in the same County; they are sad dirty Scoundrels; dont think I mean the Indians."[119]

Penn complained of the Quakers' involvement "as a distinct body of People" in the Easton Treaty, and reported the dissatisfaction of British officials that private individuals "presume to Treat with foreign Princes." He ordered Governor William Denny to prohibit Quakers, and others, from attending subsequent treaty negotiations.[120] Nevertheless, a large contingent of Quakers appeared at a 1757 conference in Lancaster with a gift "which it is said, they design to present to the Indians in their names separately."[121] When Denny relayed Penn's directions regarding Indian affairs to the Friendly Association prior to a second conference in Easton in 1757, Friends tried in vain to convince him that their interests were solely in furthering peace.[122] Despite the governor's opposition, Quakers attended the conference and discussed the Indians' grievances with them. While Denny termed the negotiations a "struggle" due to the "many Obstructions raised by a Certain set of People,"[123] Penn was pleased with the peace treaty despite the "unjust, base, and cruel" conduct of the Friends.[124]

Quakers repeatedly defended themselves against the "ill Natured warm Spirits, who cannot bear to see that Friends should have any part of the Reputation of making a Peace."[125] The Meeting for Sufferings transmitted information to London Friends "in Order to obviate the Prejudices of our Adversaries" who "industriously propagated" many "gross Misrepresentations" of their activities.[126] The Friendly Association sent materials to Penn that did help to make their conduct appear justifiable, although he continued to question their motives and activities.[127] Many Pennsylvanians, however, remained convinced Quakers were manipulating the Indians for their own ends.[128]

Pontiac's Rebellion intersected with the continuing Quaker political participation and suspicions about their relations with the Indians to transform what might have been simply a sectional controversy into a conflict that emphasized religious and ethnic antagonisms in this culturally diverse province. The bitterness and frustration of frontierspeople exploded in December 1763 when a mob of men from the vicinity of Paxton in Lancaster County descended on a long-established settlement of Christianized Indians and killed all they found. When the remnants of the community were transferred to the Lancaster jail in order to better protect them, another mob stormed the building and murdered them. The Paxton Affair culminated with a march on Philadelphia in February 1764 by frontiersmen who demanded effective protection.[129] Unlike the 1755 German march on the city, which aroused little comment, this episode was discussed and debated well into 1765. It reveals that, although Pennsylvanians normally overlooked potentially divisive differences in religious philosophy or national origins, not all colonists were without prejudices that could be brought to the surface, or exploited, by extreme situations.

Pennsylvanians of all faiths initially condemned the attack. Until the march on Philadelphia the perpetrators were simply called "Banditti," "wild Men," a "Lawless Party of Rioters," "a Riotous Wicked Com^y of Men," or similar epithets that usually did not reflect ethnic or religious traits.[130] Although several discussions of the entire series of events that were penned following the march also dealt in generalities about lawless mobs,[131] the threat to Philadelphians and the defensive measures taken against the frontiersmen triggered a paper war that focused on the divisions within society.

Warning of an expedition against Indians then in Philadelphia came first from Presbyterian minister John Elder, who added that "the minds of the Inhabitants are so exasperated against the Quakers . . . for the Singular Regard they have always shown to Savages."[132] The assembly swiftly enacted a riot act,[133] and Philadelphians were called together and requested to join in defense of the city. When the marchers reached Germantown a delegation of assemblymen, provincial councillors, and a Swedish Lutheran minister convinced them to present their complaints in writing and return home. The Indians were temporarily moved from the province under a guard of British troops to prevent further violence.[134]

As the German Lutheran minister Henry Melchior Muhlenberg phrased the aftermath of the march, "Since the militant backwoodsmen have departed, a continual paper war has been going on with printed pieces in English and German flying back and forth, and this is making the factions even more bitter."[135] Discussion of the Paxton march and the murder of the Indians was conducted primarily in religious terms. Unlike earlier disputes over defense, the major opponents were Quakers and Presbyterians.

The "official" Quaker view, expressed in a letter from the Philadelphia Meeting for Sufferings to the London Meeting for Sufferings, stated that "It may be necessary to observe that the Rioters were mostly Presbyterians from the north of Ireland and their Descendants." Although the Meeting thought that the number of marchers had been exaggerated and that there were only two or three hundred men involved, it "observe[d] with Sorrow that their wicked Intentions were approv'd by great Numbers of that Society, and some others throughout the Province."[136] In private letters and anonymous pamphlets

Friends and their supporters were less restrained. A Quaker woman dated a letter "The morning the Presbyt^{ns} came to Germant^n intending to murder the Indians."[137] Quakers detected a revival of "The old Envious presecuting Spirit of [the] last century" and expressed fears of the growth of Presbyterianism in frontier regions throughout the colonies. At the same time that Presbyterians appointed missionaries to convert the Indians, they "now plead the Authority of the Scripture for extirpating them & murder^g Such who have lived in ye profession of the Xtian Religion many years."[138] Another noted that "none were concern'd but Scotch Irish Presbyterians," and that "all orders of People" in Philadelphia "Shewd a steady resolution except the Presbyterians, (even some of them)" to defend the city.[139] Pamphlets recalled the persecution Friends had experienced from Calvinists in seventeenth-century New England, and strongly implied that Presbyterians favored persecuting individuals outside of their faith. One pamphleteer argued that throughout history *"Presbyterianism* and *Rebellion,* were twin-Sisters, sprung from Faction, and their Affection for each other, has been ever so strong, that a separation of them never could be effected." Reminding readers of the English Civil War, he termed them "Oliverians."[140]

Frontierspeople, for their part, blamed Quakers for the province's defenseless condition. When assistance had been requested from the government, the "Quaker" assembly "made light of our Sufferings, ~~saying that they were only some Scotch-Irish Presbyterians that were scalped,~~" and refused to adopt military measures on the grounds of conscience. Quakers were accused of liberally contributing to the "Savages" through the Friendly Association, and at the same time refusing to help the victims of their wrath.[141] One piece of doggerel stated this theme quite clearly:

> Go on good Christians, never spare
>   To give your Indians Clothes to wear;
> Send 'em good Beef, and Pork and Bread,
> Guns, Powder, Flints and store of Lead,
> To Shoot your Neighbours through the Head;
>   .   .   .
>
> Encourage ev'ry Friendly Savage,
> To murder, burn, destroy and ravage;
>   .   .   .

> Of Scotch and Irish let them kill
> As many Thousands as they will,
> That you may lord it o'er the Land,
> And have the whole and sole command.
>   Leave back inhabitants to starve,
> No love, no Pity they deserve;
> Let Orphan's Tears, and Widow's Cries,
> Implore in vain your Ears and Eyes;
> Pass ruthless by, enjoy their Groans,
> And force 'em to make Bread of Stones.[142]

Presbyterians and others, amazed that "Quakers took up arms in Philad[a] & made their Meet,g House a Place of Rendezvous," exploited this theme to the considerable embarrassment of the sect.[143] A cartoon depicted Quakers shouldering guns and preparing to shoot a cannon at a small group of fontiersmen. The caption explained,

> When Dangers threaten tis mere Nonsense
> To talk of such a thing as Conscience
> To Arms to Arms with one Accord
> The Sword of Quakers and the Lord
> Fill Bumpers then of Rum or Arrack
> We'll drink Success to the new Barrack.[144]

One writer concluded that "it is evident from the late Conduct of *Friends*, that the *Peaceable Testimony* which they have so long born to the World, at the Expence of the Lives and Properties of Thousands of their Fellow Subjects, is now no more—and that they have no more Scruples against taking up Arms, and Fighting than any others—Nay, that they can go into more Violent Measures to *Resist Evil* than perhaps were ever heard of in the most Warlike Nations."[145]

Germans tended to be uninvolved in both the march on the city and its defense. Their countrypeople on the frontier had suffered from Indian attacks, and many believed that the "Bethlehem Indians" then in Philadelphia had participated in the murders of backcountry inhabitants. They therefore did not volunteer to "wage war against their own suffering fellow citizens for the sake of the Quakers and Herrnhuters and their creatures or instruments, the double-dealing Indians."

Muhlenberg heard rumors that the governor thought "perhaps the

Germans might be making common cause with the malcontents or so-called rebels, etc."[146] To obviate such suspicions, a German Lutheran pastor and a Swedish Lutheran priest urged Germans who had "stood idly in the market place" when the alarm was given to take up arms to defend Philadelphia. Because of rumors that many Germans were among the Paxtonians, a Lutheran pastor went to Germantown to advise the elders of the Lutheran congregation not to join the "rebels." Paulus Brycelius, however, discovered "very few Germans" among the marchers. He considered as reasonable the Paxtonians' demands—protection and the expulsion of the "Moravian" Indians, for whose safety they offered a £10,000 bond. Nor was their behavior disorderly, for they listened to his advice not to try to enter the city in order to prevent a "great and horrible blood-bath."[147] Quakers declared that "it may be said to the Reputation of the Germans, they refused to join" in the "tumultuous Proceedings."[148]

Ethnic rifts might have widened if Germans had actively supported the Scotch-Irish. While Presbyterian William Allen was disturbed that provincial laws had been "trampled on with impunity" by the Paxton men, he was more concerned about the threat posed by the uninvolved Germans: "of all things I think a Dutch Mob the most dangerous. The Presbyterians are some of them wild and impatient under real or even imaginary injury. but by temper and prudence they may be brought to see their mistakes. If the Germans grow Seditious, and should rise up in numbers, it will be difficult to restrain their rage."[149] A Quaker stated that the Paxtonians were "principally of Irish Extraction,"[150] and a few of the pamphlets published about the episode mocked the dialect of the Scotch-Irish.[151] From the other side, an apologist for the marchers claimed that the men were "a selected Band of Gentlemen, Descendents of the Noble Eniskillers, who were the great Means of setting that great and never to be forgotten Prince King William on the Throne."[152] Such comments about the ethnic background of the men were minor in comparison with the emphasis given to their religious affiliation.

The Franklin-inspired campaign to transform Pennsylvania into a royal colony further exacerbated tensions among different segments of society, as politicians on both sides exploited ethnic and religious divisions. Central issues included defense and preservation of the religious liberties guaranteed by William Penn's frame of government.[153]

The agitation for royal government was popularly viewed as a Quaker idea. Some frontierspeople believed that it was intended solely as a means of depriving them of the protection they legitimately deserved. Since it could not be achieved rapidly, they feared that during the interregnum all provision of or responsibility for defense would dissolve.[154] Many nonfrontierspeople agreed that it was an "expedient to raise a Noise loud enough to drown" the clamors for protection, or considered it an "artifice" that would have only negative effects on "liberty & security of property."[155] Some German sectarians feared that the religious freedom for which they had emigrated to Pennsylvania would be abridged by a change of government. Christopher Schultz, a Schwenkfelder, was especially concerned about the possibility of being "subjected to Episcopal Jurisdiction and Military Actions," since among sectarians opposing oaths and war only Quakers and Moravians were protected by English laws.[156]

Most petitions supporting the change came from Friends in and near Philadelphia, while counter-petitions came primarily from outlying areas and from non-Quakers.[157] William Peters, a proprietary supporter, informed Thomas Penn that "almost every Individual of yᵉ Quakers appear to be your avowed inveterate Enemies & are most industrious in promoting the Petitions" advocating change. He noted that "They have got them sign'd by some of the Church People (tho' chiefly of yᵉ meanest sort) but I believe few or none of the Presbyterian thro' yᵉ whole Province have join'd them."[158] Nevertheless numerous Quakers feared for their religious liberties under a royal government, and opposed or only reluctantly supported the plan to alter the frame of government. They believed that British officials thought "Dessantors are farr too numerous in all the Plantations & want to ballance their strength by the Church." There was some sentiment that Franklin, the promoter of the scheme, was "att Bottom an Enemy" to the sect.[159]

Franklin's *Cool Thoughts on the Present Situation of Our Public Affairs* was intended to promote support for the proposed change. He argued that the present government was unable to preserve the peace, and cited its inability to bring the murderers of the Conestoga Indians to justice or to prevent mob action. Claiming that "Religion has happily nothing to do with our present Differences," he blamed the proprietors for the weakness of the government and argued that civil and religious liberties would be better preserved under a royal than a proprietary government.[160] George Bryan thought the essay "very artful, but Superficial,"[161] and at least on religious grounds it was. Franklin told a correspondent that he could not "conceive the Number of bitter Enemies that little Piece has rais'd me among the Irish Presbyterians."[162] To his chagrin, the proprietary party was "endeavouring to stir up the Presbyterians to join in a Petition against a Change of Government."[163]

Franklin's initiative, launched in the midst of the recriminations over the Paxton episode, set the stage for an acrimonious election that exploited ethnic and religious factors and resulted in some realignment in voting patterns. William Peters believed that if Anglicans and Presbyterians formed a coalition, "a considerable Change" might be made in the assembly that would "set every thing right in the Province."[164] Richard Penn II felt that, if all of the "obnoxious Member[s]" were removed from the assembly, the "peace & Harmony" that "all Parties (except the Quakers)" desired would follow.[165] Franklin was concerned not only about the proprietary party's success in countering the pro-royal government petition but also because "The Irish Presbyterians, too, piqu'd at the Reflections thrown on them by the Quakers for the late Riots and Murders, have join'd the Proprietary Party, by which they hope to acquire the Predominancy in the Assembly, and subdue the Quakers. Hence," he predicted, "the approaching Election will probably be a warm one."[166]

Both factions published broadsides that focused not on the issue but on the ethnic composition of the colony. Franklin's comments about Germans, who had continued to support the "Quaker" or antiproprietary party, became a campaign issue. His enemies, glossing over the disparaging remarks contained in William Smith's *Brief State*, publicized the comments Franklin had made in *Observations concerning the Increase of Mankind*, published in Boston in 1755. Arguing against alien immigration to the British colonies, Franklin had queried, "why should the Palatine Boors be suffered to swarm into our Settlements, and by herding together establish their Language and Manners to the Exclusion of ours? Why should Pennsylvania, founded by the English, become a Colony of *Aliens*, who will shortly be so numerous as to Germanize us instead of our Anglifying them, and will never adopt our Language or Customs, any more than they can acquire our Complexion." [167] "Palatine Boors" was translated as "herd of hogs," and despite efforts to demonstrate that *"Boar* may be Hogs but *Boor* is Peasant," the passage was exploited in both German and English to indicate the anti-German sentiments of Franklin and his associates. [168] Such propaganda was not without effect. A German broadside advocating election of the "New Ticket," or coalition formed to oppose Franklin and constitutional change, clinched a series of rational arguments for preserving the constitution, "and it remains undeniable, that Mr. Frk. is a true enemy to all of the German inhabitants." [169]

Reminding voters of the *"Knock down Election"* of 1742, commonly attributed to proprietary supporters, another broadside declared that that faction "advocated and palliated the horrid Crimes of the *Paxton* Rioters, murdering in cool Blood, the *Indians* at *Conestoga* Manor, and at *Lancaster*, and in their marching to this City." [170] Supporters of the "New Ticket" indignantly denied such allegations. They pointed out that their slate for Philadelphia County included three incumbents who favored the present frame of government. They experimented with ethnic balancing by nominating "two creditable *Germans*," thereby offering the Germans a share of power that the "Quaker" party had not thought proper. [171]

Proprietary supporters did not rely on literature alone. They considered a late alteration to the Lancaster County ticket in response to reports of a strong Quaker and Mennonite coalition against those opposed to constitutional change. Because the "Irish . . . Interest must be much Stronger" than that of an English candidate who was reluctantly dropped, "it would be imprudent to offend them by rejecting one of their proposing" in order to add a German candidate to strengthen the ticket. "The design is by putting in two Germans to draw such a Party of them as will turn the scale in our Favor." [172] Although attempts to formulate a ticket on which different interests could unite failed, those opposing the change in government declared "We have on our side all the Lutherin & Calvanists Dutch with many

[handwritten margin note: BF opponents = Presbyt / ½ Church Eng with d Calv German digs him but his Anti-Prop to hold maj. & Cont.]

others of the Germains, we think ourselves strong Enough for the Task we have undertaken."[173] On the other side, one contender for sheriff, "the Son of Quaker," took "infinite pains in riding about the County to secure the Interest of the Germans" in favor of a change of government.[174]

In Philadelphia County, one resident was reported to be "using all the Influence he has among the Germans in his Neighbourhood to throw Mr Franklin & his adherents out of the Assembly."[175] New Jersey Governor William Franklin tried to counteract such endeavors by keeping "open house" at Germantown for several days, "canvassing among the Germans & endeavouring to get votes by propagating the most infamous lies he could invent" in favor of his father's cause.[176] A Quaker complained that the "Presb'y Party" used "every artifice in their power that they could invent" to obtain votes, and that their ministers were "remarkably vigilant in the affr & stir'd themselves more than was ever known before."[177] Once again proprietary supporters requested the support of Swedish and German Lutheran ministers.[178]

Just before the election, Allen observed that much of the opposition to the scheme focused on Franklin himself. Many "serious Quakers" disliked both the change and Franklin, but "appear to be afraid of disobliging him, and, as I tell of them, they worship him as the Indians do the Devil, for fear[.]" The majority of Franklin's opponents was "composed cheifly [sic] of Presbyterians, one half of the Church of England, and most of the other Societys, particularly the Lutheran, and Calvinist Germans (who are now Zealous again the Change of Government, Though they compose great part of the signers of the petition they aledging that they had been imposed on by his and other's false storys)," even if in other respects the Germans wished to remain in "peace, and friendship" with the Quakers.[179]

Franklin was defeated, but the antiproprietary party retained its majority.[180] He declared that his opponents "carried (would you think it!) above 1000 Dutch from me, by printing part of my Paper . . . on Peopling new Countries where I speak of the *Palatine Boors* herding together, which they explain'd that I call'd them a *Herd* of *Hogs*. This is quite a laughing Matter."[181] Muhlenberg reported "great rejoicing and great bitterness in the political circles of the city," for one of his church trustees had been elected to the assembly. This "greatly pleased the friends of the *Proprietors*, but greatly exasperated the *Quakers* and German *Moravians*." According to his interpretation of the factions, English and German sectarians formed one party, while "the English of the High Church and the Presbyterian Church, the German Lutheran, and German Reformed joined the other party and gained the upper hand—a thing heretofore unheard of."[182] Although Muhlenberg's assessment may not be completely accurate, it appears that the "German vote," previously viewed as a unified bloc that supported the Quaker faction, was beginning to fragment.[183] Even William Smith was moved to praise the "industrious GERMANS, to whom this province is so much indebted for its flourishing state."[184]

The assembly immediately dispatched Franklin to England to lobby for a change in government.[185] A petition was prepared against this appointment, and signed at a meeting held in the Anglican church in Philadelphia. Muhlenberg, uninvolved in provincial politics, feared that the campaign for royal government and Franklin's journey to England were "likely to cause bad blood among the inhabitants."[186] Indeed, Pennsylvanians of diverse backgrounds and political philosophies were dissatisfied both with the election's outcome and with the continued agitation for constitutional change.[187]

The failure to resolve the problem led to active campaigning prior to the 1765 elections, in which ethnic and religious appeals were again prominent. One broadside declared that Franklin had "since continued, wherever he could be heard, to traduce his countrymen, especially the Germans, as an ungovernable mob." The author declared, "Our ticket is composed of honest men of various denominations; and with respect to the Germans, they have shewn themselves lovers of liberty, and the province is much indebted to their industry." Objections to the anti-Franklin faction were "only the artifice of a party who are jealous of seeing you treat these *Germans* as fellow citizens on level with yourselves, after they have treated them so many years as persons fit indeed to vote for them at elections, but not to be entrusted with any share of their power."[188] A German broadside by Christopher Sauer II, son of the printer who had supported the Quaker faction, praised the blessings of the country under the proprietary regime and accused Franklin of trying to destroy the people's privileges. "If this balance remains in the House of Assembly, I cannot see why, dear countrypeople, we should believe the terrible monsters that Mr. Franklin's friends threaten us with, such as a burdensome militia law, the fortification of the city, coming under a tyrannical Presbyterian government, becoming the serfs of the proprietors, and whatever terrifying prospects and imaginary things with which these people seek to dazzle our eyes."[189]

Franklin's supporters, for their part, reminded voters of the traditional proprietary attitude toward Germans. They stated that "The *hireling scribling Parson* who wrote the *Brief State*, according to whose plan the Germans were to be kept under and not allowed a News-Paper or Bond or Note of Hand in their Language" was hardly to be trusted with an interpretation of Franklin's "Palatine Boors" phrase. Furthermore, "great Proprietary Officers" had "turned up their Noses at the Germans, when they came to be naturalized."[190]

Campaign strategy extended beyond the bounds of literary efforts. In Bucks County proprietary supporters scheduled a meeting of Germans, Baptists, and Presbyterians, to which Philadelphia Germans and Baptists were invited "in order to attempt a general confederacy" against the antiproprietary faction. Fearing a "project" by Lancaster County Mennonites to defeat the "only good member" on the ticket, Samuel Purviance suggested that a "Lutheran or Calvinist" be nominated in place of an "English" candidate in order to maintain the good will of German voters.[191] More ominous was the plan to secure the election of four proprietary candidates in Lancaster. Once the ticket was formed, advised an anonymous writer,

let it be Spread Through the Country that all your party intend to come well armed to the Election & that you intend if there's the least partiality in either Sheriff Inspectors or Managers of the Election that you will thrash the Sheriff every Inspector Quaker & Minonist to Jelly & further I would report it that not a Menonist nor German should be admitted to give in a Ticket without being Sworn that he is naturalized & worth £50 & that he has not voted already & further that if you discovered any person attempt[g] to give in a Vote without being Naturalized or Voting twice you would that Moment deliver him up to the Mob to Chastize him, let this report be industriously spread before the Election which will Certainly keep great Numbers of Menonists at home.[192]

In contrast, a Philadelphia proprietary supporter found a way to obtain the support of unnaturalized Pennsylvanians: "I have out of my own packet spent some money for giting some people neterlizet to git some votes more. who had no mind to be neterlizet. as a thing of not much benefit to them." [193]

Franklin's faction attracted the largest number of voters in an election that saw more people than usual cast ballots. [194] According to a report sent "with great grief and miscontend" to Thomas Penn, the antiproprietary party sent men throughout the colony to tell sectarians that if a new assembly were elected its first act would be to give backcountry counties more representation. Nonpacifists would have "for ever the majority in the assembly on there side. and would make laws not favourable to all such as could not bear arms," an argument that swayed many nonpacifists, "notwithstanding. sour our printer informet them that all that was nothing but falsity." [195] Governor John Penn complained that despite the "greatest pains" taken by his allies, "There is no resisting the Intrigues of the Yearly meeting." He intimated that "much money was spent upon this occasion by *friends*" to secure the election of their candidates. [196] Muhlenberg declared that, in contrast to the previous year, "The German sectarians and English Quakers and their large following gained the upper hand in the election, and the English and German church people lost out." [197]

III

The political instability of the turbulent decade had only a limited influence on intergroup relations. If political rivals exploited religious and ethnic factors in their attempts to gain power, they did not disturb the prevailing stability and harmony of provincial society. Political contentiousness, especially in the heat of a campaign, had little impact on the daily lives of most Pennsylvanians. Disputes over who should hold office affected primarily the elite; voters continued to express their approbation of the policies of the "Quaker" party, whether its candidates were Friends or not.

The threat of warfare did bring to the surface the ambivalence with which many English-speaking, non-Quaker Pennsylvanians regarded "outsiders." German, Moravian, and Roman Catholic colonists were occasionally viewed with apprehension. Yet the fears and prejudices expressed toward these groups were superficial or rhetorical, and rapidly dissipated as they demonstrated their loyalty to the English regime. If wartime panic generated hostilities, Pennsylvanians were sufficiently openminded that their opinions could be altered by factual information.

At the outset of the French and Indian War, some Pennsylvanians questioned the allegiance of German colonists. A former governor wrote that "The Germans too I fear, from their Ignorances and Covetousness are not so averse to a French Government, as a People ought to be, who have tasted the sweets of Liberty."[198] Governor Morris believed that "the French by means of the Foreigners in this Province may possibly subject the whole Continent to their Dominion."[199] Conrad Weiser did little to allay such fears of his fellow Germans. He declared that backcountry Germans "have no notion of the English government and laws, and are themselves not always satisfied with the administration of Such[.]" Some had come from Lorraine, and therefore had been subjects of the French King; many were "papists." Because a number of German settlers did not know from whom they could obtain title to their farms, they "Will Submit themselves to those who will and can protect them." If the French offered to "tollerate them in their Religious persuasions it is my opinion Several hundreds If not tousants would Steal away" and "go over to the french to ohio."[200]

Awareness of such apprehensions led Germans to address Morris early in his governorship. The "mild Government, the incomparable Priviledges, the inestimable Liberty of Conscience, and the just Administration of the excellent Laws so happily established" in Pennsylvania had encouraged emigrants from "arbitrary Powers and Slavery" to settle there, while the "kind Reception and the actual and unexceptionable Admission to the Rights of born Brittains" had "most firmly and heartily attached" them to the British and proprietary administrations. German Protestants "unanimously" opposed the French. They asked Morris to ignore "false Defamations" against them.[201]

Although some members of the provincial elite questioned the Germans' reliability if the French invaded the frontier areas in which many of them had settled, others recognized that the vast majority of backcountry settlers suffering attacks by hostile Indians would defend themselves and support the British cause. Germans were encouraged to provide teams and wagons for Braddock's expedition by Franklin, who combined promises of payment in gold with a threat that supplies would be commandeered if voluntary support were not forthcoming.[202] Christopher Sauer I, who was not noted for being sympathetic to military affairs, reported with pleasure the extensive German contributions to the campaign, and also advised his readers to wait patiently to be paid. He reported that Braddock had sent a letter to England "in which he boasted how prompt and loyal" Pennsylvanians had been to meet the King's demands. In contrast, "other colonies indeed promised much, but kept few of their promises."[203] Germans also contributed wagons to later campaigns, although "Religious people" were somewhat reluctant to do so.[204] There were, however, some complaints about the "Baseness & Coveteousness of our Rich Dutch Farmers" who expected high prices for military provisions.[205]

Germans volunteered to serve in military units. The British government devised a plan to send German and Swiss officers to recruit and lead a 4000-man regiment of German-speaking Protestants, drawn primarily from Pennsylvania. Local men would be selected for certain positions.[206] Even though recruiters arrived "in the midst of Harvest," they had "surprizing Success" in enlisting soldiers.[207] Large numbers of Germans joined Pennsylvania companies and were placed in leadership positions, not invariably in predominantly German units.[208] Early in the war Richard Peters noted that "The dutch behave admirably well" and participated in the defense of the frontiers.[209] As they demonstrated their support of the British cause, qualms that the presence of foreigners was endangering the province diminished.

One segment of the German population, the Moravians, was viewed with particular ambivalence. Prior to the 1756 election a proprietary supporter expressed the hope that Northampton County "will never disgrace it self by putting in any Moravian whose Principles for ought we know may be Popish." Not only were they "against Defence," but they "even refused to sell Powder to Protestants tho' it is said they furnished the Indians with it."[210] The following year an esssayist queried, "can it be possible that any Subjects of a *Protestant Country*, or any true Englishman, can give their Votes for *Moravians* to be their Representatives; a sett of Men of dark and suspicious Principles, living by themselves in a separate kind of Government, whom we do not know to be *Protestants.*"[211] Many suspected that the Moravians were "on secret terms with the Frenchmen, etc." These "false and deeply imbedded rumors and imputations" could not be rooted out by "oral or written apologies, or by explanations." The "most convincing apology or the shortest refutation" of these allegations was the massacre of several Moravians by Indians at their settlement at Gnadenhütten.[212]

Only during periods of acute crisis were the extensive Moravian contacts with the Indians considered dangerous. With the outbreak of Pontiac's Rebellion, Moravians were suspected of selling gunpowder to "friendly" Indians, who then traded it with hostile ones. People were "much exasperated" with the Bethlehem settlement and so "rivetted in the Opinion, that it is almost impossible to set them right respecting it," notwithstanding evidence that the governor's orders respecting trade had been "very strictly complied therewith."[213] When mills at Bethlehem burned, arson was suspected on the part of the "neighboring inhabitants who were much embittered against the Moravians because they suspected that the Bethlehemites and their Indian friends had some part in several murders and burnings of their homes and farms."[214]

Another source of tension was religious principles. Although their main settlements were located in areas vulnerable to Indian attack, Moravians could not actively defend the province. Their pacifistic beliefs were viewed as a hindrance to organizing defense. Nevertheless, on several occasions Moravians provided information about conditions in Northampton County. Their letters to officials in Philadelphia indirectly argued for defensive measures, even suggesting sites for garrisons or forts and offering land for that purpose.[215] Although unable to serve as soldiers, Moravians were "willing to Keep watches at Home, and thereby to hinder Incendiaries, prevent barbarous Murders, and to save women, children, etc. from cruel Hands[.]"[216]

The authorities held a somewhat more positive view of the Moravians than did ordinary colonists. Governor Morris requested them to "receive into their Houses at Bethlehem all such friendly Indians as shall come to them and desire to be taken in and to support and maintain them till they have my further Orders," a task the Moravians found somewhat "inconvenient."[217] Governor Denny also asked Moravians to supply the needs of Indians who visited them, and promised that the province would defray their expenses.[218] However, popular distrust of the Moravians may have led Denny to demand information about the number of Moravians in Bethlehem in late 1756. Bishop Augustus Spangenberg returned a list of the names of all Bethlehem residents grouped by family, summarized the whereabouts of other Moravians, and mentioned several Indians residing in their settlement. A summary was presented to the council, but no further mention of the Moravians was made.[219]

The decade of war with France also brought to the surface concerns about Roman Catholic inhabitants. Because it was assumed that their religion would take precedence over other considerations, Catholics occasionally appeared to threaten provincial security. Smith's anti-Catholic rhetoric in the *Brief State* resulted in a visit to at least one proprietary supporter, Thomas Graeme, by the priest resident in Philadelphia. Father Robert Harding stated that "I am an English Man and have an English Heart," that he "should be extreamly concernd ever to see the ffrench possessed of a foot of English America," and that he would "never" desire to live under a French government. Harding "thought it not a miss to apprize you" that fewer than two thousand Catholics resided in the colony, "least their Numbers might be made use of in prejudice to your affairs." Apparently he was convincing, for Graeme informed Thomas Penn that "the Number of Roman Catholicks is much Exagerated" and related the conversation.[220]

War with an aggressive Catholic power revealed hatred of Catholicism in general and some forebodings about provincial Catholics. Shortly before news of Braddock's defeat reached Philadelphia, Philip Reading preached a sermon denouncing the "dogs of Hell, *Popish* superstition and French tyranny" on the province's borders. The "quiet and peaceful" behavior of Pennsylvania Catholics should not lull Protestants into believing that they were safe, for the "Inquisitors of Rome" were "approaching to crush us."[221] A mob threatened to destroy the Catholic church in Philadelphia following news of Braddock's defeat. But "peaceable Quakers insisting that the Catholics as well as Christians of other denominations were settled upon the faith of the Constitution, or William Penn's Charter, and that the Government were bound to protect them so long at least, as they remained inoffensive and paid dutiful regard to the Establishment," persuaded the mob to "desist."[222]

At almost the same time, Berks County justices of the peace reported the alarming news that a "very magnificent Chappel" had recently been completed at Goshenhoppen, and that there had been "large Processions" near it. Armed Indians were seen "lurking" nearby. They requested "some legal Authority to disarm or otherwise to disable the Papists from doing any Injury to other People who are not of their vile Principles." The justices expected "a Massacre whenever the Papists are ready."[223] This letter was referred to the assembly, but after investigation it concluded there was "very little foundation for that representation."[224] Perhaps in an effort to convince readers that there was no reason to fear Catholics, Sauer reported that, in this time of crisis, "the Catholic priest has demonstrated to his people that they will never have such liberties under the French as they enjoy under the present government."[225] The following year Morris received a "Confused" letter from a gentleman in Carlisle stating that five "Swiss familys were gone from York county to Joyn the French, and that many Roman Catholicks in York & Frederick counties had engaged to go off to ye Ohio." However, he believed that there did not "appear" to be "much truth in this account." When he presented this information to the council, members agreed that "there are no sufficient grounds" to believe the report.[226]

In 1757 Governor Denny, "thinking it necessary to know the exact Number of Roman Catholics within the Province," followed the precedent he had set with the Moravians and ordered the provincial secretary to request information from the Philadelphia priest. It turned out that there were only 1365 Catholics in the colony over the age of twelve. There were roughly equal numbers of German and English or Irish Catholics, and there was also a balance of men and women.[227] Perhaps the revelation that the number of Catholics was insignificant helped to quiet fears, for there was little subsequent mention of this segment of the population. In 1759 Philadelphia Catholics purchased an additional lot in the city, and opened a second church in 1763, apparently without any protest.[228] Near the end of the French and

Indian War an Anglican priest summarized the mixed response to Roman Catholic colonists. The behavior of Lancaster Catholics "in outward apearance is quiet and inoffensive; but they have been often suspected during this war of communicating intelligence to the Enemies of our Religion and Country."[229]

The panic engendered by war reflected neither the development of intolerant attitudes nor a desire to create a homogeneous society. Episodes of animosity must be weighed against the reception accorded the "French Neutrals," Acadians deported because they refused to take an oath of allegiance to England that would obligate them to fight against the French. Although willing to declare allegiance to the British Crown as well as promise not to assist the French, and despite the absence of any evidence that the Acadians had committed or contemplated disloyal or treasonous acts, Governor Thomas Lawrence of Nova Scotia exiled them in autumn 1755. They were dispersed throughout the other British colonies. Neither the Acadians nor the governors who were to receive them were notified in advance of his plans. The sudden arrival of a Catholic, French-speaking, and presumably dangerous people provides a test of the degree of toleration British colonists were disposed to demonstrate. Pennsylvania's response was not entirely satisfactory, but compared with the reception accorded the Acadians in other provinces, it was both tolerant and enlightened.[230]

Before their expulsion, the *Pennsylvania Gazette* reprinted three articles from Boston relating to the Neutrals, "*as they are very improperly called*," which implied that they seriously threatened British interests.[231] Hence, when three vessels carrying 454 Acadians arrived in Delaware Bay in November 1755, Pennsylvanians were concerned, for the colony was in the "most defenceless State immaginable." Lacking a militia and with French soldiers and Indians ravaging the frontier, "its a very unfitt time to send such People here."[232] Governor Morris penned a panic-stricken letter to General William Shirley in which he claimed to be "at a very great Loss what to do" with the Neutrals. Pennsylvanians were "very uneasy at the thoughts of having a Number of Enemys scatterd in the very Bowells of the Country, who may go off from Time to time with Intelligence and Joyn their Country Men," or "foment some Intestine Commotion in Conjunction with the Irish & German Catholicks." Because there was no provincial militia, he set a guard over them from the "Recruiting Partys" then in Philadelphia.[233]

His message to the assembly was more temperate. He requested its advice and suggested that, for health reasons, the Acadians should be landed on Province Island, where there were facilities for sick immigrants.[234] The assembly agreed, and ordered that provision be made for them out of the money granted for the King's use. It also received information that they were "in great Want of Blankets, Shirts, Stockings, and other Necessities" from Anthony Benezet, a Quaker of Huguenot background whom some members had asked to visit the Neutrals.[235] A few months later a Pennsylvanian noted that people near Philadelphia were "under apprehentions from ye Neutral French which is sent amongst us full of resentment & revenge alltho thay yet appear tolerable civil when we feed them with ye best we can afford."[236] Perhaps in part to alleviate such fears, the Neutrals presented a statement to the assembly that included a brief history of their fidelity to England following the Peace of Utrecht, which had brought them under English control, and promised continued allegiance. The confusion and haste of their displacement had prevented them from bringing anything with them, and many families had been separated. But, they declared, "blessed be God, that it was our Lot to be sent to *Pennsylvania*, where our Wants have been relieved, and we have in every Respect been received with Christian Benevolence and Charity."[237]

The assembly then began to consider a policy regarding the involuntary immigrants. Proposals envisioned not only charity but the incorporation of the Acadians into provincial society. The policies were an adaptation of steps taken in regard to voluntary immigrants or based on observations of the ways in which immigrants adjusted to life in the colony. Because maintaining the Neutrals was expensive, it devised a plan to disperse them in Philadelphia, Chester, Bucks, and Lancaster Counties in order to "give them an opportunity of exercising their own labor and industry, whereby they may procure a comfortable subsistence" for their families. Each township would receive one family, for whom overseers of the poor were to rent a farm and provide "such stock or utensils of husbandry" as would permit farming to begin. Resettlement expenses would be defrayed by the province, out of money granted to the King. Because most Acadians had been farmers, it was expected that they would become self-support-ing, "as other inhabitants of this province are known to do."[238]

This measure proved unpopular. Certain townships refused to re-ceive the Neutrals.[239] For their part, many Acadians, arguing that no matter what the authorities said they were prisoners of war who must either be supported or be transported to France or to French colonies, refused to accept farms. A more compelling reason to reject farms was that many of them were women, children, or otherwise unable to labor.[240] The only public support came from Sauer, who reminded the colonists that they should be charitable to the strangers in their midst. "They are all Catholics, and if we had been born and raised in their country, we would also be Catholic. And if we had been carried off as they were, we would be as poor as they are now. It rests in God's hand, which no one can resist. And one should act charitably toward them, as one would want to be treated by them if one were in their place. Blessed are the merciful, for they shall obtain mercy."[241]

In 1757 the assembly decided to apprentice the Acadian children so that they could learn a trade and the English language, and thereby "become reputable inhabitants entitled to the rights of British Sub-jects." Neutrals unable to earn a livelihood because of age or infirmity would be supported at the province's expense. The law dispersing them throughout the colony was repealed.[242] The Acadians, however, complained that this act was inhumane. "Being deprived of that Sub-stance which God had granted us, permit us at least to live or die with our Children, and those of our deceased Brethren."[243] In fact, the apprenticeship portion of the law was not effectively carried out.[244] Pennsylvania policy became charity. It supported the Neutrals until the eve of the Revolution. When their needs were brought to the as-sembly's attention by Quakers or the overseers of the poor, assistance was forthcoming.[245]

At the request of Lord Loudoun, five Neutrals, "suspicious and evil-minded Persons," were arrested and removed from the colony.[246] But despite frustration at the Acadians' refusal to accommodate them-selves to provincial society, Pennsylvanians expressed little fear. While newspapers reprinted negative articles about the Neutrals in other col-onies,[247] the Pennsylvania Acadians came under suspicion only once.

When the "Cannon in the Battery & Barracks" were found "spiked with hard steel Spikes," it was "apprehended that the French might have set our Neutrals to work." But it proved to be "only the Contrivance of a Shatter Brained Gimcrack to procure himself the Job of unspiking them."[248]

Friends also took a more personal interest in the Acadians, and tried to improve their situation by constructing houses for them or educating their children.[249] Beginning in 1760, Friends lobbied in England for relief for the Neutrals. Benezet drafted a petition to the King in their behalf reminding him of their integrity and fidelity. Victims of "groundless fears," he described some of the "miseries" they suffered and the "extremely wretched" conditions under which half of their number had perished from disease in Pennsylvania.[250] The governor consented to transmit this petition to England, and Quakers planned to press English Friends to use their influence in behalf of the Neutrals. A subscription was begun to pay for lobbying costs. When Benezet found some Friends reluctant to contribute because it was "a matter which the Government ought to see to," he countered that the principles of Christianity required charity toward one's neighbors.[251] He and his associates solicited the proprietors' "Christian Interposition & Influence" on behalf of people who had endured five years of suffering. The Acadians "flatter'd themselves with a Hope that at the End of the War they should be restor'd to their Possessions, which arises as we conceive in some Measure from a Consciousness, that they were dispossessed out of Political considerations, rather than by Way of Punishment for any Offence, & that the Clemency & Justice of the British Government will secure them some Favour."[252] English Quakers visited the Penns to discuss the matter and found them sympathetic, although they believed that, because British public opinion held that the Acadians were "favourers of the French & secret enemys to the English," it was unlikely that they would be relieved. In the end, their plight was ignored.[253]

IV

Despite the suspicions of "outsiders" generated by war and Indian unrest, there was a conscious effort to maintain both the official poli-

cies of religious tolerance and also the more unofficial attitudes of respect for or indifference to those who differed in beliefs. After the
war efforts to recruit immigrants resumed, despite earlier interest in
limiting the potential influence of non-English colonists. Increasing
interaction with the British culture by Continental immigrants also
helped to decrease fears of "foreigners." A fundamental social stability
minimized the disruptiveness of the political and military problems
that surfaced after 1754.

The French and Indian War seriously affected the servant trade. Once
again there were problems caused by the enlistment of indentured
servants[254] and reluctance to invest in the services of men who might
desert them. Families were undesirable, because women and children
could not defray their transportation costs themselves, while the men
responsible for them might either join the army or be unable to provide repayment because of the disorder in the backcountry. Some
merchants experienced difficulty obtaining payment from "Pallatines"
who had been extended credit for their passage, particularly from those
who settled on the province's borders, for "many of them are Scalpt
and others wholy ruind with their familys now a Begging in the more
Interior part of the province." There was no imputation that the immigrants were dishonest or trying to evade their obligations.[255] Furthermore, the hazards involved in crossing the Atlantic and frontier
disruption made emigration undesirable to potential colonists. Late in
1756 the assembly complained that "The importation of Germans is
pretty much over," and expressed apprehension about the colony's
future. People were leaving it "faster than they come into it" in search
of cheaper land, while "The Danger attending Frontier Settlement
will probably be long remembered, even after a peace may be restored."[256] Nevertheless, despite merchants' complaints a small number of immigrants arrived during the war.[257]

By the early 1760s, as the colony became more secure from the
dangers inherent in war, Pennsylvanians expected that Germans "will
transport themselves here in as great numbers as formerly." Their
services were in demand. One firm of merchants vigorously attempted
to recruit skilled laborers for an iron works. Germans were the most
qualified, although it also considered finding Welsh or Swedish metal-

workers.[258] Furthermore, "a prodigious Spirit prevails at present among the Irish to go to America, nor is it to be wonddered at as the Nine tenths of 'em are miserably poor & distressed to the last degree by Land-Lords & Clergy."[259]

With the resumption of immigration came a corresponding interest in the conditions under which passengers were transported. A London Quaker was concerned that "the little regard paid to justice, by those who transact that business, and their excessive charges, . . . rather discourage than induce" emigration.[260] Although one Quaker merchant ordered stringent measures to be taken on a ship to safeguard passengers' health,[261] the assembly delayed further attempts to regulate the servant trade.

Impetus for improving existing regulations came from the Deutsche Gesellschaft, an organization of Germans of various religious beliefs dedicated to improving the lot of their less fortunate countrypeople. Unlike other societies composed of immigrants and their descendants that were devoted to aiding impoverished newcomers from their ancestral homes in the British Isles after their arrival,[262] the Germans were interested in the broader issue of the servant trade as well as in dispensing charity.[263]

Within weeks of the Gesellschaft's founding, it petitioned the assembly for permission to introduce a supplement to the law prohibiting the transportation of too many passengers in one vessel. It requested that the person appointed to investigate shipboard conditions for compliance with provincial laws speak German or have a German-speaking deputy. Passengers should be given receipts for all of their goods placed in the hold of the vessel; if any were retained after landing as security for payment, specific receipts, listing the goods and the amount of money for which they were to be redeemed, should be provided. Passengers who paid for their passage before embarking should be discharged with all of their property immediately upon arrival. No one should be liable for the charges incurred by those who died during the voyage, nor should anyone but the head of a family be required to pay the costs of transporting other emigrants. Immigrants should be released upon arrival to try to find a means to repay their passage money; it was inhumane to confine them to ships for lengthy periods or to place them in jail as insolvent debtors unless they failed to make payments or appeared ready to abscond from the province. A registry of servants, providing information about the place each would reside, should be established. Servants should not, without their own consent, be employed by masters living in other provinces. Finally, married couples should not be separated. The petitioners were allowed to present a bill embodying the petition's provisions.[264]

Merchants involved in the servant trade then presented a lengthy counter-petition. They agreed in principle that better regulation would benefit the province and immigrants, but objected to most of the proposed remedial measures. Germans, as free agents, made contracts in their own language in Holland and insisted on their strict fulfillment during the voyage. Receipts for baggage were impracticable, for often passengers needed access to their goods during the voyage; furthermore, English customs inspectors occasionally seized illegal goods. All family members should be liable for payment of the total cost of transporting the unit, since sometimes only young adults could be sold as servants. Because of the expense involved in purchasing provisions that were worthless if unconsumed, half-payment should be collected for those who died on the voyage. Alteration in the terms under which people could leave the ships or in the laws concerning debts would increase opportunities for fraud. Although they did not object to registering servants, they reminded the assembly that Pennsylvania served a market embracing the Lower Counties and New Jersey.[265]

With little difficulty, the legislature enacted a law containing the best features listed by both groups of petitioners and addressing other issues as well. The height of the space allowed each passenger was mentioned, amending the deficiency of the previous law that specified only length and breadth. New steps were taken to regulate the cleanliness of vessels, and a surgeon with medical supplies was to be present on all ships. An interpreter would visit all incoming ships to explain the provincial regulations and ask passengers if these provisions had been met. Goods to which passengers did not have access during the voyage were to be inventoried. Passengers were to be informed if they were bringing dutiable goods, and given an opportunity to pay customs charges in order to prevent seizure. Those who could pay their transportation costs on arrival were to be discharged immediately, with their goods. The property of others could be held for thirty days as security for payment; then legal procedures for the collection of small debts could be used. Merchants could no longer arbitrarily retain property in order to defray the cost of passage to the colony. If a passenger died during the voyage, the head of a family was liable for the expenses of his dependents, and children were obligated to pay for their parents. Otherwise, no one could be forced to pay the freight of another. Immigrants could be kept on board for thirty days in order to find an employer or friends who could pay their fares; masters were obliged to provide food and drink. After thirty days, passengers were responsible for their own maintenance. Sick passengers were to be provided with the necessities to restore their health, but were liable for the costs. If passengers were permitted to go ashore, their goods could be retained to guarantee payment, but receipts specifying the terms of redemption were to be issued. Married couples could not be separated except by mutual consent. A servant registry was established that listed the master's place of residence.[266]

The assembly was sympathetic to other concerns of immigrants. One matter of interest to aliens was security of property. An attorney advised that, although an alien could purchase property, it "became escheatable and forfeited" with the alien's death.[267] In 1759 the assembly enacted a law that secured the estates of deceased aliens to their heirs. It viewed the statute as a method of encouraging immigration, and considered it proper since immigrants expected to obtain property.[268] Thomas Penn complained that the law "will be looked on as forced from us," and saw no advantages in it except that, contrary to English usage, its benefits were not limited to Protestants.[269] Royal disallowance occurred, for it deprived the proprietors of a historic right, and extended privileges more extensive than those granted in the provincial charter and in the 1740 naturalization act.[270] In 1765 the assembly received a petition requesting enactment of a similar law, but simply ordered an inquiry to be made as to whether the proprietors had ever "taken Advantage" of their right to escheat.[271]

Although naturalization conveyed important benefits, most aliens remained indifferent to the offer. Political participation and the ability to engage in overseas trade—the primary advantages of becoming a British subject—do not seem to have been important to the average

German farmer; since the Penn family did not exercise its right to escheat, their property was secure in fact if not in law. Nevertheless, editors of the *Pensylvanische Berichte* and the *Philadelphische Staatsbote* occasionally urged readers to be naturalized, and publicized the dates of court sessions where aliens could avail themselves of the simple procedures for gaining citizenship extended to them in 1740.[272] The governor and assembly occasionally resorted to provincial naturalization. In 1759 a Swedish minister was naturalized by the governor after he took oaths of allegiance. In 1763 another Swedish priest was naturalized by private act of assembly.[273] Perhaps because Swedish missionaries returned to their homeland after spending several years in the colonies, only provincial naturalization was desired, merely to protect their heirs in case they died in the province. British subject-ship would not be advantageous. But for unclear reasons other individuals, some of whom appear to have qualified under the British law, were granted provincial naturalization in 1763 and 1765.[274]

The proprietors insisted on "an universal toleration of religion" and were anxious to keep all religious groups in the colony on an equal footing in matters that affected Pennsylvanians' religious beliefs.[275] They sold or granted land on favorable terms to various religious societies for churches, schools, or meetinghouses.[276] The assembly permitted several denominations to hold lotteries to help complete construction of churches or schools. Occasionally two denominations joined in one lottery and divided the proceeds, and sometimes men outside the sponsoring denomination were chosen as managers.[277]

   The proprietors hesitated to grant charters of incorporation to religious groups, for this could be perceived as favoritism. When Presbyterian ministers petitioned for incorporation of a mutual insurance society to benefit their widows and orphans, the request was referred to the English attorney general for a legal opinion. He objected that the colony's charter did not permit the proprietors to incorporate anything but towns. More significantly, he pointed to the toleration of all faiths practiced in the province. The incorporation of one religious body might be viewed by others as an "establishment." Nevertheless, the governor granted the charter, and Penn was obliged to promise that other charitable or religious corporations would receive the same favors bestowed by this precedent.[278] Charters for individual churches were only reluctantly granted; those given to the Lutheran and Reformed congregations in Philadelphia in 1765 were done for frankly political reasons, "to engage these people to vote against the Quaker faction."[279]

Efforts to treat religious groups impartially did not please everyone. Some Anglican missionaries complained that, because local officials believed that all clergymen should benefit from the fees, marriage licenses were issued to all Protestant ministers rather than just to Anglicans.[280] On the other hand, Quakers complained when Anglican priests attempted to obtain secular governmental positions.[281] A few priests, discontented that power was in the hands of "dissenters," believed that in consequence their church had little prestige.[282] Some Anglicans noted, with varying degrees of dismay, that they were surrounded by "great Numbers of Dissenters of all Kinds"; some were especially hostile to Quakers, others to Presbyterians, who had the recognized advantage of being able to train ministers within the colonies.[283] They were particularly upset that the "unbounded Toleration" granted in the provincial constitution allowed a "great & daily Growth of popery," and consistently exaggerated its number of priests, converts, and members.[284] Nevertheless these same Anglican priests informed their superiors that "dissenters" frequently attended their services and behaved reverently. Others found that through conversation they were able to remove prejudices against the Anglican church. Conversions encouraged ministers that their church could compete with other churches.[285] But in something of a reversal, the English sheriff of Philadelphia County was "awakened" by a Swedish Lutheran pastor and joined his congregation. Although his friends were astonished, he replied that he "found too much politics and party feeling in the Philadelphia High Church, and his soul had no pleasure in such things, but took pleasure rather in the essence and practice of the Christian religion" he found in Lutheranism.[286]

German-English interaction across strict denominational lines increased during this decade, although for the most part the division between church and sect continued. Churches were generously lent to ministers of different faiths and languages. For example, German Lutherans requested permission to hold a service in an English Baptist church, the only one in the neighborhood; it was granted, on condition that an English sermon be preached as well. Reportedly, all who attended were pleased with the service.[287] On other occasions, English masters asked German ministers to preach to their servants and also include an English sermon.[288] Similarly, Lutheran and Reformed churches in Germantown were offered to an Anglican minister so that he could conduct services for the few English residents of the town.[289] Lancaster Lutherans invited an Anglican priest to preach in their church, and made no objection to his use of the Anglican liturgy.[290] But when a Moravian minister who had "been ordain'd in ye church of England" volunteered to "officiate for You" in the Lancaster Anglican church,[291] the priest was adamantly opposed. If the Moravians had no local church, he might have allowed them to hold a service, but in this case they had a suitable building. He believed that the Moravian had "forsake[n]" the Anglican communion, and concluded his letter "with That Petition of our most Excellent Liturgy, That It may please God to bring into ye Way of Truth all such as have erred & are deceived[.]"[292]

There was some interest in constructing a backcountry church to be used jointly by Anglicans and Lutherans.[293] Several Anglican clergymen reported that Lutherans and Reformed thought highly of the Church of England and that those who understood English, especially younger people, frequently came to their services.[294] Lutheran congregations discussed adoption of the English language and the translation of religious works, and a new Anglican missionary broached the topic of a *"coalition"* or union between Anglican and Lutheran churches.[295] However, a Reformed congregation that asked to be taken into the Anglican fold was rebuffed because it wished to retain a degree of independence inconsistent with episcopal jurisdiction.[296]

Lack of formal union did not prevent ministers from working together. Once when Muhlenberg was having difficulties with a congregation, he was assured by the commissary of the Anglican church that "if my German elders cast me out I should come to him and be the fourth preacher. I should also bring my sheep and lambs with me; they would find room."[297] Ministers of the German Lutheran, Swedish Lutheran, and Anglican churches frequently invited pastors of the other bodies to attend their ministerial conferences. A Swedish missionary provided the impetus for a resumption of conferences of German Lutheran ministers. Ministers also conducted services in one another's churches attended by people of the three faiths. When George Whitefield returned to preach in the Philadelphia Anglican church in the 1760s, some Lutheran ministers supported his activities.[298]

Sectarians also found some common ground with other groups, and indicated interest in the beliefs of other sects.[299] A letter from the Philadelphia Yearly Meeting condemning the slave trade was translated and published in the *Pensylvanische Berichte*. Sauer commented, "This is praiseworthy of the Quakers! One hopes there is fruit from it."[300] Pennsylvania Quakers requested books in French and German to distribute among colonists who read those languages.[301] When a history of Pennsylvania was being prepared, one Quaker believed that material about the pacifistic views of German sectarians should be included.[302]

There was some rivalry over control of higher education, especially between Presbyterians and Anglicans. The College of Philadelphia, with a board of trustees composed of men of several faiths and intended for the education of young men of all beliefs without partiality to any one religion,[303] was an institution in which advocates of different tenets competed to favor their own sect and complained of the influence, real or potential, of others. To Thomas Penn impartiality, or "the most Catholick Plan," was the only basis on which the institution should function. He disapproved of an order that students must wear gowns as well as the purchase of an organ, practices that would prevent "graver Quakers" from sending their sons to the school.[304] William Smith, the provost, while agreeing in principle that the college should remain "*catholic*," did everything he could to foster Anglicanism. He suspected that if too many Presbyterians were involved as teachers, the college's broad base would collapse.[305] Yet many Presbyterians were concerned that students might convert to Anglicanism, and feared an Anglican takeover.[306] Ironically, when an anonymous letter criticizing the college for favoritism toward Presbyterians and other "Dissenters" was sent to the Archbishop of Canterbury, Smith had to defend the institution's policies. Its lack of Anglican teachers indicated only its inability to find qualified men; there was no "Partiality" involved.[307]

By mid-century most Pennsylvanians accepted the diversity of their province and their neighbors' right to hold different religious opinions. Nevertheless, they were sensitive to proselytization or attempts to interfere in the affairs of one church by adherents of another. When a Quaker published an essay against baptism to counteract a tract he supposed published by a Presbyterian,[308] an Anglican priest wrote an "Antidote" that was apparently successful.[309] Another instance of concern about publishing religious views occurred when the Brethren printer Christopher Sauer II was criticized by members of his sect for publishing the Heidelberg Catechism for the German Reformed.[310]

More significant were the responses to an extraordinary letter written by Presbyterian ministers to support the appointment of a revivalistic Anglican minister to a Philadelphia church. When Anglican priests complained to the Synod that its members had "intermeddled in their church affairs," it denied responsibility for or approval of the action and suggested that the priests discuss it with the men involved. It hoped that "the same good understanding which has hitherto happily subsisted between us and the Reverend Gentlemen of the Church of England, may still continue."[311] The following year the Synod condemned its brethren who "acted without due consideration and improperly in that affair."[312]

In individual contacts with colonists of different beliefs, many Pennsylvanians overlooked narrow religious differences. If some remained contentious,[313] most were not. A Quaker who lodged with a Presbyterian family during a journey noted that they were "not so begited as some nor did not practise thire formal Praying or Singing nor ye man when at home would hardly say any Grace" while he and his companion were in the house. Moreover, the family was disposed to listen to Quaker books being read.[314] In frontier Pittsburgh, the Presbyterian schoolmaster "Reads y^e [Anglican] Littany & Common Prayer on ye first Days to a Congregation of different Principels," who behaved "very Grave[ly]" at the services.[315] A Lutheran pastor who baptized the children of Anglican and Baptist parents in a private ceremony at which Quakers, Presbyterians, Anglicans, and German Reformed were present, noted that the entire company was moved by the ceremony. He commented, "I can truthfully say, that for a long time nothing pleased me as much as this; when otherwise in this country everything is still far too sectarian and factious."[316]

Although warfare highlighted tensions and accentuated divisiveness, it also provided opportunities for people of diverse origins and beliefs to work together to aid distressed frontierspeople. Pacifists contributed humanitarian aid, which was approvingly reported in German and English newspapers.[317] Appeals for donations to assist those who fled from their homes noted that Presbyterian ministers had allocated £150 to be "distributed, without Partiality, or any Regard to religious Distinctions," while other appeals praised "very liberal" Quaker and Mennonite contributions. Colonists of all faiths were urged to follow these examples.[318] Moravians received a large number of frontierspeople who "fled for their life to Bethlehem, . . . leaving behind them all they had in the World."[319] Because their resources were limited, Moravians requested aid from Philadelphia Friends, who promptly began a subscription to provide food, clothing, and other provisions. They emphasized that goods should be given to all of the distressed, including Indians, strictly on the basis of need.[320] Even though the monastics at Ephrata were alarmed by rumors that many men "had bound themselves by oath not to march against the enemy until every non-combatant in the county had been massacred," whenever "poor people" sent messengers to request aid from the community, a "liberal collection" was made for them.[321]

During this decade of external crisis, internal tensions among various segments of the population became evident. Social and political stability were temporarily disrupted as Pennsylvanians were challenged by circumstances that forced them to confront fundamental differences in outlook. But dissension was limited in scope, and tended to dissipate once the immediate issue was resolved. If some Pennsylvanians objected to the presence of pacifists in the legislature, there was almost no sentiment for the removal of Quakers from all offices, as there had been in the late seventeenth and early eighteenth centuries, nor was there a significant amount of anti-Quaker voting. Fears of "outsiders," especially Germans and Roman Catholics, gradually dissolved.

That prejudice, suspicion, and hostility were expressed by individuals toward those outside of their ethnic or religious groups cannot be denied. Nevertheless, by mid-century most Pennsylvanians had become accustomed to the pluralistic nature of provincial life. Tolerance for or acceptance of differences was viewed as a means of preserving one's own interests and privileges. Cooperation with others was essential. Even in the midst of a discussion of the acrimonious factionalism in politics that arose from religious differences, a Quaker wrote, "we live in Great Charity for one another, Intermix in Conversation, in Trafick, & all ye other affairs of Life, With great friendliness."[322]

CHAPTER 8

The Revolutionary Era,
1765-1783

The pre-revolutionary years were marked by increasing interaction among different components of the population. Immigrants were welcomed to a society with diminishing religious discord. Pennsylvanians became increasingly aware of the unique nature of the society they had created, and contrasted it with other, less liberal or tolerant states. Pluralism was celebrated; no longer was it a cause for anxiety. The unity in diversity was threatened by the imperial crisis, but it survived intact and in some ways was strengthened by the experience. As advocates and antagonists of British policies strove to make their positions known to all colonists, both sides translated propaganda into German. The ethnic overtones in provincial politics present since the 1740s were deemphasized, while opportunities for men of disparate backgrounds to participate in political and military affairs were broadened. Colonists, absorbed in a struggle transcending local issues, viewed their neighbors as Pennsylvanians rather than as members of particular national or religious groups. Lines were drawn on the basis of realistic appraisals of genuine differences in religious and political philosophies rather than simple stereotypes or preconceived notions.

Despite the difficulties inherent in war, and the occasionally repressive measures directed at those who refused to participate, Pennsyl-

vanians did not attempt to transform provincial society into a less
tolerant, less pluralistic one. Instead, they broadened the philosophical basis of society and extended political rights and religious freedom.

I

The resumption of immigration following the conclusion of the French
and Indian War continued throughout the decade preceding the Revolution. Pennsylvania was not the only destination, although it remained a popular one. In 1765 the *Pennsylvania Gazette* approvingly
reported that the British government had "a very excellent plan on
foot, to better people some of our new Colonies with Palatines," and
had dispatched agents to recruit those "inclined to try their fortune in
the American World."[1] But most immigrants came on their own initiative or were encouraged to do so by private interests. Merchants
involved in the passenger and servant trade actively fostered immigration. Although many migrants defrayed their own transportation costs
themselves, large numbers could not; merchants profited from the sale
of the services of redemptioners and indentured servants. While this
had generally been the case, after William Penn's death there had
been few serious efforts to recruit settlers. Except for recruiting occasional specialized workers, Pennsylvanians had not stimulated migration, even if they had not discouraged it. By the mid-1760s, however, people were well aware of the value of industrious immigrants,
regardless of their origins, for the province's economic development.

Some merchants advertised in European newspapers.[2] Thomas
Clifford sent an emissary to visit the area in which he grew up to
"acquaint the poor labouring people with the genuine State of this
Country, & the Opportunitie, industrious honest poor men, have of
supporting themselves by their Labour here," and to make arrangements with "Young healthy People" to migrate.[3] Other merchants extolled the quality of life in Pennsylvania to the captains in their employ or to their European correspondents. One noted that a recently
arrived servant "told me how happy he was in a place," while another
man "seems to rejoice at the Day he set foot on the American Shore,
says he has a rare good place." He concluded from wider experience
that "I do not think there is one of the Servants . . . but wishes to

see more of their Distressed Countrymen in their happy Situation."[4] Another merchant declared that the colony was the "finest & best Country in the World for Labourers & Handycrafts, but the worst for what may be call'd half bred Gentlemen without Capital."[5]

Merchants venturing their capital in the servant trade were careful, or tried to be, about the characteristics of the people they transported. Clifford favored younger people, "as they are early instructed in the ways of the Country, well supplyed with all necessarys, & when their Service is ended they are qualified not only to procure themselves a comfortable Living, but stand Candidates to be valuable Members of Community, & usefully to fill the various Stations of Life."[6] The James and Drinker firm advised its correspondents to "pray be careful to know their Characters & take none that are without good Ones (of which Number we scarcely expect any Women will offer) Perhaps some Germans may offer at that Season of the year."[7]

Because German immigrants had a better reputation than Irish servants, their services were more salable. When Joseph White heard that a ship carrying many "Dutch Servants" had recently arrived, he asked a friend to select a young laborer for him. He feared that "by Delay the Opportunity may be lost."[8] A western land speculator "wish[ed] we had a number of industrious Germans, which would make this one of the finest countries in the world, allowance for ague excepted," and even the ague could be remedied by increased settlement.[9] In contrast, Clifford noted that "Irish Servants we have more trouble with than any others, few but their own Country Men chuse to have them[.]"[10] Even so, an Irish merchant writing to Cork suggested that "perhaps your Sheriff may have some Convicts in his Jail, that he might be glad to get rid of, if so, it woud be an Advantage to the Ship to have them[.]"[11]

During the 1770s, English apprehensions about massive emigration from Ireland and Scotland to its North American colonies mounted.[12] While the Pennsylvania press reported the possibility that emigration might be regulated, it sympathetically pointed out the wretched economic conditions under which the Scots and Irish lived and their hopes of improving their lives elsewhere.[13] Benjamin Franklin drafted a strong protest against restricting emigration and "confin[ing] them as Prisoners in this Island." Landlords were guilty of "fleecing and skinning" their tenants in order to live a "Life of Luxury." Britain would not be depopulated, for increased opportunities after the surplus population was drained off would encourage people to have larger families as well as discourage further emigration. Furthermore, individuals had a right to live where they pleased. Since the "Common People" of England and Ireland had paid the taxes and provided the manpower that secured an enlarged British North America, they, rather than the Germans who were "now pouring into it," ought to enjoy the new territory. A restrictive law was *unnecessary, impracticable, impolitic,* and *unjust.*"[14]

A few years later, "A Friend to Pennsylvania" declared that "The value of all estates in this country must and will depend on the number of its inhabitants." Population could increase "only in two ways, viz. by natural generation, and the influx of foreigners." Rural Pennsylvania had developed primarily because of alien immigration. However, if the colony were to continue to prosper, it needed to develop industry to attract new settlers. If "public spirited men" would turn their interests in this direction, immigration would rapidly increase, which "must of necessity enhance the value of property" and would "finally put us in a capacity to withstand every stretch of arbitrary power with more certainty of success."[15]

During this period only one individual formulated a general argument lamenting the heterogeneity of his province. William Logan believed "there never will be found any Method to recover the golden Age of America, while we have such a mixture of Inhabitants," for "different Nations have by Inheritance, by Climate and by Custom, prejudices which they never will loose."[16] On a more specific issue, another Pennsylvanian complained about the servant problem. Recent immigrants were "spoilt in a month," while the native-born were "insolent and extravagant." In particular, "The imported Dutch are to the last degree ignorant and awkward. The Irish . . . are generally thieves, and particularly drunkards; and the negroes stupid and sulky, and stink damnably."[17]

Anti-immigrant rhetoric or the expression of negative images of non-English settlers was extremely rare during the revolutionary era; in most cases it was trivial. One colonist criticized a friend's recent marriage to a German woman. She, "good woman!" thought it "bad Oeconomy in him to frequent taverns or friends' houses."[18] Germans were ridiculed for their *"pernicious Method of keeping the Sick in hot Stove-rooms, under a hot regimen,"* and for their *"Prejudices"* against smallpox inoculation.[19] Their "whole Strange Infatuation" with bloodletting on particular days was also derided.[20] After Christopher Marshall experienced difficulty finding someone to prepare the body of his black servant for burial, he declared that "wretched" Lancaster was "full of Religious Profession. but not a grain of Love or Charity, except in words, in the generality of the German inhabitants[.]"[21] When a Lutheran minister visited a glassworks established by a German, he noted that the manufacturer faced several problems. Among them, "many who envy and hate him and try to render his efforts abortive because he is only a German, not an Engl[ishman] or a Fr[enchman]. The 'superior nations' look upon the Germans as nothing but wig-blocks, which are thick and hard, to be sure, but wanting brains."[22]

Citizenship helped to integrate aliens into provincial society. Since children born in the colony "acquire all the privileges of native Englishmen," a German-born minister considered it essential that accurate baptismal records be maintained.[23] Men born abroad continued to take advantage of the 1740 British naturalization act. The assembly occasionally enacted private naturalization acts for aliens who did not precisely fit the qualifications of the British law, thus indicating approbation of immigration and recognition of some of the difficulties aliens encountered. However, in 1773 one such law was repealed by the Crown, and the assembly was forbidden to enact statutes extending all of the privileges of British citizenship to aliens beyond the colony's borders. Pennsylvania laws included the right to engage in overseas trade, which was considered "exceptionable."[24]

Positive responses to religious as well as ethnic diversity increased during the revolutionary era. The provincial government continued its efforts to treat various beliefs impartially. Land was granted to many religious societies for the construction of schools and churches, and additional grants were made for cemeteries. Non-Protestants shared in such favors; land on which a Catholic church in Lancaster had been built was confirmed to them, and additional land was sold for the "Jews Burying Ground" in Philadelphia.[25] The proprietors exercised

caution when granting charters of incorporation for educational institutions or benevolent societies, primarily because they feared that such
grants might abridge the liberty of conscience of others or be considered favoritism.[26] Marriage licenses were given to clergymen of all
faiths, including Roman Catholic priests. One official stated that when
he issued them to Catholics, "I insert one of their Names instead of
the Words [any Protestant Minister] which I always blot out with my
Pen." He did "not see any good reason why they may not marry their
own People by a Licence, as well as by publication, since they are
allowed the public Exercise of their Religion in this Province."[27]

When the assembly received several petitions in 1772, probably from
Presbyterians, declaring that their consciences forbade taking an oath
in the "common form by laying the hand upon and kissing the book
when thereto legally required," it permitted the Scottish usage of simply raising the right hand when swearing.[28] The petitioners emphasized the provincial guarantees of liberty of conscience and the colony's settlement by emigrants "from sundry Parts of *Europe*, where the
Rights of Conscience are invaded and religious Freedom is fettered,
that they might here enjoy the Sweets of Liberty, and the unham-
pered Profession of their holy Religion."[29] Benjamin Franklin was asked
to lobby in England for the law's confirmation. Although pessimistic,
since a similar law had been repealed in 1740, he was able to secure
its approval.[30]

Close cooperation to further Christianity continued, especially among
representatives of European "state" churches. Lutheran and Reformed
pastors considered organizing quarterly meetings where ministers could
meet for edification and fraternal encouragement.[31] Ministers of different faiths sometimes participated actively in such rites as the dedi-
cation of a new Lutheran church in Philadelphia or the laying of cor-
nerstones.[32] Another ceremonial activity was the composition of letters
of introduction for parishioners or neighbors traveling abroad, clergy
who were leaving the colony, or those assigned to Pennsylvania. In
many cases the person to whom the letter was written, or the author,
was of a different faith or nationality from the person introduced. One
Anglican priest even recommended "a worthy, honest Jew and principal merchant" of Lancaster to an imperial Indian agent for employment.[33]

Similar ties occurred on an institutional level. In one instance, the search for a suitable bilingual minister for a German and English settlement in Nova Scotia involved Pennsylvania's Lutheran and Anglican pastors.[34] A native of Germany, ordained by the Bishop of London to serve a frontier mission in Pennsylvania, was joyfully welcomed because of his ability to serve both German and English settlers. It was considered proper that in unessential matters he might modify Anglican practices for his German flock.[35] The Presbytery of Philadelphia admitted a Reformed minister to membership in a display of unity with the Church of Holland, and, at the request of a Reformed congregation, temporarily exercised oversight over it.[36] Meanwhile, laypeople demonstrated their good will toward neighbors of differing beliefs. Thus, the Reformed Coetus informed the Classis of Amsterdam that a new church had been completed with financial assistance "even by other denominations, [which] convinces us that that is done in America which has long and vainly been sighed for in Germany."[37]

Although a few ministers at times complained about the diversity of beliefs held by Pennsylvanians, the character of other ministers, and proselytization by a rival denomination,[38] acceptance of religious pluralism was almost universal. Clergymen concentrated on the needs of the people who chose to attend their services, and demonstrated little interest in imposing their views on others. An Anglican noted that most Carlisle residents were Presbyterians, but added that on a visit to the town he was "entertained" with "much kindness and hospitality: And of them, was my audience chiefly composed on Sunday."[39] Most ministers recognized the tendency of Pennsylvanians to be undogmatic about their denominational affiliation, attend a variety of forms of worship, and form congregations consisting of a "mixed multitude."[40]

Schools functioned as a unifying force, even though most children attended church schools.[41] A group in Philadelphia County planned to organize a township school "open indifferently to every Religious Society, without the least Distinction or Preference whatsoever,"[42] while in Germantown a school providing English instruction was opened.[43] Schwenkfelders established a nonsectarian school in the late 1760s that offered instruction in both the English and German languages. A Philadelphia Quaker supported one German child in the school, and offered to pay the expenses of another if a Schwenkfelder leader "can'st find another Such poor Child that is likely to be bene- fited" by education.[44]

Common religious or social interests helped to increase the contacts that sectarians had with other religious groups. Individuals adhering to different beliefs seem to have participated in rational discussions of "religious matters" more frequently than before.[45] Prominent Quakers and Schwenkfelders, first closely associated during the 1750s in con- junction with the Friendly Association's effort to restore peace with the Indians, exchanged books and information about the histories and tenets of their sects. One Schwenkfelder assisted in translating Quaker works into German.[46] The dissemination of Quaker literature in for- eign languages was a project that interested many Friends in England and Pennsylvania throughout the revolutionary era.[47]

Individual Quakers and some meetings occasionally sought allies among members of other religious groups who shared similar views on specific issues. Anthony Benezet sent a letter opposing the slave trade to the secretary of the Anglican Society for the Propagation of the Gospel, and requested him to bring it before the organization.[48] Concerned about the possibility of "Theatrical entertainments" in Philadelphia, its Quarterly Meeting appointed a committee to "[make] application to divers of the other Religious Denominations in this City, . . . to Unite in Discouraging the evil mentioned." As a result, re- monstrances to the governor and the assembly were signed by several hundred people of different faiths.[49]

Smaller German sects, particularly the Moravians and the monastic community at Ephrata, attracted interest and became somewhat more familiar to outsiders. The monks translated the doctrines of their founder in response to a request by Franklin, adding as a gift a compilation of music composed for use in the cloister which had taken three brothers most of a year to copy and embellish for their Vorsteher, Johann Conrad Beissel.[50] They subsequently printed several of Beissel's dis- courses. An English friend of the community was disappointed that they had been published only in German.[51] Ephrata received a num- ber of visitors curious about the way of life and religious practices of the community. One group found them "bigoted to certain forms and ceremonies" and considered their refusal to eat meat because "all Animals are their Brethren, odd whimsies," but concluded that "as they are certainly inoffensive they ought to be allowed to enjoy them in peace."[52]

Because Moravian communities entertained numerous visitors, leaders of one settlement expressed the wish that "our people might be more attentive to strangers at our services, and in general to our neighborhood."[53] Quakers attended services and engaged in religious conversation with the Moravians. Many guests were impressed by the Moravians' industry and their flourishing settlements, which were willingly shown to visitors. If some objected to the communal life in which the unmarried of both sexes lived separately, most guests were pleased by the quality of their music. Two Lutheran pastors once visited the Hebron settlement merely to hear one of the brothers play the organ, and when an organ built by a Moravian for the Lutheran congregation in Lancaster was consecrated, an instrumental ensemble from Bethlehem was invited to participate in the ceremonies.[54]

By the late 1760s Pennsylvanians articulated both theoretical and practical arguments for religious toleration. Colonists expressed more clearly the benefits that William Penn's tolerant policies had brought the province. Recognizing the colony's uniqueness, they indicated that religious liberty should be extended elsewhere in the British world.

In his notes for a commencement address at the College of Philadelphia, Provost William Smith declared that "either to hamper or imprison men, or deny them any Natural Rights, or the common Security of Life Limb or Property, because they will not think in a particular Manner, is now well understood to be repugnant to all Reason, so far as they behave as peaceable Subjects." The "happy Experiment" of Pennsylvania "has shewn that Men of various & different Persuasions may share Power, & live peaceably together." The "enlightened" and "liberal Turn of Principles" embodied in the province's constitution should be "for ever inviolably preserved."[55] A "Pious Sermon" delivered by Anglican priest Richard Peters at the consecration of a Lutheran church met with Thomas Penn's approval. He hoped that the "Catholick Spirit recommended by it may spread throughout all Professions that each individual may consider his Neighbour as a fellow Christian without too great a Partiality to his own denomination."[56] In praising the province's "extensive" religious liberty, a letter writer noted that colonists lived in peace with one another.[57] A Philadelphian, posing as a visitor to the colony, declared that "there is less religious bigotry here, than in any place I have yet visited."[58] A Schwenkfelder, describing a funeral at which people holding "many diverse religious opinions" gathered, summarized the Pennsylvania experience:

Here we mingled like fish at sea, but peaceably. He who would let it be noticed that he was inimical to another because of religion, would be regarded as a fool, although one frankly tells another his mind. A Mennonite preacher is my real neighbor; I do not wish for a better; on the other side stands a large, stone, Catholic church. The present Jesuit father here is a native of Vienna, . . . he confides more in me than in any of the bosom-children. When he encounters a difficulty he comes to me. These men have learned to adjust themselves perfectly to the time. Furthermore, the Lutherans and Reformed have their churches here. . . . On Sundays we meet each other criss-cross. That does not signify anything.[59]

Pennsylvanians generally opposed intolerance, and criticized instances of it that occurred within the colony.[60] They also took an interest in toleration, or its absence, elsewhere. Thus in the early 1770s, when Parliament attempted to remove some of the disabilities on Dissenters, articles concerning the bill chosen for reprinting in the *Pennsylvania Gazette* tended to be those favoring its passage.[61] Benjamin Franklin, commenting on contributions in the London press that argued against tolerating Dissenters because they had persecuted Anglicans in America, especially in New England, denied such charges. Pointing out that throughout history many sects had "in their turns been persecutors, and complainers of persecution," he compared Old and New England to prove that Anglicans in New England enjoyed greater rights than Dissenters in England.[62] But if Anglicans had full rights in Massachusetts, others did not. In 1774 Pennsylvania Quakers discussed the laws under which Baptists and Quakers "may be Subjected to Sufferings" with delegates to the Continental Congress. They believed that such statutes "are not warranted by their Charter wch they pretended So resolute a purpose to maintain as the Foundation of their Constitution," and hoped that officials would repeal them.[63] When in early 1774 James Madison complained to a Philadelphia acquaintance that several Virginians had been imprisoned for publishing religious views that "in the main are very orthodox,"[64] his friend replied that "Persecution is a weed that grows not in our happy soil." "Liberty," he declared, "is the Genius of Pennsylvania; and it inhabitants think speak and act with a freedom unknown" elsewhere.[65]

II

The imperial crisis challenged the fundamental harmony that subsisted among Pennsylvania's varied ethnic and religious groups. Nevertheless, a basic respect for others remained significant to the social stability that underlay the political and military disruption. Sincerely held religious views that limited participation in the opposition to English policies or required neutrality were recognized as valid, for Pennsylvania had long experience with pacifist sentiments. During the decade of debate, political beliefs or supposed beliefs became more important than national origins or religious philosophy as leaders of the pro- and anti-independence forces attempted to unite colonists in favor of their cause, although background and belief to some extent determined the level of support given to Britain or to the resistance movement, and the perceptions of it.

Responses to the Stamp Act reveal the beginnings of new patterns of interaction. By the summer of 1765 the provisions of this statute, including a double tax on foreign-language newspapers and documents,[66] had aroused considerable and widespread objections. The reluctance of some assemblymen, including John Hughes, the Stamp Agent, to approve sending a delegation to the Stamp Act Congress became an issue in the 1765 elections, and helped to unify both English- and German-speaking voters against Franklin's antiproprietary party. Denunciation of the "all too heavy and unbearable burden of the Stamp Act" was as readily found in a German election broadside as in English-language pamphlets.[67] Many suspected that Franklin had been involved in formulating the law's provisions. One of his friends reported that German clergymen were reading a letter in their churches that informed their congregations that Franklin's "Enmity to them, was so great" because he had been defeated in the 1764 election "that thou had obtaind the Additional duties, being laid on the Dutch Papers &c."[68] Another of Franklin's correspondents recounted how his enemies hoped "That the Stamp Act might give Birth, to as much prejudice, among the Ignorant, against You As the harmless Word, Boor had done last year."[69]

When the ship bearing stamped paper arrived in Philadelphia, muffled bells were rung at the State House and the Anglican church to mourn the event. Among the Lutherans, however, Henry Melchior Muhlenberg advised his church council not to consent to ringing the bells of their schoolhouse; since "we Germans are already painted black enough by the envious opposing party in England, we would be sensible to guard ourselves against this act. . . . We would do better to remain quiet and let the English act as they see fit." He further directed his parishioners "to have nothing whatsoever to do with any uprising or tumult."[70] Nevertheless, Germans demonstrated both direct and indirect support for the anti-Stamp Act movement. German and English printers met together to determine the best course of action, temporarily suspended their newspapers, and then resumed publication using unstamped paper.[71] Germans hastened to be naturalized at the court sessions immediately before the law took effect, for the newspapers reported that the cost would rise from two thalers to nine or ten pounds.[72] Franklin subsequently informed the House of Commons that the Germans were "more" dissatisfied with the act than the "English" were, "and with reason, as their stamps are, in many cases, to be double."[73]

Many observers perceived Pennsylvanians as somewhat more moderate in their resistance to this law than people in other provinces. Religious factors were taken into account, but contradictorily interpreted. According to Governor John Penn II, "There has not been so much rioting here as in the other Provinces though many of the good people called Quakers were desirous of it and endeavoured to promote it."[74] In contrast, General Thomas Gage agreed that "Philadelphia has been free of Riots," but believed "The Presbyterians, who are of the Proprietary Party, are as ripe for outrage as can be, but the contrary Party composed of Quakers and their Friends, tho' they Complain of hardship in the Stamp Act, have been for complying with the Law; And have found Means to keep Peace and Tranquility in the

City."[75] Some Quakers feared the commotions would lead to an increase in Presbyterian power, which they deplored because Presbyterians were "altogether intolerant."[76] Others implied that Presbyterians were attempting to propagate "Republican Principles," with the intention of "throwing of[f] all Connection with their Mother Country."[77] When news of the repeal of the Stamp Act reached Philadelphia, Quakers requested that magistrates use their influence to persuade the people to "keep their demonstrations of joy within bounds." To their satisfaction, there were "no tumults raised or violence attempted on those who could not join" in the illumination of the city.[78]

Contention was muted in the years between the repeal of the Stamp Act and the enactment of the so-called Intolerable Acts. The only disturbing issue was the plan to send Anglican bishops to the colonies, a matter of concern in several provinces. Almost from the beginning of their mission in America, Anglican clergymen had importuned English church authorities to establish colonial bishoprics. They hoped to strengthen the presence and prestige of their church, but also stressed such practical matters as discipline, confirmation, and ordination. After 1763 Pennsylvania missionaries emphasized the need to combat the growing numbers of Presbyterians; previously they had emphasized the threat posed by Quakerism.[79] In Pennsylvania, the question of bishops intersected with constitutional guarantees of religious liberty and apprehensions that one religious group might gain political and ecclesiastical domination and thereby disrupt the relatively stable balance of religious factions. While members of several denominations could agree that it would be beneficial for Anglican clergymen to be ordained without the risk and expense of crossing the Atlantic, and that a bishop was necessary to discipline the clergy, many worried that the extensive religious and secular prerogatives of English bishops would be imported with them. Nevertheless, Pennsylvanians were relatively moderate in their discussion of this issue. Even some Anglican priests opposed the idea of forcing a bishop on the colonists and the strident insistence by some of their brethren in other colonies that one be appointed.

Anglicans often insisted that colonists of all persuasions thought that a bishop with circumscribed functions would be useful. According to reports sent to England, only Presbyterians opposed bishops. Quakers allegedly favored the plan because of their "dread" of Presbyterian power, which they believed a stronger Anglican church could effectively "check."[80] One layman, noting the "Allarming" growth of Presbyterianism, reported that "the Quakers say as there is a Synod of the Presbetery they think there is no other way but to Introduce a Bishop in America," since "they make Presbeterian Ministers with as much ease as a Countrywoman sets Eggs under Hen & Hatches Chikkens."[81]

Not all dissenters viewed the prospect of bishops with the equanimity suggested by the Anglican clergy. Some suspected that William Smith, the ambitious, politically active priest who served as provost of the College of Philadelphia, was agitating for a colonial bishopric in order to become the first incumbent.[82] One priest reported that Francis Alison, a Presbyterian minister and vice-provost of the college, "assured" him that Presbyterian clergymen did not object to "what he Called, primitive Episcopacy, i,e, Episcopacy without any *civil* power anexed to it"; Alison "would be well contented if there was a Bishop, of this sort, in every Province in America[.]"[83] He was mistaken. When in July 1766 the *Pennsylvania Gazette* announced serious consideration of creating colonial bishoprics and a recent bequest that would help to support the new establishments,[84] Alison took the lead in opposing the plan.

Alison's primary objections were founded on the political and civil privileges that bishops enjoyed under English common law, which he believed would automatically be extended to the colonies. When he saw a 1750 plan for colonial bishops said to be under consideration in the 1760s, he noted with approval that they would have no "Coercive" power over the laity, would have no share in temporal powers such as granting marriage licenses or probating wills, and would not be settled where the government was in the hands of "Dissenters." But he appended to his summary of the bishop's functions, "Quere how Shall ye Colonies have Security that Bishops when sent among us shall become such peaceable harmless Creatures? Nothing less than an act of Parliament made in England before they embark could afford the least Security. for they have power by ye common & statute law of England to erect courts, to plague & torment us; these privileges they will claim, & what way can we prevent their claims from taking place?"[85] Alison proposed a coalition among the "anti-Episcopal Churches" to form "A firm union against Episcopal Encroachments." Denominations in the Reformed tradition would work together to preserve religious liberty and advance such uncontroversial goals as education and missions to the Indians. Churches would not be forced to conform in doctrine, practice, or church government, nor should any try to gain superiority over other bodies.[86]

Presbyterians and Congregationalists arranged intercolonial meetings designed to foster unity. They also solicited the assistance of English Dissenters in their effort to oppose bishops, and were assured that steps would be taken to frustrate the design.[87] Presbyterians denounced the spiritual and temporal powers of English bishops as inappropriate to colonial conditions and infringements upon the privileges granted by William Penn. They argued, "we *dare not yet trust Bishops with our Liberties*," and cited the bishops' opposition to repeal of the Stamp Act as an example.[88]

A group of Philadelphians prepared a series of essays in opposition to the idea of establishing bishops, but the debate they inaugurated was considerably more temperate than in other colonies.[89] The first series of articles published early in 1768 evoked little response,[90] but after the Anglicans replied in September 1768, the *Pennsylvania Gazette* was filled for the next five months with tedious but fairly rational essays arguing the merits and demerits of episcopacy in general and Anglican bishops in particular. Even some Anglicans criticized the proposals made by New Jersey missionary Thomas Bradbury Chandler in an essay published in 1767.[91] This pamphlet had instigated the debate. They hoped to prove that bishops with limited powers could be appointed and that their church would not infringe upon the religious and civil liberties of Dissenters or diminish religious freedom. Anglican attacks on Presbyterians and Independents were based primarily on the intolerance exhibited by seventeenth-century New Englanders, while opponents of episcopacy criticized the Church of England's persecution of Dissenters. They did not believe assurances that the entire English ecclesiastical structure would not be re-created in America.

In the midst of the dispute the *Gazette* published an essay urging both sides to cease arguing, and to work to heal the breaches in the Christian church.[92] The dispute ended shortly after the newspaper announced "that it is absolutely determined not to establish Episcopacy in America, for two reasons; first, because it is not thought necessary, and secondly because the Americans are not likely to submit to it."[93] The final Anglican essay pleaded for the cultivation of "*domestic harmony*" in order to better resist the "gloomy prospect that seems gathering against us on the other side of the Atlantic."[94]

Only after mid-1774 did resistance to imperial policies have a significant impact upon the ethnic and religious dimensions of provincial life. Yet until fighting broke out and independence was declared, Pennsylvanians tended to be understanding in their expectations of appropriate behavior. Revolutionary leaders struggled to achieve unity by extending the base of political participation and publicizing their views. Although the refusal of many inhabitants to compromise their religious beliefs for political ends opened the way for contention and ill-feeling, the trend was toward moderation, compromise, and accommodation. Until the goals of the anti-British agitation became clearly defined, hard lines could not be drawn. Because neither pacifists nor revolutionaries had firm notions of how they should, or could, respond to each crisis, compromise was possible.

The conflict between achieving unanimity and respecting conscience is evident in Philadelphia's response to the Intolerable Acts. In January 1774 a Pennsylvania Friend wrote of "the Uneasiness prevailing among the people here,"[95] but not until shortly before the acts went into effect did revolutionary activity begin to have ramifications for the relations among various segments of the colony's population. Contention was triggered by a report Charles Thomson, a member of the committee of correspondence, sent to the chairman of the New York committee of correspondence that "a Number of the Inhabitants from every Church & Denomination of Christians" in Philadelphia had agreed to suspend business and hold church services on 1 June, the day on which the Intolerable Acts would take effect.[96] Indeed a meeting was held, but of "most of the Different Societies."[97] The city's most influential Quakers held a separate meeting where they decided to publish a public notice that "no Person or Persons were authorized to represent us on this Occasion," and that if anyone in their fellowship "countenanced or encouraged" such a proposal, he was guilty of a breach of discipline.[98] An epistolary dispute ensued. The *Gazette* also published a statement at the request of the Anglican rector that no service had been held in his church, nor had the church bells been rung. This statement was intended to correct an inaccurate report in another newspaper.[99] Nevertheless, one revolutionary claimed that "the necessity of harmony and perfect unanimity, which all seem sensible of, has reconciled very different interests among us, and by yielding to each other, the Quakers and Presbyterians, and other contending sects, have met on this point."[100]

Over the next two years the attitudes of Quakers came to be viewed as a significant element in determining the extent of the province's participation in the resistance movement. Some Pennsylvanians blamed Quakers for the colony's lack of revolutionary fervor. "'*Their* dear delight is peace,' for which I believe . . . they have more reasons than one," declared one man.[101] Christopher Marshall thought Friends hoped "to defete the pacifick proceedings" of the Continental Congress,[102] while another critic declared that "Quakers are moving Heaven & Earth to defeat the Measures of Congress."[103]

Pacifists believed that moderate measures would be most efficacious and encouraged petitions rather than the formation of military units or other potentially violent, inflammatory measures. Although some Quakers participated in committees, supported boycotts, prepared a "spirited petition" to the Crown "in defence of their rights in the colonies," and engaged in other forms of passive resistance, their primary concern was with moderate and proper behavior. Encouraged by London Friends to continue their "prudent Conduct" and to refrain from active involvement in public affairs, Pennsylvania meetings drafted epistles reminding Friends of the sect's peaceable tenets. Illegal assemblies and violence in opposition to duly established laws and government were wrong; respectful addresses to the King and those in authority were the only means Friends could use in attempting to restore harmony between the colonies and Britain and to safeguard colonial rights. But individual decisions to remain aloof from public affairs

were not easily reached. There was a difficult balance to attain between the proper conduct of Friends and their interpretations of British policies and American liberties.[104]

Many Pennsylvanians were disturbed by the Quebec Act, but their
reactions to its religious provisions were mixed. In light of the recent
refusal to extend the privileges allowed to English Dissenters, the toleration granted to Canadian Roman Catholics was often viewed as the
government's decision to ally itself with the temporal and spiritual
bondage associated with the Church of Rome. Newspaper articles reprinted from the English press were generally negative,[105] although
the limited amount of Pennsylvania comment was more inconsistent.
One *Gazette* reader submitted an extract from a 1755 wartime sermon
denouncing the "Dogs of Hell, *Popish* Superstition and *French* Tyranny," and calling for men to unite to defend "our Protestant Religion
and our *British* Liberties[.]"[106] One Pennsylvanian believed Britain intended to "[keep] on foot a large body of popish Canadians in order
to March and oppose our Protestant Brethren in America who should
oppose their oppressive tyranical Ministerial Schems."[107] But others
considered it "very wise" to allow the Canadians to enjoy their accustomed religion and to be governed with only slight modifications from
French practices.[108] When the Continental Congress tried to gain Canadian support for the American cause, it enlisted the aid of a Pennsylvania priest.[109] Edward Shippen commented, "I hope the Natives
of Canada will be induced to place great Confidence in us all, when
they reflect upon our kind treatment of many hundreds, nay some
thousands of people in Pennsylvania &c. of their own persuasion after
our Conquest of Terra Canadensis[.]"[110]

With the prospect of war looming following the battles of Lexington
and Concord, Pennsylvanians were forced to consider creating militia
units and financing military actions. If service on a county or city
committee, support of boycotts, and similar activities had not neces-
sarily posed serious threats to conscience, military measures were a
more clear-cut issue. However, the results were mixed. Some pacifists
found the defense of American liberties more important than theolog-

ical precepts, while many individuals and sects experienced difficulties in defining the limits of participation.

Recruitment of militia units entailed considerable contact with pacifists, especially in the eastern and central counties where large numbers of Quakers and German sectarians resided. The Berks County committee once requested a pacifist to attend a meeting so that there would be a quorum, but the last issue it considered was military. When a member "said it was necessary that each member encourage the brethren in his neighborhood to make armed resistance . . . nothing further was done, for he said that I would not give my consent to such action, as he already knew."[111] Moravian delegates visited an official to explain their sect's views concerning war. They "would not *oppose* the current of events" and were "willing to bear our share of the burdens of the country," but reminded the official that their religious society enjoyed legal exemption from military service in many countries, including the British Empire.[112] Some colonists suggested that those "whose Consciences are scrupulous" contribute clothing or lend guns to poor men who were willing to join the associations but were unable to provide their own equipment. They noted that "Quakers & others of scrupulous Consciences" in Philadelphia were taking similar steps.[113]

When the Lancaster County committee received information that "divers Persons, whose religious Tenets forbid their forming themselves into Military Associations, have been mal-treated, and threatned by some violent ill-disposed people . . . notwithstanding their Willingness to contribute chearfully to the Common Cause, otherwise than by taking up of Arms," it ordered people to "discourage and prevent such licentious Proceedings, and assiduously cultivate that Harmony and Union" it deemed essential. At the same time, it warned nonassociators against "abusive, opprobrious or insulting Expressions" directed at those willing to fight. It hoped that "every Member of the Community will readily use his utmost Endeavours to promote Peace good Order and Unanimity amongst the Inhabitants of this respectable County."[114] Militiamen, however, objected to this plea for mutual respect, and refused to muster until everyone was required to do so. Committeemen, threatened with violence, promptly resigned.[115] A few days later it was rumored that the committee had been "bribed with £1500 to excuse the Quakers & Meninists from arming,"[116] which may be the reason one person noted that "the Mennonites are very much hated by the people."[117]

The new committee, which consisted of most of the former members, "recommended" that all nonpacifists "immediately" provide themselves with weapons to defend their civil and religious liberties. It also recommended that men who conscientiously opposed joining a militia unit or furnishing arms contribute £3.10 "to be applied to such uses, as by this Committee shall be deemed most advantageous to the Public Interest."[118] A delegation of Mennonites, Amish, and Baptists then warned that many members of their societies objected to this mode of raising contributions and might "prove obstinate." Because they acknowledged an obligation to "contribute towards the Support of the Rights & Liberties of their Country," they planned to request the Continental Congress to devise a "more binding" method of raising money that would be satisfactory to people of all persuasions. If Congress failed to act, the representatives proposed to "of themselves fall upon such measures as they expect will give general Satisfaction[.]"[119]

In June 1775, in response to demands by the Continental Congress for soldiers and requests from Pennsylvanians to fund defensive measures and create a military association,[120] the assembly issued a series of resolutions intended to regularize the informal organizations already in existence and to procure the necessary equipment. Money would be raised through a tax on real and personal estates. Recognizing that "many of the good People of this Province are conscientiously scrupulous of bearing Arms," the assembly recommended that associators "bear a tender and brotherly Regard towards this Class of their Fellow-Subjects and Country-Men," and that pacifists "chearfully assist, in Proportion to their Abilities" associators who could not serve their country "without great Injury to themselves and their Families."[121] Congress, "intend[ing] no Violence to their Consciences," urged pacifists to *"Contribute Liberally* in this time of universal calamity" and to perform services consistent with their religious principles.[122]

Berks County pacifists cited both declarations, as well as the provincial frame of government, in their protest against a local requirement that all men between certain ages either join the association or be "fined in such a Degree, whereby numbers of Families would be reduced to utter Ruin, and such Fines to be raised by distraint of their Goods, by military Force." The petitioners pledged that they would "do their utmost for the Welfare and Support of the common Cause" if such unconstitutional measures were repealed.[123] Moravians appointed members to make collections in compliance with the recommendations of Congress and the assembly.[124] Brethren told the collector that their money was given "for the needy." Because Congress had assured two representatives of the sect that the county committee "was to use it accordingly, we therefore did as we were ordered and had no further scruples as to how the Committee used it."[125] However, the York County committee discovered that many sectarians considered the directives to be "equally against their Consciences" as bearing arms. Yet because sectarians believed it was "a Matter of Conscience to pay the Provincial Tax," some of them offered alternative proposals that would "remove all uneasiness" about the matter.[126]

In September 1775 officers of the Philadelphia association, convinced "that People *sincerely* and *religiously* scrupulous are but few in Comparison to those who upon this Occasion, as well as others, make *Conscience a Convenience*," complained that "fatal Mischiefs" might arise from the "Lenity" shown to conscientious objectors. Because "a very considerable Share of the Property of this Province is in the Hands of People professing to be of tender Conscience in military Matters," associators thought it "extremely hard" that they should risk their lives to defend them. They requested that a plan be devised that would obligate everyone to lend his personal or financial support to the struggle and no longer leave it to the "*Inclinations*" of pacifists to contribute. A few days later the committee of safety presented a similar petition.[127]

Following the election of a new assembly in October, several petitions were presented requesting the enactment of a militia law that would require all able-bodied men to enlist, for recommendations to join associations had produced an inadequate response. Petitioners acknowledged that pacifists should not be forced to fight, but insisted that they should be required to provide financial assistance.[128] Quakers secured copies of the petitions, and in response presented a counterpetition reiterating their beliefs about war. Reminding the assembly of the guarantees of liberty of conscience set forth in the frame of government, Friends asked that this fundamental element of the constitution not be infringed.[129] This petition received replies from the Philadelphia committee, the officers of the city association, and the privates of that body. All objected to the tenor of the Quaker petition, and argued that because Quakers would share in the benefits if Americans successfully defended their liberties, therefore they must make some sacrifice. All denied an intention to violate liberty of conscience.[130]

Mennonites and German Baptists also presented an address summarizing their beliefs concerning nonresistance. They accepted the recommendation that nonassociators assist "those who are in Need and distressed Circumstances" as a statement of their religious duties. "[A]lways ready, according to CHRIST'S Command to *Peter*, to pay the Tribute, that we may offend no Man, and so we are willing to pay Taxes, and to render unto *Caesar* those Things that are *Caesar's*, and to GOD those Things that are GOD'S," they stated that they would submit to the commands of the government, with the exception of bearing arms or otherwise doing injury to any person. They requested the "Patience" of other inhabitants with respect to religious beliefs on which they differed.[131]

The assembly then formulated lengthy provisions to regularize the military associations and transform them from temporary, county units into a provincial force. Local assessors were directed to compile lists of all white male inhabitants between the ages of sixteen and fifty capable of bearing arms, excluding ministers and indentured servants. Those who refused to join an association for any reason were to be fined £2.10. Collection would be in accordance with the tax laws.[132] Although apprehensive that the tax might prove burdensome, some pacifists were pleased that they were not forced to act against their consciences by actually participating in the new military organization.[133] Militiamen, on the other hand, found several deficiencies in the regulations and presented numerous petitions proposing modifications. They also declared that the fine imposed upon nonparticipants was not a fair equivalent to personal service. Moreover, many wealthy men were over fifty, and therefore completely exempt from supporting defensive measures.[134] Revisions in the militia regulations made in April 1776 increased the fine on nonassociators to £3.10.[135]

During the two years preceding independence, there was some sentiment that Quakers were obstructing the American cause. Others hinted that Presbyterians were behind the agitation, and expressed fear of living under their governance. There were complaints about those whose consciences forbade them to accept the paper money issued to support the war effort. The designation of days of fasting and prayer aroused some ill-feeling, although officials did try to prevent violence against those whose religious beliefs precluded the recognition of appointed fast days.[136]

More important was the underlying impulse to accord, as antagonists aimed at persuasion rather than persecution. Both factions worked to solidify their positions and publicize their views. With the increase in the number of committees and military units, new positions were opened to Germans, the Scotch-Irish, and others outside of the normal channels of active participation in colonial affairs, a trend that continued and increased during the war. Members of pacifistic sects served on committees, at least until independence was declared.[137]

Efforts to deemphasize religious and ethnic distinctions were made. One man was forced to apologize before the Bucks County committee for having "uttered expressions" that were "invidious to a particular denomination of Christians" and to promise that he would behave better in the future.[138] Among the regulations governing the military association was a decree that "All National Distinctions in Dress or Name . . . be avoided, it being proper that we should now be united in this General Association for defending our Liberties and Properties, under the Sole Denomination of *Americans*."[139]

Quakers translated and distributed at least one epistle urging moderation among the Germans. County committees and the assembly translated the articles governing military associations into German, while the German version of *Common Sense*, it was reported, "Works on the Minds of those People amazingly." The German press informed those who did not understand English about the imperial problems, and the issues involved.[140] When asked by a member of Congress to write a letter urging their coreligionists in other colonies to support the American cause, German pastors refused, but in response to a similar request from Congress, the lay councils of the Philadelphia Lutheran and Reformed churches, in conjunction with the Deutsche Gesellschaft, drafted a circular letter to Germans in New

York and North Carolina to acquaint them with the issues. It included translations of many of that body's declarations and urged the Germans to support American liberty.[141]

Germans petitioned for concessions that would make them full citizens. Philadelphia privates declared that "all Persons, (not being Mercenaries) who expose their Lives in Defence of a Country, should be admitted to the Enjoyment of all the Rights and Privileges of a Citizen of that Country which they have defended and protected[.]"[142] The assembly concluded that aliens producing enlistment certificates should be "put in the same Condition, and entitled to the same Rights and Privileges, as natural-born Subjects within this Province now are."[143] It also began to draft resolutions to make "Naturalization and the Oaths or Affirmations of Allegiance unnecessary in all Cases where they are required or have been usually taken within this Colony."[144] A similar petition was presented to the provincial congress convened in June 1776 to discuss the procedures for framing a new constitution. It decided that any associator over twenty-one who had resided in the colony for one year and who paid or had been assessed for taxes would be eligible to vote in the election for members of a constitutional convention, provided that he declared that he no longer bore allegiance to the King and would not oppose the establishment of a free government. Other voters could also be required to make this declaration.[145]

III

The 1776 Pennsylvania constitution provided an opportunity for the colonists to reshape William Penn's frame of government, under which they had lived since 1701. Its authors reaffirmed religious liberty, indicating widespread acceptance of the ways in which their society had evolved. The constitution declared that "all men have a natural and unalienable right to worship Almighty God, according to the dictates of their own consciences and understanding"; that no one should be compelled to attend services or support a church against his own will, "nor can any man who acknowledges the being of a God, be justly deprived or abridged of any civil rights as a citizen, on account of his religious sentiments, or peculiar mode of religious worship"; and that "no authority can, or ought to be vested in, or assumed by any power whatever, that shall in any case interfere with, or in any manner controul the right of conscience in the free exercise of religious worship."[146]

One controversial issue involved the qualifications for officials. The first draft proposed that assemblymen simply declare "I do believe in one God the Creator and Governor of the Universe." However, people of many faiths found this apparent disrespect for Christianity objectionable.[147] A disowned Quaker declared, "(farewell Christianity when Turks. Jews. infidels. & what is worse Deists & Atheists are to make laws for our State)[.]"[148] There was some sentiment that "members of the new government should also acknowledge that God was a rewarder of the good and punisher of the wicked." A coalition of Philadelphia ministers tried to formulate a more acceptable qualification, but even some clergymen thought that belief in the Supreme Being as creator and upholder of the world was sufficient.[149] The final version of the constitution required assemblymen to declare "I do believe in one God, the creator and governor of the universe, the rewarder of the good and punisher of the wicked, and I do acknowledge the scriptures of the Old and New Testament to be given by Divine Inspiration." It also guaranteed that "no further or other religious test shall ever hereafter be required of any civil officer or magistrate in this state."[150] Even this test did not satisfy all Pennsylvanians, many of whom feared disaster would befall the state if non-Christians, especially deists and atheists, were allowed to share in government. Although the small Jewish community was excluded from full participation in civil affairs, there was apparently no question of excluding Roman Catholics.[151]

The new constitution expanded privileges tentatively extended to a limited group of aliens prior to independence. Revolutionaries were interested in incorporating aliens into the state, and achieved at least one goal that had been blocked by royal and proprietary authorities. Because all individuals "have a natural inherent right to emigrate from one state to another . . . or to form a new state in vacant countries, or in such countries as they can purchase, whenever they think that thereby they may promote their own happiness," every "foreigner" of "good character" who took the oath or affirmation of allegiance to the state was entitled to buy and sell property. After one year of residence he would be "deemed a free denizen thereof, and entitled to all the rights of a natural born subject of this state." The only restriction was a two-year residency requirement for election to the assembly.[152]

Oaths or affirmations of allegiance and abjuration, military service, and taxation were the principal sources of contention among Pennsylvania's varied ethnic and religious groups during the war. While the question of loyalism entered the discussions, the real problem involved the interplay of religious beliefs with civil war. The Revolution tested the limits to which the rulers under the new government would tolerate conscientious dissent, and the willingness of sectarians to define or compromise their beliefs.

Between 1777 and 1779 Pennsylvania enacted a series of test laws designed to separate loyalists from supporters of the American cause. The first test law, enacted in June 1777, directed all white male inhabitants over the age of eighteen to take an oath or affirmation renouncing the King, declaring allegiance to the state, and promising to do nothing prejudicial to the state's independence and to inform a justice of the peace about treason or conspiracies against it. Any adult male, subsequently redefined to include those over age sixteen, who traveled outside of the county in which he resided would be regarded as a spy, and if he refused to declare allegiance would be imprisoned without bail until he did so. Men who neglected or refused to subscribe the declaration were to be disfranchised, disarmed, and forbidden to serve on juries, sue to collect debts, and buy or sell property.[153] A new law enacted in April 1778 extended the deadline for subscribing the test, but specified even harsher penalties for noncompliance: most professionals were no longer permitted to practice their occupations, access to the legal system was curtailed, property rights were restricted, and double taxes were exacted. Individuals could be summoned by justices to take the test; refusal brought imprisonment unless the offender paid a fine not to exceed £10. If a man refused to make the declaration when he was brought before a regular court session, he could be expelled from the state and forfeit his property.[154]

The most repressive provisions of the April 1778 act were repealed eight months later. The December law gave Pennsylvanians an additional opportunity to become citizens in good standing, and excluded nonjurors only from the franchise and jury service. Furthermore, a general pardon was issued for all those confined in prison under the provisions of the previous law.[155] The last statute concerning allegiance, enacted in 1779, gave residents one final chance to declare their loyalty to the state. Those who did not "shall be forever excluded from [taking] the same, and deprived of the privileges and benefits of a citizen or citizens who shall have complied with this act."[156]

Although all statutes equated an affirmation with an oath, indicating a recognition that the refusal to swear an oath of allegiance might be based on an objection to oaths rather than to their content, many people opposed the loyalty declarations. The pleas of Moravians, Schwenkfelders, and other sectarians helped to persuade the assembly to mitigate the most severe penalties of the April 1778 law. Professing their allegiance to the state and willingness to support it in all ways consistent with their religious beliefs, they pointed out that, because of the sanctity of the affirmations of allegiance taken upon naturalization, they could not in good conscience abjure the King.[157] The assembly remained unconvinced. It considered the sectarians' arguments specious, for Pennsylvania had an old law requiring abjuration of the Stuart line to which no one had objected. Germans, in fact, had made this declaration as part of the naturalization process. The new state law was in the same form and, like the British act, did not entail an obligation to take up arms to uphold the abjuration.[158] Moravians argued, however, that Germans had never owed allegiance to the Pretender, and therefore had not transferred their allegiance to the Hanoverian line. Moreover, the abjuration was not a "proper Discrimination to distinguish the Friends from the Enemies of the Land. Whosoever can swear or affirm Allegiance to the State & act a contrary Part, such a one will not Scruple to take the Test, as it stands & do what he pleases, whatsoever his Religion or Society may be called."[159]

A few revolutionaries zealously pressed nonjurors to make the required declarations, especially during the early years of the war. Some sectarians were harassed, fined, and imprisoned.[160] Under pressure, a few pacifists yielded, but their religious societies responded by requiring erring members to retract their affirmation, apologize in the church, and repent if they wished to remain within the fellowship.[161] Persecution appears to have been conducted more typically from personal motives rather than as state policy. Some officials urged that pacifists be treated with leniency and that the laws not be abused. George Bryan, a member of the Supreme Executive Council, believed that because "these people are not to be feared, either as to numbers or malice," the government did not wish to call them to take the test without a specific reason.[162]

The most notable instance of persecution for religious beliefs was the exile of several Philadelphia Quakers in September 1777. Fearing an impending invasion of the city, Congress took umbrage at a "seditious" epistle issued by the Meeting for Sufferings in December 1776 and advised Pennsylvania authorities to "apprehend and secure all Persons, as well among the People called Quakers, as others, who have in their general Conduct and Conversation, widened a Disposition inimical to the Cause of America."[163] Warrants for the arrest of forty-one persons, including a dancing master, Anglican priests, and other non-Friends, were issued. When twenty-one Quakers refused to affirm allegiance to the state, they were ordered to be conveyed under guard to Virginia. For the next six months Pennsylvania authorities and Congress blamed each other for this clearly illegal action. Decisions on their release were delayed as petitioners in support of the prisoners were referred from one body to the other. The officials involved seemed embarrassed by their momentary panic, and tried to evade responsibility by denying that the exiles were their prisoners. Finally in April 1778 the men were released; they continued to refuse to affirm their allegiance to the new government.[164]

Very few Pennsylvanians believed that the expulsion was warranted. Quakers were outraged, especially since there was no attempt to prove that the men had engaged in any crimes or treasonable activities. "Evil Men" had conducted "Arbitrary & oppressive proceedings" against Friends, an "Unheard of Cruelty" by "wicked men."[165] The Yearly Meeting declared that the exiles had done nothing wrong, nor had they "departed from the peaceable Principles which we profess."[166] Even individuals who had belonged to the proprietary faction or had otherwise opposed Quakers in the prewar years objected to the proceedings. When the carriages with the men passed near his residence, Muhlenberg commented, "Now prepare thyself, Pennsylvania, to meet the Lord thy God!"[167] James Allen declared that "These proceedings bear the mark of the most wanton Tyranny ever exercised in any Country. . . . This civil war has rendered the minds of our Governors desperate & savage: they not only trample on the most express laws of their own Government, but those of natural Justice & humanity."[168] Indicative of the widespread sympathy for the accused Quakers was the way they were treated by guards, people in the towns through which they passed, and many Virginians. They were permitted to walk or ride around the towns in which they were lodged, granted free access to writing materials, and allowed to hold religious meetings that other Friends and visitors attended. Their guards were reported to be "very good humor'd." People with whom they came in contact were, after initial hesitance, easily convinced by their inoffensive behavior that they posed no threat.[169]

Several Anglican priests also suffered hardship and suspicion of loyalism for their refusal either to take the oath of allegiance to the state or to cease reading the prayers appointed for the King and government to which they were bound by their ordination oaths.[170] Very early in the war one priest, exaggerating somewhat, declared that "every Clergyman of the *Church of England*, who dar'd to act upon proper Principles, was mark'd out for Infamy & Insult;—In Consequence of which the *Missionaries* in particular have suffer'd greatly—Some of them have been drag'd from their Horses;—assaulted with Stones & Dirt;—duck'd in Water;—obliged to flee for their Lives;—driven from their Habitations & Families;—laid under Arrests, & imprison'd!—I believe they were all (or, at least, most of them) reduc'd to the same Necessity, with me, of shutting up their Churches[.]" Ministers, however, continued to exercise some of their functions privately. When the test laws prohibited nonjurors from crossing county lines, Anglican priests traveled near them so that women could cross and have their children baptized and instructed.[171]

The Pennsylvania constitution recognized the rights of conscientious objectors. Pacifists could not be "justly compelled" to bear arms if they would "pay such equivalent" to personal service.[172] Military laws took cognizance of the number of men who could not in good conscience bear arms. Although all men except those in certain occupations were required to enroll in the militia, and fines were levied on those who neglected or refused to attend musters, exemptions from personal service could be granted when the unit was called into active duty. Men who preferred not to serve could provide a substitute. If an individual refused to do so or could not find one, the officer was to obtain one, with the delinquent paying the costs. Anyone who refused to pay the fines or costs of a substitute was liable to distraint of goods. Subsequent laws regularized the procurement of substitutes and the methods of collecting fines, which were gradually increased, from nonparticipants.[173] A few laws required nonparticipants to pay heavier taxes than those who joined the army, but were in effect only temporarily.[174]

Resentment of men who refused to pay the fines in order to be exempted from service continued throughout the war, for some Pennsylvanians believed that they were not carrying their share of the burden. Refusal to serve in the army resulted in abuse of the laws through imprisonment, excessive seizure of property, and exorbitant rates for hiring substitutes, despite the legal safeguards intended to prevent oppression. Officials were unwilling to exempt pacifists from the fines or taxation, probably believing that exemption from personal service was a liberal, tolerant, and equitable policy. They paid little regard to what they viewed as excessive scruples of conscience that forbade monetary contributions.[175]

The variety of sects in the state makes it difficult to generalize about the experiences of pacifists, for each took a different position on the extent to which it could cooperate on military matters. Schwenkfelders, who took a moderate position, summed up the situation in mid-1779: "no one really can complain, . . . even though here and there one was fleeced, as the saying goes. The military thus far have not been able to force anyone of our people into service, . . . Nevertheless it costs horrible sums to escape the same."[176] Some sects experienced difficulty reaching a consensus, although their members frequently agreed to help each other bear the burdens of fines.[177] It appears that those whose principles enabled them to pay fines or to hire substitutes suffered less than those who adamantly refused to do so.

To these problems were added conflicts over the means of financing the war. Some "conscientiously scrupulous men" refused to accept paper money, and on occasion suffered violence for their action. But others also refused to sell their goods for inflated paper money, and some forced to accept it in payment for debts complained of being cheated.[178] Some Quakers believed that they could not pay taxes "impos'd for the support of the War," and questioned, "would it not be repugnant to reason to contribute by Taxes to the support of either party who may happen to prevail, who we could not under the present unsetled State of Affairs be free to Acknowledge?"[179] Others believed that even though "our Brethren formerly paid them; Knowledge is progressive."[180] Many Quakers, however, "freely" paid their taxes, "the greatest part of which they knew was appropriated for military purposes."[181] Other tried to distinguish between 'the taxes and the war effort. Some Friends believed that they had an obligation to aid the poor and unfortunate, and voluntarily made collections of goods and money to aid the poor or distressed.[182]

Social and religious tensions surfaced in minor issues. Most incidents were caused simply by the presence of large numbers of men congregated in one place, such as the occasional outbreaks of violence or disorder on St. Patrick's Day.[183] Others involved the refusal to observe fast days or illuminations; Quakers in particular were victims of broken windows or verbal abuse by those who believed that nonparticipation indicated loyalist sentiments.[184] Yet most Pennsylvanians recognized that Friends were merely acting consistently with long-established practices. Partially successful pleas that they be left alone were issued, or men walked the streets to keep the peace.[185]

The war entailed particular hardships for Moravian communities. On several occasions their buildings were appropriated to serve as hospitals or to house prisoners. Some instances of unnecessary harassment occurred, including plans to use a minister's house as a powder magazine and threats to blow up a church. But in other cases officials attempted to limit disruption by leaving the houses of the sisters untouched and stationing protective guards around them. In addition, officers arranged passage of troops through Moravian towns at times that would not interfere with their religious observances. Because Moravians bore their burdens with a fortitude that officials recognized, they were able to negotiate with military and civil authorities to reach accommodations that would both contribute to the American cause and preserve their distinctive beliefs and practices. They hosted some members of the Continental Congress, which allowed them to gain support for the integrity of their beliefs as they demonstrated that they were not loyalists. The use of their towns may be regarded as persecution, a sentiment that the Moravians occasionally expressed; however, there was a practical need for large buildings in a rural and healthful area.[186] It should also be remembered that many denominations found their churches and meetinghouses used as hospitals or to house troops, had their pews burned for firewood, or were otherwise damaged. Both contending parties were guilty of such destruction.[187]

Despite tensions, further evidence of harmonious relations between different religious groups emerged during the war. The refusal to draw narrow distinctions based on denominational lines was evident in the relationships between Anglicans and other groups. An Anglican candidate for the ministry became involved in a lengthy effort to secure ordination from the Lutheran Ministerium in order to supply vacant congregations. Sympathetic Lutherans in effect licensed him as a probationer. They wrote testimonials verifying his qualifications, helped him to regularize his relationship with his congregations, and expressed the opinion that he could properly administer baptism. Although reluctant, they finally concluded that he could be ordained following more particular instruction in Lutheran theology.[188] The Reformed were approached by another Anglican candidate for ordination, but after some consideration, they declined to do so unless he could unite with their church. While divisions within the visible church were regrettable, European ordination practices should be followed.[189] One Anglican priest arranged for a German Lutheran candidate for the ministry to read prayers and preach in his congregations, while he baptized, visited the sick, and conducted funerals. Together they managed to keep the congregations together during the war.[190] One Anglican church in Philadelphia was opened to use by a Baptist congregation during the war. The congregation "Impowerd the Vestry to permit any Orthodox Preacher of any Denomination to the use of the Church Occasionally in our present Situation."[191] In Lebanon, while the churches were used to house Hessian prisoners, the inhabitants requested an official to clear one of them, "in which the Ministers of the different denominations had agreed to perform divine service alternately," a request he considered "reasonable."[192]

Pennsylvanians demonstrated considerable interest in the Hessian mercenaries dispatched to help quell the American rebellion. At first, they were denounced for their barbarity in battle and for extensive plundering.[193] Later, Americans hoped to persuade Hessians to desert. Because of their long experience with Germans, Pennsylvanians played a large part in this effort.[194] Franklin suggested that some of Congress' statements about the war be translated and sent over to their camp in New Jersey in a drifting canoe. If the papers were used to wrap a bit of tobacco, he thought the soldiers would divide it as "Plunder before the Officers could know the Contents of the Paper & prevent it."[195] One emissary of German descent infiltrated a Hessian camp and attempted to induce soldiers to desert by describing the affluence of Pennsylvania Germans and the liberties and independence they enjoyed.[196] Congress declared that all foreign deserters would be guaranteed religious freedom in whatever state they chose to settle.[197] Hessians were encouraged not only to desert but to settle among their former countrypeople. They were not exchanged as readily as British prisoners, in the hope that the visual evidence of prosperity would convince them that America offered better opportunities than Germany.[198]

Following the Battle of Trenton at Christmas 1776, many Hessians were sent to the predominantly German sections of Pennsylvania.[199] While one minister noted that "they are being well provided for and also have the opportunity of hearing God's Word in both the English and German languages,"[200] the Americans considered them in more practical terms. The council of safety directed that shoemakers be put to work for the benefit of the army; other prisoners were hired out to local farmers. Although security for their good behavior and return if there were to be a prisoner exchange was required, their services were apparently in demand.[201] By the 1780s Pennsylvania had printed a blank form that included a simple declaration of allegiance to the United States to be subscribed by each Hessian prisoner who "signified his Desire to become a free Citizen of the said State."[202]

The course of the Revolution illuminated the potential tensions that could occur within a pluralistic society during a period of crisis, but there were few fundamental deviations from the course the province had taken over the previous decades. Nonparticipants suffered somewhat, yet there appears to have been little question that religious beliefs, if not political activities, should be respected. If the options open to pacifists were not always acceptable to them, the new rulers demonstrated a willingness to compromise and to modify regulations to suit individual beliefs in such ways as they believed were equitable to other citizens and responsive to the needs of the war. Guarantees of freedom of conscience remained an integral part of the new constitution. Catholics, for the first time since 1705/6, were entitled to fill major governmental positions. When in 1779 the College of Philadelphia's charter was revoked, its replacement included the senior ministers of several denominations in Philadelphia, including the Roman Catholic priest, as members of the board of trustees.[203] Futhermore, citizenship became easier to acquire, and aliens' rights to hold property were extended.

With the proclamation of peace, Pennsylvanians quickly moved to restore the harmony that had characterized their pre-revolutionary society. Interest in foreign immigration revived.[204] Presbyterians, reacting to "an apprehension" that other denominations believed members of their church "hold intolerant principles," declared that "they ever have, and still do renounce and abhor the principles of intolerance; and we do believe that every peaceable member of civil society ought to be protected in the full and free exercise of their religion."[205] The test law disabling nonjurors from the civil and legal rights of other citizens was repealed within a decade, although there was initially some reluctance to do this.[206] Jewish Pennsylvanians, arguing that the state constitution guaranteed no loss of civil rights because of religious beliefs, petitioned for a repeal of the religious declaration required of assemblymen. Their appeal for complete equality was sympathetically

greeted in the newspapers, and was granted in the new state constitution of 1790.[207] If the war tested the limits of toleration, it also
provided an opportunity for Pennsylvanians to affirm the wisdom of
the principles and policies articulated by William Penn.

CHAPTER 9

Epilogue:
The Pennsylvania Experience

The ethnic, linguistic, and religious diversity characterizing Pennsylvania in the seventeenth and eighteenth centuries may be described as a transitional state between the exclusiveness of England and most of the other colonies and the subsequent American pattern of relatively unrestricted immigration from Europe and religious freedom. While it was not the only colony settled by Europeans of diverse origins and beliefs, it did represent the extreme. Rhode Island, perhaps the closest analogue in its guarantee of religious liberty, did not attract a wide variety of non-English colonists. Other colonies experienced migration of German and Scotch-Irish peoples to their frontiers, but conceded at best only the privilege of toleration to newcomers, not the right of freedom of conscience. Only in Pennsylvania was there no "establishment" to dispense or withhold favors; if non-English immigrants were not always encouraged, and if fervent members of religious groups sometimes proved obstreperous, there were few institutional hindrances.

Underneath this harmony was a subtle mosaic of shifting attitudes and concerns, but there were few consistent hostilities expressed by one group toward another. Underlying prejudices and tensions were revealed only in extreme situations that suddenly thrust a particular group into prominence. Threats of war, intensive missionary activity, or a visible increase in immigration appeared to challenge the status quo by potentially disrupting a relatively stable balance of power or factions. But with resolution of the immediate problem, the ideology of tolerance prevailed and the colony soon reverted once again into peace.

There was initially little concern about any negative impact when large numbers of people from different cultures settled in the province. Although during one period of large-scale German immigration in the middle of the eighteenth century some concern was voiced that the "English" culture would be replaced by a "German" one, there was little pressure on immigrants to conform to a particular set of cultural norms. Only in the abortive Charity School project was there an attempt to enforce conformity.

Even without outside pressure, many settlers found it advantageous to adopt the English language. By the middle of the eighteenth century Swedish and Welsh had fallen almost completely into disuse. It is important to note, however, that the German language—continually reinforced by new immigrants and by relative isolation from English-speaking people in the backcountry—continued to be used throughout the period. Translations of important documents, laws, and proceedings of the assembly, published both by order of the assembly and on the initiative of German printers, reflected an attempt to accommodate the needs of this community and to fully incorporate it into provincial society.

Despite the continuing use of the German language, ethnic consciousness in Pennsylvania was limited. The distinctions people made in referring to themselves and others tended to be primarily of a religious nature; those based upon national group or language were less significant. Both English- and German-speaking peoples were fragmented by their religious beliefs, and individuals often extended this mode of distinction to include the way people of another national or linguistic group were viewed. To a large extent, the amount of formal interaction among different groups seems also to have been along religious lines. "Church" Germans—both Lutherans and Reformed—Swedish Lutherans, and Anglicans worked closely together; it was not uncommon for ministers to serve the needs of congregations other than those of their particular denomination. Members of sects often had common interests that cut across linguistic or theological lines.

When religious disputes arose, more often than not they centered within a particular national group and did not seriously affect intergroup relations. Germans in particular tended to factionalize into so many varieties of sects that they concerned themselves very little with their English and Scotch-Irish neighbors. Divisions within a particular denomination, such as the schism within the Presbyterian church following the Great Awakening and the seemingly endless quarrels within the German Reformed church, were also important. Religious factionalism and contention were a significant aspect of provincial society, but because they were generally restricted within linguistic or denominational groups, society as a whole was not seriously disrupted.

One area where intergroup conflicts did noisily intrude from time to time was politics. Here the issues usually derived from the disparate views of church and sect, and principally involved English-speaking Anglicans and Quakers. Fundamental differences in outlook produced contention, especially on issues related to war. Many non-Quakers believed that the Quaker-dominated assembly was attempting to impose its pacifistic beliefs on others, to the detriment of provincial security. However, politics is almost by definition the arena where conflicts are announced, occasionally created, debated, and less frequently resolved. In Pennsylvania there are significant reasons to qualify the importance of the contentious legislative record. Quakers were, after all, continually reelected to the assembly by their predominantly non-Quaker constituents. Nor was the conduct of provincial politics ever based completely upon religious beliefs. Power struggles pitted Quakers against Quakers, and neither the proprietary nor the antiproprietary faction was religiously homogeneous. Although Germans and the Scotch-Irish did not become actively involved in colonial politics until after the middle of the eighteenth century, their votes were solicited by all factions at an earlier date. Moreover, it is unclear to how great an extent political contention affected the ordinary Pennsylvanian. Social instability was rarely a consequence of the political disputes carried on by the elite.

It did take some time for settlers to adjust to what became the "custom of the country." Not all settlers were prepared for the unusual religious and ethnic heterogeneity they discovered, and the first reaction was often one of amazement or bewilderment. Some of the initial reports sent back to friends in Europe indicate that extreme pluralism, especially in religious matters, was not expected, and not always appreciated. Liberty of conscience was praised as one of the chief virtues of the colony, but at the same time there was anxiety about preserving "orthodoxy" in the midst of competing beliefs and practices and the seeming irreligion of many Pennsylvanians. There was also concern about maintaining proper standards of behavior and morality. In the abstract, life in a province distinguished by the presence of a wide variety of nationalities and beliefs may not have been considered the most desirable situation. Nevertheless, most colonists pragmatically adjusted to the conditions they found in the colony. Those discontented with their surroundings could choose to leave the colony, attempt to find a home in a fairly homogeneous portion of it, or migrate to unsettled land along the frontier. A significant portion of those who permanently settled in Pennsylvania, however, came to take pride in the way all colonists lived harmoniously with their neighbors.

As each new group of people entered the province, there seems to have been a lag of about a decade before its members fully accepted the nature of the society in which they lived or were fully integrated into it. This seems to have been especially true of religious groups and their leaders. At first there was an effort to establish "orthodoxy" and to make converts out of nonbelievers. However, missionaries who remained in the colony generally came to recognize that not only was there no possibility that the European system of state churches could be established, but also that it was almost impossible to maintain stable congregations that could gather weekly for worship. Many individuals frequented whatever services were available. Although ministers hoped to make converts and to redeem former adherents who had joined sects or lapsed into religious indifference, they soon discovered that hostile attacks on other sects or denominations were unpopular. On the contrary, the way to reach the unbeliever was to present the basics of Christian belief and morality; debates over minor points of doctrine heightened contention, but converted few. Because Pennsylvanians frowned upon intensive missionary activity, a group's acceptance increased after it ceased trying to gain influence. Sectarians interested in bringing their message to other colonists also discovered that vigorous missionary work was opposed, and their tactics underwent a change similar to that of ministers. Sectarians who came to Pennsylvania to flee from the world also seemed to undergo a gradual transformation, or if they did not accept Pennsylvania society, their neighbors recognized their right to remain different.

The widespread toleration characteristic of the province is clearly evident in the reception accorded Roman Catholics and Jews—unpopular groups in Britain and most of the other North American colonies. There was a small amount of anti-Catholic sentiment, but most of it was expressed during periods of war with the French. That Catholics lived in Pennsylvania, built churches, and were regularly visited by priests resident in the province was hardly a secret, and was frequently ignored or mentioned without evident animosity. The presence of the relatively few Jewish inhabitants was most frequently noted because of the novelty involved in meeting one. Little anti-Semitism was expressed in such comments.

When the Revolution presented an opportunity to restructure colonial institutions, Pennsylvanians reaffirmed the guarantees of liberty of conscience and equality of all white settlers articulated by William Penn almost a century earlier. The new constitution recognized the validity of pacifistic beliefs, and guaranteed an exemption from bearing arms. Naturalization became easier to acquire under the new government, and the property rights of aliens were strengthened. Although an attempt to remove restrictions on officeholding that limited certain positions to trinitarian Protestants was defeated, the framers of the first state constitution revealed an interest in enlarging still further the boundaries of liberty of conscience. Their action indicates that many Pennsylvanians had come to believe that liberty of conscience was to be valued; that even a token uniformity of religion was no longer considered essential to a stable government; and that some men believed that one's faith was a private matter and had nothing at all to do with public affairs.

I

Individuals did not immediately lose any prejudices they brought with them, nor were all colonists completely tolerant of various forms of diversity. Nevertheless, Pennsylvanians tended to ignore potentially divisive differences. The explanation lies in some mixture of a number of factors that were conducive to group interaction, tolerance, or at least indifference.

For one thing, a variety of peoples, languages, and religious beliefs characterized Pennsylvania almost from the beginning of its settlement. Sparse population, the ease with which the Swedes, Dutch, and English gained control of the Delaware Valley during the seventeenth century, the willingness to reconfirm land grants, the simple requirement of an oath of allegiance to the new rulers, and toleration for the previous settlers' religion provided an early pattern for the toleration and ethnic diversity that were to become characteristic of Pennsylvania during the eighteenth century. But these were pragmatic adjustments, unstable and fragile. New York, New Jersey, and Delaware also had non-British inhabitants when the English crown seized them. A degree of accommodation occurred in these colonies as well, but without the commitment to diversity and harmony that marked Pennsylvania.

It was only with the grant of Pennsylvania and the Lower Counties to William Penn that the ideology of tolerance, and with it a principled commitment to religious and ethnic heterogeneity, were articulated, and the earlier, pragmatic pattern became firmly established as a matter of principle. The ideals of William Penn—especially his goal of establishing a haven for individuals persecuted for their beliefs—induced him to recruit not only Quakers from all parts of the British Isles but also Dutch and German pietists and French Huguenots. Quaker beliefs that Truth had not been entirely revealed and that each person would understand it individually encouraged toleration of different systems of belief and practice as well as religious pluralism. Penn's guarantee of liberty of conscience to all who believed in God and promises of equal civil rights without regard to narrow distinctions in beliefs—as well as his decree that anyone who disturbed another because of religious ideas or practices was guilty of disturbing the peace—also fostered tolerance. Furthermore, the desire to sell large tracts of land encouraged both recruitment of individuals outside of the Quaker fellowship and concessions to alien purchasers and settlers.

Despite the liberal provisions of the various frames of government he promulgated for the colony, Penn left only a vague blueprint for the colony's subsequent development. He spent very little time in his province, and exercised no veto over legislation enacted by the assembly and deputy governor in his absence. His heirs eventually drifted from Quakerism into the Church of England. But to the credit of Penn's sons and the predominantly Quaker government, the commitment to toleration and the effort to treat all religious groups impartially remained effective, and were gradually adopted by most residents of the province.

The tolerant attitudes and policies were not achieved without difficulty; there were serious debates over the meaning of religious freedom and the extent to which it was to be practiced, especially in the early years. In the novel situation in which there was no religious establishment, those accustomed to the privileges inherent in membership in an established church believed that they were being deprived of their rights. Those outside of the traditional union of church and state, for their part, fought to obtain the rights they believed belonged to all inhabitants peaceably residing under a particular government. Nevertheless, within twenty-five years of William Penn's founding of his colony devoted to religious liberty, Pennsylvanians had reached accommodations on the major issues that had threatened the colony's existence or success. Vital compromises on the meaning of liberty of conscience, the validity of oaths and affirmations, and a method of meeting the financial demands for defense had been devised. Although these accommodations or adjustments were fragile, individuals came to recognize that if—as was guaranteed under Penn's constitution—no particular religion was to be established, or even dominant, all inhabitants must be permitted to follow the dictates of their consciences.

In effect, competition forced compromise; to protect one's right to act in accordance with individual beliefs entailed a recognition that a similar right must be accorded to those with differing beliefs and practices. Thus, once agreement had been reached on the theoretical problems involved in issues in which the conscientious beliefs of individuals conflicted, subsequent but related problems could be resolved relatively easily. Although tensions within this complex province frequently developed, the basic respect for the beliefs of others was one of the most characteristic features of provincial culture during the remainder of the colonial period.

Penn's interest in recruiting foreign immigrants played a major role in creating a diverse society. Yet in his absence this, too, could have been thwarted by restrictive laws or by a generally hostile attitude toward aliens. Perhaps because Penn's early colonists were themselves drawn from several countries and entered an area already settled by people of Dutch, Swedish, Finnish, and English descent, by the time massive Scotch-Irish and German immigration commenced, Pennsylvanians had already adjusted to the reality of living in a heterogeneous society. If dismay over the sheer number of immigrants and their purported attributes was occasionally expressed, the sole restrictive measure enacted was a duty on Irish servants and German passengers, a law repealed within a year of its passage. More significant, and typical, were the positive responses that indicated a willingness to accept all Europeans into provincial society. The assembly passed laws to naturalize aliens, liberalized the provisions of the 1740 English general naturalization act, and enacted measures intended to protect the health and interests of Pennsylvania-bound immigrants. Naturalized foreigners enjoyed all of the civil and political rights of the native-born, and the unnaturalized suffered no discrimination or restriction except for a denial of the franchise.

Another major component in the toleration that characterized the colony was the individualism displayed by many of its inhabitants. In religious terms, it took the form of acceptance of the idea that no one had a right to impose his views upon another. This concept was especially prevalent among sectarians, although it was subsequently adopted by churchmen. There was another aspect to individualism, however. Eighteenth-century settlers, whose motives for emigration tended to be more economic than religious, seem often to have chosen to come to Pennsylvania for the opportunities it offered to improve the standard of living for themselves and their families. Such immigrants were more interested in inexpensive, fertile land and the minimal demands of government than in the nature of provincial society or the characteristics of their neighbors. Landowners were more concerned about a person's ability to purchase land or to pay rent for it than in his origins or beliefs. Although there were numerous complaints that German and Scotch-Irish immigrants were squatters and unwilling or unable to purchase land, there was at the same time a belief that continued prosperity depended upon continual immigration. In particular, the contributions of German farmers were recognized as a valuable asset in the rapid development of the provincial economy.

Individualism was accentuated by the patterns of immigration and settlement. Very few colonists emigrated in groups; those who did were primarily sectarians who arrived in the late seventeenth and early eighteenth centuries. Migration by individuals and families could help to break down the awareness of belonging to a particular religious or regional group, as well as make it more difficult to retain distinctive traits. Many emigrants were unable to defray the costs incurred in sailing to the province, and thus came as indentured servants or redemptioners. The prevalence of servitude frequently resulted in acquaintance with those of a different language, culture, or religion, on the part of both master and servant. It was commonly believed that service in an English family would help German immigrants to acquire the English language and to become acculturated. Young people of all backgrounds were desired as servants, for it was thought that they could most easily adjust to colonial mores and become useful citizens when their terms expired.

The settlement pattern of dispersed farms, rather than compact villages, further reinforced the isolation of individuals from those who might naturally form a distinct community. Penn's refusal to allow the ethnic enclaves desired by early Welsh and German colonists, while it caused hard feelings at the time, in the long run probably contributed to mutual toleration as individuals acquired neighbors of different backgrounds and beliefs. Perhaps because of continual interaction with "outsiders," firm stereotypes tended not to develop. Preconceived notions about a particular group broke down as its members were viewed as individuals.

Finally, many people were affected by the inability to transfer European institutions to the colony and by the disintegrating impact of scattered settlements along the frontier. Sectarians had a distinct advantage in being able to organize their congregations locally without reference to European authorities or dependence upon an educated clergy. Church groups, which included the majority of the population during the eighteenth century, suffered throughout the period from a shortage of ministers, particularly in the early years of settlement. Although ministers, when they finally arrived, were extremely critical of the religious diversity of Pennsylvania and of the unwillingness of its inhabitants to receive the sacraments, pay salaries to the clergy, or otherwise participate in the forms of organized religion, they also reported that adherents of many sects or denominations attended their services. Many individuals reacted to the shortage of readily available public worship by losing interest in religion or by taking advantage of whatever preachers or services were convenient. Strong denominational consciousness was characteristic primarily of ministers; the average lay person, if he or she had religious inclinations, was more interested in similarities than in differences. Many seemed to have only hazy ideas about the theological concepts held by various congregations, and there was a continual drift of individuals in quest of spiritual peace from one sect to another. The variety of forms of worship allowed colonists an unparalleled opportunity to find their way to salvation. If some individuals became confused by the diversity and lost faith altogether, others found the answer to their particular needs.

II

One of the first historians to recognize the significance of these developments was Frederick Jackson Turner, who cited the experiences of the Middle Colonies in general, and Pennsylvania in particular, as those most closely related to American life over the next century of the country's development. Turner had in mind the influence of economic individualism and a cosmopolitan national identity fashioned from the gradual accommodation of diverse peoples.[1] He was correct in making the association, and in suggesting that the difficulties of maintaining European institutions in a frontier environment fostered the continuity between the colonial and national periods. However, all of the British colonies underwent changes caused by the disruptive effects of the frontier and economic conditions conducive to individualism. The Pennsylvania experience, however much it was affected by the factors cited by Turner, was unique. Although it became in time a tradition that would influence the ways in which groups and individuals would interact in a national culture, that tradition in turn had sources that did not in fact continue to play a dominant role in the nineteenth and twentieth centuries.

In retrospect, these sources were above all religious, not social or economic. Because group identity in Pennsylvania during the eighteenth century was religious rather than ethnic, it was easier for national groups such as the Germans to maintain their separate cultural institutions and languages without pressure to conform to the English norms. Yet at the same time, similar religious interests encouraged interaction among people of different cultures. Furthermore, because the dominant religious ideals were individualistic and undogmatic, it was impossible for any group to mold colony-wide institutions to which individuals could be forced to conform. Other colonies shared Pennsylvania's ethnic diversity, economic individualism, and frontier conditions, but only Pennsylvania had the enduring legacy of William Penn. Only in Pennsylvania was there a firm, if not unwavering, commitment to the ideology of liberty of conscience and toleration and the settlement of peoples of diverse origins and beliefs that provided the opportunity to explore fully the practical aspects of those ideals.

Abbreviations for Periodicals

ACHR   American Catholic Historical Researches
AG   Americana Germanica
AHR   American Historical Review
BFHA   Bulletin of Friends' Historical Association
CH   Church History
DH   Delaware History
FH   Fides et Historia
GAA   German American Annals
HMPEC   Historical Magazine of the Protestant Episcopal Church
JAH   Journal of American History
JLCHS   Journal of the Lancaster County Historical Society
JPHS   Journal of the Presbyterian Historical Society
LCQ   Lutheran Church Quarterly
PAJHS   Publications of the American Jewish Historical Society
PAPS   Proceedings of the American Philosophical Society
PGFS   Pennsylvania German Folklore Society
PGSPA   Pennsylvania-German Society Proceedings and Addresses
PH   Pennsylvania History
PLCHS   Papers of the Lancaster County Historical Society
PMHB   Pennsylvania Magazine of History and Biography
PSQ   Political Science Quarterly
QH   Quaker History
SPHQ   Swedish Pioneer Historical Quarterly
TAPS   Transactions of the American Philosophical Society
TMHS   Transactions of the Moravian Historical Society
3WMQ   William and Mary Quarterly, 3d series

Abbreviations for Manuscript Repositories

A.P.S.   American Philosophical Society
E.R.H.S.   Evangelical and Reformed Historical Society
F.H.L.   Friends Historical Library, Swarthmore College
H.S.P.   Historical Society of Pennsylvania
L.C.   Library of Congress
L.C.P.   Library Company of Philadelphia
M.A.   Moravian Archives
P.H.M.C.   Pennsylvania Historical and Museum Commission
P.H.S.   Presbyterian Historical Society
Q.C.H.C.   Quaker Collection, Haverford College
S.L.   Schwenkfelder Library
V.P.L.   Van Pelt Library, University of Pennsylvania

Notes

1. Prologue: Pennsylvania and American Pluralism

1. U. S. Bureau of the Census, *Historical Statistics of the United States, Colonial Times to 1970*, Bicentennial ed. (Washington, D.C., 1975), pt. 2, p. 1168. These statistics have recently been the subject of considerable debate. See Forrest McDonald and Ellen Shapiro McDonald, "The Ethnic Origins of the American People, 1790," 3*WMQ*, 37 (1980), 179–199, especially Table V (p. 198); Thomas L. Purvis, "The European Ancestry of the United States Population, 1790," *Ibid.*, 41 (1984), 85–101, especially Table II (p. 98); Donald H. Akenson, "Why the Accepted Estimates of the Ethnicity of the American People, 1790, Are Unacceptable," *Ibid.*, pp. 102–119. Purvis, Akenson, and the McDonalds continue the debate in "Commentary," *Ibid.*, pp. 119–135. To make assumptions about person's ethnic (or religious) background on the basis of surname analysis is risky. Regardless of which set of figures or combination thereof the reader finds most acceptable, all of them indicate that Pennsylvania was the least "English" state in 1790.

2. Native Americans and blacks, although a component of provincial society, will be considered only insofar as they affected the relationships among white settlers from various Western European cultures. Racism is a somewhat different question from ethnic or religious prejudice.

3. Lester J. Cappon, ed., *Atlas of Early American History: The Revolutionary Era 1760–1790* (Princeton, 1976), p. 38. This enumeration of various religious congregations appears to omit small sects and may not include groups such as the Amish that did not worship in churches or meetinghouses.

4. A glance at the notes to this book (or the more heavily documented dissertation, "'A Mixed Multitude': Religion and Ethnicity in Colonial Pennsyvania," Harvard University, 1981) will reveal the author's indebtedness to other students of Pennsylvania history; their books, dissertations, and articles were invaluable for interpreting the writings of contemporary Pennsylvanians. They have, however, asked different questions about provincial society. Although a collection of essays edited by Michael Zuckerman,

Friends and Neighbors: Group Life in America's First Plural Society (Philadelphia, 1982), has recently been published, neither it nor other works have addressed the nature of ethnic and religious pluralism in Pennsylvania.

5. A convenient introduction to these issues may be found in the thematic essays contained in Stephan Thernstrom, ed., *Harvard Encyclopedia of American Ethnic Groups* (Cambridge, Mass., 1980).

6. Patricia U. Bonomi has explored the nature of the religious experience throughout colonial America in *Under the Cope of Heaven: Religion, Society, and Politics in Colonial America* (New York, 1986).

2. William Penn's Ideals and Goals

1. Background on the pre-Penn settlements and the sources of religious and ethnic diversity may be found in Sally Schwartz, "Society and Culture in the Seventeenth-Century Delaware Valley," *DH*, 20 (1982), 98–122.

2. William C. Braithwaite, *The Beginnings of Quakerism* (London, 1912), and *The Second Period of Quakerism* (London, 1919); Christopher Hill, *The World Turned Upside Down: Radical Ideas During the English Revolution* (New York, 1972), especially pp. 186–207; Barry Reay, *The Quakers and the English Revolution* (London, 1985); "The Author's Life," *A Collection of the Works of William Penn. In Two Volumes. To Which is Prefixed A Journal of His Life. With Many Original Letters and Papers Not Before Published* (London, 1726), I, 1–4.

3. Melvin B. Endy, Jr., *William Penn and Early Quakerism* (Princeton, 1973), pp. 315–316. Quakers did not originate the concepts of liberty of conscience or religious toleration, nor were they the only advocates of these ideas. Richard Burgess Barlow, *Citizenship and Conscience: A Study in the Theory and Practice of Religious Toleration During the Eighteenth Century* (Philadelphia, 1962); W. K. Jordan, *The Development of Religious Toleration in England*, 4 vols. (Cambridge, Mass., 1932–1940); A. A. Seaton, *The Theory of Toleration Under the Later Stuarts* (Cambridge, Eng., 1911; reprint ed., New York, 1972).

4. William Wistar Comfort, "William Penn's Religious Background," *PMHB*, 68 (1944), 341–358; William I. Hull, *William Penn: A Topical Biography* (New York, 1937), pp. 15–31, 65–83.

5. Penn was sent down from Oxford in 1662 as a result of a vague nonconformity to the established church and to the religious requirements of his college, and had experienced difficulties with his father over religious matters, but this was the first instance of civil action taken against him in consequence of his affirmation of a particular set of beliefs or for attending an illegal meeting. Mary Maples Dunn, *William Penn: Politics and Conscience* (Princeton, 1967), pp. 4–5.

6. "Life," Penn, *Works*, I, 2.

7. William Penn to Earl of Orrery, [November] 1667, *The Papers of William Penn*, 14 reels (Philadelphia, 1975 [microfilm]), I, 57.

8. Hugh Barbour, "William Penn, Model of Protestant Liberalism," *CH*, 48 (1979), 163–167; William Corbyn Obert Beatty, *William Penn as Social Philosopher* (New York, 1939), pp. 122–162; Dunn, *Politics and Conscience*.

9. William Penn, "The Great Case of Liberty of Conscience. Once more briefly Debated and Defended, by the Authority of Reason, Scripture, and Antiquity . . ." (1670), *Works*, I. 443–467, quotes pp. 443–444, 447, 449, 452, 457, 467.

10. William Penn, "England's Present Interest Considered, with Honour to the Prince and Safety to the People . . ." (1675), *Ibid.*, pp. 672–711, quotes pp. 691, 688, 689, 701.

11. William Penn, "An Address to Protestants of All Perswasions; more Especially the Magistracy and Clergy, for the Promotion of Virtue and Charity. In Two Parts" (1679), *Ibid.*, pp. 717–818, quotes pp. 718 (preface to 2d ed.), 751–752, 796.

12. William Penn, "A Perswasive to Moderation to Church-Dissenters, in Prudence and Conscience: Humbly submitted to the King and His Great Council" (1686), *Ibid.*, II, 727–749, quote pp. 734–735.

13. *Ibid.*, p. 729.

14. This seems to be the spirit, if not the letter, of many of his works, see also Dunn, *Politics and Conscience*, pp. 67–69.

15. Penn's "An other Form of Bill for the better Preserving, & maintaining English Property, being the true Foundation of English Government," n.d. [1674?], proposed a test that could be taken by Protestant dissenters but which specifically disavowed the Church of Rome. Penn, *Papers*, I, 559–560. He proposed another form of test in "One Project for the Good of England, That is, Our Civil Union is our Civil Safety: Humbly Dedicated to the Great Council, The Parliament of England" (1679), *Works*, II, 689–690.

16. *Ibid.*, pp. 682–691; Penn, "England's Great Interest," *Ibid.*, pp. 678–682; William Penn, "Good Advice to the Church of England, Roman-Catholick, and Protestant Dissenter . . ." (1687), *Ibid.*, pp. 749–773.

17. William Penn, "Truth Exalted, in a Testimony, against all those Religions, Faiths and Worships, that have been formed and followed in the Darkness of Apostacy . . ." (1668, with a 1671 postscript), *Ibid.*, I, 239–248, quote p. 242. Penn examined many of the central tenets of the Roman Catholic church, in a more rational manner, in "A Seasonable Caveat against Popery, or A Pamphlet entituled, An Explanation of the Roman Catholick Belief, briefly Examined" (1670), *Ibid.*, pp. 467–486.

18. In "Good Advice to the Church of England," he remarked that "That Part of *Popery*, which the Church of *England* with most Success objects against, is her *Violence*." *Ibid.*, II, 753.

19. Penn, "Address to Protestants of All Perswasions," *Ibid.*, I, 777; Penn, "England's Great Interest," *Ibid.*, II, 681; Penn, "England's Present Interest," *Ibid.*, I, 690–696; Penn, "Great Case of Liberty of Conscience," *Ibid.*, p. 454.

20. Penn, "One Project for the Good of England," *Ibid.*, II, 683–684. The threat that there would be attempts to restore Catholicism called forth some of Penn's most extreme statements against Catholics and Catholicism, such as "An Address to Protestants of All Perswasions," "England's Great Interest," and "One Project for the Good of England," all written in 1679. However, the crises of James' reign saw the publication of his "Perswasive to Moderation" and "Good Advice to the Church of England," which reminded his readers that Catholics, Anglicans, and Dissenters were all Englishmen.

21. Penn, "England's Great Interest," *Works*, II, 681.

22. Penn, "Good Advice to the Church of England," *Ibid.*, p. 766 (quotes); Penn, "Perswasive to Moderation," *Ibid.*, pp. 733–734.

23. Penn, "England's Present Interest," *Ibid.*, I, 684–688 (quote p. 686); Penn, "Good Advice to the Church of England," *Ibid.*, II, 766.

24. This statement concluded a letter to [Richard Langhorne], written in Newgate in 1671, that was an offer to debate articles of religion with a Roman Catholic (preferably with a priest or a Jesuit). Penn, *Papers*, I, 289.

25. Vincent Buranelli, *The King and the Quaker: A Study of William Penn and James II* (Philadelphia, 1962), explores this friendship in depth.

26. See, for example, "Good Advice to the Church of England," *Works*, II, 768–770, where Penn argues that Catholics should be satisfied with toleration and not insist upon being granted liberty of conscience.

27. Penn, "One Project for the Good of England," *Ibid.*, pp. 687–690; Penn, "Another Form of Bill for the Better Preserving, & Maintaining English Property," n.d. [1674?], Penn, *Papers*, I, 559–560.

28. Joseph J. Casino, "Anti-Popery In Colonial Pennsylvania," *PMHB*, 105 (1981), 284–292.

29. Penn, First Speech to a Committee of Commons, 22 March 1678, in "Life," *Works*, I, 118–119.

30. William I. Hull, *Benjamin Furly and Quakerism in Rotterdam* (n.p., 1941); Hull, *William Penn*, pp. 120–122; Julius F. Sachse, "Benjamin Furly," *PMHB*, 19 (1895), 277–306.

31. The only extensive account of these journeys is William Penn, "Travels in Germany and Holland" (1677), in "Life," *Works*, I, 50–116.

32. In 1677 William Penn wrote "A Tender Visitation, in the Love of God, that overcometh the World, to all People in the High and Low-Dutch Nations . . . ," in "Appendix to Life," *Ibid.*, pp. 216–223. Julius F. Sachse, comp., "Title Pages of Books and Pamphlets that Influenced German Emigration to Pennsylvania, Reproduced in Fac-simile for The Pennsylvania-German Society," *PGSPA*, 7 (1896), 199–256, includes translations of several of Penn's works, for example on pp. 202, 204, and 229.

33. William Penn, "A Letter To the Council and Senate of the City of Embden" (dated 14 December 1674; published 1674), *Works*, I, 609–611, quotes p. 611.

34. Penn to King of Poland, [4 or 5 August 1677], printed in "Travels in Germany and Holland," in "Life," *Ibid.*, pp. 56–58, quotes pp. 57, 58.

35. Penn to Prince Eector Palatine of Heidelberg, 25 August 1677, *Ibid.*, pp. 74–76.

36. Penn to Prince of Orange, draft, 26 February 1679/80, Penn, *Papers*, II, 774–777, quote p. 776.

37. Penn, "England's Present Interest," *Works*, I, 693 (cultural diversity); Penn, "Great Case of Liberty of Conscience," *Ibid.*, pp. 457–462; Penn, "Perswasive to Moderation," *Ibid.*, II, 727–749; Penn to Lord Arlington, 1 July 1669, in "Appendix to Life," *Ibid.*, I, 152–153.

38. Toleration united Dutch Protestants, thus strengthening the country against a reimposition of Roman Catholicism. Penn, "Good Advice to the Church of England," *Ibid.*, II, 773; Penn, "One Project for the Good of England," *Ibid.*, p. 686; Penn, "Good Advice to the Church of England," *Ibid.*, p. 773.

39. Penn, "One Project for the Good of England," *Ibid.*, pp. 685–686; Penn, "Perswasive to Moderation," *Ibid.*, pp. 742–743.

40. Penn, "An Act for the Preserving of the Subjects Properties, & for the repealing of Several penal Laws, by which the lives & properties of the subjects were subject to be forfeited for things not in their power to be avoyded," n.d. [1674?], Penn, *Papers*, I, 559 (quotes); Penn to [Richard Butler, Earl of Arran?], 9 January 1683/4, *Ibid.*, IV, 697–698; Penn, "Perswasive to Moderation," *Works*, II, 741.

41. Penn, "Perswasive to Moderation," *Ibid.*, pp. 742–743. He stated that the "downright *Toleration* in most of the Kings *Plantations* abroad, prove the Assertion, *That Toleration is not dangerous to Monarchy.* For Experience tells us, where it is in any Degree admitted, the King's Affairs prosper most; *People, Wealth* and *Strength* being sure to follow such *Indulgence.*" *Ibid.*, p. 734.

42. Rufus Jones, with Isaac Sharpless and Amelia M. Gummere, *The Quakers in the American Colonies* (1911; reprint ed., New York, 1966), pp. 357–390, 417–436. The charter or patent to Penn was granted on 4 March 1680/1, and is most conveniently found in Staughton George, Benjamin M. Nead, and Thomas McCamant, eds., *Charter to William Penn, and Laws of the Province of Pennsylvania, Passed between the Years 1682 and 1700 . . .* (Harrisburg, 1879), pp. 81–90 [hereafter *Charter and Laws*]. Two grants from the Duke of York, 24 August 1682, conveyed the lands along the Delaware River south of Pennsylvania—what became Delaware—to Penn. *Ibid.*, p. 467.

43. Penn to Roger Mompesson, 17 February 1704/5, Penn, *Papers*, XI, 512 (first quote); Penn to ?, July 1681, *Ibid.*, III, 248 (second quote).

44. Penn to the Inhabitants of Pennsylvania, 8 April 1681, *Ibid.*, pp. 218–220, quote p. 218. They were also told that any quitrents due on their holdings would now be paid to Penn. A royal proclamation of the grant to Penn was sent to the inhabitants of Pennsylvania on 2 April 1681, *Charter and Laws*, p. 466.

45. Joseph E. Illick, *Colonial Pennsylvania: A History* (New York, 1976), pp. 30–31. William Markham, whom Penn sent to act as governor until his arrival, did make arrangements with the Swedes to sell some land or to exchange it for larger tracts further back in the country *(Ibid., p. 31)*; this occurred, for example, with the site for Philadelphia. Disputes over these transactions, and over the new surveys Penn ordered of these settlers' land, continued into the eighteenth century; see below, ch. 3, 4.

46. Penn to William Crispin, John Bezar, and Nathaniel Allen, 30 September 1681, Penn, *Papers*, III, 310.

47. See [Philip Ford], *A Vindication of William Penn, Proprietary of Pensilvania, from the late Aspersions spread abroad to Defame him. . . .* (London, 1683), for an abstract of Penn's letter to Ford, 1 November 1682, which describes the rituals the inhabitants performed in giving Penn possession of the land and of their promises to be faithful subjects. See also Penn to [Butler?], 9 January 1683/4, Penn, *Papers*, IV, 697.

48. The relations between Penn's settlers and the previous inhabitants are discussed in chapter 3. In Penn's mind, they seem to be undistinguished from each other or from his colonists by their language or religious beliefs.

49. Sydney V. James, *Colonial Rhode Island: A History* (New York, 1975), pp. 33–47; Gary B. Nash, *Quakers and Politics: Pennsylvania, 1681–1726* (Princeton, 1968), pp. 13–14.

50. The Carolina proprietors were particularly interested in recruiting Huguenots, whom Penn also found quite desirable. Despite Penn's efforts to recruit Huguenots and the advantages such as religious liberty that he offered, few chose to emigrate to Pennsylvania, a decision that the most recent historian of the Huguenots finds "puzzling." Jon Butler, *The Huguenots in America: A Refugee People in New World Society* (Cambridge, Mass., 1983), pp. 48, 52–53, quote p. 53.

51. Hope Frances Kane, "Notes on Early Pennsylvania Promotional Literature," *PMHB*, 63 (1939), 144–168.

52. William I. Hull, *William Penn and the Dutch Quaker Migration to Pennsylvania* (Swarthmore, Pa., 1935), pp. 310–316, 329–336; Julius F. Sachse, ed. and trans., "Daniel

Falckner's *Curieuse Nachricht from Pennsylvania: The Book that Stimulated the Great German Immigration to Pennsylvania in the Early Years of the* XVIII. Century," *PGSPA*, 14 (1903), 8–21; Julius F. Sachse, ed. and trans., *Letters Relating to the Settlement of Germantown in Pennsylvania, 1683–4 From the Könneken Manuscript in the Ministerial-Archive of Lübeck* (Lübeck and Philadelphia, 1903), pp. v–xii; Albert Cook Myers, *Immigration of the Irish Quakers into Pennsylvania 1682–1750 With Their Early History in Ireland* (Swarthmore, Pa., 1902), pp. 53–54. Several of the most important English-language promotional pieces are reprinted in Albert Cook Myers, ed., *Narratives of Early Pennsylvania, West New Jersey, and Delaware, 1630–1707* (New York, 1912), pp. 197–448. His introductions usually indicate the translations or reprinting of each tract.

53. Hull, *Dutch Quaker Migration*, pp. 310–316.

54. Willem Sewel to Penn, 24 August 1686, Penn, *Papers*, V, 502; English translation, *Ibid.*, p. 504.

55. In addition to the material cited in n. 52 above, see: "An Abstract of a Letter from Thomas Paschall of Pennsilvania To his Friend J. J. of Chippenham" (1683), Myers, *Narratives of Pennsylvania*, pp. 250–254; letter of Francis Daniel Pastorius, 7 March 1684, Sachse, *Letters Relating to Germantown*, pp. 7–29; Pastorius to his parents, 7 March 1684, *Ibid.*, pp. 3–5; letter of Joris Wertmuller, 16 March 1684, trans. Samuel W. Pennypacker, *The Settlement of Germantown Pennsylvania and the Beginning of German Emigration to North America* (Philadelphia, 1899), pp. 100–102; Cornelis Bom to Jan Laurens, 12 October 1684, trans. *Ibid.*, pp. 103–107.

56. Not all Quakers approved of emigration to the colonies; see Joseph E. Illick, "The Flight to Pennsylvania: Affirmation or Denial of Quakerism?" *QH*, 59 (1970), 104–105, and a letter from Richard Davis to Penn (7 July 1684), where he stated that many feared Quakerism would fail in Wales because so many Welsh Quakers were emigrating to the colonies (Penn, *Papers*, IV, 954). Migrants, not only of the Quaker persuasion, came from other New World colonies as well as from Europe. Carl Bridenbaugh, "The Old and New Societies of The Delaware Valley in the Seventeenth Century," *PMHB*, 100 (1976), 163–164.

57. Penn to [Charles Townshend], 4 April 1710, Penn, *Papers*, XIV, 115–116; Business Collection, James Claypoole Letterbook, 1681–1684, H.S.P.; Hull, *Dutch Quaker Migration*, pp. 254–256.

58. Penn to Thomas Lloyd, 2 October 1685, Penn, *Papers*, V, 286 (quote); Penn to James Harrison, n.d. [c. September-October 1686], *Ibid.*, p. 544.

59. Penn to Lloyd, John Simcock, and others, 13 July-17 August 1685, *Ibid.*, p. 219 (quote); Penn to Commissioners of State, 21 October 1687, *Ibid.*, p. 841; Penn to James Logan, 26 June 1709, *Ibid.*, XIII, 789.

60. In addition to the Welsh and German attempts to establish separate colonies discussed below, a similar plan seems to have been proposed by prospective Scottish investors and by Robert Barclay, Penn's representative in that country. Barclay to Penn, 17 December 1681, *Ibid.*, III, 376. Apparently satisfactory arrangements were never made. Scottish Quakers focused their attention primarily on East Jersey. Ned C. Landsman, *Scotland and its First American Colony, 1683–1760* (Princeton, 1985).

61. Charles H. Browning, *The Welsh Settlement of Pennsylvania* (Philadelphia, 1912), pp. 26–27, 32–36; John E. Pomfret, "The First Purchasers of Pennsylvania, 1681–1700," *PMHB*, 80 (1956), 156–158.

62. Inhabitants of the Welsh Tract to Penn and Commissioners of Property, 23 April

1688, Penn, *Papers*, VI, 8; Inhabitants of the Welsh Tract to Commissioners of Property, n.d. [c. 13 December 1690], *Ibid.*, p. 520 (quote); Welsh Settlers to Penn, 15 May 1691, *Ibid.*, p. 590. Penn's promises were only verbal, so there is no firm evidence for the exact agreement he made with the Welshmen. Arthur H. Dodd points out that the Welsh emigrants were not being forced out of their country by poverty or persecution; perhaps this induced them to demand greater concessions from Penn before they would purchase land and to be more vocal in their disappointment when the conditions were not fulfilled. *The Character of Early Welsh Emigration to the United States*, 2d ed. (Cardiff, 1957), pp. 12–13.

63. Penn to Thomas Holme, 13 November 1684, Penn, *Papers*, IV, 773; Governor's Instructions, read at a meeting of the Board of Property, 13 May 1687, John B. Linn and William H. Egle, eds., *Pennsylvania Archives*, 2d ser., 19 vols. (Harrisburg, 1876–1893), XIX, 6–7 [hereafter *Pa. Arch.*]; Penn to Commissioners of Property, 10 January 1689/90, Penn Manuscripts, Governor John Blackwell Manuscripts, 1689–1690, p. 1, H.S.P. (quote). The Welsh settlements were divided between Chester and Philadelphia counties.

64. Holme to Penn, 24 May 1687, Gary B. Nash, ed., "The First Decade in Pennsylvania: Letters of William Markham and Thomas Holme to William Penn," *PMHB*, 90 (1966), 492; Welsh Settlers to Penn, 15 May 1691, Penn, *Papers*, VI, 590–591; Minutes, Commissioners of Property, 13 May 1687–1 December 1701, *Pa. Arch.*, 2d ser., XIX, 6–7, 14–15, 47–48, 55, 67, 70–71, 202.

65. The difficulties of the Welsh settlers are discussed in detail in Browning, *Welsh Settlement*, pp. 26–27, 33–36, and especially pp. 331–345. He argues that Penn was consciously trying to defraud the Welsh. Penn undoubtedly made many verbal promises while engaged in negotiations to sell land, and they were probably interpreted by the Welsh (and to a lesser extent by the Germans and Dutch) as granting more definite conditions than were intended. But the disorganization of Penn's initial venture, the lack of men to survey tracts of land promptly and accurately, and Penn's subsequent changes in land policies to increase his revenue from quitrents, when added to his general failure to think about how his colony should be structured, probably accounted for these problems. See also Illick, *Colonial Pennsylvania*, p. 41.

66. Hull, *Dutch Quaker Migration*, pp. 254–256. Pomfret, in "First Purchasers of Pennsylvania" (*PMHB*, 80 [1956], 155), notes that six men purchased a total of 18,000 acres but were not joined in a single company.

67. Hull, *Dutch Quaker Migration*, p. 180. The company later purchased an additional 10,000 acres.

68. Letter of Pastorius, 7 March 1684, Sachse, *Letters Relating to Germantown*, pp. 22–23; Francis Daniel Pastorius, "Umständige Geographische Beschreibung Der zu Allerletzt erfundenen Provintz Pensylvaniae. . . ." (1700), trans. Myers, *Narratives of Pennsylvania*, p. 381 (quote).

69. Letter of Pastorius, 7 March 1684, Sachse, *Letters Relating to Germantown*, pp. 20–25; Jacobus van der Walle to Penn, 24 August 1684, Penn, *Papers*, IV, 1069–1073.

70. Illick, *Colonial Pennsylvania*, pp. 40–41.

71. Stephanie Grauman Wolf, *Urban Village: Population, Community, and Family Structure in Germantown, Pennsylvania 1683–1800* (Princeton, 1976).

72. Edwin B. Bronner, *William Penn's "Holy Experiment": The Founding of Pennsylvania 1681–1701* (New York, 1962), p. 27.

73. Negotiations and contracts with alien purchasers who intended to recruit colo-

nists from their homelands are discussed in Penn to William Clark and William Rodney, 21 July 1700, Penn, *Papers*, VIII, 521–522; Penn to Logan, 16 January 1704/5, *Ibid.*, XI, 475.

74. Penn to Harrison, 25 August 1681, *Ibid.*, III, 272–273; Penn to Board of Trade, 14 August 1683, *Ibid.*, IV, 428; Penn to Provincial Council, 13 June 1691, *Ibid.*, VI, 621 (quote).

75. Sachse, "Benjamin Furly," *PMHB*, 19 (1895), 277–306. A translation of Furly's comments is printed *Ibid.*, pp. 297–306.

76. The tendency to use these terms loosely occurred throughout the colonies. James H. Kettner, *The Development of American Citizenship, 1608–1870* (Chapel Hill, 1978), pp. 7–10, 78–80, 83, 91. Since Pennsylvanians intended to bestow on aliens all of the rights of natural-born Englishmen, and used the term "naturalize," I shall follow their usage. This "naturalization" was valid only in Pennsylvania.

77. Laws Agreed Upon in England, 5 May 1682, art. 2, *Charter and Laws*, p. 99.

78. Great Body of Laws, 7 December 1682, ch. 57, *Ibid.*, pp. 121–122.

79. Frame of Government, 7 November 1696, art. 3, *Ibid.*, pp. 247–248.

80. 6 December 1682, Gertrude MacKinney and Charles F. Hoban, eds., *Pennsylvania Archives*, 8th ser., 8 vols., *Votes and Proceedings of the House of Representatives of the Province of Pennsylvania, 1682–1776* (Harrisburg, 1931–1935), I, 5–6 [hereafter Assembly, *Votes*].

81. An Act for Naturalization, 7 December 1682, *Charter and Laws*, pp. 105–106, quotes p. 105.

82. Ch. 141, March 1683, *Ibid.*, p. 154. The naturalization act was again declared fundamental on 8 April 1689, *Minutes of the Provincial Council of Pennsylvania, From the Organization to the Termination of the Proprietary Government*, 16 vols. (Philadelphia and Harrisburg, 1851–1853), I, 277 [hereafter Council, *Minutes*]. This law was not, however, among those reenacted as a result of the Petition of Right, 1693, *Charter and Laws*, pp. 190–191.

83. Sachse, "Benjamin Furly," *PMHB*, 19 (1895), 297.

84. Frame of Government, 2 April 1683, art. 21, *Charter and Laws*, p. 160. This provision was also contained in the 1696 Frame of Government as ch. 13, 7 November 1696, *Ibid.*, pp. 252–253.

85. Penn to Board of Trade, n.d. [September-October 1700?], Penn, *Papers*, VIII, 570.

86. Penn to [Earl of Sunderland], 18th Curr^t [1709], *Ibid.*, XIII, 643–644. Penn was a supporter of the parliamentary general naturalization act of 1709, which remained in effect for three years. *Ibid.*; Penn to Logan, 3 March 1708/9, *Ibid.*, p. 701; Kettner, *American Citizenship*, pp. 73–74.

87. Ch. 30, 27 November 1700, James T. Mitchell and Henry Flanders, comps., *The Statutes at Large of Pennsylvania from 1682 to 1801*, 16 vols. (Harrisburg, 1896–1911), II, 29–31, quote p. 31 [hereafter *Statutes*]. The cost of naturalization was increased by this law. Henceforth the provincial secretary and keeper of the seal would each receive 6s. for processing the certificate, and the governor would be paid 20s. by aliens resident prior to passage of this law and 30s. by those who subsequently immigrated.

88. Ch. 88, 27 November 1700, *Ibid.*, pp. 121–122.

89. *Ibid.*, pp. 31n., 492, quote p. 492.

90. Ch. 88, 27 November 1700, *Ibid.*, p. 122. According to 7–8 Wm. III, ch. 22, no proprietor could dispose of land to other than natural-born subjects of England

without the King's express license for that purpose. Pennsylvanians routinely violated this law. William Robert Shepherd, *History of Proprietary Government in Pennsylvania* (New York, 1896), pp. 65–66.

91. Kettner, *American Citizenship*, pp. 117–118.

92. Penn to Logan, 29 September 1708, Penn, *Papers*, XIII, 560–561. Although alien property was not mentioned in the 1701 Frame of Government, Penn here implies that it was.

93. [7 November 1704], Assembly, *Votes*, I, 454.

94. Another petition, 15 May 1706, had requested clarification of the property laws and also that those who had not yet promised allegiance to the British government might be allowed to do so. Council, *Minutes*, II, 241–242. When the legislature finally acted on this petition in 1709, it expressed its appreciation of the contributions foreign Protestants made to the colony's prosperity. 17 August 1709, *Ibid.*, p. 480; 31 August 1709, *Ibid.*, p. 488; 29 September 1709, *Ibid.*, pp. 493–494; ch. 167, 29 September 1709, *Statutes*, II, 297–300.

95. Penn to [Butler?], 9 January 1683/4, Penn, *Papers*, IV, 697.

96. Penn to Mompesson, 17 February 1704/5, *Ibid.*, XI, 512.

97. For a somewhat different interpretation of Penn's intentions, see J. William Frost, "Religious Liberty in Early Pennsylvania," *PMHB*, 105 (1981), 424–431.

98. Charter to William Penn, 4 March 1680/1, *Charter and Laws*, pp. 81–90; the religious provision is printed pp. 89–90, quote p. 90.

99. "The Fundamentall Constitutions of Pennsylvania as they were Drawn up Settled and Signed by William Penn Proprietary and Governour, and Consented to and Subscribed by all the First Adventurers and Free Holders of that Province, as the Ground and Rule of all future Government," *PMHB*, 20 (1896), 286–287. Other drafts are in Penn Manuscripts, VIII, 49–149, H.S.P.

100. These examples are drawn from the Great Body of Laws, 7 December 1682, *Charter and Laws*, pp. 106–123.

101. Laws Agreed Upon in England, 5 May 1682, art. 35, *Ibid.*, pp. 102–103.

102. *Ibid.*, art. 36, p. 103. This law and the one cited directly above, combined into one, were reenacted by the first assembly. Great Body of Laws, 7 December 1682, ch. 1, *Ibid.*, pp. 107–108. This law was declared fundamental in March 1683, ch. 141, *Ibid.*, p. 154.

103. At the end of the seventeenth century sabbatarianism seems to have been more characteristic of Continental pietists than of English sectarians, so perhaps this law did not appear to be important to Penn.

104. Laws Agreed Upon in England, 5 May 1682, art. 34, *Charter and Laws*, p. 102.

105. Great Body of Laws, 7 December 1682, *Ibid.*, p. 108. This law, however, was not among those declared fundamental in March 1683, ch. 141, *Ibid.*, p. 154.

106. Petition of Right, 1693, *Ibid.*, pp. 188–192; Frost, "Religious Liberty," *PMHB*, 105 (1981), 434. The provisions of the Toleration Act of 1689 (1 Wm. III, ch. 18) are discussed in Barlow, *Citizenship and Conscience*, pp. 22–24. It is ironic that the Toleration Act, which resulted in liberal reforms in England and in many colonies, was used to restrict religious freedom in Pennsylvania.

107. Frame of Government, 7 November 1696, ch. 1, sects. 3, 4, *Charter and Laws*, pp. 246–249. The Frame is printed *Ibid.*, pp. 245–253.

108. Ch. 1, 27 November 1700, *Statutes*, II, 3–4, quote p. 4. This law also required observance of the First Day.

109. Opinion of Attorney General, 1705, *Ibid.*, p. 489. It should be noted that the Toleration Act did not repeal the laws under which dissenters could be persecuted; these laws were merely suspended for individuals willing to fulfill certain conditions.

110. Ch. 28, 27 November 1700, *Ibid.*, pp. 24–25. This law was also repealed, *Ibid.*, p. 25n.

111. Frame of Government, 28 October 1701, art. 1, Council, *Minutes*, II, 55. The attestations or oaths were those enacted in ch. 33, 27 November 1700, *Statutes*, II, 39–42, a law subsequently repealed by the Crown.

112. Frame of Government, 28 October 1701, art. 2, Council, *Minutes*, II, 56.

113. Ch. 137, 12 January 1705/6, *Statutes*, II, 219–220. This assembly also enacted a law concerning the observation of the First Day. With the exception of food preparation and serving the needs of travelers, almost all forms of labor were forbidden. Fines of 20s. could be levied on offenders, who were to be prosecuted within ten days of the offense. Ch. 119, 12 January 1705/6, *Ibid.*, pp. 175–177.

114. Ch. 115, 12 January 1705/6, *Ibid.*, p. 171.

115. Penn "Good Advice to the Church of England," *Works*, II, 772.

116. In a letter to Logan, Penn reported "a Complaint agst your Govr^{mt} that you suffer public Mass in a scandalous manner." Laconically he requested "ye matter of facts for ill use is made of it agst us here." 29 September 1708, Penn, *Papers*, XIII, 564. Logan does not seem to have replied, and the question was not raised again.

117. See "The Christianity Of the People commonly Called, Quakers Asserted, Against the Unjust Charge of their being No Christians, upon several Questions relating to those Matters, wherein their Christian Belief is questioned" (London; reprint ed., Philadelphia, 1690), Broadside Collection, H.S.P., and a petition to the King, 20 May 1696 (Penn, *Papers*, VII, 183–184), a defense of Friends against charges made by their (political) opponents, which also contains a brief statement of the Quaker faith.

118. Penn to Robert Harley, n.d. [c. April 1701], *Ibid.*, IX, 165–168, quote p. 167.

119. Penn to Provincial Council, 11 September 1691, *Ibid.*, VI, 631.

3. Penn's Province, 1681–1718

1. These estimates are derived from James T. Lemon, *The Best Poor Man's Country: A Geographical Study of Early Southeastern Pennsylvania* (Baltimore, 1972), p. 23.

2. [Philip Ford], *A Vindication of William Penn, Proprietary of Pensilvania, from the late Aspersions spread abroad to Defame him. . . .* (London, 1683).

3. An Act of Union, 7 December 1682, Staughton George, Benjamin M. Nead, and Thomas McCamant, eds., *Charter to William Penn, and Laws of the Province of Pennsylvania, Passed between the Years 1682 and 1700 . . .* (Harrisburg, 1879), p. 104 [hereafter *Charter and Laws*].

4. Edwin B. Bronner, *William Penn's "Holy Experiment": The Founding of Pennsylvania 1681–1701* (New York, 1962), pp. 33–35.

5. Act of Settlement, 10 March 1683, preamble, *Charter and Laws*, pp. 124–125; Frame of Government, 2 April 1683, arts. 1, 2, 13, 15, *Ibid.*, pp. 156–158; Frame of Government, 7 November 1696, art. 2, *Ibid.*, p. 246; Frame of Government, 28 October 1701, art. 2, *Minutes of the Provincial Council of Pennsylvania, From the Organization to the Termination of the Proprietary Government*, 16 vols. (Philadelphia and Harrisburg, 1851–1853), II, 55–56 [hereafter Council, *Minutes*]; Joseph E. Illick, *Colonial Pennsylvania: A History* (New York, 1976), p. 173.

6. Joseph Growden to William Penn, 28 April 1691, *The Papers of William Penn*, 14 reels (Philadelphia, 1975 [microfilm]), VI, 576.

7. Declaration of the Council of the Three Lower Counties, 6 April 1691, *Ibid.*, pp. 548–549.

8. John A. Munroe, *Colonial Delaware: A History* (Millwood, N.Y., 1978), pp. 96–116.

9. Frame of Government, 28 October 1701, Council, *Minutes*, II, 57–58, quote p. 57.

10. Governor to Assembly, n.d., Gertrude MacKinney and Charles F. Hoban, eds., *Pennsylvania Archives*, 8th ser., 8 vols., *Votes and Proceedings of the House of Representatives of the Province of Pennsylvania, 1682–1776* (Harrisburg, 1931–1935), I, 406–407 [hereafter Assembly, *Votes*]; correspondence among the governor, Pennsylvania representatives, and Delaware representatives, 12–13 April 1704, *Ibid.*, pp. 408–410.

11. Robert W. Johannsen, "The Conflict Between the Three Lower Counties on the Delaware and the Province of Pennsylvania, 1682–1704," *DH*, 5 (1952), 96–132.

12. See, for example: Illick, *Colonial Pennsylvania*, pp. 39, 64; Gary B. Nash, *Quakers and Politics: Pennsylvania, 1681–1726* (Princeton, 1968), pp. 67–69, 73–74, 82–83.

13. Penn to Jasper [Batt], 5 February 1682/3, Penn, *Papers*, IV, 45–47, quote p. 45.

14. 12 March 1682/3, Assembly, *Votes*, I, 13.

15. Penn to James Harrison, 8 September 1687, Penn, *Papers*, V, 814; Penn to Commissioners of State, 21 October 1687, *Ibid.*, p. 841.

16. Penn to [Batt], 5 February 1682/3, *Ibid.*, IV, 45 (quote); Penn to William Penn Jr., 2 January 1700/1, *Ibid.*, IX, 8; Penn, Memorial to Queen Anne, n.d. [31 July 1710], *Ibid.*, XIV, 157.

17. Penn to Harrison, 8 September 1687, *Ibid.*, V, 814 (quote); Penn to Commissioners of State, 18 September 1688, *Ibid.*, VI, 101; Penn to Lord Somers, 22 October 1700, *Ibid.*, VIII, 610–611; James LaVerne Anderson, "The Governors' Councils of Colonial America: A Study of Pennsylvania and Virginia, 1660–1776" (Ph.D. diss., University of Virginia, 1967), pp. 120–122, 132–134, Appendix A.

18. Penn to Robert Turner, 29 November 1692, Penn, *Papers*, VI, 681–686.

19. Penn to Robert Harley, 9 February 1703/4, *Ibid.*, XI, 146–147 (quote); Directions to Agents intended to be sent to England ab^t restoring this Governm^t to W: Penn &c, n.d. [c. 1693–1694], Norris Papers, Norris of Fairhill Family Letters, I, 120, H.S.P.

20. David Lloyd to Dolobran Quarterly Meeting, 2 November 1684, Roberts Collection, Pennsylvania Governors, Q.C.H.C.; Philadelphia Monthly Meeting to Penn, 7 August 1706, Penn, *Papers*, XII, 806; James Logan to Penn, 25 May 1712, *Ibid.*, XIV, 391.

21. Philadelphia Friends to Penn, 23 May 1711, *Ibid.*, pp. 275–276; Griffith Owen to Penn, 24 June 1711, *Ibid.*, pp. 284–285 (quote p. 285).

22. Turner to Penn, 15 April 1697, *Ibid.*, VII, 459.

23. Robert Suder to [Francis Nicholson], 20 November 1698, William Stevens Perry, ed., *Historical Collections Relating to the American Colonial Church*, vol. 2, *Pennsylvania* (Hartford, 1871), p. 12 (quote); Deborah Mathias Gough, "Pluralism, Politics, and Power Struggles: The Church of England in Colonial Philadelphia, 1695–1789" (Ph.D. diss., University of Pennsylvania, 1978), pp. 21–78.

24. John Blackwell to Penn, 1 May 1689, Penn, *Papers*, VI, 309.

25. Petition of the Protestant Subjects living in Pennsylvania to King William, n.d. [1696?], *Ibid.*, XIII, 637–638 (quote p. 638); Suder to [Nicholson], 20 November 1698,

Perry, *Colonial Church*, pp. 9–12; A Brief Narrative of the Proceedings of William Penn, n.d. [c. 1701], *Ibid.*, pp. 2–4; Robert Quary to Board of Trade, 7 December 1702, Herman V. Ames, ed., "Pennsylvania and the English Government, 1699–1704," *PMHB*, 24 (1900), 73–75.

26. Gough, "Pluralism, Politics, and Power Struggles," pp. 52–53, 59–61.

27. Philadelphia Yearly Meeting Epistle, 17–20 September 1710, Philadelphia Yearly Meeting Collection, Miscellaneous Epistles and Papers, 1703–1714, Q.C.H.C.

28. Gough, "Pluralism, Politics, and Power Struggles," pp. 52–56.

29. Isaac Norris, "Friendly Advice to the Inhabitants of Pennsylvania" (1710; reprint ed., [Philadelphia, 1728]), Broadside Collection, H.S.P.; Isaac Norris to J[ames] L[ogan], 25 September 1710, Norris Papers, Isaac Norris Sr. Letterbook, 1709–1716, pp. 213–214, H.S.P.

30. Philadelphia Yearly Meeting Epistle, 17–20 September 1710, Philadelphia Yearly Meeting Collection, Miscellaneous Epistles and Papers, 1703–1714, Q.C.H.C.

31. Norris to Penn, 23 November 1710, Penn, *Papers*, XIV, 172.

32. William Penn, "A Treatise of Oaths, containing several weighty Reasons why the People called Quakers refuse to Swear . . ." (1675), *A Collection of the Works of William Penn. In Two Volumes. To Which is Prefixed A Journal of His Life. With Many Original Letters and Papers Not Before Published* (London, 1726), I, 612–672 (quote p. 615); J. William Frost, "The Affirmation Controversy and Religious Liberty," Richard S. Dunn and Mary Maples Dunn, eds., *The World of William Penn* (Philadelphia, 1986), pp. 303–322.

33. Penn, Memorandum of Additional Instructions to William Markham, William Crispin, and John Bezar, 28 October 1681, Penn, *Papers*, III, 369a.

34. Laws Agreed Upon in England, 5 May 1682, arts. 6, 26, *Charter and Laws*, pp. 100 (quote), 101–102; Great Body of Laws, 7 December 1682, ch. 36, *Ibid.*, pp. 116–117; ch. 66, 10 March 1683, *Ibid.*, p. 128; Laws enacted under Benjamin Fletcher, 1 June 1693, ch. 9, *Ibid.*, p. 228. The law enacted under Fletcher was apparently never repealed and continued in force despite the repeal of subsequent, similar laws. Norris to Logan, 14 July 1707, Norris Papers, Isaac Norris Sr. Letterbook, 1706–1709, p. 83, H.S.P.

35. Penn to Board of Trade, n.d. [c. 30 November 1702], Penn, *Papers*, X, 627.

36. Nash, *Quakers and Politics*, pp. 205–208.

37. Winfred Trexler Root, *The Relations of Pennsylvania with the British Government, 1696–1765* (New York, 1912), p. 235.

38. Frame of Government, 7 November 1696, ch. 1, sect. 4, *Charter and Laws*, pp. 247–249. This exemption did not apply to anyone required by acts of trade and navigation to swear an oath.

39. Petition to the King from Pennsylvania, 20 May 1696, Penn, *Papers*, VII, 183; Anthony Morris, D. Lloyd, and others to Penn, 25 April 1697 (postscript to a letter of 22 March 1696/7), *Ibid.*, p. 431.

40. An Act for Preventing Frauds & Regulating Abuses in Trade, Within the Province of Pennsilvania & Counties Annexed, 10 May 1698, *Charter and Laws*, pp. 268–274.

41. Ch. 33, 27 November 1700, James T. Mitchell and Henry Flanders, comps., *The Statutes at Large of Pennsylvania from 1682 to 1801*, 16 vols. (Harrisburg, 1896–1911), II, 39–42 [hereafter *Statutes*].

42. A Brief Narrative of the Proceedings of William Penn, n.d. [c. 1701], Perry, *Colonial Church*, pp. 2–4.

43. Ch. 99, 27 November 1700, *Statutes*, II, 133.

44. Ch. 160, 12 January 1705/6, *Ibid.*, pp. 266–272; ch. 171, 28 February 1710/11, *Ibid.*, pp. 355–357; ch. 209, 28 May 1715, *Ibid.*, III, 58–60; ch. 235, 31 May 1718, *Ibid.*, pp. 198–214; ch. 281, 9 May 1724, *Ibid.*, pp. 427–431.

45. Petition of the Protestant Subjects living in Pennsylvania to King William, n.d. [1696?], Penn, *Papers*, XIII, 637–638 (first quote p. 637); A Brief Narrative of the Proceedings of William Penn, n.d. [c. 1701], Perry, *Colonial Church*, pp. 2–4 (last three quotes p. 3); Logan to Penn, 12 December 1705, Penn, *Papers*, XII, 445; George Willcox to Board of Trade, [6 November 1706], *Statutes*, II, 514–518 (second–third quotes p. 515); Charles Gookin to Bishop of London, 21 May 1711, *Records of the Society for the Propagation of the Gospel in Foreign Parts*, 27 reels (East Ardsley, Wakefield, England, 1964 [microfilm]), Letterbook, A6, no. 92.

46. Suder to [Nicholson], 20 November 1698, Perry, *Colonial Church*, p. 10; George Keith to Thomas Bray, 24 February 1702/3, *S.P.G. Letterbooks*, A1, no. 87 (first quote); Logan to Penn, 24 June 1703, Penn, *Papers*, X, 1002–1003; William Poppel to Penn, 23 July 1703, *Ibid.*, p. 1059 (second quote); Penn to Logan, 27 August 1703, *Ibid.*, XI, 5–6; Logan to Penn, 11 September 1703, *Ibid.*, pp. 26–27; Norris to Martha Barker, 3 May 1711, Norris Papers, Isaac Norris Sr. Letterbook, 1709–1716, p. 253, H.S.P.; Robert Assheton to Penn, 15 December 1711, Penn, *Papers*, XIV, 344; Logan to Henry Goldney, 21 July 1718, Logan Papers, James Logan Letterbook, 1717–1728, p. 30, H.S.P.

47. Logan to Penn, 29 September 1703, Penn, *Papers*, XI, 64.

48. Assembly to George Whitehead, William Mead, and Thomas Lower, 15 October 1708, Penn Letters and Ancient Documents, II, 436, A.P.S.

49. Logan to Penn, n.d. [answering a letter of 26 August 1703], Logan Papers, James Logan Letterbook, I, 104–105, H.S.P. (first quote p. 104); D. Lloyd to Whitehead, Mead, and Lower, 3 October 1704, Penn, *Papers*, XI, 392 (second quote).

50. Samuel Carpenter to Penn, 26 April 1696, *Ibid.*, VII, 167; Logan to Penn, 11 September 1703, *Ibid.*, XI, 27; Norris to Penn, 30 July 1707, *Ibid.*, XIII, 250; Penn to Poppel, 14 August 1707, *Ibid.*, p. 261.

51. 9 January 1705/6, Council, *Minutes*, II, 225–227, quote p. 227.

52. Logan to Penn, 25 May 1712, Penn, *Papers*, XIV, 391.

53. Morris, D. Lloyd, and others to Penn, 25 April 1697 (postscript to a letter of 22 March 1696/7), *Ibid.*, VII, 431; D. Lloyd to Whitehead, Mead, and Lower, 3 October 1704, *Ibid.*, XI, 392 (quote).

54. Ch. 236, 31 May 1718, *Statutes*, III, 199–214; Board of Trade to King, 1 May 1719, *Ibid.*, pp. 438–439; Minutes of Privy Council, 26 May 1719, *Ibid.*, p. 437.

55. Ch. 281, 9 May 1724, *Ibid.*, pp. 427–431; Minutes of Privy Council, 27 March 1725, *Ibid.*, p. 514.

56. Norris to John Askew, 24 November 1715, Norris Papers, Isaac Norris Sr. Letterbook, 1709–1716, p. 536, H.S.P.

57. Resolution of Assembly, [24 May 1718], Assembly, *Votes*, II, 1265. The assembly's petition, [21 May 1718], is printed *Ibid.*, pp. 1260–1262.

58. The assembly subsequently altered the forms of oaths to accommodate the conscientious beliefs of other settlers and allowed aliens to affirm their loyalty in order to be naturalized (see below, ch. 4, 6, 8).

59. Charter of the Province of Pennsylvania, 4 March 1680/1, *Charter and Laws*, p. 88.

60. Peter Brock, *Pacifism in the United States From the Colonial Era to the First World*

War (Princeton, 1968), pp. 83–86; Hermann Wellenreuther, "The Political Dilemma of the Quakers in Pennsylvania, 1681–1748," *PMHB*, 94 (1970), 143–147. Throughout the colony's history a deputy usually served as the local chief executive rather than a member of the proprietary family, even after William Penn's heirs drifted away from Quakerism toward or into the Church of England. Contemporaries referred to the Penns' representative as the governor; I shall follow their usage.

61. Report of Board of Trade on Penn's Petition, 1, 3 August 1694, E. B. O'Callaghan and B. Fernow, eds., *Documents Relative to the Colonial History of the State of New-York . . .* , vols. 1–12 (Albany, 1856–1877), IV, 108–109 [hereafter *NYCD*]; Revocation of Benjamin Fletcher's Commission as Governor of Pennsylvania, 20 August 1694, *Ibid.*, p. 110.

62. The Case of William Penn, Requesting the Removal of Gov. Fletcher, n.d. [c. July 1694?], Penn, *Papers*, VI, 841.

63. Report of Board of Trade on Penn's Petition, 1, 3 August 1694, *NYCD*, IV, 108–109 (quote p. 108).

64. May–June 1693, Assembly, *Votes*, I, 127–154; Laws enacted under Benjamin Fletcher, 1 June 1693, ch. 1, *Charter and Laws*, pp. 221–224.

65. Benjamin Fletcher to William Blathwayt, 12 June 1693, *NYCD*, IV, 31–32 (first quote p. 31); Fletcher to Board of Trade, 9 October 1693, *Ibid.*, p. 56 (second quote).

66. Governor to Assembly, 23 May 1694, Assembly, *Votes*, I, 159–160 (quotes); Resolution of the Committee of the House, [26 May 1694], *Ibid.*, pp. 176–177.

67. Fletcher to Markham, 12 June 1695, Penn Letters and Ancient Documents, II, 294, A.P.S.; September 1695, Assembly, *Votes*, I, 177–184.

68. 27 October-[7 November 1696], *Ibid.*, pp. 185–186, 192. The assembly considered this an emergency situation and raised money "upon the Credit of this Act," advancing it to Fletcher before it could be collected through the new tax law. It explained its failure to act the previous year by citing the disruption caused by the restoration of the colony to Penn, the consequent need for a new frame of government, and the unexpected brevity of its session. Assembly to Penn, 7 November 1696, Penn, *Papers*, VII, 242–243.

69. Penn to Arthur Cook, John Simcock, and others, 5 November 1695, *Ibid.*, VI, 983–984.

70. Governor to Assembly, 2 June 1709, Assembly, *Votes*, II, 857.

71. Assembly to Governor, 8 June 1709, *Ibid.*, pp. 862–863, quote p. 862.

72. Governor to Assembly, 9 June 1709, *Ibid.*, pp. 864–866 (quote p. 865); [14 June 1709], *Ibid.*, p. 874.

73. Norris to Goldney, 3 June 1709, Norris Papers, Isaac Norris Sr. Letterbook, 1709–1716, pp. 26–27, H.S.P. (quote p. 27); Anderson, "Governors' Councils," pp. 81–82.

74. Assembly to Governor, 8 June 1709, Assembly, *Votes*, II, 862; Logan to Penn, 14 June 1709, Penn, *Papers*, XIII, 772; Assembly to Governor, 29 July 1709, Assembly, *Votes*, II, 877. An embittered Gookin suggested that the Queen turn this paltry gift over to the S.P.G. to support its missionary work. To the Secretary, 27 August 1709, *S.P.G. Letterbooks*, A5, no. 38.

75. Whitehead, Mead, and Lower to D. Lloyd and other Friends in the assembly, 30 September 1709, Wharton-Willing Papers, Box 1, H.S.P.

76. Norris to Logan, 20 July 1711, Norris Papers, Isaac Norris Sr. Letterbook, 1709–1716, p. 282, H.S.P. (first two quotes); Norris to Logan, 28 August 1711, *Ibid.*, p. 286 (third quote).

77. 2–4 November 1689, Council, *Minutes*, I, 306–311, quotes pp. 306, 310.

78. Petition of severall of The ffreemen of This Province willing and Ready to bear Armes in Defence of The same, 24 April 1690, *Ibid.*, p. 334.

79. Minutes of the Provincial Council, 22 April 1699 [misdated; should be 24 April 1690], Robert Proud Collection, Box 2, H.S.P.

80. Petition of the Protestant Subjects living in Pennsylvania to King William, n.d. [1696?], Penn, *Papers*, XIII, 637–638, quote p. 637.

81. Petition to the King from Pennsylvania, 20 May 1696, *Ibid.*, VII, 183.

82. Suder to [Nicholson], 20 November 1698, Perry, *Colonial Church*, p. 10.

83. Root, *Relations with the British Government*, pp. 272, 276–278.

84. Quary to Board of Trade, 31 March 1702, Ames, "Pennsylvania and the English Government," *PMHB*, 24 (1900), 67.

85. Keith to the Secretary, 4 September 1703, *S.P.G. Letterbooks*, A1, no. 121.

86. Logan to Penn, 29 July 1702, Penn, *Papers*, X, 400 (first two quotes); Andrew Hamilton to Penn, 19 September 1702, *Ibid.*, p. 502 (last two quotes); Logan to Penn, 1 December 1702, Logan Papers, James Logan Letterbook, I, 64–66, H.S.P. (third–fifth quotes).

87. Penn to John Evans, 9 August 1703, Penn, *Papers*, X, 1079.

88. Logan to Penn, 28 September 1704, *Ibid.*, XI, 370–371 (quotes); Judith M. Diamondstone, "The Philadelphia Corporation 1701–1776" (Ph.D. diss., University of Pennsylvania, 1969), pp. 103–104.

89. J. Evans to Board of Trade, 9 November 1705, Penn, *Papers*, XII, 378–380, quote p. 379.

90. D. Lloyd to Whitehead, Mead, and Lower, 16 August 1706, Dreer Collection, Additional Manuscripts, H.S.P. (quote); Penn to J. Evans, 15 May 1707, Penn, *Papers*, XIII, 177–181.

91. Logan to Penn, 11 May 1709, *Ibid.*, p. 757 (quote); Bronner, "*Holy Experiment*," pp. 186, 192–205.

92. Munroe, *Colonial Delaware*, pp. 124–125.

93. Penn to Markham and the Council, 5 September 1697, Penn, *Papers*, V, 535–536.

94. Norris to Thomas Lloyd, 13 May 1709, Norris Papers, Isaac Norris Sr. Letterbook, 1709–1716, p. 12, H.S.P. (first quote); Norris to Benjamin Coole, 24 May 1709, *Ibid.*, p. 15 (second quote); Norris to Joseph Wyeth, 26 August 1709, *Ibid.*, p. 62 (third–fifth quotes).

95. Logan to Penn, 19 July 1708, Howland Collection, Q.C.H.C. While still nominally a Quaker, George Keith had raised similar questions in *An Appeal from the Twenty Eight Judges To the Spirit of Truth & true Judgment In all Faithful Friends, called Quakers, that meet at this Yearly Meeting at Burlington, the 7 Month, 1692* [Philadelphia, 1692], p. 7.

96. Logan to Penn, 11 May 1709, Penn, *Papers*, XIII, 757.

97. Draft complaints against Gov. John Blackwell, n.d. [c. 1689], *Ibid.*, VI, 195.

98. Ch. 25, 27 November 1700, *Statutes*, II, 21–23.

99. Penn to Charlewood Lawton, 21 October 1700, Penn, *Papers*, VIII, 700–701; Henry Compton to Board of Trade, 29 December 1701, *Statutes*, II, 458 (quote).

100. Penn to Nicholson, 31 October 1700, Penn, *Papers*, VIII, 743–745, quotes p. 745.

101. Ch. 109, 28 October 1701, *Statutes*, II, 161–162.

102. Jon Butler, "Power, Authority, and the Origins of American Denominational Order: The English Churches in the Delaware Valley 1680–1730," *TAPS*, 68, pt. 2 (1978), 27–31.

103. The only complete biography of Keith is Ethyn Williams Kirby, *George Keith (1638–1716)* (New York, 1942). Several pamphlets written by participants in the controversy have been reprinted in J. William Frost, ed., *The Keithian Controversy in Early Pennsylvania* (Norwood, Pa., 1979).

104. Philadelphia Yearly Meeting to London Yearly Meeting, 15–19 September 1695, Philadelphia Yearly Meeting Collection, Philadelphia Yearly Meeting Minutes, 1681–1746, p. 52a, Q.C.H.C. (quote); Jon Butler, "Into Pennsylvania's Spiritual Abyss: The Rise and Fall of the Later Keithians, 1693–1703," *PMHB*, 101 (1977), 157–162, 168–170.

105. Hugh Roberts to Penn, n.d. [c. 1693–1694], Meta Vaux and Thomas Stewardson, eds., "Hugh Roberts of Merion: His Journal and a Letter to William Penn," *Ibid.*, 18 (1894), 205–206.

106. Caleb Pusey, *Satans Harbinger Encountered* (Philadelphia, 1700), p. 58, quoted in Edward J. Cody, "The Price of Perfection: The Irony of George Keith," *PH*, 39 (1972), 15.

107. Kirby, *George Keith*, pp. 71–72.

108. Philadelphia Yearly Meeting to London Yearly Meeting, 23 September 1696, Philadelphia Yearly Meeting Collection, Philadelphia Yearly Meeting Minutes, 1681–1746, pp. 58–59, Q.C.H.C. (quotes p. 58); Butler, "Into Pennsylvania's Spiritual Abyss," *PMHB*, 101 (1977), 157–162.

109. Bronner, *"Holy Experiment,"* pp. 199–203.

110. Quary and others to Nicholson, 18 January 1696/7, Perry, *Colonial Church*, p. 6.

111. Thomas Clayton to the Clergy, 29 November 1698, *Ibid.*, pp. 13–14; Norman Sykes, *From Sheldon to Secker: Aspects of English Church History 1660–1768* (Cambridge, Eng., 1959), pp. 68–104.

112. John Watts and others to Clayton, 11 March 1698/9, Morgan Edwards, *Materials Towards a History of the Baptists in Pennsylvania Both British and German, Distinguished into Firstday Baptists[,] Keithian Baptists[,] Seventhday Baptists[,] Tuncker Baptists[,] Mennonist Baptists*, vol. 1 (Philadelphia, 1770), Appendix 3, pp. 99–103, quote p. 100.

113. Thomas Martin to Clayton, 16 September 1698, Perry, *Colonial Church*, pp. 12–13, quotes p. 12.

114. Kirby, *George Keith*, pp. 113–147.

115. 12 February–10 March 1701/2, Edgar Legare Pennington, ed., "The Journal of the Reverend George Keith, 1702–1704," *HMPEC*, 20 (1951), 414–416; Keith to Bray, 24 February 1702/3, *S.P.G. Letterbooks*, A1, no. 87.

116. Norris to Jonathan Dickinson, 8 November 1702, Norris Papers, Isaac Norris Sr. Letterbook, 1702–1704, p. 11, H.S.P. (first quote); William Hudson to J. and Mary Dickinson, 19 April 1703, Maria Dickinson Logan Family Papers, Letters, 1682–1890, H.S.P. (second quote).

117. 21 September 1702, Keith, "Journal," *HMPEC*, 20 (1951), 424.

118. "An Account of the State of the Church in North America, by Mr. George Keith and Others [November 1702]," in *Ibid.*, pp. 368–370, quotes pp. 369, 370.

119. John Kendall Nelson, "Anglican Missions in America, 1701–1725: A Study of the Society for the Propagation of the Gospel in Foreign Parts" (Ph.D. diss., North-

western University, 1962), pp. 411–412. Penn thought that "G K's H[ypo]crisy first open'd ye way for this Violent spirit" of militant Anglicanism. Penn to Lawton, 10 December 1700, Penn, *Papers*, VIII, 664–665, quote p. 665.

120. Keith to Bray, 24 February 1702/3, *S.P.G. Letterbooks*, A1, no. 87.

121. John Talbot to Richard Gillingham, 10 April 1703, *Ibid.*, no. 119 (first quote); Talbot to the Secretary, 10 January 1707/8, *Ibid.*, A3, no. 186 (second quote). Although there is no firm evidence about Roman Catholic services in Philadelphia at this date, John Tracy Ellis believes that "In all likelihood it was true" that Jesuit priests from Bohemia Manor, Maryland, made occasional visits to Pennsylvania and Delaware to seek out scattered Catholic families after 1706. *Catholics in Colonial America* (Baltimore, 1965), pp. 373–374.

122. George Ross to the Secretary, 22 January 1711/2, *S.P.G. Letterbooks*, A7, p. 502.

123. Talbot to the Secretary, 7 April 1704, *Ibid.*, A1, no. 181.

124. Vestry of Oxford Church to the Secretary, 5 September 1713, *Ibid.*, A8, pp. 493–494.

125. St. Paul's Church, Chester, to the Secretary, 1705, *Ibid.*, A2, no. 135 (quote); Ross to the Secretary, 30 June 1712, *Ibid.*, A7, pp. 508–509.

126. "Account of the State of the Church," Keith, "Journal," *HMPEC*, 20 (1951), 370–371; Talbot to Keith, 20 October [1704], *S.P.G. Letterbooks*, A2, no. 23; John Clubb to the Secretary, 24 July 1710, *Ibid.*, A5, no. 149; Ross to the Secretary, 30 June 1712, *Ibid.*, A7, p. 509 (quote).

127. "Account of the State of the Church," Keith, "Journal," *HMPEC*, 20 (1951), 371.

128. Talbot to the Secretary, 1 September 1703, *S.P.G. Letterbooks*, A1, no. 125.

129. Evan Evans, A Memorial Of the State of the Church in Pensylvania, 18 September 1707, Dreer Collection, H.S.P.

130. Quary and others to Nicholson, 18 January 1696/7, Perry, *Colonial Church*, p. 6 (first quote); Wardens of Trinity Church, Oxford, to the Secretary, 25 June 1718, *S.P.G. Letterbooks*, A13, p. 271 (second quote).

131. Evans, Memorial Of the State of the Church, 18 September 1707, Dreer Collection, H.S.P. (quote); Pennsylvania Clergy to the Secretary, 1712, *S.P.G. Letterbooks*, A8, p. 475.

132. Ross to the Secretary, 22 January 1711/2, *Ibid.*, A7, p. 502.

133. Evans, Memorial Of the State of the Church, 18 September 1707, Dreer Collection, H.S.P.; Ross to the Secretary, 28 August 1716, *Ibid.*, A11, pp. 236–237 (quotes).

134. Gough, "Pluralism, Politics, and Power Struggles," pp. 21–22, 47–53, 68–72.

135. A Brief Narrative of the Proceedings of William Penn, n.d. [c. 1701], Perry, *Colonial Church*, p. 4.

136. Logan to Penn, 2 December 1701, Penn, *Papers*, IX, 896–897, quote p. 897.

137. See *S.P.G. Letterbooks* and Perry, *Colonial Church*.

138. Penn to Harley, n.d. [c. April 1701], Penn, *Papers*, IX, 166–168 (quotes); Penn to Logan, 29 September 1708, *Ibid.*, XIII, 558.

139. Logan to Penn, 11 May 1702, Logan Papers, Extracts from the Correspondence of James Logan, I, 34–35, H.S.P.

140. Logan to Penn, 3 April 1704, Penn, *Papers*, XI, 218.

141. Logan to Thomas Callowhill, 30 May 1705, Logan Papers, James Logan Letterbook, II, 60–61, H.S.P.

142. Philadelphia Monthly Meeting to Penn, 7 August 1706, Penn, *Papers*, XII, 806.

143. Penn to Assheton, 1 November 1700, *Ibid.*, VIII, 624.

144. Penn to Lawton, 10 December 1700, *Ibid.*, pp. 664–665.

145. Penn to Logan, 29 September 1708, *Ibid.*, XIII, 558; Gough, "Pluralism, Politics, and Power Struggles," pp. 56–57.

146. Penn to S. and Hannah Carpenter, 16 September 1708, Penn, *Papers*, XIII, 539.

147. Penn to J. Evans, 26 February 1704/5, *Ibid.*, XI, 533.

148. Edwards, *Baptists in Pennsylvania*, p. 45.

149. Watts and others to Jedidiah Andrews and others, 30 October 1698, *Ibid.*, Appendix 4, pp. 104–106, quotes pp. 105, 106.

150. Presbyterians to Baptists, 3 November 1698, *Ibid.*, p. 107; Baptists to Presbyterians, 19 November 1698, *Ibid.*, pp. 108–109; note by Watts, n.d., *Ibid.*, p. 109 (quote).

151. *Ibid.*, p. 45.

152. Clayton to [Nicholson], 29 November 1698, Perry, *Colonial Church*, p. 15.

153. Keith to Bray, 26 February 1702/3, *S.P.G. Letterbooks*, A1, no. 88.

154. Talbot to the Secretary, 5 December 1716, *Ibid.*, A12, p. 180.

155. Clayton to [Nicholson], 29 November 1698, Perry, *Colonial Church*, p. 15.

156. John Humphreys to the Secretary, 10 December 1711, *S.P.G. Letterbooks*, A7, pp. 499–500; Humphreys to the Secretary, 12 October 1714, *Ibid.*, A9, p. 322 (quote).

157. Henry Nichols to the Secretary, 10 June 1706, *Ibid.*, A2, no. 169.

158. Clubb to the Secretary, 24 July 1710, *Ibid.*, A5, no. 149.

159. Letter of Francis Daniel Pastorius, 7 March 1684, trans. Julius F. Sachse, ed., *Letters Relating to The Settlement of Germantown in Pennsylvania, 1683–4 From the Könneken Manuscript in the Ministerial-Archive of Lübeck* (Lübeck and Philadelphia, 1903), p. 11.

160. Morgan Evans to ?, 30 October 1714, "Notes and Queries," *PMHB*, 42 (1918), 177.

161. Alan Tully, ed., "One Quaker's View: William Fishbourn's Remarks on the Settlement of Pennsylvania [1739]," *QH*, 66 (1977), 56. He was referring to the first decade of the colony's history, prior to the Keithian Schism which, in his opinion, destroyed the harmony.

162. Letter of Joris Wertmuller, 16 March 1684, trans. Samuel W. Pennypacker, *The Settlement of Germantown Pennsylvania and the Beginning of German Emigration to North America* (Philadelphia, 1899), pp. 100–102, quote p. 101.

163. Francis Louis Michel to John Rudolf Ochs, 20/30 May 1704, William J. Hinke, ed. and trans., Report of a Journey of Francis Louis Michel from Berne, Switzerland, to Virginia, October 2, 1701–December 2, 1702, pt. 3, p. 20, William J. Hinke Collection, Miscellaneous Letters and Documents relating to the Reformed Church in Pennsylvania, 1700–1806, XX, E.R.H.S.

164. Julius Friedrich Sachse, ed. and trans., "Daniel Falckner's *Curieuse Nachricht from Pennsylvania:* The Book that Stimulated the Great German Immigration to Pennsylvania in the Early Years of the XVIII. Century," *PGSPA*, 14 (1903), 22–30.

165. Question 10, *Ibid.*, pp. 96–97.

166. Question 55, *Ibid.*, pp. 160–163. For German Philadelphianism, see F. Ernest Stoeffler, *German Pietism During the Eighteenth Century* (Leiden, 1973), pp. 208–216.

167. Question 75, Falckner, "*Curieuse Nachricht*," *PGSPA*, 14 (1903), 190–191.

168. Question 99, *Ibid.*, pp. 224–225.

169. Question 80, *Ibid.*, pp. 200–201.

170. Logan to Penn, 24 June 1703, Penn, *Papers*, X, 1003.

171. Penn to [Richard Butler, Earl of Arran?], 9 January 1683/4, *Ibid.*, IV, 697.

172. "An Abstract of a Letter from Thomas Paschall of Pennsilvania To his Friend J. J. of Chippenham" (1683), Albert Cook Myers, ed., *Narratives of Early Pennsylvania, West New Jersey, and Delaware, 1630–1707* (New York, 1912), pp. 250–252; William Penn, "Letter from William Penn, Proprietary and Governour of Pennsylvania in America, to the Committee of the Free Society of Traders of that Province, residing in London" (1683), *Ibid.*, pp. 237–238; Gabriel Thomas, "An Historical and Geographical Account of the Province and Country of Pensilvania; and of West-New Jersey in America" (1698), *Ibid.*, pp. 316–317.

173. Penn, "Letter to the Free Society of Traders," *Ibid.*, pp. 237–238, quotes p. 237.

174. Letter of Pastorius, 7 March 1684, Sachse, *Letters Relating to Germantown*, p. 13.

175. "Letter from Paschall To J. J.," Myers, *Narratives of Pennsylvania*, p. 251.

176. Carl Bridenbaugh, in "The Old and New Societies of the Delaware Valley in the Seventeenth Century," *PMHB*, 100 (1976), 150–151, points out the pioneer nature of the agricultural practices of the Dutch and Swedish colonists.

177. Henry J. Cadbury, ed., "Caleb Pusey's Account of Pennsylvania [c. 1723]," *QH*, 64 (1975), 45–46, quote p. 46.

178. Penn to Lord Keeper North, 24 July 1683, Penn, *Papers*, IV, 314.

179. "Letter from Paschall To J. J.," Myers, *Narratives of Pennsylvania*, pp. 250–252, quotes pp. 251–252.

180. Penn, "Letter to the Free Society of Traders," *Ibid.*, pp. 237–238.

181. Francis Daniel Pastorius, "Umständige Geographische Beschreibung Der zu Allerletzt erfundenen Provintz Pensylvaniae. . . ." (1700), trans. *Ibid.*, pp. 385–386; Penn to Earl of Sunderland, 28 July 1683, Penn, *Papers*, IV, 343.

182. Bronner, *"Holy Experiment,"* pp. 61–62.

183. Penn to the Inhabitants of Pennsylvania, 8 April 1681, Penn, *Papers*, III, 218–220; Israel Acrelius, *A History of New Sweden; or, the Settlements on the River Delaware*, trans. William M. Reynolds (Philadelphia, 1876), pp. 125–127.

184. Petition, Swedes belonging to Wicaco Parish to Markham, n.d. [c. 1692], Society Miscellaneous Collection, Box 4A, H.S.P.

185. Benjamin Chambers to Penn, 1 February 1699/1700, Penn Manuscripts, Penn-Physick Manuscripts, Correspondence, I, 11, H.S.P.

186. [1 June 1709], Assembly, *Votes*, II, 856 (first quote); 11 June 1709, Council, *Minutes*, II, 465–466; 7 August 1709, *Ibid.*, pp. 479–482 (second–fifth quotes pp. 480, 481).

187. Minutes, Commissioners of Property, 14 September 1709, William H. Egle and John B. Linn, eds., *Pennsylvania Archives*, 2d ser., 19 vols. (Harrisburg, 1876–1893), XIX, 501–502 [hereafter *Pa. Arch.*].

188. Acrelius, *New Sweden*, pp. 127–128.

189. Lord Leyonberg to Penn, 25 May 1686, Penn, *Papers*, V, 445; Acrelius, *New Sweden*, pp. 115, 185–186.

190. 2 December 1696, Luther Martin, trans., "Diary of Rev. Andrew Rudman, July 15, 1696–June 14, 1697," *GAA*, n.s., 4 (1906), 366; Frick Biörck to Israel Kolmodin, 29 October 1697, Thomas Campanius Holm, *A Short Description of the Province of New Sweden. . . .* [1702], trans. Peter S. DuPonceau (Philadelphia, 1834), p. 98.

191. C. A. Weslager, ed., "The Swedes' Letter to William Penn [30 October 1697]," *PMHB*, 83 (1959), 93–94, quotes p. 93.

192. Letter from C. Leyoncrona, 3 August 1699, Horace Burr, trans., *The Record of Holy Trinity (Old Swedes) Church, Wilmington, Del., From 1697 to 1773. . . . With an Abstract of the English Records from 1773 to 1810* (Wilmington, Del., 1890), p. 73; 29 November 1699, *Ibid.*, p. 70; 7 December 1699, *Ibid.*, p. 75 (quote).

193. Acrelius, *New Sweden*, pp. 179–181, quote p. 180.

194. B. Fernow, ed., "Domine Rudolphus Varick in Philadelphia, 1690," *PMHB*, 13 (1889), 249–250.

195. Acrelius, *New Sweden*, pp. 181–189; Jeannette Eckman, *Crane Hook on the Delaware, 1677–1699: An Early Swedish Lutheran Church and Community With the Historical Background of the Delaware River Valley* (Newark, Del., 1958), pp. 71–76 (quote p. 74).

196. Andrew Rudman to Jacob Arrhenius, 20 October 1697, trans. Holm, *Short Description of New Sweden*, pp. 102–103; Biörck to Kolmodin, 29 October 1697, *Ibid.*, pp. 98–101 (first and third quotes, pp. 100, 99), and Eckman, *Crane Hook*, pp. 116–118 (second quote pp. 116–117).

197. Letter of Rudman, 1700, Ruth L. Springer and Louise Wallman, eds. and trans., "Two Swedish Pastors Describe Philadelphia, 1700 and 1702," *PMHB*, 84 (1960), 204; Ira Oliver Nothstein, ed. and trans., *The Planting of the Swedish Church in America: Graduation Dissertation of Tobias Eric Biörck* [1731] (Rock Island, Ill., 1943), pp. 20–23.

198. Letter of Rudman, 1700, Springer and Wallman, "Swedish Pastors Describe Philadelphia," *PMHB*, 84 (1960), 206.

199. Biörck, *Planting of the Swedish Church*, p. 30.

200. Letter of Andreas Sandel, 17 June 1702, Springer and Wallman, "Swedish Pastors Describe Philadelphia," *PMHB*, 84 (1960), 213.

201. Biörck, *Planting of the Swedish Church*, pp. 30–32, quotes pp. 31, 32.

202 Letter of Sandel, 17 June 1702, Springer and Wallman, "Swedish Pastors Describe Philadelphia," *PMHB*, 84 (1960), 213.

203. Biörck, *Planting of the Swedish Church*, pp. 30–31, quotes p. 31.

204. 13 May 1715, Andrew Hesselius, Journal, 1711–1724, p. 46, H.S.P.

205. 1 September–31 November [sic] [1708], Burr, *Holy Trinity Record*, pp. 128–130, quote p. 128. This episode appears to have been an anomaly in Swedish-Quaker relations.

206. Letter of Rudman, 1700, Springer and Wallman, "Swedish Pastors Describe Philadelphia," *PMHB*, 84 (1960), 208.

207. *Ibid.*; Letter of Sandel, 17 June 1702, *Ibid.*, pp. 213–214; Biörck, *Planting of the Swedish Church*, pp. 30–32.

208. Robert Meredith Gabler Libby, "Anglican-Lutheran Ecumenism in Early American History," *HMPEC*, 36 (1967), 219–220, 230–231; Nelson Rightmyer, "Swedish-English Relations in Northern Delaware," *CH*, 15 (1946), 101–115.

209. May 1712, Burr, *Holy Trinity Record*, pp. 142–143, quote p. 143.

210. Bishop of London to E. Evans, 8 February 1711/2, *Ibid.*, p. 143.

211. William Arnold Bultmann, "The Society for the Propagation of the Gospel in Foreign Parts and the Foreign Settler in the American Colonies" (Ph.D. diss., University of California, Los Angeles, 1951), pp. 17–19, 24–25; Rightmyer, "Swedish-English Relations," *CH*, 15 (1946), 103; Joyce L. White, "The Affiliation of Seven Swedish Lutheran Churches with the Episcopal Church," *HMPEC*, 46 (1977), 172–176.

212. 25 February 1703, Andreas Sandel, Brief Review of my Journey to West India,

1701–1719, trans. B. Elfving, pp. 111–112, H.S.P.; November 1708, *Ibid.*, pp. 144–145.

213. Bultmann, "S.P.G. and the Foreign Settler," pp. 29–30, 45–46, 317–318.

214. Butler, "Into Pennsylvania's Spiritual Abyss," *PMHB*, 101 (1977), 159–161.

215. Julius Friedrich Sachse, ed. and trans., "The Missive of Justus Falckner, Germantown, Concerning the Religious Condition of Pennsylvania in the Year 1701," *PMHB*, 21 (1897), 217–223 (first five quotes pp. 218, 219, 221); Julius Friedrich Sachse, ed., and George T. Ettinger, trans., "A Contribution to Pennsylvania History: Missives to Rev. August Herman Francke from Daniel Falckner, Germantown, April 16, 1702, and Justus Falckner, New York, 1704," *PGSPA*, 18 (1907), 4–13 (sixth quote p. 9 [letter of D. Falckner]).

216. Frank Ried Diffenderffer, "The German Exodus to England in 1709," *Ibid.*, 7 (1896), 265–266; Henry Eyster Jacobs, "The German Emigration to America 1709–1740," *Ibid.*, 8 (1897), 137–141; Julius Friedrich Sachse, *The German Pietists of Provincial Pennsylvania, 1694–1708* (Philadelphia, 1895), pp. 66–68.

217. Sachse, "Missive of Justus Falckner," *PMHB*, 21 (1897), 218–221, quotes pp. 218, 220.

218. D. Falckner to Francke, 16 April 1702, Sachse and Ettinger, "Contribution to Pennsylvania History," *PGSPA*, 18 (1907), 6–11, quotes p. 9.

219. Letter of Pastorius, 7 March 1684, Sachse, *Letters Relating to Germantown*, p. 25; Markham to Penn, 22 August 1686, Penn, *Papers*, V, 483; Logan to Penn, 7 April 1709, *Ibid.*, XIII, 744.

220. 6 February 1693/4, Council, *Minutes*, I, 436.

221. 11 June 1707, Assembly, *Votes*, I, 777–778 (quote p. 777); 15–22 July 1707, Council, *Minutes*, II, 385–386, 390. Colonists seem to have equated "French" and "Roman Catholic," but at least one prominent family of traders, the LeTorts, were Huguenots. Evelyn A. Benson, "The Huguenot LeTorts: First Christian Family on the Conestoga," *JLCHS*, 65 (1961), 92–105; Marian Wallace Reninger, "Ann Letort," *Ibid.*, 64 (1960), 49–52.

222. Logan to Penn, 18 June 1708, Penn, *Papers*, XIII, 468.

223. See, for instance, 12 May 1686, Council, *Minutes*, I, 179, for an investigation of complaints by French immigrants about a breach of contract. For the council's involvement in naturalization, see 15 April 1704, 3 April 1705, 15 May 1706, 1 March 1708/9, 17 August 1709, 29 September 1709, *Ibid.*, II, 131, 184–185, 241–242, 430–432, 480, 493–494.

224. Minutes, Commissioners of Property, 29–30 November 1691, 26 December 1691, *Pa. Arch.*, 2d ser., XIX, 78–81; 19 November 1712, 21 December 1715, *Ibid.*, pp. 538–539, 595–596.

225. Owen to Penn, 9 November 1705, Penn, *Papers*, XII, 392.

226. London Yearly Meeting to Philadelphia Yearly Meeting, 3 October 1709, Philadelphia Yearly Meeting Collection, Miscellaneous Epistles and Papers, 1703–1714, Q.C.II.C.

227. Germantown Friends' Protest Against Slavery, 1688, quoted in Mary Anne Shafer, "Francis Daniel Pastorius: His Influence Outside of Germantown" (M.A. thesis, Pennsylvania State University, 1977), p. 42.

228. See also the discussion of promotional tracts and letters in ch. 2, 4.

229. Cornelis Bom to Jan Laurens, 12 October 1684, trans. Pennypacker, *Germantown*, pp. 102–107, quote p 104.

230. Report of Louis Michel, pt. 2, p. 22, Hinke Collection, Letters and Documents, XX, E.R.H.S.

231. Letter of Pastorius, 7 March 1684, Sachse, *Letters Relating to Germantown*, p. 17.

232. William Penn, "A Further Account of the Province of Pennsylvania and its Improvements, for the Satisfaction of those that are Adventurers, and enclined to be so" (1685), Myers, *Narratives of Pennsylvania*, p. 260.

233. Richard Frame, "A Short Description of Pennsilvania, Or, a Relation What things are known, enjoyed, and like to be discovered in the said Province" (1692), *Ibid.*, pp. 300–305.

234. Michel to Ochs, 20/30 May 1704, Report of Louis Michel, pt. 3, pp. 20–22, Hinke Collection, Letters and Documents, XX, E.R.H.S., quote p. 20.

235. Question 22, Falckner, *"Curieuse Nachricht," PGSPA*, 14 (1903), 96–99, quote p. 99.

236. Question 70, *Ibid.*, pp. 182–183. See also Questions 49, 71, 72, and 75, *Ibid.*, pp. 152–153, 184–185, 186–187, 190–191.

237. Francis Paul Jennings, "Miquon's Passing: Indian-European Relations in Colonial Pennsylvania, 1674 to 1755" (Ph.D. diss., University of Pennsylvania, 1965), pp. 163–165.

238. Memorial of the Amish to Penn and the Deputy Governor, 20 May 1718, Samuel Hazard, ed., *The Register of Pennsylvania. . . .* , 16 vols. (Philadelphia, 1828–1835), VII, 151 and n.

239. John Jones to Hugh Jones, 1708, "Philadelphia in 1682," *PMHB*, 13 (1889), 228.

240. The Yearly Meeting was not pleased with this arrangement, but agreed to allow the Welsh meetings to remain within the same quarterly meeting. 24 September 1701, Philadelphia Yearly Meeting Collection, Philadelphia Yearly Meeting Minutes, 1681–1746, p. 83, Q.C.H.C.

241. Barry John Levy, "The Light in the Valley: The Chester and Welsh Tract Quaker Communities and the Delaware Valley, 1681–1750" (Ph.D. diss., University of Pennsylvania, 1976), pp. 51–53, 57–58, 60–63.

242. Edwards, *Baptists in Pennsylvania*, pp. 19–21.

243. Abel Morgan to church at Blaenegwent, 12 April 1712, Horatio Gates Jones, "The Rev. Abel Morgan," *PMHB*, 6 (1882), 306.

244. Bultmann, "S.P.G. and the Foreign Settler," pp. 6, 66–111.

245. Council to Penn, 11 August 1715, Penn, *Papers*, XIV, 532–535, quotes pp. 535, 533.

246. Pastorius to his children, n.d., quoted in Pennypacker, *Germantown*, p. 61.

247. Sachse, "Missive of Justus Falckner," *PMHB*, 21 (1897), 219–220; Oswald Seidensticker, ed. and trans., "The Hermits of the Wissahickon," *Ibid.*, 11 (1887), 440; and above.

248. Questions 72–74, 77, Falckner, *"Curieuse Nachricht," PGSPA*, 14 (1903), 186–189, 194–195.

249. Johannes Kelpius to Johannes Fabricius, 23 July 1705, Julius Friedrich Sachse, ed. and trans., "The Diarium of Magister Johannes Kelpius," *Ibid.*, 25 (1914), 80–83, quote p. 80.

250. Substance of a letter from Pastorius to Rowland Ellis, 25 March 1717, Pastorius Papers, Letterbook, 1700–1719, p. 22, H.S.P.

4. Immigration, 1717–1740

1. Data on immigration to Pennsylvania are imprecise. The number of immigrants, their places of origin, and the years during which the greatest numbers arrived in the colony have been variously interpreted on the basis of incomplete records. The studies that best illuminate major periods of migration are: R. J. Dickson, *Ulster Emigration to Colonial America 1718–1775* (London, 1966), pp. 23–24, 32–35, 55–59, 96–97, 224–227, Appendices A, C, D, E; James G. Leyburn, *The Scotch-Irish: A Social History* (Chapel Hill, 1962), pp. 168–175, 179–183; and Marianne Wokeck, "The Flow and the Composition of German Immigration to Philadelphia, 1727–1775," *PMHB*, 105 (1981), 249–278, especially Table 1 (pp. 260–261). The exact number of arrivals in the province each year is relatively unimportant for the purposes of this book, which is primarily concerned with attitudes and perceptions, although, of course, a sudden increase in immigration did sharpen awareness of the pluralistic nature of society.

2. Dickson, *Ulster Emigration;* Wayland F. Dunaway, *The Scotch-Irish of Colonial Pennsylvania* (1944; reprint ed., London, 1962); E. R. R. Green, ed., "The 'Strange Humours' That Drove the Scotch-Irish to America, 1729," 3*WMQ*, 12 (1955), 113–123.

3. Frank Ried Diffenderffer, "The German Emigration into Pennsylvania Through the Port of Philadelphia from 1700 to 1775," *PGSPA*, 10 (1899), 32–54, and "The German Exodus to England in 1709," *Ibid.*, 7 (1896), 257–413; Julius Friedrich Sachse, "The Fatherland (1450–1700) . . . ," *Ibid.*, pp. 33–256. For convenience, immigrants from German-speaking countries will be termed "Germans" or "Palatines," even though there was no "Germany" prior to 1871 and not all immigrants came from the region commonly designated as the Palatinate. To contemporary Pennsylvanians, they were "Germans," "Palatines," or "Dutch."

4. Dunaway, *Scotch-Irish*, pp. 47–48.

5. Matthias Henry Richards, "The German Emigration from New York Province into Pennsylvania," *PGSPA*, 9 (1898), 347–447.

6. Christopher Sauer to [Robert Hunter Morris], 15 March 1755, Donald F. Durnbaugh, ed., *The Brethren in Colonial America: A Source Book on the Transplantation and Development of the Church of the Brethren in the Eighteenth Century* (Elgin, Ill., 1967), p. 32 (quote); Green, "'Strange Humours,'" 3*WMQ*, 12 (1955), 115–119; Russell Sage Nelson, Jr., "Backcountry Pennsylvania (1704–1774): The Ideals of William Penn in Practice" (Ph.D. diss., University of Wisconsin, 1968), pp. 5–9.

7. R. W. Kelsey, ed. and trans., "An Early Description of Pennsylvania. A Letter of Christopher Sower, Written in 1724, Describing Conditions in Philadelphia and Vicinity, and the Sea Voyage from Europe," *PMHB*, 45 (1921), 249.

8. Sauer to Wittgenstein Friends, 1 August 1725, trans. Durnbaugh, *Brethren in Colonial America*, pp. 33–39, quotes pp. 35, 36.

9. John Adam Gruber to Berleburg Friends, 28 October 1730, trans. *Ibid.*, p. 118.

10. Esther Werndtlin to Ursula Oehrin, 24 November 1736, Albert B. Faust, ed., "Documents in Swiss Archives relating to Emigration to American Colonies in the Eighteenth Century," *AHR*, 22 (1916), 124.

11. Durs Thommen to Burgomaster and Council of Basel, 3 October 1737, *Ibid.*, p. 117.

12. John George Käsebier to Count Casimir, 7 November 1724, trans. Durnbaugh, *Brethren in Colonial America*, pp. 30–31; Sauer to Wittgenstein Friends, 1 August 1725, *Ibid.*, pp. 34–38; Robert [Parke] to Mary Valentine, December 1725, Chester County

Miscellaneous Papers, 1684–1847, p. 87, H.S.P.; David Seibt to Brother, 20 December 1734, Andrew S. Berky, ed. and trans., *The Journals and Papers of David Shultze*, 2 vols. (Pennsburg, Pa., 1952), I, 52–54; Hans Georg Gerster to Friends, "den alten Winter-monat" 1737, Leo Schelbert and Hedwig Rappolt, eds., *Alles ist ganz anders hier: Auswandererschicksale in Briefen aus zwei Jahrhunderten* (Breisgau, Switzerland, 1977), pp. 119–121.

13. Jonathan Dickinson to Ezekiel Gomersall, 2 September 1717, Jonathan Dickinson Letterbook, 1715–1721, p. 135, L.C.P. (second and third quotes); Dickinson to Joshua Crosby, [September 1717], *Ibid.*, p. 136 (first and fourth quotes).

14. Isaac Norris Sr. to William Wragg, 13 September 1717, Norris Papers, Isaac Norris Sr. Letterbook, 1716–1730, p. 99, H.S.P.

15. Logan feared that "by the same Routes and methods" many Swedes "might be pourd in upon us, & that nation . . . has made some Claim to this Countrey alledging they were the first Settlers of it." James Logan to Henry Goldney, Joshua Gee, and others, 25 September 1717, Logan Papers, James Logan Letterbook, IV, 60, H.S.P. For Logan's views on immigration and its implications for the province a few years later, see Logan to Hannah Penn, 29 March 1720, Penn Manuscripts, Official Correspondence, I, 89, H.S.P.

16. Dickinson to John Askew, 22 November 1717, Jonathan Dickinson Letterbook, 1715–1721, p. 163, L.C.P.

17. Logan to Askew, 28 November 1717, Logan Papers, James Logan Letterbook, IV, 81, H.S.P.

18. The assembly did resolve to extend the most recent tax law of *"One Penny per Pound*, and *Four Shillings per* Head," to all Palatines who were of taxable age; they also became subject to county taxes. But the tax commissioners were given discretionary power to rebate the taxes according to individual circumstances. [11 January 1717/8], Gertrude MacKinney and Charles F. Hoban, eds., *Pennsylvania Archives*, 8th ser., 8 vols., *Votes and Proceedings of the House of Assembly of the Province of Pennsylvania, 1682–1776* (Harrisburg, 1931–1935), II, 1235 [hereafter Assembly, *Votes*].

19. 17 September 1717, *Minutes of the Provincial Council of Pennsylvania, From the Organization to the Termination of the Proprietary Government*, 16 vols. (Philadelphia and Harrisburg, 1851–1853), III, 29 [hereafter Council, *Minutes*]. Because some of the immigrants were "said to be Menonists," they were expressly allowed to give "Equivalent assurances" of allegiance in their own manner.

20. Governor to Assembly, [15 October 1717], Assembly, *Votes*, II, 1223.

21. Assembly to Governor, [8 January 1717/8], *Ibid.*, p. 1229.

22. Governor to Assembly, [10 January 1717/8], *Ibid.*, p. 1232.

23. Logan to Askew, 28 November 1717, Logan Papers, James Logan Letterbook, IV, 81, H.S.P.

24. James Steel to Isaac Taylor, 27 September 1717, Taylor Papers, XIV, no. 2861, H.S.P.; Minutes, Commissioners of Property, 21 November 1717, William H. Egle and John B. Linn, eds., *Pennsylvania Archives*, 2d ser., 19 vols. (Harrisburg, 1876–1893), XIX, 679 [hereafter *Pa. Arch.*]; 22 November 1717, *Ibid.*, p. 624 (quotes).

25. Alan Tully, *William Penn's Legacy: Politics and Social Structure in Provincial Pennsylvania, 1726–1755* (Baltimore, 1977), pp. 3–11.

26. Norris to Joseph Pike, 22 June 1724, Norris Papers, Isaac Norris Sr. Letterbook, 1716–1730, pp. 377–378, H.S.P., quote p. 377.

27. Logan to H. Penn, 1 January 1725/6, Penn Manuscripts, Official Correspondence, I, 185, H.S.P.

28. Logan to I. Taylor, 1 February 1719/20, Taylor Papers, XIV, no. 2935, H.S.P. (quote); Logan to H. Penn, 9 February 1724/5, Penn Manuscripts, Official Correspondence, I, 313, H.S.P.

29. Norris to Pike, 22 June 1724, Norris Papers, Isaac Norris Sr. Letterbook, 1716–1730, pp. 377–378, H.S.P.

30. Norris to Pike, 21 June 1721, Ibid., pp. 261–262, quotes p. 262.

31. Nelson, "Backcountry Pennsylvania," p. 17.

32. 14–21 September 1727, Council, Minutes, III, 282–283, quote p. 282.

33. Petition, December 1727, Society Miscellaneous Collection, Box 4A, H.S.P.

34. Logan to John Penn, 6 December 1727, Logan Papers, James Logan Letterbook, IV, 167, H.S.P.

35. Patrick Gordon to Duke of Newcastle, 8 December 1727, Penn Manuscripts, Additional Miscellaneous Letters, I, 29, H.S.P.

36. Logan to ?, 23 September 1727, Logan Papers, James Logan Letterbook, IV, 145, H.S.P.

37. [27 January 1727/8], Assembly, Votes, III, 1869–1870.

38. [17 April 1728], Ibid., pp. 1875–1876.

39. Assembly to Governor, 18 April 1728, Ibid., p. 1877.

40. Logan to J. Penn, 11 September 1728, Penn Manuscripts, Official Correspondence, II, 21, H.S.P.

41. Governor to Assembly, 17 December 1728, Council, Minutes, III, 342. The assembly had briefly worried about the arrival of "great Numbers of Convicts, and some Irish Servants of ill Character," and the expectation of more of the same, at its meeting on [14 January 1725/6], Assembly, Votes, II, 1727.

42. Because many emigrants from Ireland debarked at New Castle rather than Philadelphia, the assembly asked Gordon to recommend similar restrictions to the assembly of the Lower Counties. Assembly to Governor, [20 December 1728], Ibid., III, 1915–1917.

43. Gordon to Springett and J. Penn, 16 May 1729, Penn Manuscripts, Official Correspondence, II, 75, H.S.P.

44. Ch. 307, 10 May 1729, James T. Mitchell and Henry Flanders, comps., The Statutes at Large of Pennsylvania from 1682 to 1801, 16 vols. (Harrisburg, 1896–1911), IV, 135–140, quote p. 135 (preamble) [hereafter Statutes].

45. [21 August 1729], Assembly, Votes, III, 1966–1967; [14–15 January 1729/30], Ibid., pp. 1983–1984.

46. [15 October 1729], Ibid., p. 1976. After a "long Debate" on [16 October 1729], a committee was appointed to draft a bill to repeal the objectionable clauses. Ibid., p. 1977.

47. [16 January 1729/30], Ibid., pp. 1984–1986; ch. 314, 14 February 1729/30, Statutes, IV, 164–171 (quotes). This act was repealed by a new statute for similar purposes, ch. 354, 3 February 1742/3, Ibid., pp. 360–370.

48. Gordon to [the Proprietors], 20 May 1730, Penn Manuscripts, Official Correspondence, II, 111, H.S.P.

49. [16 April 1728], Assembly, Votes, III, 1870; [12–20 February 1728/9], Ibid., pp. 1925–1926, 1930; [23 January 1729/30], Ibid., p. 1987.

50. 15 January 1729/30, Council, *Minutes*, III, 374; Governor to Assembly, 16 January 1729/30, *Ibid*. (quotes).

51. Gordon to the Proprietors, 25 March 1731, Penn Manuscripts, Official Correspondence, II, 155, H.S.P.

52. Ch. 309, 14 February 1729/30, *Statutes*, IV, 147–150.

53. Karl Frederick Geiser, *Redemptioners and Indentured Servants in the Colony and Commonwealth of Pennsylvania* (New Haven, 1901), pp. 26–27.

54. Philadelphia Yearly Meeting Epistle, 17–21 September 1726, Philadelphia Yearly Meeting Collection, Philadelphia Yearly Meeting Minutes, 1681–1746, pp. 316–317, Q.C.H.C.

55. Logan to Elisha Gatchel, 1 June 1727, Logan Papers, James Logan Letterbook, III, 103, H.S.P.

56. Norris to Pike, 28 October 1728, Norris Papers, Isaac Norris Sr. Letterbook, 1716–1730, pp. 515–516, H.S.P.

57. Logan to Steel, 18 November 1729, Logan Papers, X, 46, H.S.P.

58. Samuel Blunston to Thomas Penn, 3 March 1737/8, Lancaster County Papers, 1724–1772, p. 33, H.S.P.

59. Logan to S. Penn, 8 December 1727, Logan Papers, James Logan Letterbook, IV, 168, H.S.P.

60. Steel to J. Penn and others, 2 August 1731, Logan Papers, James Steel Letterbook, II, 25, H.S.P.

61. Dickinson to Walter Newberry, 25 November 1717, Jonathan Dickinson Letterbook, 1715–1721, p. 165, L.C.P. (second quote); Dickinson to Crosby, 17 November 1719, *Ibid*., p. 295 (first quote). However, as late as [9 January 1722/3] the assembly had read a petition from inhabitants of Philadelphia County requesting "that our Port may be freed of Taxes, and Foreigners encouraged." Assembly, *Votes*, II, 1467.

62. [Logan] to [J. Penn], 25 November 1727, *Pa. Arch.*, 2d ser., VII, 96–97, quote p. 96.

63. Norris to Pike, 28 October 1728, Norris Papers, Isaac Norris Sr. Letterbook, 1716–1730, p. 515, H.S.P.

64. Logan to the Proprietors, 14 November 1731, Penn Manuscripts, Official Correspondence, II, 213, H.S.P.

65. Steel to the Proprietors, 28 November 1737, *Ibid.*, III, 63.

66. [Logan] to [J. Penn], 25 November 1727, *Pa. Arch.*, 2d ser., VII, 97.

67. Norris to Pike, 28 October 1728, Norris Papers, Isaac Norris Sr. Letterbook, 1716–1730, p. 515, H.S.P.

68. Logan to the Proprietors, 17 April 1731, Penn Manuscripts, Official Correspondence, II, 165, H.S.P.

69. Norris to Pike, 28 October 1728, Norris Papers, Isaac Norris Sr. Letterbook, 1716–1730, p. 515, H.S.P.

70. S. Blunston to T. Penn, 3 March 1737/8, Lancaster County Papers, 1724–1772, p. 33, H.S.P.

71. Logan to T. Penn, 14 June 1733, Gratz Collection, Case 2, Box 32, H.S.P.

72. Logan to Joseph Houston, 14 April 1730, Logan Papers, James Logan Letterbook, III, 150–151, H.S.P. (quotes); Logan to James Anderson, 23 December 1730, *Ibid.*, IV, 213.

73. Logan to Adam Boyd, 29 February 1731/2, Maria Dickinson Logan Family Pa-

pers, Jonathan Dickinson/James Logan Letterbook, James Logan Section, pp. 41–42, H.S.P.

74. Logan to Anderson, 22 January 1735/6, Logan Papers, X, 55, H.S.P.

75. Peter Baynton to Benjamin Faneuil, 31 July 1729, Sequestered Baynton-Wharton-Morgan Papers, Box 1, Peter Baynton Letterbook, 1729, P.H.M.C.

76. Norris to Pike, 28 October 1728, Norris Papers, Isaac Norris Sr. Letterbook, 1716–1730, p. 515, H.S.P.

77. Dickinson to John Herriot, 12 November 1719, Jonathan Dickinson Letterbook, 1715–1721, p. 288, L.C.P.

78. Logan to J. Chalmers, n.d. [c. 1729], Logan Papers, Selections from the Correspondence of James Logan, V, 308, H.S.P. Among the "villanies" perpetrated by Irishmen was the importation of counterfeit coins and bills of credit.

79. Gordon to S. and J. Penn, 16 May 1729, Penn Manuscripts, Official Correspondence, II, 75, H.S.P.

80. Logan to James Kirkpatrick, 2 August 1729, Logan Papers, Selections from the Correspondence of James Logan, V, 278–280, H.S.P., quotes p. 279. He did, however, once find a "very well recommended gentleman" from Ireland, whom he referred to a surveyor for a land grant. Logan to J[ohn] T[aylor], 15 March 1730/1, Logan Papers, James Logan Letterbook, III, 171, H.S.P.

81. Logan to T. Penn, 22 December 1730 (postscript to a letter of 18 December 1730), Ibid., p. 334 (first two quotes); Steel to J. Penn, 25 March 1731, Logan Papers, James Steel Letterbook, II, 19, H.S.P. (third quote).

82. S. Blunston to T. Penn, 13 August 1734, Lancaster County Papers, 1724–1772, p. 7, H.S.P.

83. Logan to Steel, 18 November 1729, Logan Papers, X, 46, H.S.P.

84. Logan to [J. Penn], 13 August 1729, Logan Papers, James Logan Letterbook, III, 304, H.S.P. (first quote); Logan to John Wright and S. Blunston, 2 September 1730, Logan Papers, James Logan Correspondence, I, 96, H.S.P. (second quote); Logan to Edward Shippen, 3 September 1730, Ibid., p. 98.

85. 17 September 1717, Council, Minutes, III, 29.

86. Alien immigration could have been restricted or discouraged, while that from Ireland could not be, since the Scotch-Irish were British subjects. Thus Pennsylvanians occasionally discussed limiting German immigration, although they appeared to have had greater antipathy toward the emigrants from Ireland.

87. [Logan] to [J. Penn], 25 November 1727, Pa. Arch., 2d ser., VII, 96.

88. Norris to J. and T. Penn, 15 November 1731, Penn Manuscripts, Official Correspondence, II, 203, H.S.P.

89. J. Penn to Logan, 17 April 1727, Penn Manuscripts, Letters of the Penn Family to James Logan, II, 19, H.S.P.; Logan to James Mitchell and Galbraith, September 1728, Logan Papers, James Logan Letterbook, III, 119–120, H.S.P.; S. Blunston to T. Penn, 3 March 1737/8, Lancaster County Papers, 1724–1772, p. 33, H.S.P.

90. Dickinson to Joseph Farmer, 29 July 1720, Jonathan Dickinson Letterbook, 1715–1721, p. 341, L.C.P.

91. J. Penn to Logan, 22 March 1727/8, Penn Manuscripts, Letters of the Penn Family to James Logan, II, 22, H.S.P.; the Proprietors to Richard Hill, Norris, Samuel Preston, and Logan, 11 November 1728, Ibid., p. 70.

92. Margaretta Freame to [J. Penn?], 22 March 1736/7, Penn Manuscripts, Private

Correspondence, II, 163, H.S.P.; Thomas Freame to [J. Penn?], 22 March 1736/7, *Ibid.*, p. 17.

93. He noted sympathetically that they had been expelled from their homeland because they refused to swear oaths and to bear arms. Dickinson to Isaac Gale, 14 November 1719, Jonathan Dickinson Letterbook, 1715–1721, p. 291, L.C.P.

94. J. Penn to Logan, 10 February 1730/1, Penn Manuscripts, Thomas Penn Letterbook, I, 22–23, H.S.P.; J. Penn to T. Penn, 1 October 1732, *Ibid.*, pp. 63–64.

95. J. Penn to T. Penn, 28 January 1732/3, *Ibid.*, p. 70.

96. Francis Paul Jennings, "Miquon's Passing: Indian-European Relations in Colonial Pennsylvania, 1674 to 1755" (Ph.D. diss., University of Pennsylvania, 1965), pp. 217–218, 231–234, 292–294; Thomas Wendel, "The Keith-Lloyd Alliance: Factional and Coalition Politics in Colonial Pennsylvania," *PMHB*, 92 (1968), 297–298.

97. Logan to S. Penn, 24 November 1725, Logan Papers, Selections from the Correspondence of James Logan, III, 319, A.P.S. (first quote); Logan to H. Penn, 1 January 1725/6, Penn Manuscripts, Official Correspondence, I, 185, H.S.P. (second quote).

98. 5 June 1728, Council, *Minutes*, III, 323–324.

99. [Logan] to [J. Penn], 25 November 1727, *Pa. Arch.*, 2d ser., VII, 94–95.

100. Jennings, "Miquon's Passing," pp. 193–196.

101. Logan to Andrew Hamilton, 12 February 1724/5, Logan Papers, James Logan Letterbook, II, 254–255, H.S.P., quotes p. 255.

102. Norris to S. Clements, 30 April 1725, Norris Papers, Isaac Norris Sr. Letterbook, 1716–1730, p. 422, H.S.P.

103. [4 March 1724/5], Assembly, *Votes*, II, 1673–1674.

104. Norris to Clements, 30 April 1725, Norris Papers, Isaac Norris Sr. Letterbook, 1716–1730, p. 422, H.S.P.

105. [29 April 1724], Assembly, *Votes*, II, 1568–1569 (quote p. 1569); [5 March 1724/5], *Ibid.*, p. 1675.

106. Governor to Assembly, 18 March 1724/5, *Ibid.*, pp. 1678–1680, quotes p. 1679.

107. Resolution of Assembly, 18 March 1724/5, *Ibid.*, p. 1680; Logan to Hamilton, 24 March 1724/5, Logan Papers, James Logan Letterbook, II, 270, H.S.P..

108. Governor to Assembly, [10 August 1725], Assembly, *Votes*, II, 1695–1696; [11 August 1725], *Ibid.*, p. 1697 (quote).

109. [23 November–8 December 1725], *Ibid.*, pp. 1715–1718, 1721–1722; ch. 291, 5 March 1725/6, *Statutes*, IV, 57–59.

110. Roy N. Lokken, *David Lloyd, Colonial Lawmaker* (Seattle, 1959), pp. 196–224; Wendel, "Keith-Lloyd Alliance," *PMHB*, 92 (1968), 289–305.

111. [4–6 June 1726], Assembly, *Votes*, II, 1759, 1764.

112. Logan to Wright and James Blunston, 30 October 1727, Logan Papers, James Logan Letterbook, III, 111, H.S.P.

113. Logan to Anderson and Galbraith, 2 March 1730/1, *Ibid.*, p. 170.

114. Dickinson to Richard Champion, 28 August 1721, Jonathan Dickinson Letterbook, 1715–1721, p. 385, L.C.P.

115. Logan to I. Taylor, 25 September 1724, Taylor Papers, XV, no. 2997, H.S.P.

116. "The Remainder of the Observations promised in the *Mercury*" [1735], Broadside Collection, L.C.P.

117. [11–19 January 1721/2], Assembly, *Votes*, II, 1397 (quote), 1402–1403.

118. Report on the Petition of the Swedes, 28 February 1721/2, Samuel Hazard, ed., *Pennsylvania Archives*, [1st ser.], 12 vols. (Philadelphia, 1852–1856), I, 172–177,

quotes pp. 172, 176. Emigration from Sweden was not legally restricted until 1739, but very few Swedes chose to emigrate to the Delaware Valley after 1700. William Arnold Bultmann, "The Society for the Propagation of the Gospel in Foreign Parts and the Foreign Settler in the American Colonies" (Ph.D. diss., University of California, Los Angeles, 1951), p. 14. As early as 1693, only 21% of all Swedish heads of households had been born in Sweden. Susan Klepp, "Five Early Pennsylvania Censuses," *PMHB*, 106 (1982), 486.

119. Logan to ?, [12 December 1726], Logan Papers, James Logan Letterbook, IV, 123–124, H.S.P.

120. Petition, December 1727, Society Miscellaneous Collection, Box 4A, H.S.P.

121. Kelsey, "Early Description of Pennsylvania," *PMHB*, 45 (1921), 249. Sauer neglected to mention the English inhabitants of the colony.

122. Letter of Caspar Wistar, 8 November 1732, trans. Henry Eyster Jacobs, "The German Emigration to America 1709–1740," *PGSPA*, 8 (1897), 142.

123. Seibt to Brother, 20 December 1734, Berky, *David Shultze Papers*, I, 52.

124. Anonymous letter, 16 November 1738, Waldemar Westergaard, ed. and trans., "Two Germantown Letters of 1738," *PMHB*, 56 (1932), 13.

125. "Authentic Open Letter from Pennsylvania in America. . . ." (1739), trans. Durnbaugh, *Brethren in Colonial America*, pp. 41–53, quotes pp. 43, 44, 46, 51.

126. Ch. 62, 27 November 1700, *Statutes*, II, 80.

127. Governor to Assembly, 2 January 1738/9, Council, *Minutes*, IV, 315.

128. Assembly to Governor, 2 January 1738/9, *Ibid.*, pp. 316–317.

129. [9–10 August 1739], Assembly, *Votes*, III, 2501–2503.

130. He believed the "Violent distemper" had resulted from overcrowding. J. Penn to T. Penn, 28 March 1739, Penn Manuscripts, Thomas Penn Letterbook, I, 287, H.S.P.; J. Penn to George Thomas, 29 March 1739, *Ibid.*, p. 296 (quote).

131. Logan to Kirkpatrick, 2 August 1729, Logan Papers, Selections from the Correspondence of James Logan, V, 279–280, H.S.P.

132. T. Penn to Ferdinand John Paris, 5 July 1740, Penn Manuscripts, Official Correspondence, III, 121, H.S.P.

133. Ch. 320, 6 February 1730/1, *Statutes*, IV, 208–210.

134. The date the first priest, Joseph Greaton, permanently settled in the city and the date for the completion of the church are uncertain. John Tracy Ellis, *Catholics in Colonial America* (Baltimore, 1965), p. 374.

135. 25 July 1734, Council, *Minutes*, II, 589.

136. 31 July 1734, *Ibid.*, p. 608.

137. Perhaps there was only slight awareness of the presence of Roman Catholics because there were so few in the province. Joseph J. Casino states that there were only thirty-seven Catholics in Philadelphia in 1732 ("Anti-Popery In Colonial Pennsylvania," *PMHB*, 105 [1981], 293), a number that does, however, seem too small to justify the construction of a chapel and to have a resident priest.

138. Robert Weyman to the Secretary, 3 August 1728, William Stevens Perry, ed., *Historical Collections Relating to the American Colonial Church*, vol. 2, *Pennsylvania* (Hartford, 1871), pp. 162–163.

139. John Humphreys to the Secretary, 30 November 1719, *Records of the Society for the Propagation of the Gospel in Foreign Parts*, 27 reels (East Ardsley, Wakefield, England, 1964 [microfilm]), Letterbook A13, pp. 307–308; Archibald Cummings to the Secretary, 7 June 1728, *Ibid.*, A21, p. 246.

140. William Skinner to the Secretary, 30 November 1720, *Ibid.*, A13, pp. 103–104, quotes p. 103.

141. Vestry of St. Paul's Church, Chester, to the Secretary, 16 March 1732, *Ibid.*, A24, pp. 372–373 (quotes); Richard Backhouse to the Secretary, 7 November 1732, *Ibid.*, pp. 370–371.

142. Pennsylvania Clergy to the Secretary, n.d. [late 1720], *Ibid.*, A14, pp. 100–101.

143. William Lindsay to the Secretary, 14 November 1735, *Ibid.*, A26, p. 115.

144. Backhouse to the Secretary, 12 March 1728, *Ibid.*, A21, p. 275.

145. Backhouse to the Secretary, 30 October 1734, *Ibid.*, A25, pp. 205–206. Others were concerned with growing infidelity and freethinking in the 1730s. William Becket to the Secretary, 25 August 1736, Becket Manuscripts, pp. 52–53, H.S.P. (transcript).

146. Griffith Hughes to the Secretary, 2 March 1733/4, *S.P.G. Letterbooks*, A25, pp. 193–194, quotes p. 193.

147. Alexander Howie to the Secretary, 27 April 1734, *Ibid.*, p. 197.

148. George Ross to the Secretary, 8 October 1733, *Ibid.*, A24, pp. 392–394.

149. Howie to the Secretary, 28 July 1732, *Ibid.*, p. 353 (second quote); Howie to the Secretary, 27 April 1734, *Ibid.*, A25, p. 197 (first quote).

150. Weyman to the Secretary, n.d. [1728], *Ibid.*, A21, pp. 21–22.

151. Backhouse to the Secretary, 15 March 1736/7, *Ibid.*, A26, p. 346.

152. Backhouse to the Secretary, 10 May 1729, *Ibid.*, B6, p. 246.

153. Backhouse to the Secretary, 30 October 1734, *Ibid.*, A25, p. 205.

154. Lindsay to the Secretary, 9 March 1736/7, *Ibid.*, A26, p. 343.

155. Becket to the Secretary, 29 March 1738, Becket Manuscripts, p. 82, H.S.P.

156. 1720, Horace Burr, trans., *The Record of Holy Trinity (Old Swedes) Church, Wilmington, Del., From 1697 to 1773. . . . With an Abstract of the English Records from 1773 to 1810* (Wilmington, Del., 1890), pp. 257–258.

157. Howie to the Secretary, 28 July 1732, *S.P.G. Letterbooks*, A24, p. 354.

158. Pennsylvania Clergy to the Secretary, n.d. [late 1720], *Ibid.*, A14, p. 101. Swedish ministers were unlike "other foreign Ministers on ye Main of America who instead of Aiming as they do, at Incorporating with us are Strenuous bettors of ye Separation."

159. Secretary to Andrew Hesselius and Abraham Lidenius, 8 May 1721, *Ibid.*, A15, pp. 87–88; A. Hesselius and Lidenius to the Secretary, 1722, *Ibid.*, A16, p. 163 (quotes). Statements of the dates and places that Swedish ministers preached may be found scattered throughout the Pennsylvania sections of the *S.P.G. Letterbooks*, series A and B.

160. July 1729–December 1731, Burr, *Holy Trinity Record*, pp. 310–331, 336–339, quotes pp. 320, 324–325. Although Samuel Hesselius was assigned to the Christina (New Castle, Del.) church, his preaching in Pennsylvania churches was part of the issue, and several Pennsylvanians were involved in the dispute.

161. Weyman to the Secretary, 4 April 1723, *S.P.G. Letterbooks*, A17, p. 173 (first quote); Weyman to the Secretary, 26 July 1725, *Ibid.*, A19, pp. 128–130 (second–third quotes p. 129).

162. Hughes to the Secretary, 3 December 1734, *Ibid.*, A25, pp. 213–214; Inhabitants of Conestoga to the Secretary, 1734, *Ibid.*, pp. 215–217 (quote p. 215); Hughes to Bishop of London, 10 September 1735, *Ibid.*, A26, pp. 113–114.

163. Guy Soulliard Klett, *Presbyterians in Colonial Pennsylvania* (Philadelphia, 1937), pp. 48–49.

164. 24 May 1738, Minutes of the Presbytery of Philadelphia, 1733–1746, pp. 53–54, P.H.S.; 22 April 1740, *Ibid.*, pp. 82–83 (quote).

165. Leonard J. Trinterud, *The Forming of an American Tradition: A Re-examination of Colonial Presbyterianism* (Philadelphia, 1949), pp. 1–52.

166. Anderson to John Sterling, 1 August 1716, Wodrow Letters, no. 115, National Library of Scotland, Edinburgh (microfilm at P.H.S.) (last two quotes); Anderson to Sterling, 8 August 1717, *Ibid.*, no. 116 (first two quotes).

167. Anderson to Sterling, 29 November 1725, *Ibid.*, no. 123.

168. Martin E. Lodge, "The Crisis of the Churches in the Middle Colonies, 1720–1750," *PMHB*, 95 (1971), 199–200.

169. For example: Jonathan Dickinson, *The Vanity of Human Institutions in the Worship of God. A Sermon Preached at Newark, June 2, 1736. To which are added, some little Enlargements* (New York, 1736), and *The Reasonableness of Non-Conformity to the Church of England in Point of Worship. A Second Defence of a Sermon* (Boston, 1738).

170. Joseph Henry Dubbs, "The Reformed Church in Pennsylvania," *PGSPA*, 11 (1900), 63–65; Klett, *Presbyterians in Pennsylvania*, pp. 48–49, 226–227.

171. Jedidiah Andrews to Thomas Prince, 14 October 1730, Samuel Hazard, ed., *The Register of Pennsylvania*. . . . , 16 vols. (Philadelphia, 1828–1835), XV, 201 (quotes); John Philip Boehm to Classis of Amsterdam, [8 July 1744], trans. William J. Hinke, ed., *Life and Letters of the Rev. John Philip Boehm Founder of the Reformed Church in Pennsylvania 1683–1749* (Philadelphia, 1916), p. 408.

172. James E. Ernst, "Ephrata: A History," *PGFS*, 25 (1961), 101–105.

173. Jacobus Van Ostade to Dutch Reformed Church of New York, 1 December 1731, trans. William J. Hinke Collection, Miscellaneous Letters and Documents relating to the Reformed Church in Pennsylvania, 1700–1806, II, E.R.H.S.

174. Van Ostade to Gerard Bolwerck, 30 September 1731, trans. *Ibid.*

175. Falckner Swamp, Skippack, and Whitemarsh churches to Classis, July 1728, trans. Hinke, *John Philip Boehm*, pp. 161–162. Lutherans similarly complained that "We live in a land full of heresy and sects; our souls are in the utmost need and poverty." Letter of Daniel Weissiger, 28 January 1734, Johann Ludewig Schulze, ed., *Nachrichten von den vereinigten Deutschen Evangelisch-Lutherischen Gemeinen in Nord-America, absonderlich in Pensylvanien*, 2 vols. (Halle, 1787), I, 4–5.

176. Henry Gotchius to Herr Werdmuller, 21 July 1735, Hinke Collection, Letters and Documents, IV, E.R.H.S.

177. Boehm to Classis, 12 November 1730, *Ibid.*, III.

178. "Report and Instructions Concerning and to the Colony and Church of Pennsylvania. Composed and Published by the Deputies of the Reverend Christian Synod of South Holland, together with the Commissioners of the Reverend Classis of Delft and Delfsland and Schieland" (1731), pp. 3–5, *Ibid.*, II, quotes p. 4.

179. Van Ostade to Bolwerck, 30 September 1731, *Ibid.* (quote); Bolwerck to Van Ostade, 1 October 1731, trans. *Ibid.*

180. Peter Henry Dorsius to Synodical Deputies, 1 March 1738, trans. *Ibid.*, VI.

181. "Report and Instructions," p. 6, *Ibid.*, II.

182. Arent Hassert Jr. to Van Ostade, 9 January 1733, trans. *Ibid.*

183. Ernst, "Ephrata," *PGFS* 25 (1961), 101–105, 197–199; Charles H. Glatfelter, "The Colonial Pennsylvania German Lutheran and Reformed Clergyman" (Ph.D. diss., Johns Hopkins University, 1952), pp. 25–26; Lodge, "Crisis of the Churches," *PMHB*, 95 (1971), 197.

184. John B. Frantz, "The Awakening of Religion among the German Settlers in the Middle Colonies," 3 *WMQ*, 33 (1976), 270. Lodge, in "Crisis of the Churches" (*PMHB*, 95 [1971], 199), gives slightly different numbers of effective ministers in the province in 1741, three Reformed and one Lutheran.

185. Dorsius to Synodical Deputies, 1 March 1738, Hinke Collection, Letters and Documents, VI, E.R.H.S.

186. Boehm to Classis, 12 November 1730, *Ibid.*, III.

187. Morgan Edwards, *Materials Towards a History of the Baptists in Pennsylvania Both British and German, Distinguished into Firstday Baptists[,] Keithian Baptists[,] Seventhday Baptists[,] Tuncker Baptists[,] Mennonist Baptists*, vol. 1 (Philadelphia, 1770), pp. 64–66; Howard Wiegner Kriebel, "The Schwenkfelders in Pennsylvania, A Historical Sketch," *PGSPA*, 13 (1902), 26–70; C. Henry Smith, "The Mennonite Immigration to Pennsylvania In the Eighteenth Century," *Ibid.*, 35 (1924), 75–277.

188. Anonymous letter, 16 November 1738, Westergaard, "Two Germantown Letters of 1738," *PMHB*, 56 (1932), 13.

189. Durnbaugh, *Brethren in Colonial America*, pp. 61–111; Edwards, *Baptists in Pennsylvania*, pp. 94–95; Walter C. Klein, *Johann Conrad Beissel: Mystic and Martinet 1690–1768* (Philadelphia, 1942), pp. 60–66; Julius Friedrich Sachse, *The German Sectarians of Pennsylvania 1708–1742: A Critical and Legendary History of the Ephrata Cloister and the Dunkers*, vol. 1 (Philadelphia, 1899), pp. 129–133, 148–154, 156–159, 292–293; John C. Wenger, *History of the Mennonites of the Franconia Conference* (Telford, Pa., 1937), pp. 89–93, 116–118.

190. Georg Neisser, *A History of the Beginnings of Moravian Work in America*, ed. and trans. William N. Schwarze and Samuel H. Gapp (Bethlehem, Pa., 1955), pp. 11–12, 23–25 (Appendix II).

191. An exception occurred when the Classis of Amsterdam warned a minister to "guard . . . against all manner of errorists, and also against the Moravians, which spread themselves everywhere, even in foreign lands," since many of their doctrines controvened the fundamentals of the Reformed church. Classis to Boehm, 13 January 1739, trans. Hinke Collection, Letters and Documents, II, E.R.H.S.

192. Logan to Josiah Martin, 2 August 1737, Logan Papers-Alverthorpe, James Logan Letterbook A, pp. 23–24, H.S.P.

193. Logan to Martin, [November 1737], *Ibid.*, pp. 35–36, quotes p. 36.

194. Logan to Martin, 17 October 1738, *Ibid.*, Letterbook B, p. 2.

195. Augustus Gottlieb Spangenberg to David Nitschmann, 7 March 1739, trans. Durnbaugh, *Brethren in Colonial America*, p. 278.

196. Spangenberg to Herrnhut, 14 May 1736, trans. *Ibid.*, pp. 271–273; Christopher Wiegner and George Böhnisch to Herrnhut, 7 November 1737, trans. *Ibid.*, pp. 269–270; Spangenberg to Nicholas von Zinzendorf, 1738, trans. *Ibid.*, p. 277 (quote).

197. Br. Lamech and Agrippa, comps., *Chronicon Ephratense, Enthaltend den Lebens-Lauf des ehrwürdigen Vaters in Christo Friedsam Gottrecht, Weyland Stiffiers und Vorstehers des geistl. Ordens der Einsamen in Ephrata in der Graffschaft Lancaster in Pennsylvania* (Ephrata, Pa., 1786), trans. J. Max Hark (Lancaster, Pa., 1889), pp. 44–45; Ernst, "Ephrata," *PGFS*, 25 (1961), 76–77.

198. Lamech and Agrippa, *Chronicon Ephratense*, pp. 86–87; Ernst, "Ephrata," *PGFS*, 25 (1961), 114–115.

199. Lamech and Agrippa, *Chronicon Ephratense*, pp. 82–83; Ernst, "Ephrata," *PGFS*, 25 (1961), 117.

200. Ch. 311, 14 February 1729/30, *Statutes*, IV, 152–154.

201. Pennsylvania Clergy to the Secretary, 16 April 1730, *S.P.G. Letterbooks*, A23, pp. 176–178, quotes pp. 177, 178.

202. Backhouse to the Secretary, 14 May 1730, *Ibid.*, pp. 156–158, quotes p. 157.

203. Becket to Bishop of London, 15 March 1727/8, Becket Manuscripts, pp. 7–8, H.S.P. He made a similar complaint to the Secretary, 2 August 1737 (*Ibid.*, p. 72), after a new governor continued Gordon's practice.

204. Minutes of the Synod of Philadelphia, 24 September 1734, William Morrison Engles, ed., *Records of the Presbyterian Church in the United States of America Embracing the Minutes of the Presbytery of Philadelphia, from A.D. 1706 to 1716: Minutes of the Syond [sic] of Philadelphia, from A.D. 1717 to 1758: Minutes of the Synod of New York, from A.D. 1745 to 1758: Minutes of the Synod of New York and Philadelphia, from A.D. 1758 to 1788* (Philadelphia, 1841), p. 111 (quote); Minutes of the Synod of Philadelphia, 19 September 1735, *Ibid.*, pp. 115–116.

205. Philadelphia Yearly Meeting Epistle, 15–19 September 1733, Philadelphia Yearly Meeting Collection, Philadelphia Yearly Meeting Minutes, 1681–1746, p. 372, Q.C.H.C.

206. See above, ch. 3.

207. Norris to Pike, 22 June 1724, Norris Papers, Isaac Norris Sr. Letterbook, 1716–1730, p. 379, H.S.P.; 3 May 1725, Philadelphia Yearly Meeting Collection, Philadelphia Quarterly Meeting Minutes, 1723–1772, p. 15, Q.C.H.C.; 2 August 1725, *Ibid.*, p. 16; Philadelphia Quarterly Meeting to William Keith, 2 May 1725, *Ibid.*, p. 17; Keith to Philadelphia Quarterly Meeting, 10 May 1725, *Ibid.*, p. 18.

208. Norris to Pike, 10 July 1725, Norris Papers, Isaac Norris Sr. Letterbook, 1716–1730, pp. 432–434, H.S.P. The assembly received a petition from the Wardens of Christ Church, Philadelphia, opposing passage of the act, and a petition from Quakers requesting that an affirmation law be passed; these were discussed on [29 November 1723 and 4 December 1723], Assembly, *Votes*, II, 1557–1558.

209. Oaths, 1732, "A Collection of Christian and Brotherly Advices, Given forth from time to time BY THE Yearly Meetings of Friends FOR Pennsylvania & New Jersey Held alternately At Burlington & Philadelphia," p. 175, Church and Meeting Collection, H.S.P.; Oaths, 1733, *Ibid.*, pp. 175–176; Oaths, 1738, *Ibid.*, p. 176.

210. Richard Peters to [J. Penn?], 30 August 1740, Peters Papers, Richard Peters Letterbook, p. 18, H.S.P.

211. J. and Richard Penn to T. Penn, 26 November 1740, Penn Manuscripts, Thomas Penn Letterbook, I, 339–340, H.S.P. (quotes p. 339); J. Penn to Thomas, 26 November 1740, *Ibid.*, pp. 343–344.

212. 5 April 1739, Minutes of the Presbytery of Donegal, 1732–1750, pp. 176–177, P.H.S.; [10 May 1739], Assembly, *Votes*, III, 2482 (quote).

213. [12 May 1739], *Ibid.*, p. 2485; ch. 351, 19 May 1739, *Statutes*, IV, 337–338 (quotes).

214. *Ibid.*, p. 338n.; Paris to T. Penn, 30 April 1740, Penn Manuscripts, XII, H.S.P. (quotes).

215. [F. Hall], *The Importance of the British Plantations in America to this Kingdom* . . . (London, 1731), preface, pp. 89–90, quote p. 89.

216. Seibt to Brother, 20 December 1734, Berky, *David Shultze Papers*, I, 53.

217. *Pennsylvania Gazette*, 6–13 May 1736.

218. Andrew Hamilton, Speech to the Assembly, 1739, quoted in Joshua Francis Fisher, "Andrew Hamilton, Esq., of Pennsylvania," *PMHB*, 16 (1892), 7.

219. "A Layman," preface to "A Letter to a Friend in the Country, Containing the Substance of a Sermon Preach'd at Philadelphia, in the Congregation of The Rev. Mr. Hemphill, Concerning the Terms of Christian and Ministerial Communion" (1735), Leonard W. Labaree, *et al.*, eds., *The Papers of Benjamin Franklin*, 25 vols. to date (New Haven, 1959–), II, 66–67.

5. Religious Awakening in the 1740s

1. Jon Butler has argued that "Historians should abandon the term 'the Great Awakening' because it distorts the character of eighteenth-century American religious life and misinterprets its relationship to prerevolutionary American society and politics" ("Enthusiasm Described and Decried: The Great Awakening as Interpretative Fiction," *JAH*, 69 [1982], 305–325, quote p. 322). While I agree that the term has been made to carry too much of the burden of interpreting colonial history, a general term to describe the upsurge of interest in experiential religion in Western Europe and the colonies during the middle third of the eighteenth century remains useful. The "Great Awakening" in Pennsylvania was of limited long-run significance, but because it had an impact on the interaction of religious groups, it merits brief discussion.

2. 6 November 1739, Iain Murray, ed., *George Whitefield's Journals* ([London], 1960), p. 342.

3. Albert D. Belden, *George Whitefield—The Awakener: A Modern Study of the Evangelical Revival* (New York, 1953); William Howland Kenney, 3d, "George Whitefield and Colonial Revivalism: The Social Sources of Charismatic Authority. 1737–1770" (Ph.D. diss., University of Pennsylvania, 1966); Martin Ellsworth Lodge, "The Great Awakening in the Middle Colonies" (Ph.D. diss., University of California, Berkeley, 1964).

4. 4–10 November 1739, Whitefield, *Journals*, pp. 341–346; Archibald Cummings to the Secretary, 14 November 1739, William Stevens Perry, ed., *Historical Collections Relating to the American Colonial Church*, vol. 2, *Pennsylvania* (Hartford, 1871), p. 210 (quote).

5. 11 November 1739, Whitefield, *Journals*, pp. 345–346.

6. 25 November 1739, *Ibid.*, pp. 356–357.

7. 9 January 1739/40, *Ibid.*, pp. 386–388, quote p. 387. Friendly meetings with Baptist and Presbyterian ministers are mentioned on 5 November 1739, 6 November 1739, 10 November 1739, 22 November 1739, *Ibid.*, pp. 342, 345, 354–355.

8. 15 April 1740, *Ibid.*, pp. 406–407; Cummings to the Secretary, 31 July 1740, Perry, *Colonial Church*, pp. 210–211.

9. Lodge, "Great Awakening," pp. 220–222.

10. 20 April 1740, Whitefield, *Journals*, pp. 409–410 (quotes p. 410); 11 May 1740, *Ibid.*, pp. 421–422.

11. Richard Backhouse to the Secretary, 23 August 1740, Perry, *Colonial Church*, p. 206 (first quote); Backhouse to the Secretary, 13 October 1741, *Records of the Society for the Propagation of the Gospel in Foreign Parts*, 27 reels (East Ardsley, Wakefield, England, 1964 [microfilm]), Letterbook B9, no. 106 (second quote).

12. William Currie to the Secretary, 7 July 1740, Perry, *Colonial Church*, pp. 208–209.

13. Alexander Howie to the Secretary, 17 July 1740, *Ibid.*, p. 207.

14. Cummings to the Secretary, 31 July 1740, *Ibid.*, p. 211; Currie to the Secretary, 2 May 1741, *S.P.G. Letterbooks*, B9, no. 110.

15. Deborah Mathias Gough, "Pluralism, Politics, and Power Struggles: The Church of England in Colonial Philadelphia, 1695–1789" (Ph.D. diss., University of Pennsylvania, 1978), pp. 165–166; Lodge, "Great Awakening," pp. 218–221.

16. Currie to the Secretary, 2 May 1741, *S.P.G. Letterbooks*, B9, no. 110 (first quote); Currie to the Secretary, 28 September 1741, *Ibid.*, no. 111 (second quote).

17. Backhouse to the Secretary, 25 July 1741, *Ibid.*, no. 104.

18. Howie to the Secretary, 17 July 1740, Perry, *Colonial Church*, p. 208.

19. Currie to the Secretary, 28 September 1741, *S.P.G. Letterbooks*, B9, no. 110. He requested additional copies to distribute to his parishioners.

20. For example: Backhouse to the Secretary, 14 June 1742, *Ibid.*, B10, no. 123; Richard Locke to the Secretary, 29 September 1748, *Ibid.*, B16, no. 108.

21. He noted that "In his conversation I could perceive very little of the scholar or gentleman. I really think he is enthusiastically mad, &c." Cummings to the Secretary, 14 November 1739, Perry, *Colonial Church*, p. 210.

22. Howie to the Secretary, 17 July 1740, *Ibid.*, pp. 207–208, quotes p. 207.

23. Currie to the Secretary, 7 July 1740, *Ibid.*, pp. 208–209, quotes p. 209.

24. 17 April 1740, Whitefield, *Journals*, pp. 407–408.

25. Patricia U. Bonomi, *Under the Cope of Heaven: Religion, Society, and Politics in Colonial America* (New York, 1986), pp. 139–149; Elizabeth I. Nybakken, "New Light on the Old Side: Irish Influences on Colonial Presbyterianism," *JAH*, 68 (1982), 813–832; Leonard J. Trinterud, *The Forming of an American Tradition: A Re-examination of Colonial Presbyterianism* (Philadelphia, 1949), pp. 53–165.

26. 10 November 1739, Whitefield, *Journals*, pp. 344–345 (first quote); 22 November 1739, *Ibid.*, pp. 354–355 (second quote p. 354).

27. Kenney, "George Whitefield," pp. 101–107.

28. *Pennsylvania Gazette*, 9 March 1743/4.

29. Frederick B. Tolles, "Quietism Versus Enthusiasm: The Philadelphia Quakers and the Great Awakening," *PMHB*, 69 (1945), 26–49.

30. 9 September 1739, Whitefield, *Journals*, p. 333; 30 September 1739, *Ibid.*, p. 335.

31. 4–6 November 1739, *Ibid.*, pp. 341–343 (quotes p. 342); 25 November 1739, *Ibid.*, p. 357.

32. 9 January 1739/40, *Ibid.*, p. 387.

33. 11 May 1740, *Ibid.*, pp. 422–423.

34. Letter of James Pemberton, quoted in Tolles, "Quietism Versus Enthusiasm," *PMHB*, 69 (1945), 31.

35. John Smith to J. Pemberton, 29 November 1739, General Manuscript Collection, Box 9, Rare Books Room, V.P.L. As a Quaker, though, he disapproved of Whitefield's compliance with such Anglican customs as wearing a surplice and singing psalms.

36. Richard Hockley to Bernard Hannington, 8 June 1740, Richard Hockley Letterbook, 1739–1742, p. 20, Q.C.H.C.

37. James Logan to Peter [Collinson], 10 or 12 December 1740, Logan Papers Alverthorpe, James Logan Letterbook B, pp. 19–20, H.S.P., quotes p. 20.

38. J. Pemberton to Smith, 17 July 1741, John Jay Smith Papers, Smith Manuscripts, I, 196, L.C.P.

39. Judah Foulke to Smith, 21 May 1740, *Ibid.*, p. 183.

40. Melvin H. Buxbaum, *Benjamin Franklin and the Zealous Presbyterians* (University Park, Pa., 1975), pp. 122–150; Anna Janney DeArmond, *Andrew Bradford: Colonial Journalist* (Newark, Del., 1949), pp. 124–130.

41. 11 May 1740, Whitefield, *Journals*, p. 423.
42. William L. Turner, "The Charity School, the Academy, and the College," *TAPS*, n.s., 43 (1951), 179.
43. *Pennsylvania Gazette*, 5 February 1744/5.
44. 27 November 1739, Whitefield, *Journals*, pp. 357–358.
45. 24 April 1740, *Ibid.*, p. 412.
46. Lodge, "Great Awakening," pp. 237–239.
47. Peter Böhler to Nicholas von Zinzendorf, 20 April 1740, Albert F. Jordan Collection, Box 3 (Translations of Peter Böhler Letters in the Library of Congress), M.A.
48. 22 April 1740, Whitefield, *Journals*, p. 411.
49. P. Böhler to Zinzendorf, 25 March 1741, Jordan Collection, Box 3, M.A.
50. Gilbert Tennent to [Ebenezer] Pemberton, 1741, Tennent Papers, P.H.S. (typescript) (quotes); Keith J. Hardman, "Jonathan Dickinson and the Course of American Presbyterianism, 1717–1747" (Ph.D. diss., University of Pennsylvania, 1971), pp. 252–253.
51. *Pennsylvania Gazette*, 12 August 1742.
52. *Ibid.*, 2 September 1742.
53. Samuel Finley, Some Extracts of my conversation wth Some moravians, at Willm Price's house, 22 December 1742, Hazard Family Papers, H.S.P.
54. Finley to "Brother" [a fellow minister], 18 January 1742/3, *Ibid.*
55. Tennent to George Whitefield, 5 June 1742, Pennsylvania 1740s and Lischy Box, Pennsylvania Controversies Folder, M.A.
56. Whitefield to Christopher Pyrlaeus, 19 September 1742, *Ibid.*, Folder 5.
57. Whitefield to Trustees of the New Building, 19 September 1742, *Ibid.*
58. Whitefield to Finley, September 1742, *Ibid.*
59. Whitefield to Tennent, 27 February 1742, *Ibid.* (first quote); Whitefield to Tennent, 13 September 1742, *Ibid.* (second quote).
60. P. Böhler to Zinzendorf, 26 January/6 February 1742/3, Jordan Collection, Box 3, M.A.
61. John Frederick Cammerhoff to Zinzendorf, 10–16 February 1748 (n.s.), Letters of Bishop Cammerhoff to Count Zinzendorf, p. 127, H.S.P. (transcript).
62. See, among others: Samuel Finley, *Satan strip'd of his angelick Robe. Being The Substance of several Sermons Preach'd at Philadelphia, January 1742–3 . . .* (Philadelphia, 1743); Gilbert Tennent, *Some Account of the Principles of the Moravians . . .* (London, 1743); Jonathan Dickinson, *Familiar Letters to a Gentleman, Upon a Variety of seasonable and important Subjects in Religion* (Boston, 1745), pp. 182–210.
63. *Pennsylvania Gazette*, 14 April 1743. All authorized essays would be signed by Peter Böhler, who would deposit the originals with the printer.
64. *Ibid.*, 7 April 1743 (quotes), 19 May 1743, 30 June 1743, 7 July 1743.
65. *Ibid.*, 2 August 1753 (quotes); *Pensylvanische Berichte*, 16 August 1753.
66. John Penn II to Thomas Penn, 19 August 1753, Penn Manuscripts, Private Correspondence, IV, 119, H.S.P.
67. T. Penn to [J. Penn], 29 January 1754, Penn Manuscripts, Thomas Penn Letterbook, III, 283, H.S.P.
68. Despite contacts with English-speaking people, however, Moravianism was predominantly German. John R. Weinlick, "Colonial Moravians, Their Status Among the Churches," *PH*, 26 (1959), 221–222.
69. 6 June 1742, John Philipp Maurer's Journal to Pennsylvania, 25 February–15

June 1742, Journal Collection, JC IV 2a, M.A.; 6/17 June 1742, Kenneth G. Hamilton, ed. and trans., *The Bethlehem Diary*, vol. 1 *(1742–1744)* (Bethlehem, Pa., 1972), p. 14.

70. 20 June/1 July 1742, *Ibid.*, p. 28.

71. P. and Elisabeth Böhler to Zinzendorf, 28 July 1742, Jordan Collection, Box 3, M.A.

72. *Pennsylvania Gazette*, 2 September 1742.

73. P. Böhler to Zinzendorf, 1 November 1743 (n.s.), Jordan Collection, Box 3, M.A.

74. David Bruce, A List of those places Where hitherto English has been preached & where the Englis Welsh & Irish reside, 1746, Journal Collection, JA I 9d, M.A.

75. 20 June/1 July 1742, 17/28 October 1742, 3 June 1743, 19 October 1743, Hamilton, *Bethlehem Diary*, pp. 28–29 (quote p. 28), 101, 150, 168.

76. 1 August 1742, Br. [John] Okely's Journal, 1–17 August 1742, Journal Collection, JD II 1a, M.A.

77. 2 August 1742, *Ibid.*

78. 23 May 1743, Br. John Okeley's Journal of his Visit in West New Jersey, 1743, *Ibid.*, JD II 1b.

79. 5 March 1746/7, Auszuge aus [Christian Henry] Rauch's Diarium, 23 January–30 June 1747, *Ibid.*, JD VII.

80. John Wade to Cammerhoff, 17 February 1747/8, *Ibid.*, JF IV 4c.

81. 12 November 1743, Diarium von der Reise der 2 Brüder [Leonard] Schnell und Hussey die nach Georgien besuchen gingen, 6 November 1743–10 April 1744, *Ibid.*, JE I 3.

82. Richard Utley's Nachricht von Neshamony, n.d., *Ibid.*, JF II 1.

83. 3 August 1742, Okely, Journal, 1742, *Ibid.*, JD II 1a.

84. 24 May 1743, Okeley, Journal, 1743, *Ibid.*, JD II 1b.

85. 8 June 1742, Maurer, Journal, 1742, *Ibid.*, JC IV 2a.

86. Conrad Weiser to Richard Peters, 10 March 1748/9, Peters Papers, II, 116, H.S.P.

87. Peters to [T. Penn], 17 February 1749/50, Peters Papers, Richard Peters Letterbook, pp. 397–398, H.S.P.

88. Logan to Josiah Martin, 31 May 1742, Logan Papers-Alverthorpe, James Logan Letterbook B, pp. 27–28, H.S.P.

89. Logan to [J. Martin], 19–20 November 1742, *Ibid.*, p. 29.

90. Among the most important discussions of land transactions are: Okely to ?, 16 May 1752, Provincial Council Records, H.S.P., T. Penn to Peters, 2 February 1753, Penn Manuscripts, Thomas Penn Letterbook, III, 212, H.S.P.; Peters to T. Penn, 3 May 1753, Penn Manuscripts, Official Correspondence, VI, 49, H.S.P.; Augustus Gottlieb Spangenberg to T. Penn, 15 October 1753, *Ibid.*, p. 117; T. Penn to Peters, 21 October 1753, Penn Manuscripts, XVII, 67, H.S.P.

91. For early Moravian interest in the Indians, see John Heckewelder, *A Narrative of the Mission of the United Brethren among the Delaware and Mohegan Indians* . . . (Philadelphia, 1820). Early visitors to the Indians reported that the "Irish" were "trying to make the Indians suspicious" of the Moravians, but without success. 23 October 1743, Hamilton, *Bethlehem Diary*, p. 169.

92. George Thomas to Weiser, 26 February 1741/2, Peters Papers, I, 73, H.S.P.

93. Logan to George Clarke, 30 March 1742, Logan Papers-Alverthorpe, James Logan Letterbook D, p. 20, H.S.P.

94. Peters to [T. Penn], 21 November 1742, Peters Papers, Richard Peters Letterbook, pp. 157–158, H.S.P. Needless to say, their request was denied.

95. T. Penn to Peters, 24 February 1749/50, Penn Manuscripts, XVII, 39, H.S.P.; T. Penn to Peters, 30 May 1750, Ibid., p. 41.

96. 24 June 1752, Minutes of the Provincial Council of Pennsylvania, From the Organization to the Termination of the Proprietary Government, 16 vols. (Philadelphia and Harrisburg, 1851–1853), V, 575–576, quotes p. 576.

97. 22 March 1742/3, Hamilton, Bethlehem Diary, p. 143.

98. 15/26 August 1742, Ibid., p. 75.

99. 27 August/7 September 1742, Ibid., pp. 80–81. The legal battles in which the Moravians were involved with Lutheran and Reformed congregations may have been another reason for studying provincial laws.

100. 30 August/10 September 1742, Ibid., p. 83.

101. The most complete analysis of Zinzendorf's ideas and his plans for Pennsylvania is found in A. J. Lewis, Zinzendorf The Ecumenical Pioneer: A Study in the Moravian Contribution to Christian Mission and Unity (Philadelphia, 1962), especially pp. 98–108, 139–150. It was not unusual for "pietists" of various sorts to drift from one church to another or to organize "conventicles" composed of members drawn from several denominations. Earlier pietists in Pennsylvania, such as the Falckner brothers and Bernhard Köster (above, ch. 3), also exhibited this cross-denominational fellowship. Church structure and dogmatic adherence to the tenets of a particular denomination or sect were not as important as the experience of grace and the reformation of outward life. Pietistic ideas also flowed easily from various groups, and regions, to others in both the old world and the new. The religious freedom and diversity of Pennsylvania did provide increased opportunities for these types of movements than were available in Europe. Dietmar Rothermund, The Layman's Progress: Religious and Political Experience in Colonial Pennsylvania, 1740–1770 (Philadelphia, 1961), pp. 1–15; F. Ernest Stoeffler, German Pietism During the Eighteenth Century (Leiden, 1973); F. Ernest Stoeffler, The Rise of Evangelical Pietism (Leiden, 1965).

102. John R. Weinlick, "Moravianism in the American Colonies," F. Ernest Stoeffler, ed., Continental Pietism and Early American Christianity (Grand Rapids, Mich., 1976), pp. 135, 139.

103. Henry Antes, Call for a meeting of Christians, 15 December 1741, William J. Hinke Collection, Miscellaneous Letters and Documents relating to the Reformed Church in Pennsylvania, 1700–1806, VI, E.R.H.S.; Lewis, Zinzendorf, pp. 143–146.

104. 30 June/11 July 1742, Hamilton, Bethlehem Diary, pp. 35–36.

105. 13/24 June 1742, Ibid., pp. 15–17, quotes p. 16.

106. Letter of unknown Brethren (or possibly Mennonite) to Germany, 15 November 1742, trans. Donald F. Durnbaugh, ed., The Brethren in Colonial America: A Source Book on the Transplantation and Development of the Church of the Brethren in the Eighteenth Century (Elgin, Ill., 1967), pp. 302–303.

107. George Adam Martin, Autobiography, trans. Ibid., p. 287.

108. Caspar Kriebel to Christopher Schultz, 7 March 1742, VK 1–10, pp. 3218–3224, S.L., quote p. 3219.

109. Extracts from the minutes of the synods and Zinzendorf's statements, trans. Durnbaugh, Brethren in Colonial America, pp. 285–286.

110. Anonymous Brethren letter, 15 November 1742, Ibid., p. 303.

111. Extracts from the minutes of the synods and Zinzendorf's statements, *Ibid.*, pp. 286–287.

112. Henry Antes, "Well-Founded Reminders," trans. *Ibid.*, pp. 316–317, quote p. 316.

113. Spangenberg to Herrnhut, 14 May 1736, trans. *Ibid.*, pp. 271–273.

114. Spangenberg to David Nitschmann, 8 November 1738, trans. *Ibid.*, pp. 273–274, quote p. 274.

115. Spangenberg to Zinzendorf, 1738, trans. *Ibid.*, p. 277 (first two quotes); Spangenberg to Nitschmann, 7 March 1739, trans. *Ibid.*, p. 278 (third quote).

116. Br. Lamech and Agrippa, comps., *Chronicon Ephratense, Enthaltend den Lebens-Lauf des ehrwürdigen Vaters in Christo Friedsam Gottrecht, Weyland Stiffiers und Vorstehers des geistl. Ordens der Einsamen in Ephrata in der Graffschaft Lancaster in Pennsylvania* (Ephrata, Pa., 1786), trans. J. Max Hark (Lancaster, Pa., 1889), pp. 105, 145–152; James E. Ernst, "Ephrata: A History," *PGFS*, 25 (1961), 204–207; Walter C. Klein, *Johann Conrad Beissel: Mystic and Martinet 1690–1768* (Philadelphia, 1942), pp. 101–107.

117. Ernst, "Ephrata," *PGFS*, 25 (1961), 209–210.

118. P. Böhler to Zinzendorf, 16/27 December 1743, Jordan Collection, Box 3, M.A.; Christopher Sauer to Henry Antes, 6 September 1743, Henry Antes 1741–1750 Box, M.A.; Antes to ?, November 1743, *Ibid.*; Sauer to Melchior Schultz, 13 December 1743, *Ibid.* Sauer's wife had joined the monastic community, and in a letter written to German friends c. 1750 he seems to have been sympathetic to the sect. Durnbaugh, *Brethren in Colonial America*, pp. 120, 121. He also may have been receiving assistance from the monks in his publication of the Bible (see below).

119. John B. Frantz, "The Awakening of Religion among the German Settlers in the Middle Colonies," 3*WMQ*, 33 (1976), 279–280; Leonard Richard Riforgiato, "Missionary of Moderation: Henry Melchior Muhlenberg and the Lutheran Church in English America" (Ph.D. diss., Pennsylvania State University, 1971), pp. 14, 107.

120. Riforgiato, "Missionary of Moderation," pp. 93–96; Nachricht von den neuesten Umständen, Johann Ludewig Schulze, ed., *Nachrichten von den vereinigten Deutschen Evangelisch-Lutherischen Gemeinen in Nord-America, absonderlich in Pensylvanien*, 2 vols. (Halle, 1787), I, 129–142 [hereafter *Hallesche Nachrichten*]; 29 December 1742, Theodore G. Tappert and John W. Doberstein, eds. and trans., *The Journals of Henry Melchior Muhlenberg*, 3 vols. (Philadelphia, 1942–1958), I, 75–76 (quote p. 76).

121. "A Protestation of the several Members of the Protestant Lutheran and Reformed Religions in the City of Philadelphia . . ." [1742], Broadside Collection, H.S.P.; *Pennsylvania Gazette*, 26 August 1742.

122. Peters to [T. Penn], 15 January 1742/3, Peters Papers, Richard Peters Letterbook, p. 165, H.S.P.; T. Penn to Peters, 4 May 1743, Penn Manuscripts, Thomas Penn Letterbook, II, 42, H.S.P.

123. 29–31 December 1742, Muhlenberg, *Journals*, I, 76–81, 14 February 1742/3, *Ibid.*, p. 90 (quote).

124. Israel Acrelius, *A History of New Sweden; or, the Settlements on the River Delaware*, trans. William M. Reynolds (Philadelphia, 1876), pp. 241–242.

125. Letter of Henry Melchior Mühlenberg, 28 June 1747, *Hallesche Nachrichten*, I, 69–71, quotes pp. 70, 71.

126. Lawrence Nyberg to [Paulus] Brycelius, Spring 1745, trans. Rothermund, *Layman's Progress*, pp. 154–158; Acrelius, *New Sweden*, pp. 246–247.

127. 12 December 1745, Muhlenberg, *Journals*, I, 109–110 (quotes p. 109); [8 January 1745/6], Gertrude MacKinney and Charles F. Hoban, eds., *Pennsylvania Archives*, 8th ser., 8 vols., *Votes and Proceedings of the House of Assembly of the Province of Pennsylvania, 1682–1776* (Harrisburg, 1931–1935), IV, 3073; letter of Mühlenberg, 28 June 1747, *Hallesche Nachrichten*, I, 71–75.

128. *Pensylvanische Berichte*, 16 February 1745/6, 16 March 1745/6, 16 May 1746, 16 June 1746.

129. 24 June 1747, Muhlenberg, *Journals*, I, 156–158; 28 June 1747, *Ibid.*, p. 166; 6–7 July 1747, *Ibid.*, pp. 169–174; letter of Johann Friederich Handschuch, 7 October 1748, *Hallesche Nachrichten*, I, 67–69; Jerome H. Wood, Jr., *Conestoga Crossroads: Lancaster, Pennsylvania 1730–1790* (Harrisburg, 1979), pp. 186–187, 191–193.

130. John Philip Boehm to Classis of Amsterdam, 25 July 1741, trans. William J. Hinke, ed., *Life and Letters of the Rev. John Philip Boehm Founder of the Reformed Church in Pennsylvania 1683–1749* (Philadelphia, 1916), p. 323.

131. John Philip Boehm, *Getreuer Warnungs Briefe an die Hochteutsche Evangelisch Reformirten Gemeinden und alle deren Glieder, in Pensylvanien* . . . (Philadelphia, 1742), Hinke Collection, Pamphlets, E.R.H.S. (copy); John Philip Boehm, "Abermahlige treue Warnung und Vermahnung an meine sehr werthe und theuer geschâtzte Reformirte Glaubens-verwandte, wie auch alle andere die den herren Jesum lieb haben . . ." (1743), Broadside Collection, H.S.P.

132. Boehm to Synods of North and South Holland, 18 March 1743/4, Hinke Collection, Letters and Documents, VII, E.R.H.S.

133. Boehm, Report on Conditions in Pennsylvania, [8 July 1744], trans. Hinke, *John Philip Boehm*, pp. 417–418, 421–422, quotes pp. 417, 421.

134. 15 February 1745/6, Lischy's und Rauchs Relation, 1745, Journal Collection, JC II 1, M.A. Schnorr was later dismissed from the ministry because of misconduct. *Pensylvanische Berichte*, 16 May 1746, 16 October 1749.

135. Weinlick, "Colonial Moravians," *PH*, 26 (1959), 219–220.

136. Rothermund, *Layman's Progress*, p. 40n.

137. The men apologized. 30 November 1742, Muhlenberg, *Journals*, I, 68.

138. Letter of Mühlenberg, 12 August 1743, *Hallesche Nachrichten*, I, 12–17, quote p. 17.

139. January 1754, Fortgesetzter Bericht des Herrn Pastor Mühlenbergs von seiner Amtsführung vom Jahr 1753 und Anfang des Jahrs 1754, *Ibid.*, p. 606.

140. 14 February 1742/3, Muhlenberg, *Journals*, I, 90.

141. Letter of Mühlenberg, 1 July 1743, *Hallesche Nachrichten*, I, 22.

142. March 1747, Muhlenberg, *Journals*, I, 141–142.

143. Neuesten Umständen, *Hallesche Nachrichten*, I, 145.

144. April–May 1747, Muhlenberg, *Journals*, I, 143–144 (quotes p. 144); Mühlenberg, Peter Brunnholtz, and Handschuch to Friederich Michael Ziegenhagen and Johann Gotthilf Francke, 9 July 1754, *Hallesche Nachrichten*, I, 665–670.

145. Mühlenberg to Ziegenhagen and Francke, 29 December 1749, *Ibid.*, pp. 373–381, quote p. 374.

146. February 1750, Muhlenberg, *Journals*, I, 236.

147. June 1748, *Ibid.*, pp. 196–197.

148. January 1749/50, *Ibid.*, pp. 234–235.

149. 20 June 1747, *Ibid.*, p. 154; October 1751, *Ibid.*, pp. 312–313; and, for example,

Pensylvanische Geschicht-Schreiber, 16 August 1744; *Pensylvanische Berichte*, 16 October 1746, 16 December 1746, 1 April 1753.

150. Letter of Brunnholtz, 1745, *Hallesche Nachrichten*, I, 52.

151. Anfang des Berichts des Herrn Past. Mühlenbergs von seiner Amtsführung, vom Anfang derselben, nemlich vom Jahr 1742 an, bis in das Jahr 1746; nebst einem Brief, darinnen noch einige Nachricht von eben dieser Zeit ertheilet wird, *Ibid.*, pp. 157–158.

152. January 1747/8, Mühlenbergs Amtsführung, 1747–1748, *Ibid.*, pp. 256–257, quote p. 257.

153. March 1748/9, Auszuge aus des Herrn Pastor Handschuchs Tageregister vom 7ten Sept. 1748 bis den 15ten May 1750, *Ibid.*, p. 399, / March 1750, *Ibid.* (quotes).

154. Mühlenbergs Amtsführung, 1742–1746, *Ibid.*, pp. 155–156; April–May 1747, Muhlenberg, *Journals*, I, 147; February 1748, *Ibid.*, p. 180. There are numerous "merkwürdige Exempel" of individuals drawn into the Lutheran church scattered throughout Muhlenberg's *Journals* and the *Hallesche Nachrichten*.

155. For example: April–May 1747, Muhlenberg, *Journals*, I, 146; June 1748, *Ibid.*, pp. 196–198; September 1748, *Ibid.*, p. 202; October–November 1748, *Ibid.*, p. 204.

156. See, for example: 12 May 1748, Auszug aus des Herrn Pastor Handschuchs Tageregister, so er auf der Reise von England nach Pensylvanien geführet [1747–1748], *Hallesche Nachrichten*, I, 103; 28 March 1749, Handschuchs Tageregister, 1748–1750, *Ibid.*, p. 400; Brunnholtz to Ziegenhagen and Francke, 11 April 1749, *Ibid.*, p. 384; 31 July 1749, Handschuchs Tageregister, 1748–1750, *Ibid.*, pp. 407–408; 22 July 1753, Herrn Pastor Mühlenbergs Nachricht von seiner Reise nach Raritan vom 12ten bis 23sten Julii 1753, *Ibid.*, p. 622; Mühlenberg to Ziegenhagen and Francke, 18 June 1754, *Ibid.*, pp. 649–654.

157. 10 January 1742/3, Muhlenberg, *Journals*, I, 85; September 1748, *Ibid.*, p. 202; 1749, *Ibid.*, p. 213.

158. 22 June 1748, Handschuchs Reise nach Pensylvanien, 1747–1748, *Hallesche Nachrichten*, I, 108.

159. 25 March 1745, 30 June 1745, Extract from Brunnholtz' diary, *Ibid.*, pp. 57–58.

160. 2 May 1750, Muhlenberg, *Journals*, I, 241.

161. Boehm to Synod, 9 July 1744, Hinke Collection, Letters and Documents, VII, E.R.H.S.

162. George Michael Weiss to Hermann Barthold Hoedmaker, 1 October 1752, *Ibid.*, X.

163. Although this discussion has focused on the Lutheran experience, the situation among the Reformed appears to be similar. Documentation for the work of the Lutheran pastors is much more complete than for that of the Reformed, notably Muhlenberg's *Journals* and the *Hallesche Nachrichten*. In addition, Muhlenberg was dispatched to the colony in 1742, while Michael Schlatter was not sent to investigate conditions among the Reformed for the Dutch Reformed church until 1746.

164. *Pensylvanische Berichte*, 16 May 1746, 1 August 1749, 16 October 1749.

165. *Ibid.*, 1 August 1749, 16 January 1749/50, 1 February 1749/50, 16 February 1749/50, 16 March 1749/50; *Pennsylvania Gazette*, 16 November 1749, 5 April 1750, 26 December 1752. The work of the arbiters may be followed in the diary of John Smith (IX, John Jay Smith Papers, L.C.P.), 13 February–6 March 1749/50.

166. Locke to the Secretary, 11 April 1747, *S.P.G. Letterbooks*, B15, no. 143.

167. Logan to [J. Martin], 19–20 November 1742, Logan Papers-Alverthorpe, James Logan Letterbook B, p. 29, H.S.P.

168. Thomas to Bishop of Exeter, 23 April 1748, *S.P.G. Letterbooks*, B16, no. 164.

169. 28 December 1742, Muhlenberg, *Journals*, I, 75.

170. 14 August 1748, *Ibid.*, pp. 201–202; letter of Brunnholtz, 16/27 November 1748, *Hallesche Nachrichten*, I, 81–83.

171. March 1748, Mühlenbergs Amtsführung, 1747–1748, *Ibid.*, pp. 265–268; 31 May 1748, *Ibid.*, pp. 277–278; Mühlenberg to Ziegenhagen and Francke, 18 May 1754, *Ibid.*, p. 654.

172. 1 January 1742/3, Muhlenberg, *Journals*, I, 83; 18 February 1742/3, *Ibid.*, p. 92; letter of Handschuch, 12 August 1743, *Hallesche Nachrichten*, I, 13; Fortsetzung der Kurtzen Nachricht von einigen Evangelischen Gemeinen in America, *Ibid.*, pp. 34–35.

173. Nyberg to Brycelius, Spring 1745, Rothermund, *Layman's Progress*, pp. 154–158; Acrelius, *New Sweden*, pp. 246–249. Kock was instrumental in preventing Moravian inroads into the Swedish Lutheran church in Philadelphia and in assisting Muhlenberg in his various problems with Zinzendorf. 30–31 December 1742, Muhlenberg, *Journals*, I, 79–81.

174. 1747, Mühlenbergs Amtsführung, 1747–1748, *Hallesche Nachrichten*, I, 248–249; Brunnholtz to Ziegenhagen, 21 May 1750, *Ibid.*, p. 391.

175. Brunnholtz to Ziegenhagen and Francke, 21 May 1750, *Ibid.*, p. 391; Neuesten Umständen, *Ibid.*, pp. 129–130.

176. 17 January 1742/3, Muhlenberg, *Journals*, I, 86; Charles H. Glatfelter, "The Colonial Pennsylvania German Lutheran and Reformed Clergyman" (Ph.D. diss., Johns Hopkins University, 1952), pp. 37–38; Lodge, "Great Awakening," pp. 42–43.

177. 15 October 1746, William J. Hinke, ed. and trans., "Diary of the Rev. Michael Schlatter: June 1–December 15, 1746," *JPHS*, 3 (1905), 158–159, quote p. 159.

178. Synodical Deputies to Reformed Churches in Pennsylvania, 20 September 1743, trans. Hinke Collection, Letters and Documents, II, E.R.H.S.

179. Peter Henry Dorsius to Synods, 16 February 1743/4, *Ibid.*, VII; Minutes of the Synod of Philadelphia, 25 May 1744, William Morrison Engles, ed., *Records of the Presbyterian Church in the United States of America Embracing the Minutes of the Presbytery of Philadelphia, from A.D. 1706 to 1716: Minutes of the Syond [sic] of Philadelphia, from A.D. 1717 to 1758: Minutes of the Synod of New York, from A.D. 1745 to 1758: Minutes of the Synod of New York and Philadelphia, from A.D. 1758 to 1788* (Philadelphia, 1841), p. 176.

180. Boehm and Consistories of his churches to Synod, 18 March 1744, Hinke Collection, Letters and Documents, VII, E.R.H.S. Despite reluctance to unite formally, in 1742 several Germans in Lancaster requested that their minister, Conrad Templeman, be ordained by the Presbyterians. Because the "Calvinist" minister in Lancaster branded him as a "presumptuous intruder into [the] sacred work and office of the ministry," and because ministers were available "of his own Chh & nation," the request was denied. 7 April 1742, Minutes of the Presbytery of Donegal, 1732–1750, p. 240, P.H.S.

181. Francis McHenry to Synod, 14 June 1744, Hinke Collection, Letters and Documents, VII, E.R.H.S. (quote); Robert Cross to Rev. Kennedy of Rotterdam, 16 October 1747, *Ibid.*, VIII.

182. Trinterud, *Forming an American Tradition*, pp. 109–110, 118, 122–131, 136–142.

183. Backhouse to the Secretary, 25 July 1741, *S.P.G. Letterbooks*, B9, no. 104 (quotes); St. Paul's Church, Chester, to the Secretary, read 16 November 1741, *Ibid.*, no. 108.

184. Dorsius to Synod, June 1749, Hinke Collection, Letters and Documents, IX, E.R.H.S.

185. Cammerhoff to Zinzendorf, 8–23 March 1746/7, Cammerhoff-Zinzendorf Letters, p. 16, H.S.P.

186. Backhouse to the Secretary, 21 September 1744, *S.P.G. Letterbooks*, B12, no. 55.

187. 19 July 1748, Handschuchs Reise nach Pensylvanien, 1747–1748, *Hallesche Nachrichten*, I, 109; letter of Handschuch, 7 October 1748, *Ibid.*, p. 68; Handschuch to Ziegenhagen and Francke, 18 May 1754, *Ibid.*, pp. 643–644

188. 1747, Mühlenbergs Amtsführung, 1747–1748, *Ibid.*, p. 218; T. Penn to Peters, 13 February 1749/50, Peters Papers, III, 4, H.S.P. Stipends for teachers were also granted on occasion. Thomas Cookson to T. Penn, 4 December 1749, Lancaster County Papers, 1724–1772, p. 65, H.S.P.; T. Penn to [James Hamilton], 9 January 1753, Penn Manuscripts, Penn-Hamilton Correspondence, 1748–1770, p. 23, H.S.P.

189. Henry Neal to the Provincial, 25 April 1741, Thomas Hughes, ed., *History of the Society of Jesus in North America Colonial and Federal*, [vol. 3], *Documents, Vol. 1, Part 1, Nos. 1–140 (1605–1838)* (London, 1908), p. 342.

190. Hockley to T. Penn, 1 November 1742, Penn Manuscripts, Official Correspondence, III, 241, 243, H.S.P.

191. T. Penn to Hockley, 26 February 1742/3, Penn Manuscripts, Thomas Penn Letterbook, II, 37, H.S.P.

192. T. Penn to Thomas, 26 February 1742/3, *Ibid.*, p. 32 (first quote); T. Penn to Thomas, 8 February 1743/4, *Ibid.*, p. 75 (second quote).

193. T. Penn to Thomas, 21 August 1743, *Ibid.*, p. 47. Indeed, a Roman Catholic ship captain was "often at the Gov^rs club." Hockley to T. Penn, 1 November 1742, Penn Manuscripts, Official Correspondence, III, 241, H.S.P.

194. Peters to the Proprietors, 17 November 1742, Peters Papers, Richard Peters Letterbook, p. 132, H.S.P.; Peters to T. Penn, 28 October 1749, Penn Manuscripts, Official Correspondence, IV, 243, H.S.P. In his letter to the proprietors, Peters mentioned that Hamilton's generosity had been used against him by his political opponents.

195. T. Penn to Cookson, 26 February 1742/3, Penn Manuscripts, Thomas Penn Letterbook, II, 33–34, H.S.P., quotes p. 33.

196. Backhouse to the Secretary, 23 August 1740, Perry, *Colonial Church*, p. 206.

197. Janney to the Secretary, 14 November 1745, *Ibid.*, pp. 236–237.

198. AEneas Ross to the Secretary, The Acco^t of the Churches of Oxford & White Marsh from 29th September 1743 to 25th March 1744, *S.P.G. Letterbooks*, B12, no. 46.

199. Weiss to Classis, 25 April 1742, trans. Hinke Collection, Letters and Documents, II, E.R.H.S.

200. 17 April 1749, Handschuchs Tageregister, 1748–1750, *Hallesche Nachrichten*, I, 401.

201. *Pennsylvania Gazette*, 19 May 1743, 7 August 1746 (first quote), 28 August 1746, 21 November 1751 (second quote), 19 December 1752, 5 April 1753, 5 December 1754; *Pensylvanische Berichte*, 1 August 1749, 16 July 1750, 16 November 1750.

202. *Pennsylvania Gazette*, 13 November 1746.

203. Locke to the Secretary, 11 April 1747, *S.P.G. Letterbooks*, B15, no. 143.

204. 8 June 1744, Carl Bridenbaugh, ed., *Gentleman's Progress: The Itinerarium of Dr.*

Alexander Hamilton, 1744 (Chapel Hill, 1948), p. 20; 18 September 1744, *Ibid.*, p. 191; Edwin Wolf 2d and Maxwell Whiteman, *The History of the Jews of Philadelphia from Colonial Times to the Age of Jackson* (Philadelphia, 1957), pp. 15–16, 19–21, 31–33, 47, 49, 53–54.

205. John Reynell to Daniel Flexney, 12 July 1746, Coates and Reynell Papers, John Reynell Letterbook, 1745–1747, H.S.P.

206. *Pennsylvania Gazette*, 29 August 1751.

207. This unnamed Jew lived in the house of a deacon of the congregation. 28 November 1742, Muhlenberg, *Journals*, I, 67.

208. February 1747, *Ibid.*, p. 139. Muhlenberg noted that there were "only a few Jews" in the colony, and considered them "practical atheists."

209. 5 October 1749, Handschuchs Tageregister, 1748–1750, *Hallesche Nachrichten*, I, 411.

210. Lamech and Agrippa, *Chronicon Ephratense*, pp. 82–83.

211. *Pensylvanische Geschicht-Schreiber*, 16 July 1744. Other newspaper articles about the cloister include *Pensylvanische Berichte*, 16 October 1745, 16 March 1745/6, 16 May 1746.

212. J. Pemberton to Israel Pemberton, 24 June 1744, Pemberton Papers, III, 120, H.S.P.

213. J. Penn to T. Penn, 19 August 1753, Penn Manuscripts, Private Correspondence, IV, 119, H.S.P.

214. 7–13 March 1742/3, 19 October 1743, October 1743, Charles Evans Collection, Edmund Peckover Journal, 1742–1744, pp. 28, 58, 60 (quote), Q.C.H.C.

215. For example: Backhouse to the Secretary, 25 July 1741, *S.P.G. Letterbooks*, B9, no. 104; Ross to the Secretary, 20 October 1752, *Ibid.*, B20, no. 131.

216. George Craig to the Secretary, 16 June 1752, *Ibid.*, no. 124.

217. For example: John Gordon to the Secretary, 3 October 1743, *Ibid.*, B11, no. 177; Backhouse to the Secretary, 26 June 1748, *Ibid.*, B16, no. 100 (quote).

218. Craig to the Secretary, 24 June 1753, George Craig Letterbook, 1751–1775, p. 4, H.S.P. Muhlenberg also noted that on the two Sundays each month when the minister was absent from Lancaster serving another congregation, many of its members "go to the Moravian church because they want a sermon every Sunday." 20 June 1747, *Journals*, I, 153.

219. Howie to the Secretary, 29 September 1741, *S.P.G. Letterbooks*, B9, no. 109.

220. *Pennsylvania Gazette*, 24 March 1742 (quote); Julius Friedrich Sachse, *The German Sectarians of Pennsylvania 1742–1800: A Critical and Legendary History of the Ephrata Cloister and the Dunkers*, vol. 2 (Philadelphia, 1900), pp. 1–68.

221. 6 March 1744/5, Muhlenberg, *Journals*, I, 96; *Pensylvanische Berichte*, 16 October 1745.

222. To the Committee For Foreign Needs of the Dutch Mennonite Church, 19 October 1745, trans. Richard K. MacMaster, Samuel L. Horst, and Robert F. Ulle, eds., *Conscience in Crisis: Mennonites and Other Peace Churches in America, 1739–1789: Interpretation and Documents* (Scottdale, Pa., 1979), pp. 84–87; Lamech and Agrippa, *Chronicon Ephratense*, pp. 209–210, 213–214; Martin G. Weaver, *Mennonites of Lancaster Conference Containing Biographical Sketches of Mennonite Leaders; Histories of Congregations, Missions, and Sunday Schools; Record of Ordinations; and Other Interesting Historical Data* (Scottdale, Pa., 1931), pp. 20–21, 28–29.

223. 6 August 1750, Philadelphia Yearly Meeting Collection, Philadelphia Quarterly Meeting Minutes, 1723–1772, p. 145, Q.C.H.C.

224. Philadelphia Yearly Meeting to London Yearly Meeting, 15–19 September 1750, Philadelphia Yearly Meeting Collection, Philadelphia Yearly Meeting Minutes, 1747–1779, pp. 20–21, Q.C.H.C. (quote); Smith to John Hunt, 6 July 1751, John Smith Letterbook, 1750–1752, Q.C.H.C.

225. *Pennsylvania Gazette*, 19 January 1747/8. This essay, penned by Ebenezer Kinnersley, is discussed in J. A. Leo Lemay, *Ebenezer Kinnersley: Franklin's Friend* (Philadelphia, 1964), pp. 42–44.

226. *Pennsylvania Gazette*, 6 August 1752. This article was printed under a dateline of London, which may explain the constraint on absolute liberty of conscience.

227. *Pensylvanische Berichte*, 16 February 1746/7.

228. *Ibid.*, 16 March 1746/7.

229. *Pensylvanische Geschicht-Schreiber*, 16 April 1744.

230. *Pensylvanische Berichte*, 16 August 1747. Sauer also recognized the economic freedoms of the colony in this essay.

231. "The Sum of Religion" (Philadelphia, [1740]), Broadside Collection, H.S.P.

232. *Pensylvanische Berichte*, 16 May 1749.

6. Religious and Ethnic Politics, 1739–1755

1. Between 1709 and 1773 Pennsylvania enacted thirteen naturalization acts for approximately 575 individuals. Edward A. Hoyt, "Naturalization under the American Colonies: Signs of a New Community," *PSQ*, 67 (1952), 249.

2. James H. Kettner, *The Development of American Citizenship, 1608–1870* (Chapel Hill, 1978), pp. 74–75, 103; Simon Rosendale, ed., "An Act allowing Naturalization of Jews in the Colonies," *PAJHS*, 1 (1893), 93–98 (quotes p. 94).

3. [27–29 May 1742], Gertrude MacKinney and Charles F. Hoban, eds., *Pennsylvania Archives*, 8th ser., 8 vols., *Votes and Proceedings of the House of Representatives of the Province of Pennsylvania, 1682–1776* (Harrisburg, 1931–1935), IV, 2752, 2764, 2766 [hereafter Assembly, *Votes*]; *Pennsylvania Gazette*, 3 June 1742.

4. George Thomas to [the Proprietors], 4 June 1742, Penn Manuscripts, Official Correspondence, III, 219, H.S.P.

5. Thomas Penn to Thomas, 17 September 1742, Penn Manuscripts, Thomas Penn Letterbook, II, 9, H.S.P.

6. [29 October–3 November 1742], Assembly, *Votes*, IV, 2824–2825, 2827. The British government consistently disallowed laws to protect the property holdings of deceased aliens passed by the Pennsylvania legislature.

7. Governor to Assembly, 11 January 1742/3, *Minutes of the Provincial Council of Pennsylvania, From the Organization to the Termination of the Proprietary Government*, 16 vols. (Philadelphia and Harrisburg, 1851–1853), IV, 627 [hereafter Council, *Minutes*].

8. Assembly to Governor, [13 January 1742/3], Assembly, *Votes*, IV, 2854.

9. Governor to Assembly, 14 January 1742/3, Council, *Minutes*, IV, 629.

10. Ch. 359, 3 February 1742/3, James T. Mitchell and Henry Flanders, comps., *The Statutes at Large of Pennsylvania from 1682 to 1801*, 16 vols. (Harrisburg, 1896–1911), IV, 391–394 [hereafter *Statutes*].

11. T. Penn to Mr. Speaker[?], 9 March 1746/7, Penn Manuscripts, Thomas Penn Letterbook, II, 181, H.S.P.

12. Board of Trade to Privy Council, 5 December 1746, *Statutes*, IV, 511–512, quote p. 512.

13. *Pensylvanische Berichte*, 16 October 1747; Kettner, *American Citizenship*, p. 75.

14. John Philip Boehm to Classis of Amsterdam, 25 July 1741, trans. William J. Hinke, ed., *Life and Letters of the Rev. John Philip Boehm Founder of the Reformed Church in Pennsylvania 1682–1749* (Philadelphia, 1916), pp. 334–335, quote p. 334. On 13 May 1751, Lutheran ministers decided to hold communion services prior to 10 April and 10 September, "on account of naturalization." A. Spaeth, H. E. Jacobs, and G. F. Spicker, eds. and trans., *Documentary History of the Evangelical Lutheran Ministerium of Pennsylvania and Adjacent States. . . .* (Philadelphia, 1898), pp. 34–35.

15. This is the first issue of a German-language newspaper that survives following passage of the 1740 law. *Pensylvanische Geschicht-Schreiber*, 16 February 1741/2.

16. *Pennsylvania Gazette*, 14 April 1743.

17. *Pensylvanische Berichte*, 1 June 1751, 16 March 1755 (quote), 1 April 1755, 1 July 1755.

18. *Pensylvanische Geschicht-Schreiber*, 16 August 1743.

19. *Pensylvanische Berichte*, 16 June 1747.

20. *Ibid.*, 16 September 1748, 16 September 1749, 16 September 1750, 1 September 1754, 16 July 1755, 1 September 1755.

21. Kettner, *American Citizenship*, pp. 117–119.

22. T. Penn to Richard Peters, 13 February 1749/50, Penn Manuscripts, Thomas Penn Letterbook, II, 299, H.S.P.

23. Rosendale, "Act allowing Naturalization of Jews," *PAJHS*, 1 (1893), 98. Not until 1773 was British policy clarified; men naturalized under the 1740 statute were permitted to hold office, except in Great Britain and Ireland. Kettner, *American Citizenship*, p. 77.

24. Peters to the Proprietors, 26 October 1749, Penn Manuscripts, Official Correspondence, IV, 245, H.S.P.

25. Lists of aliens naturalized under this law were to be transmitted annually to England, but only fragmentary lists remain. Kettner estimates that 92 percent of the 6911 naturalizations in the mainland colonies under this law and its supplements between 1740 and 1776 occurred in Pennsylvania. *American Citizenship*, pp. 74–75. By 1740, and increasingly thereafter, native-born "Germans" coming to maturity were entitled to the rights of British subjects without being naturalized. English-speaking Pennsylvanians rarely distinguished between immigrant and native-born German-speaking people.

26. [Robert Hunter Morris] to [Thomas Robinson], 9 April 1755, Samuel Hazard, ed., *Pennsylvania Archives*, [1st ser.], 12 vols. (Philadelphia and Harrisburg, 1852–1856), II, 285 [hereafter *Pa. Arch.*].

27. William T. Parsons, *The Pennsylvania Dutch: A Persistent Minority* (Boston, 1976), pp. 77–80.

28. Stephen Brobeck, "Changes in the Composition and Structure of Philadelphia Elite Groups, 1756–1790" (Ph.D. diss., University of Pennsylvania, 1973), pp. 28–33, 250–251.

29. John Penn to Thomas, 2 August 1739, Penn Manuscripts, Thomas Penn Letter-

book, I, 306–307, H.S.P. (quotes); J. Penn to T. Penn, 2 August 1739, *Ibid.*, pp. 308–309.

30. Governor to Assembly, [16 October 1739], Assembly, *Votes*, III, 2512–2513.

31. Resolution of Assembly, [17 October 1739], *Ibid.*, p. 2513.

32. Governor to Assembly, 18 October 1739, *Ibid.*, p. 2514.

33. William Allen to J. Penn, 17 November 1739, Penn Manuscripts, Official Correspondence, III, 91, H.S.P.

34. Thomas to [the Proprietors], 5 November 1739, *Ibid.*, p. 89,

35. Assembly to Governor, [5 January 1739/40], Assembly, *Votes*, III, 2529–2531, quotes pp. 2529–2530.

36. [5 January 1739/40], *Ibid.*, p. 2532.

37. Governor to Assembly, 10 January 1739/40, *Ibid.*, pp. 2535–3538, quote p. 2536.

38. Assembly to Governor, [19 January 1739/40], *Ibid.*, pp. 2540–2545, quotes p. 2545.

39. Governor to Assembly, 23 January 1739/40, *Ibid.*, pp. 2547–2551; Assembly to Governor, [26 January 1739/40], *Ibid.*, pp. 2555–2557; [28 January 1739/40], *Ibid.*, p. 2559.

40. Robert L. D. Davidson, *War Comes to Quaker Pennsylvania 1682–1756* (New York, 1957), pp. 27–28 and n.

41. Governor to Assembly, 6 May 1740, Assembly, *Votes*, III, 2562–2563; Assembly to Governor, [9 May 1740], *Ibid.*, p. 2569; Governor to Assembly, 10 May 1740, *Ibid.*, p. 2578; [14–15 May 1740], *Ibid.*, pp. 2586–2587.

42. Governor to Assembly, [2 July 1740], *Ibid.*, pp. 2588–2593.

43. Assembly to Governor, [7 July 1740], *Ibid.*, p. 2593.

44. [8–11 July 1740], *Ibid.*, pp. 2594–2597, including messages from the governor to the assembly.

45. Assembly to Governor, [31 July 1740], *Ibid.*, pp. 2600–2603, quotes pp. 2602, 2603.

46. Governor to Assembly, 2 August 1740, *Ibid.*, pp. 2605–2611, quotes pp. 2607, 2609.

47. [4–9 August 1740], *Ibid.*, pp. 2611–2631, including messages from the governor to the assembly and from the assembly to the governor and Thomas Penn. See also Governor to Assembly, 26 August 1740, *Ibid.*, pp. 2632–2638; Assembly to Governor, 29 August 1740, *Ibid.*, pp. 2648–2659; Governor to Assembly, 3 September 1740, *Ibid.*, p. 2660.

48. Peters to [J. Penn?], 31 July 1740, Peters Papers, Richard Peters Letterbook, p. 16, H.S.P.

49. John Reynell to Daniel Flexney, 30 August 1740, Coates and Reynell Papers, John Reynell Letterbook, 1738–1741, H.S.P.

50. Thomas to [J. Penn], 4 November 1740, Penn Manuscripts, Official Correspondence, III, 129, H.S.P.

51. James Logan to Thomas Story, 8 November 1740, Norman Penny, ed., "The Correspondence of James Logan and Thomas Story, 1724–1741," *BFHA*, 15, no. 2 (1926), 82.

52. Israel Pemberton to John Fothergill, 4 November 1740, Pemberton Papers, XXXIV, 1, H.S.P.

53. Thomas to Board of Trade, 20 October 1740, *Statutes*, IV, 470–471.

54. I. Pemberton to Fothergill, 4 November 1740, Pemberton Papers, XXXIV, 1, H.S.P.

55. Allen to [the Proprietors], 27 March 1741, Penn Manuscripts, Official Correspondence, III, 143, H.S.P.

56. Matthias Aspden to Reynell, 4 July 1741, Reynell Papers, Box 2, Folder 16, H.S.P.

57. 24 September 1740, Philadelphia Yearly Meeting Collection, Philadelphia Yearly Meeting Minutes, 1681–1746, p. 420, Q.C.H.C.

58. Flexney to Reynell, 14 February 1740/1, Reynell Papers, Box 2, Folder 13, H.S.P.

59. Thomas to Board of Trade, 20 October 1740, Statutes, IV, 468–477, quotes pp. 469, 470.

60. Governor to Assembly, 6 January 1740/1, Assembly, Votes, III, 2665–2667; Assembly to Governor, 8 January 1740/1, Ibid., pp. 2668–2670; [21 April 1741], Ibid., p. 2671; [26 May–6 June 1741], Ibid., pp. 2672–2680, 2685, including messages between the governor and assembly; [19–22 August 1741], Ibid., pp. 2687–2692, including messages to the governor and to and from Thomas Penn.

61. Petition to Assembly, [5 June 1741], Ibid., pp. 2680–2681.

62. Committee Report, [6 June 1741], Ibid., pp. 2683–2684; Resolution of Assembly, [6 June 1741], Ibid., p. 2684 (quotes).

63. Petition of Merchants and Other Inhabitants of Pennsylvania to the King, n.d. [c. 1741], John Jay Smith Papers, Smith Manuscripts, I, 191, L.C.P.

64. T. Penn to J. and Richard Penn, 23 March 1740/1, Penn Manuscripts, Thomas Penn Letterbook, 1739–1741, pp. 38–41, H.S.P., quote p. 39.

65. James Pemberton to [John Smith], 15 September 1741, John Jay Smith Papers, Smith Manuscripts, I, 199, L.C.P. There was, however, an infectious disease in Philadelphia during the late summer and early autumn of 1741.

66. Thomas Cookson to [Conrad Weiser], 12 September 1741, Weiser Papers, Correspondence, I, 6–7, H.S.P., quotes p. 6.

67. Peters to T. Penn, 8 October 1741, Peters Papers, Richard Peters Letterbook, p. 29, H.S.P. (first quote); Conrad Weiser, A Serious and Seasonable Advice to our Countreymen yᵉ Germans in Pennsylvania, 20 September 1741, Society Miscellaneous Collection, H.S.P., Weiser's translation (remaining quotes).

68. Anonymous Answer to Conrad Weiser's Letter to the Germans, 29 September 1741, Penn Manuscripts, Official Correspondence, III, 199, H.S.P.; William Reed Steckel, "Pietist in Colonial Pennsylvania: Christopher Sauer, Printer 1738–1758" (Ph.D. diss., Stanford University, 1949), pp. 142–144.

69. Samuel Noble to J. Smith, 3 October 1741, John Jay Smith Papers, Smith Manuscripts, I, 200, L.C.P.

70. Peters to T. Penn, 8 October 1741, Peters Papers, Richard Peters Letterbook, p. 29, H.S.P.

71. Richard Partridge to John Kinsey, 28 June 1742, Pemberton Papers, III, 51, H.S.P.

72. J[ames] L[ogan], "To Robert Jordan and others of the Friends of the Yearly Meeting for Business, now conven'd in Philadelphia," 22 September 1741, Ibid., p. 48 (printed copy).

73. Peters to [J. Penn], reporting the comments of Quaker Robert Strettel, [20 October 1741], Penn Manuscripts, Official Correspondence, III, 135, H.S.P.

74. 23 September 1741, Philadelphia Yearly Meeting Collection, Philadelphia Yearly Meeting Minutes, 1681–1746, p. 425, Q.C.H.C.

75. Peters to [J. Penn], [20 October 1741], Penn Manuscripts, Official Correspondence, III, 135, H.S.P.

76. Allen to T. Penn, 24 October 1741, *Ibid.*, p. 201.

77. Fothergill to I. Pemberton Jr., 8 April 1742, Pemberton Papers, XXXIV, 2, H.S.P. He did, however, urge Quaker assemblymen to moderate their behavior.

78. Philadelphia Quarterly Meeting to London Meeting for Sufferings, 3 May 1742, Philadelphia Yearly Meeting Collection, Philadelphia Yearly Meeting Minutes, 1747–1779, pp. 55–56, Q.C.H.C.

79. Committee of London Meeting for Sufferings to Samuel Preston, Robert Jordan, Kinsey, and I. Pemberton, 1741, Philadelphia Yearly Meeting Collection, Miscellaneous Epistles and Letters, 1740–1745, Q.C.H.C.

80. Fothergill to I. Pemberton Jr., 8 April 1742, Pemberton Papers, XXXIV, 2, H.S.P.

81. Partridge to Kinsey, 28 June 1742, *Ibid.*, III, 51.

82. Board of Trade to Privy Council, 8 July 1742, Levick Papers, 1674–1782, H.S.P.

83. Thomas to Weiser, 9 September 1742, Peters Papers, I, 94, H.S.P.

84. Peters to the Proprietors, 17 November 1742, Peters Papers, Richard Peters Letterbook, pp. 131–132, H.S.P.

85. Ch. 350, 19 May 1739, *Statutes*, IV, 331–336; Norman S. Cohen, "The Philadelphia Election Riot of 1742," *PMHB*, 92 (1968), 310–311.

86. This account has been drawn from the depositions collected by the assembly and from letters written by observers with different perspectives. See the forty-nine depositions printed in Assembly, *Votes*, IV, 2957–3009 (second quote from the deposition of John Mitchell, p. 2988); Richard Hockley to T. Penn, 1 November 1742, Penn Manuscripts, Official Correspondence, III, 241, 243, H.S.P. (first quote p. 241); Peters to the Proprietors, 17 November 1742, Peters Papers, Richard Peters Letterbook, pp. 131–139, H.S.P.; Reynell to Flexney, 20 November 1742, Coates and Reynell Papers, John Reynell Letterbook, 1741–1744, H.S.P.

87. Isaac Norris Jr. to Robert Charles, 21 November 1742, Norris Papers, Isaac Norris Sr. and Jr. Letterbook, 1719–1756, p. 13, H.S.P.

88. Partridge to Kinsey, 13 May 1743, Pemberton Papers, III, 62, H.S.P. (first quote); Fothergill to I. Pemberton Jr., 14 May 1743, *Ibid.*, XXXIV, 4 (second quote).

89. Mayor and Common Council of Philadelphia to the King, 23 October 1744, *Minutes of the Common Council of the City of Philadelphia, 1704 to 1776* (Philadelphia, 1847), pp. 440–441 (quotes p. 441); Judith M. Diamondstone, "The Philadelphia Corporation 1701–1776" (Ph.D. diss., University of Pennsylvania, 1969), pp. 232–239.

90. Philadelphia Quarterly Meeting to London Meeting for Sufferings, 5 November 1744, Philadelphia Yearly Meeting Collection, Philadelphia Yearly Meeting Minutes, 1747–1779, pp. 57–58, Q.C.H.C.

91. Evidence of accommodation may be seen in the passage of the affirmation law for alien naturalization and resolution of the dispute over providing facilities for sick passengers during the 1742–1743 sessions.

92. Governor to Assembly, 31 July 1744, Assembly, *Votes*, IV, 2934–2938, quotes p. 2935.

93. Assembly to Governor, [10 August 1744], *Ibid.*, pp. 2942–2943, quote p. 2942.

94. Governor to Assembly, 26 February 1744/5, *Ibid.*, p. 3025; Assembly to Governor, [28 February 1744/5], *Ibid.*, pp. 3027–3028.

95. Governor to Assembly, 4 June 1745, *Ibid.*, p. 3036; Assembly to Governor, [6 June 1745], *Ibid.*, p. 3038; Governor to Assembly, 23 July 1745, *Ibid.*, pp. 3039–3040; Resolution of Assembly, [24 July 1745], *Ibid.*, p. 3042; Assembly to Governor, [24 July 1745], *Ibid.*, pp. 3042–3043 (quotes).

96. Governor to Assembly, 8 January 1745/6, *Ibid.*, pp. 3064–3065; Assembly to Governor, [15 January 1745/6], *Ibid.*, p. 3071 (quote).

97. [3–5 February 1745/6], *Ibid.*, pp. 3079–3081; [20–21 May 1746], *Ibid.*, pp. 3089–3092; [10–25 June 1746], *Ibid.*, pp. 3093–3105, all including messages between the governor and the assembly.

98. John Swift to John White, 13 July 1747, John Swift Letterbook, 1747–1751, H.S.P.

99. 13 July 1747, John Jay Smith Papers, John Smith Diary, III, L.C.P. (quotes); 22 July 1747, Council, *Minutes*, V, 89–93 (when reports and minutes of a meeting held on 13 July 1747 were laid before the full council).

100. 14 July 1747, John Jay Smith Papers, John Smith Diary, III, L.C.P.

101. Davidson, *War Comes to Pennsylvania*, p. 46.

102. [Benjamin Franklin], "Plain Truth: or, Serious Considerations On the Present State of the City of Philadelphia, and Province of Pennsylvania" (1747), Leonard W. Labaree, *et al.*, eds., *The Papers of Benjamin Franklin*, 25 vols. to date (New Haven, 1959–), III, 188–204, quotes pp. 195, 200.

103. *Pennsylvania Gazette*, 26 November 1747.

104. [25 November 1747], Assembly, *Votes*, IV, 3167–3168; 26 November 1747, Council, *Minutes*, V, 158; Council to the Proprietors, 27 November 1747, *Ibid.*, p. 161.

105. *Pennsylvania Gazette*, 12 December 1747.

106. Gilbert Tennent, *The late Association for Defence, encourag'd, Or The lawfulness of a Defensive War. Represented in a Sermon Preach'd At Philadelphia December 24, 1747*, 2d ed. (Philadelphia, [1748]), quote p. 35. The sermon was moderate in regard to the Quakers and their principles.

107. 1 January 1747/8 (quote), 12 January 1747/8, 15 January 1747/8, 22 January 1747/8, John Jay Smith Papers, John Smith Diary, IV, L.C.P.; John Smith, *The Doctrine of Christianity, As held by the People called Quakers, Vindicated: In Answer to Gilbert Tennent's Sermon On The Lawfulness of War* (Philadelphia, 1748).

108. 23 January 1747/8, John Jay Smith Papers, John Smith Diary, IV, L.C.P.

109. Gilbert Tennent, *The late Association for Defence Farther Encouraged: Or, Defensive War Defended; And its Consistency with True Christianity Represented. . . .* (Philadelphia, 1748).

110. *Pensylvanische Berichte*, 16 January 1747/8 (quotes), 16 February 1747/8; Peter Brock, *Pacifism in the United States From the Colonial Era to the First World War* (Princeton, 1968), pp. 127–128, 174–175.

111. *Pensylvanische Berichte*, 16 December 1747.

112. Logan to T. Penn, 14 November 1749, Logan Papers, James Logan Letterbook, 1748–1750, p. 28, H.S.P.

113. Hockley to [T. Penn], 22 July 1748, Penn Manuscripts, Additional Miscellaneous Letters, I, 60, H.S.P.

114. *Pennsylvania Gazette*, 28 February 1748/9.

115. 25 August 1748, Council, *Minutes*, V, 330–332.

116. I. Pemberton to Thomas Gawthorpe, 14 October 1748, Pemberton Papers, Copies of Letters, 1740–1780, p. 156, H.S.P.

117. December 1748, Theodore G. Tappert and John W. Doberstein, eds. and trans., *The Journals of Henry Melchior Muhlenberg*, 3 vols. (Philadelphia, 1942–1958), I, 212.

118. 20 September 1749, Auszug aus den Herrn Pastor [Johann Friederich] Handschuchs Tageregister vom 7ten Sept. 1748 bis den 15ten May 1750, Johann Ludewig Schulze, ed., *Nachrichten von den vereinigten Deutschen Evangelisch-Lutherischen Gemeinen in Nord-America, absonderlich in Pensylvanien*, 2 vols. (Halle, 1787), I, 410–411 [hereafter *Hallesche Nachrichten*]. Germans had for some time been active in politics in both the borough and county of Lancaster. Jerome H. Wood, Jr., *Conestoga Crossroads: Lancaster, Pennsylvania 1730–1790* (Harrisburg, 1979), pp. 23–46, 173–178.

119. [16–17 October 1749], Assembly, *Votes*, IV, 3279–3280, 3286–3287; [22–25 November 1749], *Ibid.*, pp. 3288–3296; [2–5 January 1749/50], *Ibid.*, pp. 3297–3299; Assembly to Sheriff and Inspectors of Lancaster County, [6 January 1749/50], *Ibid.*, pp. 3299–3301; [26 January 1749/50], *Ibid.*, p. 3316.

120. *Pensylvanische Berichte*, 16 August 1750.

121. Hans Hamilton, Remonstrance, [16 October 1750], Assembly, *Votes*, IV, 3357. The council decided that the riot was not due to Hamilton's behavior, and the governor reappointed him as sheriff "during his Pleasure" on 8 October 1750, Council, *Minutes*, V, 468.

122. [17–18 October 1750], Assembly, *Votes*, IV, 3358–3359, quote p. 3359.

123. [16 January 1750/1], *Ibid.*, p. 3398.

124. Benjamin Schwoop, Deposition, 8 October 1750, *Pa. Arch.*, [1st ser.], II, 50–51.

125. Thomas Graeme to T. Penn, 6 November 1750, Penn Manuscripts, Official Correspondence, V, 83, H.S.P.

126. Ch. 392, 11 March 1751/2, *Statutes*, V, 133–140; ch. 393, 11 March 1751/2, *Ibid.*, pp. 140–147; *Pensylvanische Berichte*, 1 March 1751/2, 16 April 1752.

127. Draft Resolution of Christopher Schultze, 28 September 1752, trans. Dietmar Rothermund, "The German Problem of Colonial Pennsylvania," *PMHB*, 84 (1960), 9–10, quotes p. 10.

128. James Hamilton to T. Penn, 18 March 1751/2, Penn Manuscripts, Official Correspondence, V, 227, H.S.P.

129. T. Penn to J. Hamilton, 13 July 1752, Penn Manuscripts, Thomas Penn Letterbook, III, 143, H.S.P. (first quote); T. Penn to Peters, 17 July 1752, *Ibid.*, p. 150 (remaining quotes).

130. Russell Sage Nelson, Jr., "Backcountry Pennsylvania (1704–1774): The Ideals of William Penn in Practice" (Ph.D. diss., University of Wisconsin, 1968), pp. 253–254.

131. Peters to J. Penn, 20 October 1741, Peters Papers, Richard Peters Letterbook, pp. 35–36, H.S.P., quote p. 36.

132. J. Hamilton to T. Penn, 29 April 1749, Hamilton Papers, Box 2, James Hamilton Letterbook, 1749–1783, H.S.P.

133. [T. Penn] to J. Hamilton, 31 July 1749, Penn-Hamilton Correspondence, 1747–1771, p. 47, A.P.S.

134. Wayne L. Bockelman, "Local Government in Colonial Pennsylvania," Bruce C. Daniels, ed., *Town and Country: Essays on the Structure of Local Government in the American Colonies* (Middletown, Conn., 1978), pp. 231–232.

135. Logan to Clement Plumsted, 25 August 1741, Logan Papers-Alverthorpe, James Logan Letterbook D, p. 15, H.S.P.

136. Samuel Finley to Peters, 15 November 1755, quoted in Alan Tully, *William Penn's Legacy: Politics and Social Structure in Provincial Pennsylvania 1726–1755* (Baltimore, 1977), p. 110.

137. Paul A. W. Wallace, *Conrad Weiser, 1696–1760: Friend of Colonist and Mohawk* (Philadelphia, 1945), p. 251.

138. Graeme to T. Penn, 18 March 1751/2, Penn Manuscripts, Official Correspondence, V, 223, H.S.P.

139. A. D. Chidsey, Jr., "William Parsons, Easton's First Citizen," *PH*, 7 (1940), 92, 93. He eventually lost his hostility toward the Moravians, and, at his request, was buried by a Moravian minister, the husband of one of his daughters. *Ibid.*, pp. 100–101.

140. William Parsons to Peters, 2 October 1754, Northampton County Papers, Miscellaneous Manuscripts, 1727–1758, p. 137, H.S.P.

141. [William Smith], "A Brief History of the Rise and Progress of the Charitable Scheme . . ." (1755), *Pennsylvania Gazette*, 25 February 1755; Henry Harbaugh, *The Life of Rev. Michael Schlatter . . .* (Philadelphia, 1857), pp. 261–262. Schlatter's "A True History of the Real Condition of the Destitute Churches in Pennsylvania" (1752) is translated *Ibid.*, pp. 87–234.

142. Hermann Barthold Hoedmaker to T. Penn, 4 May 1751, Penn Manuscripts, Official Correspondence, V, 139, H.S.P.

143. Michael Schlatter to T. Penn, 3 June 1751, *Ibid.*, p. 17.

144. T. Penn to Hoedmaker, 12 June 1751, *Ibid.*, p. 149; T. Penn to [Schlatter], 12 June 1751, *Ibid.* (last two quotes); T. Penn to David Thomson, 13 June 1751, *Ibid.* (first three quotes).

145. Schlatter to T. Penn, 10 August 1751, *Ibid.*, p. 171.

146. Bernhardinus de Moor to Schlatter, 22 October 1752, William J. Hinke Collection, Miscellaneous Letters and Documents relating to the Reformed Church in Pennsylvania, 1700–1806, IX, E.R.H.S.

147. Report of a committee of the Assembly of the Church of Scotland, 22 May 1752, *Ibid.*, X (quotes); Extracts from the Annals of the Assembly of the Church of Scotland, May 1752, *Ibid.*

148. An Abstract of Two Letters from the Rev. Mr. Hoedmaker, and the Rev. Mr. Pielat, Ministers at the Hague, and Deputies of the Synod of South Holland, containing what they offer to the Consideration of the Ministers of His Majesty's Dutch Chapel at St. James's, and the Dutch Ministers of London, and what they desire of them in Behalf of the Palatines in Pensilvania, n.d., *Records of the Society for the Propagation of the Gospel in Foreign Parts*, 27 reels (East Ardsley, Wakefield, England, 1964 [microfilm]), Letterbook B16, no. 167.

149. T. Penn to Peters, 9 January 1753, Penn Manuscripts, Thomas Penn Letterbook, III, 188, H.S.P. (quote); Joseph Henry Dubbs, "The Founding of the German Churches of Pennsylvania," *PMHB*, 17 (1893), 257.

150. Samuel Chandler to Duke of Newcastle, 2 February 1753, Hinke Collection, Letters and Documents, XI, E.R.H.S.

151. 4 June 1753, Extract from the Annals of the Assembly of the Church of Scotland, *Ibid.*, XII.

152. [W. Smith], "Rise and Progress of the Charitable Scheme," *Pennsylvania Gazette*,

25 February 1755 (quotes); T. Penn to Peters, 9 March 1754, Penn Manuscripts, Thomas Penn Letterbook, III, 307, H.S.P.

153. T. Penn to Peters, 16 August 1753, *Ibid.*, p. 253.

154. William Smith to the Society for the Propagating of Christian Knowledge among the Germans, [13 December 1753] (draft), Labaree, *Franklin Papers*, V, 214–218, quotes p. 215.

155. Peter Collinson to Benjamin Franklin, 26 January 1754, *Ibid.*, p. 190.

156. W. Smith to Peters and Franklin, [February 1754], *Ibid.*, pp. 206–214, quotes pp. 208, 209.

157. Chandler to J. Hamilton, Allen, Peters, Franklin, Weiser, and W. Smith, 15 March 1754, Rev. William Smith Papers, VI, Minutes of the Charity School Society, pp. 2–5, H.S.P., quotes pp. 4, 2. According to Thomas Penn, the London managers thought it best if Schlatter were not a trustee and "that he should appear to act by their direction," but the trustees were to consult with him regularly. To Peters, 26 July 1754, Penn Manuscripts, Thomas Penn Letterbook, III, 351, H.S.P.

158. See, for example, Conrad Weiser, Thoughts of the french encroachment, 1754, Indian and Military Affairs, 1737–1755, pp. 273–274, A.P.S. Franklin's anti-German views are well known, although like the other trustees, he was not consistently anti-German. Whitfield J. Bell, Jr., "Benjamin Franklin and the German Charity Schools," *PAPS*, 99 (1955), 381–387; Glenn Weaver, "Benjamin Franklin and the Pennsylvania Germans," 3*WMQ*, 14 (1957), 536–559.

159. W. Smith to Chandler, 30 May 1754, Rev. William Smith Papers, VI, Minutes of the Charity School Society, pp. 6–10, H.S.P., quote p. 8.

160. 10 August 1754, *Ibid.*, pp. 9–10, quote p. 10.

161. T. Penn to Peters, 21 February 1755, Penn Manuscripts, Thomas Penn Letterbook, IV, 40–41, H.S.P.

162. Parsons to Peters, 23 November 1754, Northampton County Papers, Miscellaneous Manuscripts, 1727–1758, p. 145, H.S.P.

163. *Pensylvanische Berichte*, 16 March 1750, 16 April 1750.

164. *Ibid.*, 16 June 1754.

165. *Ibid.*, 1 September 1754. Sauer concluded by reminding his readers of the blessings of liberty they had found in the province, and urged them to vote for assemblymen who would preserve liberty and not enact unnecessary taxes.

166. *Ibid.*, 16 February 1755, trans. Peters Papers, IV, 84, H.S.P. This issue of the *Pensylvanische Berichte* does not appear in the microfilm edition of the newspaper.

167. Christopher Sauer to [Weiser], 16 September 1755, trans. Rothermund, "German Problem," *PMHB*, 84 (1960), 14–16, quotes p. 14.

168. Chandler to Thomson, 11 July 1755, Hinke Collection, Letters and Documents, XIII, E.R.H.S.

169. Protocol of Coetus, 9–11 April 1755, William J. Hinke, ed. and trans., *Minutes and Letters of The Coetus of the German Reformed Congregations in Pennsylvania 1747–1792, Together with Three Preliminary Reports of Rev. John Philip Boehm, 1737–1744* (Philadelphia, 1903), p. 130.

170. Pennsylvania Coetus to Classis of Amsterdam, June 1755, *Ibid.*, pp. 137–139 (quotes p. 138); W. Smith to T. Penn, 2 July 1755, Penn Manuscripts, Official Correspondence, VII, 81, H.S.P.

171. Henry Melchior Mühlenberg to Friederich Michael Ziegenhagen and Johann Gotthilf Francke, 18 June 1754, *Hallesche Nachrichten*, I, 660–661, quote p. 661.

172. Muhlenberg to Franklin, 3 August 1754, Rev. William Smith Papers, VI, Minutes of the Charity School Society (10 August 1754), pp. 12–18, H.S.P.; 10 August 1754, *Ibid.*, pp. 20–22 (quote p. 21); W. Smith to T. Penn, 2 July 1755, Penn Manuscripts, Official Correspondence, VII, 81, H.S.P. Although Muhlenberg volunteered to oversee the press, the editor of the newspaper that was eventually published was not Muhlenberg but another Lutheran minister, Johann Friederich Handschuch. Rothermund, "German Problem," *PMHB*, 84 (1960), 16–17.

173. Petition of Germans in Easton to the Trustees, 31 July 1755, Northampton County Papers, Miscellaneous Manuscripts, 1727–1758, p. 159, H.S.P.; Petition of Germans in Lower Saucon Township to Parsons, *Ibid.*, p. 161. Other petitions are recorded in the Minutes of the Charity School Society, Rev. William Smith Papers, VI, H.S.P.

174. W. Smith to T. Penn, 10 April 1755, Penn Manuscripts, Official Correspondence, VII, 23, H.S.P.; W. Smith to T. Penn, 2 July 1755, *Ibid.*, p. 81.

175. Sauer to [Weiser], 16 September 1755, Rothermund, "German Problem," *PMHB*, 80 (1964), 15–16.

176. Dietmar Rothermund, *The Layman's Progress: Religious and Political Experience in Colonial Pennsylvania, 1740–1770* (Philadelphia, 1961), p. 119.

177. Parsons to Peters, 23 November 1754, Northampton County Papers, Miscellaneous Manuscripts, 1727–1758, p. 145, H.S.P.

178. T. Penn to Peters, 31 July 1754, Penn Manuscripts, Thomas Penn Letterbook, III, 365, H.S.P.

179. T. Penn to J. Hamilton, 26 February 1755, *Ibid.*, IV, 54–55, quote p. 54.

180. T. Penn to Peters, 22 March 1755, *Ibid.*, p. 75.

181. Bell, "Franklin and the Charity Schools," *PAPS*, 99 (1955), 385–387.

182. Peters to J. Penn, 20 October 1741, Peters Papers, Richard Peters Letterbook, p. 31, H.S.P.

183. [22 August 1741], Assembly, *Votes*, III, 2691. He was to file a written report of the "State of each Vessel" he visited.

184. Council Minutes of 14 September 1741, copied into Assembly, *Votes*, IV, 2710–2713 (21 October 1741), quotes pp. 2712, 2713.

185. Governor to Assembly, 5 January 1741/2, Council, *Minutes*, IV, 507–508 (26 January 1741/2).

186. Assembly to Governor, 7 January 1741/2, *Ibid.*, pp. 509–510 (26 January 1741/2), quotes p. 509.

187. Governor to Assembly, 8 January 1741/2, *Ibid.*, pp. 510–511 (26 January 1741/2); Assembly to Governor, 16 January 1741/2, *Ibid.*, pp. 511–514 (26 January 1741/2); [14 January 1741/2], Assembly, *Votes*, IV, 2723–2734; 17 May 1742, Council, *Minutes*, IV, 524–540; Governor to Assembly, 17 May 1742, *Ibid.*, pp. 540–543; Assembly to Governor, [24 May 1742], Assembly, *Votes*, IV, 2752–2754.

188. Logan to Collinson, 10 July 1742, Logan Papers-Alverthorpe, James Logan Letterbook B, p. 28, H.S.P. (quote); Logan to Daniel Brown, 24 July 1742, *Ibid.*, Letterbook D, p. 25.

189. Governor to Assembly, 16 August 1742, Council, *Minutes*, IV, 598.

190. Assembly to Governor, 20 August 1742, *Ibid.*, p. 614.

191. [6 November 1742], Assembly, *Votes*, IV, 2834.

192. [18–29 January 1742/3], *Ibid.*, pp. 2856–2858, 2862–2863.

193. Ch. 357, 3 February 1742/3, *Statutes*, IV, 382–388, quotes p. 387. This session

of the assembly also enacted a new law to prevent the importation of "poor and impotent persons." People unfit to be disposed of as servants because of age, handicap, or insanity could be ordered to Province Island, as could anyone suspected of carrying an "infectious distemper." Ch. 354, 3 February 1742/3, *Ibid.*, pp. 360–369. This law, however, was repealed by the Crown in 1746 (*Ibid.*, p. 370n.).

194. "The Letter To the Free-Holders of the Province of Pennsylvania, Continued" [1743?], Broadside Collection, H.S.P.

195. [22 November 1743], Assembly, *Votes*, IV, 2906–2907, quotes p. 2907. No further consideration of the petition has been found in the assembly's minutes.

196. *Pensylvanische Geschicht-Schreiber*, 16 February 1745.

197. Reynell and Benjamin Shoemaker to Flexney and Samuel Wragg, 18 December 1744, Coates and Reynell Papers, John Reynell Letterbook, 1744–1745, H.S.P.

198. Winthrop P. Bell, *The "Foreign Protestants" and the Settlement of Nova Scotia: The History of an Arrested British Colonial Policy in the Eighteenth Century* (Toronto, 1961), pp. 86–87.

199. 11 September 1749, Council, *Minutes*, V, 410 (quote); *Pensylvanische Berichte*, 16 September 1749. The most graphic description of conditions aboard immigrant vessels is Gottlieb Mittelberger's *Journey to Pennsylvania* (1756), ed. and trans. Oscar Handlin and John Clive (Cambridge, Mass., 1960), pp. 7–32, 99–102.

200. [22 November 1749], Assembly, *Votes*, IV, 3287–3288.

201. [15–26 January 1749/50], *Ibid.*, pp. 3306, 3311–3313; 27 January 1749/50, Council, *Minutes*, V, 427 (quote). The assembly also ordered "That the Trustees of the *Province Island*, do, as soon as conveniently they can, built [sic] Pest-houses, on that Island to the Value of *One Thousand Pounds*, for the convenient Reception of sick Strangers imported into this Province" on [26 January 1749/50], Assembly, *Votes*, IV, 3316.

202. Ch. 381, 27 January 1749/50, *Statutes*, V, 94–97, quote p. 95.

203. Peters to the Proprietors, 16 February 1749/50, Penn Manuscripts, Official Correspondence, IV, 189, H.S.P.

204. T. Penn to Peters, 30 May 1750, Penn Manuscripts, Thomas Penn Letterbook, II, 313, H.S.P. (second quote); T. Penn to J. Hamilton, 2 July 1750, *Ibid.*, p. 320 (first quote).

205. J. Hamilton to T. Penn, 24 September 1750, Penn Manuscripts, Official Correspondence, V, 53, H.S.P.

206. Board of Trade to Privy Council, 22 April 1751, *Statutes*, V, 498–499. Confirmation of the law occurred on 13 May 1751, *Ibid.*, p. 97n.

207. *Pensylvanische Berichte*, Der Blätgen zum I^ten Februari [1749/50].

208. *Ibid.*, 1 December 1752.

209. [14 February 1754], Assembly, *Votes*, V, 3647.

210. 13 November 1754, Council, *Minutes*, VI, 169; 15 November 1754, *Ibid.*, pp. 170–173 (first quote p. 172); Memorandum to Morris from Graeme and Thomas Bond, 2 December 1754, *Ibid.*, pp. 173–175; Jacob Shoemaker, Deposition, 14 November 1754, *Ibid.*, pp. 175–176 (second quote p. 175).

211. Governor to Assembly, 12 December 1754, Assembly, *Votes*, V, 3766.

212. Norris to Charles, 21 December 1754, Norris Papers, Isaac Norris Sr. and Jr. Letterbook, 1719–1756, pp. 60–61, H.S.P., quotes p. 61.

213. Petition of Germans, read in Council 21 December 1754, *Pa. Arch.*, [1st ser.], II, 217.

214. [23 December 1754], Assembly, *Votes*, V, 2794–2795, quotes p. 2794.

215. *Pensylvanische Berichte*, 1 December 1754, 1 January 1755 (quote).

216. 1 January 1755, Council, *Minutes*, VI, 225–226.

217. 3–8 January 1755, *Ibid.*, pp. 226, 236, 242–244; 1–4 April 1755, *Ibid.*, pp. 344–351, 354–356; 14–17 May 1755, *Ibid.*, pp. 382–388, 393, including messages between the governor and assembly.

218. T. Penn to Morris, 2 July 1755, Penn Manuscripts, Thomas Penn Letterbook, IV, 105, H.S.P.

219. Sauer to William Denny, 15 March 1755, trans. Martin Grove Brumbaugh, *A History of the German Baptist Brethren in Europe and America* (Mount Morris, Ill., 1899), p. 376–382, quote p. 377.

220. Sauer to Denny, 12 May 1755, trans. *Ibid.*, pp. 382–387, quote p. 387.

221. Logan to Settiplace Bellers, 10 August 1741, Logan Papers-Alverthorpe, James Logan Letterbook B, p. 24, H.S.P.

222. J. Hamilton to T. Penn, 8 August 1749, Hamilton Papers, Box 2, James Hamilton Letterbook, 1749–1783, H.S.P.

223. Peters to T. Penn, 16 March 1751/2, Penn Manuscripts, Official Correspondence, V, 217–219, H.S.P., quote p. 217.

224. Peters to [the Proprietors], 15 January 1742/3, Peters Papers, Richard Peters Letterbook, p. 167, H.S.P. (quote); Samuel Smith to J. Smith, 13 March 1753, John Jay Smith Papers, Smith Manuscripts, IV, 110, L.C.P.

225. Parsons to Samuel Rhoads, n.d., Northampton County Papers, Miscellaneous Manuscripts, 1727–1758, p. 59, H.S.P. (quote); Parsons to Rhoads, 17 August 1751, *Ibid.*

226. Account of the Riot of the Germans, at Mr Allen's Iron Works, 20 February 1754, Penn Manuscripts, Official Correspondence, VI, 159, H.S.P. The iron works were located in New Jersey, but the moral was applied to the Pennsylvania situation. Isaac Norris, too, thought that "our latter Importations have raked the Jails thrô Germany & Ireland," and consequently brought to the colony "Inconcievable [sic] numbers of beggars & destempers almost equal to the plague." To Charles, 21 December 1754, Norris Papers, Isaac Norris Sr. and Jr. Letterbook, 1719–1756, p. 60, H.S.P.

227. [15 January 1750/1], Assembly, *Votes*, IV, 3396–3397, quote p. 3396.

228. Irish servants were of interest as well, but not as important as German ones. Sharon Vineberg Salinger, "Labor and Indentured Servants in Colonial Pennsylvania" (Ph.D. diss., University of California, Los Angeles, 1980), pp. 85–90, 128–131.

229. Memorandum, At John Reading's, 2 April 1742, Logan-Fisher-Fox Collection, I, H.S.P.

230. John Pemberton to I. Pemberton Jr., 11 August 1750, Pemberton Papers, VI, 83, H.S.P.

231. Peters to Weiser, 19 September 1751, Peters Papers, III, 47, H.S.P.; Peters to T. Penn, 14 December 1752, Penn Manuscripts, Official Correspondence, V, 313, H.S.P.

232. J. Hamilton to T. Penn, 20 November 1751, *Ibid.*, p. 193. Since Hamilton "prefer[red] the Dutch to the Irish Settlers," Penn suggested that he allow money for a schoolmaster to "teach the Dutch English, or Children to read & write" in order to attract them to the town. To J. Hamilton, 9 January 1753, Penn Manuscripts, Thomas Penn Letterbook, III, 180, H.S.P.

233. Peters to T. Penn, 9 February 1753, Penn Manuscripts, Official Correspondence, VI, 3, H.S.P. He added, "I fear he is dispirited."

234. Peters to T. Penn, 20 June 1752, *Ibid.*, V, 249.

235. Cookson to T. Penn, 4 December 1749, Lancaster County Papers, 1724–1772, p. 65, H.S.P.

236. [George Stevenson] to [Peters], 26 October 1754, John B. Linn and William H. Egle, eds., *Pennsylvania Archives*, 2d ser., 19 vols. (Harrisburg, 1876–1903), VII, 247–249, quotes pp. 247, 249.

237. *Pennsylvania Gazette*, 7 December 1742.

238. *Ibid.*, 19 December 1749.

239. William Bowdoin to James Pemberton, 16 May 1750, Pemberton Papers, VI, 31, H.S.P.

240. *Pennsylvania Gazette*, 8 August 1754.

241. Bell, "*Foreign Protestants.*"

242. *Pennsylvania Gazette*, 21 November 1754.

243. 24 February 1750/1, *Some Cursory Remarks Made by James Birket in his Voyage to North America 1750–1751* (New Haven, 1916), p. 62.

244. William Douglass, *A Summary, Historical and Political, of the First Planting, Progressive Improvements, and Present State of the British Settlements in North-America*, 2 vols. (Boston; reprint ed., London, 1755), II, 119–120, 326 (quotes).

245. Thomas to Bishop of London, 23 April 1748, *S.P.G. Letterbooks*, B16, no. 164.

246. J. Hamilton to T. Penn, 24 September 1750, Penn Manuscripts, Official Correspondence, V, 53, 55, H.S.P., quotes p. 55.

7. Wartime Disruption, 1755–1765

1. Robert L. D. Davidson, *War Comes to Quaker Pennsylvania 1682–1756* (New York, 1957), pp. 90–112.

2. 14 February 1753, Gertrude MacKinney and Charles F. Hoban, eds., *Pennsylvania Archives*, 8th ser., 8 vols., *Votes and Proceedings of the House of Assembly of the Province of Pennsylvania, 1682–1776* (Harrisburg, 1931–1935), V, 3637–3646 (quotes p. 3641 from a letter from the Earl of Holderness, 28 August 1753) [hereafter Assembly, *Votes*]; 19–[20] February 1754, *Ibid.*, p. 3650; [27 February–9 March 1754], *Ibid.*, pp. 3653–3685; 3–13 April 1754, *Ibid.*, pp. 3686–3697; 7–[18 May 1754], *Ibid.*, pp. 3697–3718; [7–16 August 1754], *Ibid.*, pp. 3719–3731, all including copies of letters from England and exchanges between the governor and the assembly.

3. Thomas Penn to James Hamilton, 29 January 1754, Penn Manuscripts, Thomas Penn Letterbook, III, 289, H.S.P.

4. Governor to Assembly, [7 August 1754], Assembly, *Votes*, V, 3721–3722; [8 August 1754], *Ibid.*, pp. 3724–3725 (quote p. 3724).

5. Davidson, *War Comes to Pennsylvania*, pp. 91–196; Alan Tully, *William Penn's Legacy: Politics and Social Structure in Provincial Pennsylvania, 1726–1755* (Baltimore, 1977), pp. 129–133.

6. Essay by "Philanthropos," *Pennsylvania Gazette*, 5 September 1754.

7. Advertisement, *Ibid.*, 12 September 1754.

8. Advertisement, *Ibid.*, 19 September 1754.

9. Advertisement, *Ibid.*

10. Isaac Norris Jr. to [Robert] Charles, 29 April [1755], (postscript to a letter of 28 April 1755), Norris Papers, Isaac Norris Sr. and Jr. Letterbook, 1719–1756, p. 70, H.S.P.

11. *Pensylvanische Berichte*, 16 October 1754, trans. Peters Papers, IV, 84, H.S.P. This issue does not appear in the microfilm edition of the newspaper.

12. Richard Hockley to T. Penn, 3 October 1754 (postscript to a letter of 1 October 1754), Penn Manuscripts, XVIII, 75, H.S.P.

13. Norris to Charles, 7 October 1754, Norris Papers, Isaac Norris Sr. and Jr. Letterbook, 1719–1756, pp. 55–57, H.S.P., quotes p. 55.

14. Philadelphia Quarterly Meeting to London Meeting for Sufferings, 5 May 1755, copied into Philadelphia Yearly Meeting Collection, Philadelphia Meeting for Sufferings Minutes, 1755–1775, pp. 13–16, Q.C.H.C., quotes pp. 15, 16 (2 June 1756).

15. Norris to Charles, 7 October 1754, Norris Papers, Isaac Norris Sr. and Jr. Letterbook, 1719–1756, pp. 55–57, H.S.P., quote p. 56.

16. Governor to Assembly, [15 October 1754], Assembly, *Votes*, V, 3741–3742, quote p. 3742.

17. Assembly to Governor, [18 October 1754], *Ibid.*, pp. 3751–3752, quotes p. 3751.

18. Governor to Assembly, 3 December 1754, *Ibid.*, pp. 3755–3757. Several letters concerning the situation, including one containing royal directions, were presented to the assembly following the speech, *Ibid.*, pp. 3757–3759.

19. James Pemberton to Henton Brown, 15 January 1755, Pemberton Papers, X, 75, H.S.P.

20. [5 December 1754], Assembly, *Votes*, V, 3761.

21. [10 December 1754–3 January 1755], *Ibid.*, pp. 3764–3839, including letters from British officials and exchanges of messages between the governor and the assembly, quote p. 3839.

22. Resolution of Assembly, [10 January 1755], *Ibid.*, p. 3856.

23. 18–[28 March 1755], *Ibid.*, pp. 3857–3872, including messages between the governor and the assembly, quote p. 3857.

24. Governor to Assembly, 1 April 1755, *Ibid.*, p. 3874; [2 April 1755], *Ibid.*, pp. 3877–3878.

25. Governor to Assembly, 16 May 1755, *Ibid.*, pp. 3894–3895, quote p. 3894. See the assembly's justification of its actions in its address to the governor, [17 May 1755], *Ibid.*, pp. 3896–3903.

26. [14–28 June 1755], *Ibid.*, pp. 3904–3924; ch. 402, 28 June 1755, James T. Mitchell and Henry Flanders, comps., *The Statutes at Large of Pennsylvania from 1682 to 1801*, 16 vols. (Harrisburg, 1896–1911), V, 189–193 [hereafter *Statutes*].

27. William Foster to John Smith, 14 October 1755, John Jay Smith Papers, Smith Manuscripts, IV, 238, L.C.P.

28. 24 July–22 August 1754, Assembly, *Votes*, V, 3926–4007 (quote p. 3934); 24 September 1755, *Ibid.*, pp. 4016–4022; [29 September 1755], *Ibid.*, pp. 4025–4050, all including messages between the governor and the assembly. The bill, with the governor's proposed amendments, is printed *Ibid.*, pp. 4072–4080.

29. [Robert Hunter Morris] to Secretary of State, July 1755, Indian and Military Affairs, 1737–1775, pp. 331–333, A.P.S., quote p. 332.

30. [31 July–1 August 1755], Assembly, *Votes*, V, 3935; [7 August 1755], *Ibid.*, p. 3940.

31. For example: Governor to Assembly, 30 December 1754, *Ibid.*, p. 3806; Governor to Assembly, 3 April 1755, *Ibid.*, p. 3879; Governor to Assembly, 24 July 1755, *Ibid.*, pp. 3926–3928; Governor to Assembly, 9 August 1755, *Ibid.*, pp. 3949–3950; Governor to Assembly, 21 August 1755, *Ibid.*, p. 4003.

32. Governor to Assembly, 29 July 1755, *Ibid.*, p. 3932; Governor to Assembly, 6 August 1755, *Ibid.*, p. 3939.

33. Assembly to Governor, [3 January 1755], *Ibid.*, p. 3833.

34. J. Smith to Richard Wells, 22 August 1755, John Smith Letterbook, 1752–1760, p. 70, Q.C.H.C.

35. [R. H. Morris] to Secretary of State, July 1755, Indian and Military Affairs, 1737–1775, pp. 332–333, A.P.S.

36. Governor to Assembly, [24 September 1755], Assembly, *Votes*, V, 4020.

37. Assembly to Governor, [29 September 1755], *Ibid.*, pp. 4032–4033.

38. J. Smith to Wells, 22 August 1755, John Smith Letterbook, 1752–1760, p. 70, Q.C.H.C.

39. "Philadelphus," "To the Freemen of Pennsylvania, and more especially to those of the City and County of Philadelphia" [1755], Broadside Collection, H.S.P.

40. [Christopher Sauer I], "Eine Zu dieser Zeit höchstnöthige Warnung und Erinnerung an die freye Einwohner der Provintz Pensylvanien von Einem, dem die Wohlfahrt des Landes angelegen und darauf bedacht ist" [1755], *Ibid.* The proposals discussed in this essay were derived from William Smith's *Brief State*, discussed below.

41. *Pensylvanische Berichte*, 16 September 1755.

42. Norris to Charles, 5 October 1755, Norris Papers, Isaac Norris Sr. and Jr. Letterbook, 1719–1756, pp. 83–84, H.S.P., quotes p. 83.

43. [James Pemberton] to Richard Partridge, 7 October 1755, Pemberton Papers, XI, 9½, H.S.P.

44. ? to John Fothergill, 17 December 1755, Etting Collection, Pemberton Papers, II, 8, H.S.P.

45. William Smith to Archbishop of Canterbury, 22 October 1755, William Stevens Perry, ed., *Historical Collections Relating to the American Colonial Church*, vol. 2, *Pennsylvania* (Hartford, 1871), pp. 557–558, quotes p. 557.

46. Thomas Willing to Thomas Willing of London, 22 November 1755, Business Collection, Willing Letterbook, 1754–1761, p. 148, H.S.P.

47. W. Smith to T. Penn, [1755], Penn Manuscripts, Official Correspondence, VII, 211, H.S.P.

48. William Allen to Ferdinand John Paris, 25 October 1755, Burd-Shippen-Hubley Family Papers, William Allen/Edward Shippen Letterbook, H.S.P.

49. John Potts, Conrad Weiser, and others to R. H. Morris, 31 October 1755, Horsfield Papers, I, 33, A.P.S.

50. 3–18 November 1755, Assembly, *Votes*, V, 4094–4122, including messages from the governor to the assembly, quote p. 4099.

51. Assembly to Governor, [11 November 1755], *Ibid.*, pp. 4113–4115, quotes p. 4113.

52. [19–25 November 1755], *Ibid.*, pp. 4130–4133, 4151, 4158–4159; ch. 405, 25 November 1755, *Statutes*, V, 197–201 (quotes).

53. [Benjamin Franklin], "A Dialogue between X, Y, and Z," 18 December 1755, Leonard W. Labaree, *et al.*, eds., *The Papers of Benjamin Franklin*, 25 vols. to date (New Haven, 1959–), VI, 296–306, quotes pp. 301, 305. A translation of the dialogue was printed in the *Pensylvanische Berichte* on 16 January 1756.

54. W. Allen and Joseph Turner to David Barclay and Sons, 25 November 1755, Allen and Turner Letterbook, 1755–1774, L.C.P.

55. R. H. Morris to the Proprietors, presented to council for approval on 26 Novem-

ber 1755, *Minutes of the Provincial Council of Pennsylvania, From the Organization to the Termination of the Proprietary Government*, 16 vols. (Philadelphia and Harrisburg, 1851–1853), VI, 741 [hereafter Council, *Minutes*].

56. Board of Trade to Privy Council, 15 April 1756, *Statutes*, V, 540–541; Recommendation of Privy Council, 24 June 1756, *Ibid.*, pp. 542–543; Meeting of King and Council, 7 July 1756, *Ibid.*, p. 532.

57. 3–[24 November] 1755, Assembly, *Votes*, V, 4095–4145, including messages between the governor and the assembly.

58. 24–[27 November 1755], *Ibid.*, pp. 4150–4169; ch. 406, 27 November 1755, *Statutes*, V, 201–212.

59. Willing to Willing of London, 17 December 1755, Business Collection, Willing Letterbook, 1754–1761, p. 154, H.S.P.

60. W. Smith to T. Penn, 27 November 1755, Penn Manuscripts, Official Correspondence, VII, 173, H.S.P.

61. J. Fothergill to Israel Pemberton, 8 July 1755, Etting Collection, Pemberton Papers, II, 3, H.S.P.

62. T. Penn to Hamilton, 10 June 1754, Penn-Hamilton Correspondence, 1747–1771, p. 347, A.P.S.

63. R. H. Morris to T. Penn, [26 December 1754], Penn Manuscripts, Official Correspondence, VI, 257, H.S.P.

64. George Thomas to Richard Peters, 15 January 1755, Peters Papers, IV, 1, H.S.P.

65. William Callender and Norris to London Meeting for Sufferings, 12 January 1755, Norris Papers, Isaac Norris Sr. and Jr. Letterbook, 1719–1756, p. 61, H.S.P. (quote); Norris and Callender to Partridge and Charles, 12 January 1755, *Ibid.*, p. 62.

66. [William Smith], *A Brief State of the Province of Pennsylvania, in which The Conduct of their Assemblies for several Years past is impartially examined* . . . (London, 1755), quotes pp. 5, 8, 26, 28, 32, 33, 14.

67. R. H. Morris to T. Penn, [26 December 1754], Penn Manuscripts, Official Correspondence, VI, 257, H.S.P.; T. Penn to R. H. Morris, 26 February 1755, Penn Manuscripts, Thomas Penn Letterbook, IV, 63, H.S.P. (first three quotes); T. Penn to R. Peters, 25 October 1755, *Ibid.*, p. 176 (fourth quote).

68. Brown to James Pemberton, 11 June 1755, Pemberton Papers, X, 130, H.S.P.

69. John Reynell to Elias Bland, 25 June 1755, Coates and Reynell Papers, John Reynell Letterbook, 1754–1756, H.S.P.; John Pemberton to Samuel Fothergill, 4 July 1757, Pemberton Papers, XXXIV, 57, H.S.P.

70. Partridge to James Pemberton, 20 June 1755, *Ibid.*, p. 137b.

71. Norris to Charles, 28 April 1755, Norris Papers, Isaac Norris Sr. and Jr. Letterbook, 1719–1756, pp. 66–67, H.S.P., quotes p. 67.

72. ? to J. Fothergill, 19 May 1755, Etting Collection, Pemberton Papers, II, 2, H.S.P.

73. W. Allen to Evan Patterson, 23 December 1754, Burd-Shippen-Hubley Family Papers, Allen/Shippen Letterbook, H.S.P.

74. R. H. Morris to Robert Dinwiddie, 3 September 1755, George Edward Reed, ed., *Pennsylvania Archives*, 4th ser., 12 vols. (Harrisburg, 1900–1902), II, 493 [hereafter *Pa. Arch.*].

75. R. H. Morris to William Shirley, 19 August 1755, Indian and Military Affairs, 1737–1775, pp. 351–352, A.P.S.

76. Willing to John Perks, 22 November 1755, Business Collection, Willing Letterbook, 1754–1761, p. 150, H.S.P. An assemblyman allegedly told back inhabitants "that if they kill an Indian they will be prosecuted by the Assembly." Such Quaker leaders were "worse than the Rebles of Scotland; for they, only Ruined themselv's: & these, will destroy Thousands of better, & more honnest Men." Willing to Willing of London, 22 November 1755, *Ibid.*, pp. 148–149.

77. W. Allen and Turner to Barclay and Sons, 24 October 1755, Allen and Turner Letterbook, 1755–1774, L.C.P. (first quote); Petition to King, considered by Board of Trade 26 February 1756, Charles J. Stillé, ed., "The Attitude of the Quakers in the Provincial Wars," *PMHB*, 10 (1886), 294–296 (last two quotes p. 294).

78. W. Allen to Paris, 25 October 1755, Burd-Shippen-Hubley Family Papers, Allen/Shippen Letterbook, H.S.P. (first two quotes); W. Allen and Turner to Barclay and Sons, 7 December 1755, Allen and Turner Letterbook, 1755–1774, L.C.P. (third quote).

79. T. Penn to R. Peters, 13 August 1755, Peters Papers, Letters of Thomas Penn to Richard Peters, 1752–1772, H.S.P.

80. T. Penn to Hamilton, 27 January 1756, Penn-Hamilton Correspondence, 1747–1771, p. 371, A.P.S. (quote); T. Penn to W. Allen, 14 February 1756, Penn Manuscripts, XVII, 101, H.S.P.

81. Brown to James Pemberton, 18 February 1756, Pemberton Papers, Copies of Letters, 1752–1775, pp. 78–79, H.S.P.

82. Minutes of Board of Trade, 18 February 1756, Stillé, "Attitude of Quakers," *PMHB*, 10 (1886), 298–315; T. Penn to R. Peters, 13 March 1756, Penn Manuscripts, Thomas Penn Letterbook, IV, 254, H.S.P. (quote).

83. Board of Trade to Privy Council, 3 March 1756, *Pennsylvania Gazette*, 21 October 1756.

84. T. Penn to R. Peters, 13 March 1756, Penn Manuscripts, Thomas Penn Letterbook, IV, 254, H.S.P.

85. T. Penn to W. Allen, 7 April 1756, *Ibid.*, pp. 262–263.

86. J. Fothergill to ?, 16 March 1756, Etting Collection, Pemberton Papers, II, 10, H.S.P.

87. Brown to James Pemberton, 11 March 1756, Pemberton Papers, XI, 55, H.S.P.; London Meeting for Sufferings to Quarterly Meetings in Pennsylvania, 11 June 1756, Philadelphia Yearly Meeting Collection, Philadelphia Meeting for Sufferings Minutes, 1755–1775, pp. 38–40 (11 December 1756), Q.C.H.C.

88. [4 June 1756], Assembly, *Votes*, V, 4245.

89. Norris to J. Fothergill, 16 June 1756, Norris Papers, Isaac Norris Sr. and Jr. Letterbook, 1719–1756, pp. 99–100, H.S.P.

90. R. Peters to T. Penn, 3 June 1756, Penn Manuscripts, Official Correspondence, VIII, 97, H.S.P. (first quote); R. Peters to T. Penn, 5 June 1756, *Ibid.*, p. 7 (second quote).

91. Willing to Perks, 10 June 1756, Business Collection, Willing Letterbook, 1754–1761, p. 196, H.S.P. (last two quotes); Willing to Willing of London, 15 June 1756, *Ibid.*, p. 200 (first two quotes).

92. ? to J. Fothergill, 26 July 1756, Etting Collection, Pemberton Papers, II, 15, H.S.P.

93. *Pennsylvania Gazette*, 10 June 1756.

94. *Philadelphia Journal and Weekly Advertiser*, 27 May 1756, reprinted in Frederick B.

Tolles, ed., "The Twilight of the Holy Experiment: A Contemporary View," *BFHA*, 45 (1956), 34–37, quote p. 35.

95. *Pensylvanische Berichte*, 16 June 1756.

96. R. Peters to T. Penn, 4 September 1756, Penn Manuscripts, Official Correspondence, VIII, 151, H.S.P.

97. Edward Shippen Jr. to Edward Shippen Sr., 19 September 1756, Burd-Shippen Papers, Box 2 (transcripts), P.H.M.C.

98. R. Peters to T. Penn, 2 October 1756, Penn Manuscripts, Official Correspondence, VIII, 167, H.S.P. (second quote); R. Peters to T. Penn, 30 October 1756, *Ibid.*, p. 181 (first quote).

99. R. H. Morris to Capt. Morris, 8 October 1756, *Ibid.*, p. 169.

100. *Pennsylvania Gazette*, 7 October 1756.

101. [16 October 1756], Assembly, *Votes*, VI, 4385–4386.

102. R. Peters to T. Penn, 30 October 1756, Penn Manuscripts, Official Correspondence, VIII, 181, H.S.P.; [James Pemberton] to S. Fothergill, November 1756, Pemberton Papers, XXXIV, 43, H.S.P.

103. J. Fothergill to ?, 21 February 1757, Etting Collection, Pemberton Papers, II, 20, H.S.P.

104. *Pennsylvania Gazette*, 12 May 1757.

105. W. Allen to Samuel Chandler, 4 February 1758, Penn Manuscripts, Official Correspondence, IX, 5, H.S.P.

106. 5 July 1758, George Bryan, Diary, 1764, L.C. He declared that eighteen of thirty-six assemblymen were Quakers.

107. John Pemberton to William Logan, 12 December 1761, Pemberton Papers, Copies of Letters, 1740–1780, p. 208, H.S.P.; Wayne L. Bockelman and Owen S. Ireland, "The Internal Revolution in Pennsylvania: An Ethnic-Religious Interpretation," *PH*, 41 (1974), 127–148.

108. Foster to J. Smith, 14 October 1755, John Jay Smith Papers, Smith Manuscripts, IV, 238, L.C.P.

109. Jack D. Marietta, *The Reformation of American Quakerism, 1748–1783* (Philadelphia, 1984), pp. 152–156, 158–164, 166–168, 170–174.

110. Ch. 409, 15 April 1756, *Statutes*, V, 219–221; ch. 414, 4 November 1756, *Ibid.*, pp. 266–269; ch. 417, 18 January 1757, *Ibid.*, pp. 281–283; ch. 425, 19 August 1757, *Ibid.*, pp. 311–313; ch. 430, 8 April 1758, *Ibid.*, pp. 334–337; ch. 443, 21 April 1759, *Ibid.*, pp. 424–427; ch. 457, 12 April 1760, *Ibid.*, VI, 51–53; ch. 464, 14 March 1761, *Ibid.*, pp. 91–93; ch. 501, 8 July 1763, *Ibid.*, pp. 297–301; ch. 507, 22 October 1763, *Ibid.*, pp. 320–325; ch. 514, 30 May 1764, *Ibid.*, pp. 367–371. The debates may be followed in Assembly, *Votes*, and Council, *Minutes*.

111. Quakers tried to dissuade Governor Morris from declaring war and, after he did so, to persuade him to rescind the decree, but to no avail. Marietta, *Reformation of Quakerism*, pp. 156–158.

112. Bylaws, 1 December 1756, Minutes of the Friendly Association for Regaining and Preserving Peace with the Indians by Pacific Measures, H.S.P.

113. Letter of Christopher Schultz, 2 November 1756, Andrew S. Berky, ed. and trans., *The Journals and Papers of David Shultze*, 2 vols. (Pennsburg, Pa., 1952), I, 187 (quote); Minutes of a Schwenkfelder Conference, 13 November 1756, *Ibid.*, pp. 187–189; Caspar Kriebel and Schultz to I. Pemberton, 23 May 1757, *Ibid.*, pp. 205–206, with note that funds were first collected on 31 May 1757.

114. Christopher Sauer I to I. Pemberton, 25 April 1756, Richard K. MacMaster, Samuel L. Horst, and Robert F. Ulle, eds., *Conscience in Crisis: Mennonites and Other Peace Churches in America, 1739–1789: Interpretation and Documents* (Scottdale, Pa., 1979), p. 136 (quote); *Pensylvanische Berichte*, 16 August 1756; [Friendly Association] to Michael Ziegler, Dielman Kolb, and other Mennonites near Skippack, 8 April 1757, Mac-Master, *Conscience in Crisis*, pp. 142–143.

115. J. Edwin Hendricks, *Charles Thomson and the Making of a New Nation, 1729–1824* (Cranbury, N.J., 1979), pp. 14–29.

116. 26 July 1756, Minutes of the Friendly Association, H.S.P. Quakers were not, however, opposed to Moravians or their mission among the Indians. On 28 July 1756 several of them visited Moravian settlements and were "highly delighted" with what they saw. *Ibid.*

117. R. Peters to [T. Penn], 4 August 1756, Gratz Collection, Case 2, Box 33a, pp. 72–73, H.S.P.

118. R. Peters to [T. Penn], 14 February 1757, *Ibid.*, pp. 144–145.

119. Willing to Robert Morris, November 1756, Business Collection, Willing Letter-book, 1754–1761, p. 240, H.S.P.

120. T. Penn to William Denny, 10 March 1757, Penn Manuscripts, Thomas Penn Letterbook, V, 94–95, H.S.P. He also informed Peters that he had discussed the Quakers' "Cabals" at the Easton Treaty with the Board of Trade, who "much censored those people for their intrusion on the rights of Government[.]" 29 March 1757, Peters Papers, IV, 87, H.S.P.

121. E. Shippen to James Burd, 14 May 1757, Burd-Shippen Family Collection, Box 2, P.H.M.C.

122. 11–15 July 1757, Minutes of the Friendly Association, H.S.P. The messages between the Friendly Association and Denny were published as a four-page pamphlet, "The Address of the Trustees and Treasurer of the Friendly Association for regaining and preserving Peace with the Indians by Pacific Measures"; a copy is included at the end of the volume of Minutes.

123. Denny to Earl of Loudoun, 10 November 1757, Croghan Papers, Typescripts and Photostats, 1753–1806, Folder 2, H.S.P.

124. T. Penn to R. Peters, 14 November 1757, Peters Papers, IV, 122, H.S.P.

125. Reynell to Thomas Saunders, 29 January 1757, Coates and Reynell Papers, John Reynell Letterbook, 1756–1759, H.S.P.

126. 10 August 1757, Philadelphia Yearly Meeting Collection, Philadelphia Meeting for Sufferings Minutes, 1755–1775, pp. 95–96, Q.C.H.C.

127. T. Penn to Logan, 9 December 1757, Penn Manuscripts, Thomas Penn Letter-book, V, 235–237, H.S.P.; T. and Richard Penn I to Friendly Association, 5 September 1760, Cox-Parrish-Wharton Papers, XII, 18, H.S.P.

128. R. Peters to [John Forbes], 12 July 1758, Sylvester K. Stevens, Donald H. Kent, and Autumn I. Leonard, eds., *The Papers of Henry Bouquet*, vol. 2, *The Forbes Expedition* (Harrisburg, 1951), pp. 197–199; 11 October 1758, Benjamin Chew, Journal of a Journey to Easton [October 1758 Indian Conference], H.S.P.; 17 October 1758, *Ibid.*; George Croghan to Henry Bouquet, 17 July 1763, Croghan Papers, Typescripts and Photostats, 1753–1806, Folder 7, H.S.P.

129. Brooke Hindle, "The March of the Paxton Boys," 3*WMQ*, 3 (1946), 461–486.

130. See, among others: 27 December 1763, George Churchman, Journal, 1759–1766, p. 68, Q.C.H.C. (first quote); David Henderson to Joseph Galloway, 8 p.m., 27

December [1763], Roberts Collection, Colonial Americans, Q.C.H.C. (second quote); John Penn II to John Elder, 29 December 1763, John Elder Photostats, P.H.S. (third quote); J. P[emberton] to Robert Valentine and Richard Downing, 29 December 1763, Cox-Parrish-Wharton Papers, XII, 27, H.S.P. (fourth quote). The only exception I have found is Logan to J. Smith, 30 December 1763, (John Jay Smith Papers, Smith Manuscripts, VI, 102, L.C.P.), in which the rioters were termed "Irish." However, at the most acute stage of the crisis Elder complained that Presbyterians "are wronged at their being charged in bulk" with the murders of the Indians "under the name of Scotch Irish, and other ill natur'd titles." He believed that "Reports, however groundless are spread by designing men on purpose to inflame matters, & enrage the parties ag^t each other, and various means used to accomplish their pernicious ends." Elder to Col. Shippen, 1 February 1764, Elder Photostats, P.H.S.

131. For example: 7 February 1764, Howard M. Jenkins, ed., "Fragments of a Journal Kept by Samuel Foulke, of Bucks County, While a Member of the Colonial Assembly of Pennsylvania, 1762–3–4," *PMHB*, 5 (1881), 70–72; Joseph Shippen Jr. to Burd, 9 February 1764, Shippen Papers, VI, 87, H.S.P.; William Cox to ?, 22 March 1764, Cox-Parrish-Wharton Papers, XI, 33, H.S.P. Exceptions among the polemics that were unconcerned about the ethnic or religious characteristics of the men include [Benjamin Franklin], "A Narrative of the Late Massacres, in Lancaster County, Of a Number of Indians, Friends of this Province, By Persons unknown. With some Observations of the Same" (1764), John R. Dunbar, ed., *The Paxton Papers* (The Hague, 1957), pp. 55–75, and "Copy of a Letter From Charles Read, Esq: To the Hon: John Ladd, Esq: And his Associates, Justices of the Peace for the County of Gloucester" (1764), *Ibid.*, pp. 77–84.

132. Elder to Col. Shippen, 1 February 1764, Elder Photostats, P.H.S.

133. 3 February 1764, Foulke, "Journal," *PMHB*, 5 (1881), 69; ch. 508, 3 February 1764, *Statutes*, VI, 325–328.

134. 1 February 1764, Theodore G. Tappert and John W. Doberstein, eds. and trans., *The Journals of Henry Melchior Muhlenberg*, 3 vols. (Philadelphia, 1942–1958), II, 18–19; 7 February 1764, *Ibid.*, pp. 22–24.

135. 21 February 1764, *Ibid.*, p. 34.

136. Philadelphia Meeting for Sufferings to London Meeting for Sufferings, 25 February 1764, Philadelphia Yearly Meeting Collection, Philadelphia Meeting for Sufferings Minutes, 1755–1775, p. 234, Q.C.H.C.

137. Elizabeth Morris to I. Pemberton, 5 February 1764, Pemberton Papers, Copies of Letters, 1752–1775, p. 207, H.S.P.

138. James Pemberton to J. Fothergill, 7 March 1764, Pemberton Papers, XXXIV, 125–126, H.S.P., quotes p. 125.

139. Richard Waln to Nicholas Waln, 10 March 1764, Waln Collection, Richard Waln Letterbook, 1762–1766, H.S.P.

140. [Isaac Hunt], "A Looking-Glass for Presbyterians. Or A brief Examination of their Loyalty, Merits, and other Qualifications for Government. With some Animadversions on the Quaker unmask'd" (1764), Dunbar, *Paxton Papers*, pp. 246–250, 253–255, quotes p. 246.

141. "Apology of the Paxton Volunteers" (1764), draft manuscript, H.S.P.

142. "The Cloven Foot Discovered" (n.d.), Dunbar, *Paxton Papers*, pp. 85–86, quote p. 85.

143. John Harris to Burd, 1 March 1764, Shippen Papers, VI, 95, H.S.P. (quote);

Hugh Neill to the Secretary, 25 June 1764, *Records of the Society for the Propagation of the Gospel in Foreign Parts*, 27 reels (East Ardsley, Wakefield, England, 1964 [microfilm]), Letterbook B21, no. 120. Quakers were largely unsuccessful in their efforts to persuade men who had taken up arms of the sinfulness of their action, yet inconsistently—and to the discredit of the sect—most offenders were not disciplined or disowned. Marietta, *Reformation of Quakerism*, pp. 194–195.

144. [James Claypoole Jr.], cartoon, 1764, Cartoon Collection, L.C.P.

145. [Thomas Barton], "The Conduct of The Paxton-Men, Impartially represented; The Distresses of the Frontiers, and the Complaints and Sufferings of the People fully stated; and the Methods recommended by the wisest Nations, in such Cases, seriously consider'd. With Some Remarks upon the Narrative, of the Indian-Massacre, lately publish'd" (1764), Dunbar, *Paxton Papers*, pp. 274–282, quote pp. 277–278.

146. 1 February 1764, Muhlenberg, *Journals*, II, 18–19.

147. 6 February 1764, *Ibid.*, pp. 20–22.

148. Philadelphia Meeting for Sufferings to London Meeting for Sufferings, 25 February 1764, Philadelphia Yearly Meeting Collection, Philadelphia Meeting for Sufferings Minutes, 1755–1775, p. 234, Q.C.H.C.

149. W. Allen to Benjamin Chew, 13 April 1764, David A. Kimball and Miriam Quinn, eds., "William Allen-Benjamin Chew Correspondence, 1763–1764," *PMHB*, 90 (1966), 222–223, quotes p. 222.

150. 7 February 1764, George Churchman, Journal, 1759–1766, p. 71, Q.C.H.C.

151. "A Dialogue, Between Andrew Trueman, and Thomas Zealot; About the killing the Indians At Cannestogoe and Lancaster" (n.d.), Dunbar, *Paxton Papers*, pp. 89–90.

152. "An Historical Account, of the late Disturbance, between the Inhabitants of The Back Settlements; Of Pennsylvania, and the Philadelphians, &c." (n.d.), *Ibid.*, p. 128 (quote); [Barton], "Conduct of the Paxton-Men," *Ibid.*, p. 272.

153. The movement for royal government has been fully studied by James H. Hutson, *Pennsylvania Politics 1746–1770: The Movement for Royal Government and Its Consequences* (Princeton, 1972).

154. 29 March 1764, Muhlenberg, *Journals*, II, 54–55.

155. Circular letter of Gilbert Tennent, Francis Alison, and John Ewing, 30 March 1764, Documents Relating to the Province of Pennsylvania and to the American Revolution, no. 26, A.P.S.; 19 March 1764, George Bryan, Diary, 1764, L.C. (second and third quotes); 13 April 1764, *Ibid.* (first quote).

156. Schultz to I. Pemberton, 4 April 1764, VOC-S⁹, S.I.

157. Hutson, *Pennsylvania Politics*, pp. 124–132, 152–168.

158. William Peters to T. Penn, 4 June 1764, Penn Manuscripts, Official Correspondence, IX, 226, H.S.P.

159. Barclay to I. Pemberton, 5 July 1764, Cox-Parrish-Wharton Papers, XI, 34, H.S.P.

160. [Benjamin Franklin], "Cool Thoughts on the Present Situation of Our Public Affairs. In a Letter to a Friend in the Country" (1764), Labaree, *Franklin Papers*, XI, 157–173, quote p. 161.

161. 26 April 1764, George Bryan, Diary, 1764, L.C.

162. Benjamin Franklin to William Strahan, 1 September 1764, Labaree, *Franklin Papers*, XI, 331–332.

163. Franklin to Richard Jackson, 12 July 1764, *Ibid.*, p. 256.

164. W. Peters to T. Penn, 4 June 1764, Penn Manuscripts, Official Correspondence, IX, 226, H.S.P.

165. Richard Penn II to T. Penn, 21 September 1764, *Ibid.*, p. 258.

166. Franklin to Jackson, 1 September 1764, Labaree, *Franklin Papers*, XI, 327–328, quotes p. 327.

167. Benjamin Franklin, "Observations concerning the Increase of Mankind, Peopling of Countries, &c." (1755), *Ibid.*, IV, 227–234, quote p. 234.

168. See, for example: "The Scribbler, Being a Letter From a Gentleman in Town To his Friend in the Country, concerning the present State of Public Affairs; with a Lapidary Character" (1764), *Ibid.*, XI, 385–387; [Hugh Williamson], "What is Sauce for a Goose is also Sauce for a Gander. Being A small Touch in the Lapidary Way. . . ." (1764), *Ibid.*, pp. 381–382; "An Answer to the Plot" (1764), Broadside Collection, H.S.P.; "The Plot. By Way of a Burlesk. To turn F———n out of the Assembly; between H. and P; Proprietary Officers, being two of the Wiser Sort" (1764), Broadside Collection, L.C.P. (quote).

169. "Höret ihr deutsche Bürger in Philadelphia, dass auch Gott auch höre!" [Germantown, 1764], Broadside Collection, H.S.P.

170. "To the Freeholders and other Electors for the City and County of Philadelphia, and Counties of Chester and Bucks" [1764], *Ibid.*

171. "To the Freeholders and Electors Of the City and County of Philadelphia" [1764], *Ibid.*

172. Samuel Purviance Jr. to Burd, 10 September 1764, Shippen Papers, VI, 107, H.S.P.

173. [Burd] to [Purviance], 17 September 1764, *Ibid.*, p. 109.

174. This man was one of the two most successful candidates in the election, and thus eligible to be appointed sheriff. At least one man thought it inconceivable that Governor John Penn would select a man who campaigned "against his own Family & Government." J. Shippen Jr. to Burd, 6 October 1764, *Ibid.*, p. 113.

175. John Penn II to T. Penn, 22 September 1764, Penn Manuscripts, Official Correspondence, IX, 260, H.S.P. This man, William Young, was subsequently commended by Thomas Penn for his "endeavours with your Country people to restore peace to the Province, by opening the Eyes of the deluded multitude[.]" 28 September 1765, Penn Manuscripts, Thomas Penn Letterbook, VIII, 315, H.S.P.

176. J. Penn to T. Penn, 20 October 1764, Penn Manuscripts, Official Correspondence, IX, 278, H.S.P.

177. Benjamin Marshall to Joseph G. Wanton, 5 October 1764, Thomas Stewardson, ed., "Extracts from the Letter-Book of Benjamin Marshall, 1763–1766," *PMHB*, 20 (1896), 207–208, quotes p. 207.

178. Michael F. Metcalf, "Dr. Carl Magnus Wrangel and Prerevolutionary Pennsylvania Politics," *SPHQ*, 27 (1976), 251, 253–254.

179. W. Allen to T. Penn, 25 September 1764, Penn Manuscripts, Official Correspondence, IX, 270, H.S.P.

180. Hutson, *Pennsylvania Politics*, pp. 170–177.

181. Franklin to Jackson, 11 October 1764, Labaree, *Franklin Papers*, XI, 397.

182. 3 October 1764, Muhlenberg, *Journals*, II, 123.

183. Hutson, *Pennsylvania Politics*, pp. 173–176.

184. [William Smith], "An Answer to Mr. Franklin's Remarks, on a Late Protest" (1764), Labaree, *Franklin Papers*, XI, 504–505, quote p. 505.

185. Hutson, *Pennsylvania Politics*, pp. 180–181.

186. 26 October 1764, Muhlenberg, *Journals*, II, 140.

187. Hutson, *Pennsylvania Politics*, pp. 178–191.

188. "To the Freeholders and Electors Of the Province of Pennsylvania" [1765], Broadside Collection, H.S.P.

189. Christopher Sauer II, "Wertheste Landes-Leute, Sonderlich in Philadelphia Bucks und Bercks-County!" [Germantown, 1765], *Ibid*. He also printed a list of the men who voted for and against attending the Stamp Act Congress in this broadside. Those who opposed sending a delegation should not, in his opinion, be reelected.

190. "To the Freeholders And other Electors of Assembly-Men, for Pennsylvania" [1765], Broadside Collection, L.C.P.

191. Purviance to Burd, 20 September 1765, Shippen Papers, VI, 127, H.S.P.

192. Letter without author, addressee, or date, attached to letter cited above, n. 191.

193. William Young to T. Penn, 14 October 1765, Penn Manuscripts, Private Correspondence, V, 75, H.S.P.

194. Hutson, *Pennsylvania Politics*, pp. 200–203.

195. Young to T. Penn, 14 October 1765, Penn Manuscripts, Private Correspondence, V, 75, H.S.P.

196. J. Penn to T. Penn, 14 October 1765, Penn Manuscripts, Additional Miscellaneous Letters, I, 121, H.S.P.

197. 1 October 1765, Muhlenberg, *Journals*, II, 272.

198. Thomas to R. Peters, 15 January 1755, Peters Papers, IV, 1, H.S.P.

199. R. H. Morris to Dinwiddie, 4 July 1755, *Pa. Arch.*, 4th ser., II, 422–423, quote p. 423.

200. Weiser, Thoughts of the french encroachment, 1754, Indian and Military Affairs, 1737–1775, pp. 273–274, A.P.S. (first four quotes); [Weiser] to ?, incomplete letter, n.d., Weiser Papers, Correspondence, II, 25, H.S.P. (last two quotes).

201. Address of German Protestants to R. H. Morris, 20 November 1754, Samuel Hazard, ed., *Pennsylvania Archives*, [1st ser.], 12 vols. (Philadelphia and Harrisburg, 1852–1856), II, 200–202 [hereafter *Pa. Arch.*]. They subsequently requested permission to publish the address in the German and English newspapers. Henry Antes to R. Peters, 24 December 1754, *Ibid.*, pp. 225–226.

202. Davidson, *War Comes to Pennsylvania*, pp. 135–137.

203. *Pensylvanische Berichte*, 1 November 1755.

204. E. Shippen to Bouquet, 4 June 1758, Stevens, *Bouquet Papers*, II, 30–31; Weiser to Bouquet, [14 June 1758], *Ibid.*, pp. 90–91 (quote p. 91); *Pensylvanische Berichte*, 25 November 1758, 23 May 1760.

205. E. Shippen to James Sinclair, 27 August 1759, Shippen Papers, Edward Shippen Letterbook, 1758–1759, A.P.S.

206. Appendix to Votes of Assembly from October 1755 to October 1756 (letters discussing proposed plans to organize a "German" corps), Assembly, *Votes*, V, 4376–4380.

207. R. Peters to [T. Penn], 13 August 1756, Gratz Collection, Case 2, Box 33a, p. 76, H.S.P.

208. Several lists of recruits that indicated the birthplaces of enlistees in a variety of provincial militia units between 1756 and 1759 are included in Shippen Papers, IX, pt. 1, H.S.P., for example, on pp. 5, 19, 63–87, 91–95, 143, 151, and 253. Christian Busse (to Weiser, 21 February 1756, Weiser Papers, Correspondence, I, 81, H.S.P.) empha-

sized the importance of selecting a particular German candidate who spoke English to command a company drawn from an area largely settled by the Scotch-Irish.

209. R. Peters to T. Penn, 8 November 1755, Gratz Collection, Case 2, Box 33a, p. 10, H.S.P.

210. W. Smith to Mr. Vernon, 15 October 1756, Logan Papers, X, 95, H.S.P.

211. "A Letter From a Gentleman in Philadelphia, to a Freeholder in the County Northampton" [Philadelphia, 1757], Broadside Collection, H.S.P.

212. 31 March 1756, Muhlenberg, *Journals*, I, 387–388, quotes p. 387.

213. Hamilton to Timothy Horsfield, 20 September 1763, Horsfield Papers, II, 487, A.P.S. (quotes); Edmund DeSchweinitz, *The Life and Times of David Zeisberger The Western Pioneer and Apostle of the Indians* (Philadelphia, 1870), pp. 274–306.

214. 22 November 1763, Muhlenberg, *Journals*, I, 709. He continued "However, it is very difficult to prove, and still more difficult to remove the people's suspicions."

215. Augustus Gottlieb Spangenberg to R. Peters, 2 December 1755, Hazard Family Papers, H.S.P. (copy); Spangenberg to Chew, 17 October 1760, Spangenberg Papers, I, Sp A V, M.A.

216. Moravian Brethren in Bethlehem, Nazareth, and other places to "Your Honor," n.d., *Ibid.*, II, Folder 1–5. Schwenkfelders also opposed war, but some were willing to financially support an "Independent Guard" intended to offer protection to isolated farmers in their neighborhood. Circular letter of John Mack and Schultz in reply to circular letter of Christopher Weber, Kriebel, Christopher Dresher, and Joseph Leukken dated 2 March 1756, n.d., Berky, *David Shultze Papers*, I, 169–173.

217. R. H. Morris to Horsfield, 22 June 1756, Horsfield Papers, I, 135, A.P.S. (first quote); R. H. Morris to Horsfield, 11 July 1756, *Ibid.*, p. 217 (second quote). Spangenberg subsequently told Denny that Indians were "troublesome guests." 29 November 1756, *Pa. Arch.*, [1st ser.], III, 69.

218. Denny to Spangenberg, 2 December 1756, Horsfield Papers, I, 343, A.P.S.

219. Spangenberg to Denny, 29 November 1756, *Pa. Arch.*, [1st ser.], III, 69-76; 5 December 1756, Council, *Minutes*, VII, 353. Amended lists, reflecting changes in the settlement, were prepared on 26 July 1757 and 22 August 1757. *Pa. Arch.*, [1st ser.], III, 242–244.

220. Thomas Graeme to T. Penn, 1 July 1755, Penn Manuscripts, Official Correspondence, VII, 67, H.S.P.

221. Philip Reading, "The Protestant's Danger and the Protestant's Duty," preached on 22 June 1755, quoted in "Fear of Catholicism in Colonial Pennsylvania, 1755–6," *ACHR*, 17 (1900), 75–76, quotes p. 76.

222. [23 July 1755], Mrs. Conway Robinson Howard, ed., "Extracts from the Diary of Daniel Fisher, 1755," *PMHB*, 17 (1893), 273–274, quote p. 274.

223. Letter from Berks County Justices of the Peace, 23 July 1755, considered in Council on 28 July 1755, *Minutes*, VI, 503. The justices further noted that the priest informed local Catholics that his next visit would be delayed, "Whereupon some imagine they've gone to consult with our Enemies at Du Quesne."

224. 28 July 1755, *Ibid.*, p. 504; Assembly to Governor, 8 August 1755, *Ibid.*, pp. 533–534 (15 August 1755) (quote p. 534).

225. *Pensylvanische Berichte*, 1 August 1755.

226. R. H. Morris to R. Peters, 28 April 1756, *Pa. Arch.*, [1st ser.], II, 647 (first four quotes); R. Peters to R. H. Morris, 6 May 1756, *Ibid.*, p. 654 (fifth quote).

227. 21 March 1757, Council, *Minutes*, VII, 447–448 (quote p. 447); *Pa. Arch.*, [1st ser.], III, 144–145.

228. John Tracy Ellis, *Catholics in Colonial America* (Baltimore, 1965), p. 378.

229. Thomas Barton to the Secretary, 8 November 1762, Perry, *Colonial Church*, p. 343.

230. N. E. S. Griffiths, ed., *The Acadian Deportation: Deliberate Perfidy or Cruel Necessity?* (Toronto, 1969); Émile Lauvrière, *La Tragédie d'un Peuple: Histoire du Peuple Acadien de ses Origines à Nos Jours*, 2 vols. (Paris, 1922).

231. *Pennsylvania Gazette*, 3 July 1755 (quote), 24 July 1755, 6 November 1755.

232. Willing to Perks, 19 November 1755, Business Collection, Willing Letterbook, 1754–1761, pp. 143–144, H.S.P. (first quote p. 144); Willing to Whatley, Meyler, and Hall, 19 November 1755, *Ibid.*, p. 144 (second quote).

233. R. H. Morris to Shirley, 20 November 1755, Penn Manuscripts, Official Correspondence, VII, 161, H.S.P.

234. Governor to Assembly, 24 November 1755, Assembly, *Votes*, V, 4150.

235. [24–25 November 1755], *Ibid.*, pp. 4159–4161 (quote p. 4161); [1 December 1755], *Ibid.*, p. 4167. The Acadians were also assisted by Fr. Robert Harding. Lauvrière, *Tragédie d'un Peuple*, II, 129–130.

236. [John Bartram] to Peter [Collinson], 4 February 1756, Bartram Papers, I, 44, H.S.P. One Anglican priest complained that "some hundreds" of the Neutrals "constantly attend Mass." George Craig to the Secretary, 10 November 1756, George Craig Letterbook, 1751–1775, pp. 12–13, H.S.P. (photocopy).

237. John Baptiste Galerm, in behalf of the Acadians, to the Assembly, [12 February 1756], Assembly, *Votes*, V, 4189–4193, quote p. 4192.

238. Ch. 408, 5 March 1756, *Statutes*, V, 215–219, quotes pp. 215, 217. Several of the commissioners appointed to find homes for the Neutrals have French surnames (i.e., DeNormandie, LeFevre), and perhaps could speak French. Frontier counties were not obliged to receive Neutrals, probably for security reasons.

239. [10 April 1756], Assembly, *Votes*, V, 4216.

240. [27 August 1756], *Ibid.*, pp. 4293–4295; 2 September 1756, Council, *Minutes*, VII, 239–241.

241. *Pensylvanische Berichte*, 1 March 1756, 1 April 1756 (quote).

242. Ch. 416, 18 January 1757, *Statutes*, V, 278–280, quote p. 279. A supplementary law directed the way in which those who could not support themselves were to be maintained. Ch. 426, 27 September 1757, *Ibid.*, pp. 313–315.

243. 7 February 1757, Council, *Minutes*, VII, 408; 8 February 1757, Assembly, *Votes*, VI, 4509–4512, quote p. 4509.

244. 27 February 1761, *Ibid.*, p. 5206. The committee inquiring into the condition of the Neutrals noted that parents opposed this law "on Account of their Religion."

245. References to the Neutrals are scattered throughout Council, *Minutes*, and Assembly, *Votes*; they are last mentioned on 21 September 1775, *Ibid.*, VIII, 7253.

246. 21 March 1757, Council, *Minutes*, VII, 446 (quote from the arrest warrant); petition from Mrs. John Baptiste Galerm to Denny, presented 23 March 1758, Indian and Military Affairs, 1737–1775, pp. 587–590, A.P.S.

247. *Pennsylvania Gazette*, 18 December 1755, 11 March 1756, 3 August 1758; *Pensylvanische Berichte*, 16 February 1756.

248. E. Shippen Sr. to E. Shippen Jr., 17 April 1765, Burd-Shippen Family Collection, Box 2, P.H.M.C.

249. Wilton Paul Ledet, "Acadian Exiles in Pennsylvania," *PH*, 9 (1942), 125–126.

250. Extract of a memorial to the King, drafted by Anthony Benezet, 1760, George S. Brookes, *Friend Anthony Benezet* (Philadelphia, 1937), pp. 477–478, quotes p. 478.

251. Benezet to J. Smith, 1 August 1760, *Ibid.*, pp. 239–242, quote pp. 240–241.

252. Benezet, James Pemberton, and Evan Morgan to T. and R. Penn I, 26 August 1760, Etting Collection, Pemberton Papers, I, 51, 99, H.S.P., quotes p. 51.

253. T. Penn to I. Pemberton and others, 9 January 1761, Etting Collection, Early Quakers and Penn Family, p. 16, H.S.P.; J. Fothergill to I. Pemberton, 10 January 1761, Etting Collection, Pemberton Papers, II, 45, H.S.P. (quote); Lauvrière, *Tragédie d'un Peuple*, II, 134.

254. The assembly addressed the governor on the question of enlisting servants, which he referred to General Shirley. He replied, however, that the King had a right to the services of anyone who voluntarily enlisted. R. H. Morris to Shirley, 16 February 1756, Charles H. Lincoln, ed., *Correspondence of William Shirley Governor of Massachusetts and Military Commander in America 1731–1760*, 2 vols. (New York, 1912), II, 391–392; Shirley to R. H. Morris, 20 February 1756, *Ibid.*, pp. 391n.–392n.; R. H. Morris to Shirley, 24 February 1756, *Ibid.*, pp. 399n.–400n.

255. W. Allen and Turner to Barclay and Sons, 23 April 1756, Allen and Turner Letterbook, 1755–1774, L.C.P.

256. R. Peters to T. Penn, 29 April 1756, Penn Manuscripts, Official Correspondence, VIII, 79, H.S.P.; Reasons offered to the Governor, by a Committee of Assembly, at a second Conference, in Answer to the Governor's Objections to the Bill for granting Sixty Thousands Pounds to the King's Use, [14 September 1756], Assembly, *Votes*, V, 4322 (quotes); W. Allen and Turner to Jacob Bosanquet, September 1756, Allen and Turner Letterbook, 1755–1774, L.C.P.

257. Advertisements for indentured servants may be found in many issues of the *Pennsylvania Gazette* and *Pensylvanische Berichte* during this period.

258. For some examples, see: W. Allen and Turner to John Allen, 21 October 1761 (two letters of this date), Allen and Turner Letterbook, 1755–1774, L.C.P.; W. Allen and Turner to Lynford Lardner, 13 December 1762, *Ibid.*; James Pemberton to John Hunt, 27 October 1763, Pemberton Papers, John Hunt Correspondence, H.S.P. (quote); Abel James and Henry Drinker to Neate, Pigou, and Booth, 20 October 1764, Drinker Papers, James and Drinker Letterbook, 1764–1765, p. 12, H.S.P.

259. George Armstrong to T. Penn, 30 October 1764, Penn Manuscripts, Official Correspondence, IX, 284, H.S.P.

260. Hunt to James Pemberton, 10 December 1763, Pemberton Papers, John Hunt Correspondence, H.S.P.

261. Thomas Clifford and Joseph Morris to Samuel Smith, 22 November 1764, Pemberton Papers, XXVII, Thomas and John Clifford Letterbook, 1759–1766, H.S.P.

262. See, for example: Minutes of the St. Andrews Society, 1749–1776, A.P.S.; Minutes of the St. George's Society, 1772–1812, H.S.P. The bylaws of these organizations declared that national societies arose not out of exclusiveness but because the need for charity was so great that it had to be channeled. Ties to the homeland were "natural" extensions of the "family."

263. Erna Risch, "Immigrant Aid Societies before 1820," *PMHB*, 60 (1936), 18–29;

Oswald Seidensticker, *Geschichte der Deutschen Gesellschaft von Pennsylvanien, von der Zeit der Gründung 1764 bis zum Jahre 1876* (Philadelphia, 1876), pp. 1–52.

264. 11 January 1765, Assembly, *Votes*, VII, 5696–5699; 16 January 1765, *Ibid.*, p. 5707.

265. 24 January 1765, *Ibid.*, pp. 5715–5722.

266. Ch. 527, 18 May 1765, *Statutes*, VI, 432–440.

267. Advice of Benjamin Chew, 16 June 1759, Council, *Minutes*, VIII, 355.

268. Ch. 345, 20 June 1759, *Statutes*, V, 443–445.

269. T. Penn to R. Peters, 9 February 1760, Penn Manuscripts, Thomas Penn Letterbook, VI, 206, H.S.P.

270. Objections to the act for the relief of the heirs of deceased aliens, n.d., *Statutes*, V, 669–670; Board of Trade to Privy Council, 24 June 1760, *Ibid.*, pp. 724–726; Repeal by King in Council, 2 September 1760, *Ibid.*, pp. 653–655.

271. 10 January 1765, Assembly, *Votes*, VII, 5692–5693; 16 January 1765, *Ibid.*, p. 5706 (quote).

272. *Pensylvanische Berichte*, 16 March 1755, 3 September 1757, 20 July 1759; *Philadelphische Staatsbote*, 22 March 1762, 20 September 1762.

273. Certificate of Naturalization for Frick Unander, 30 November 1759, *Pa. Arch.*, [1st ser.], III, 692–693; ch. 493, 4 March 1763, *Statutes*, VI, 270–272.

274. 13 January 1763, Assembly, *Votes*, VI, 5373; 18 January 1763, *Ibid.*, pp. 5375–5376; 1 February 1763, *Ibid.*, pp. 5391–5392; ch. 493, *Statutes*, VI, 270-272; 12 January 1765, Assembly, *Votes*, VII, 5700; ch. 521, 2 February 1765, *Statutes*, VI, 399–401.

275. T. Penn to R. H. Morris, 3 July 1755, Gratz Collection, Case 2, Box 33, H.S.P.

276. For example: T. Penn to John Armstrong, 4 June 1760, Penn Manuscripts, Thomas Penn Letterbook, VI, 250, H.S.P.; T. Penn to W. Smith, 8 March 1765, *Ibid.*, VII, 225–226; T. Penn to W. Allen, 13 July 1765, *Ibid.*, pp. 271–273.

277. Harold E. Gillingham, "Lotteries in Philadelphia Prior to 1776," *PH*, 5 (1938), 89–90, 94–100.

278. Petition of Presbyterian Synod of Philadelphia to T. and R. Penn I, 10 February 1757, Penn Manuscripts, Additional Miscellaneous Letters, I, 101, H.S.P.; Attorney General C. Pratt's opinion on the Presbyterian Charter, 15 October 1758, *Statutes*, V, 636–646; T. Penn to R. Peters, 12 April 1759, Penn Manuscripts, Thomas Penn Letterbook, VI, 84, H.S.P.

279. The Anglican church in Philadelphia had earlier received a charter. T. Penn to W. Smith, 8 March 1765, *Ibid.*, VIII, 225–226; J. Penn to T. Penn, 14 October 1765, Penn Manuscripts, Additional Miscellaneous Letters, I, 121, H.S.P. (quote); Nachricht von der Gemeine in Philadelphia, Johann Ludewig Schulze, ed., *Nachrichten von den vereinigten Deutschen Evangelisch Lutherischen Gemeinen in Nord-America, absonderlich in Pensylvanien*, 2 vols. (Halle, 1787), II, 1235–1240, 1256–1260 [hereafter *Hallesche Nachrichten*].

280. E. Shippen to R. Peters, 20 May 1754, Shippen Papers, I, 155, H.S.P.; Alexander Murray to the Secretary, 25 January 1764, *S.P.G. Letterbooks*, B21, no. 101.

281. Benjamin Lightfoot to ?, 11 November 1763, Cox-Parrish-Wharton Papers, XI, 32, H.S.P.

282. George Craig to the Secretary, 4 April 1756, George Craig Letterbook, 1751–1775, p. 11, H.S.P.; William Thompson to the Secretary, 25 December 1762, *S.P.G.*

Letterbooks, B21, no. 290; Thomas Barton to the Secretary, 16 November 1764, *Ibid.*, no. 14.

283. Barton to the Secretary, 6 December 1760, *Ibid.*, no. 8; Neill to the Secretary, 5 June 1762, *Ibid.*, no. 118; Murray to the Secretary, 25 January 1764, *Ibid.*, no. 101; Craig to the Secretary, 3 August 1764, George Craig Letterbook, 1751–1775, p. 27, H.S.P. (quote).

284. Craig to the Secretary, 10 November 1756, *Ibid.*, pp. 12–13 (quotes p. 12); W. Smith to the Secretary, 26 August 1760, *S.P.G. Letterbooks*, B21, no. 248; Barton to the Secretary, 8 November 1762, *Ibid.*, no. 12. Conversions to Protestantism were not, however, unknown. 25 March 1763, Auszuge aus Hrn. Pastor Mühlenbergs Tageregister vom Jahr 1763, *Hallesche Nachrichten*, II, 1093.

285. Barton to the Secretary, 8 November 1756, *S.P.G. Letterbooks*, B21, no. 1; Thompson to the Secretary, 10 March 1762, *Ibid.*, no. 288; Murray to the Secretary, 9 April 1763, *Ibid.*, no. 100; Thompson to the Secretary, 25 March 1765, *Ibid.*, no. 292; Neill to the Secretary, 25 June 1765, *Ibid.*, no. 122.

286. 6 March 1763, Muhlenberg, *Journals*, I, 602.

287. 18 October 1759, *Ibid.*, p. 418. Members of the Baptist congregation also asked Muhlenberg to conduct "a private service of edification" later that day.

288. 7 August 1763, *Ibid.*, p. 661.

289. Neill to the Secretary, 12 May 1760, *S.P.G. Letterbooks*, B21, no. 110.

290. Barton to the Secretary, 10 November 1766, Perry, *Colonial Church*, pp. 409–410.

291. Jacob Rogers to Craig, 4 April 1755, copied in letter from Rogers to Spangenberg, 9 April 1755, Journal Collection, JD IV 2a, M.A.

292. Craig to Rogers, 5 April 1755, copied in *Ibid.*

293. 25 January 1765, Muhlenberg, *Journals*, II, 201.

294. Craig to the Secretary, 17 July 1760, George Craig Letterbook, 1751–1775, pp. 19–20, H.S.P.; Neill to Secretary, 8 June 1761, *S.P.G. Letterbooks*, B21, no. 112.

295. 26 August 1763, Muhlenberg, *Journals*, I, 665–666 (quote p. 665); Heinrich P. Suhr, ed. and trans., "Muhlenberg's Opinion on the Introduction of English in the Swedish Churches, 1761," *LCQ*, 13 (1940), 79–85.

296. St. George's Church, Philadelphia, to Archbishops of Canterbury and York, 21 October 1764, Perry, *Colonial Church*, pp. 396–398.

297. 12 September 1763, Muhlenberg, *Journals*, I, 670.

298. 3 October 1764, *Ibid.*, II, 123; Charles H. Glatfelter, "The Colonial Pennsylvania German Lutheran and Reformed Clergyman" (Ph.D. diss., Johns Hopkins University, 1952), pp. 83–85, 124–129.

299. Dietmar Rothermund, "The German Problem of Colonial Pennsylvania," *PMHB*, 84 (1960), 17–18.

300. *Pensylvanische Berichte*, 16 November 1754. Another antislavery article was published *Ibid.*, 13 February 1761.

301. 19 April 1759, Philadelphia Yearly Meeting Collection, Philadelphia Meeting for Sufferings Minutes, 1755–1775, p. 156, Q.C.H.C.; 17 April 1760, *Ibid.*, p. 176.

302. Benezet to S. Smith, 17 May 1765, Anthony Benezet Papers, Q.C.H.C.

303. Anne Dexter Gordon, "The College of Philadelphia, 1747–1779: Impact of an Institution" (Ph.D. diss., University of Wisconsin, 1975), pp. 17–18, 26, 31–32; Deborah Mathias Gough, "Pluralism, Politics, and Power Struggles: The Church of England in Colonial Philadelphia, 1695–1789" (Ph.D. diss., University of Pennsylvania,

1978), pp. 398–402. For the religious affiliation of graduates of the college and their families, see Gordon, "College of Philadelphia," pp. 118, 119, 221.

304. T. Penn to Hamilton, 18 October 1760, Penn Manuscripts, Thomas Penn Letterbook, VI, 309, H.S.P. (second quote); T. Penn to R. Peters, 10 December 1762, *Ibid.*, VII, 235 (first quote).

305. W. Smith to R. Peters, 10 July 1762, Rev. William Smith Papers, II, 91, H.S.P. (quote); W. Smith to R. Peters, 2 March 1763, *Ibid.*, p. 120; W. Smith to R. Peters, 17 June 1763, *Ibid.*, p. 141.

306. Gough, "Pluralism, Politics, and Power Struggles," pp. 413–417.

307. W. Smith to R. Peters, 11 August 1763, Rev. William Smith Papers, II, 143, H.S.P. (second quote); W. Smith to R. Peters, 25 August 1763, *Ibid.*, pp. 146–147 (first quote); Archbishop of Canterbury to Jacob Duché, 17 September 1763, Perry, *Colonial Church*, pp. 389–390.

308. George Churchman Jr. to J. Smith, 26 December 1761, John Jay Smith Papers, Smith Manuscripts, I, 94, L.C.P.

309. Neill to the Secretary, 2 May 1763, S.P.G. Letterbooks, B21, no. 117.

310. Henry Schlingluff and others to Christopher Sauer II, August 1764, trans. Donald F. Durnbaugh, ed., *The Brethren in Colonial America: A Source Book on the Transplantation and Development of the Church of the Brethren in the Eighteenth Century* (Elgin, Ill., 1967), pp. 202–206.

311. 28 May 1760, Minutes of the Synod of New York and Philadelphia, William Morrison Engles, ed., *Records of the Presbyterian Church in the United States of America Embracing the Minutes of the Presbytery of Philadelphia, from A.D. 1706 to 1716: Minutes of the Syond [sic] of Philadelphia, from A.D. 1717 to 1758: Minutes of the Synod of New York, from A.D. 1745 to 1758: Minutes of the Synod of New York and Philadelphia, from A.D. 1758 to 1788* (Philadelphia, 1841), p. 306.

312. 25 May 1761, *Ibid.*, p. 311; 26 May 1761, *Ibid.*, p. 312 (quote). See also Gilbert Tennent's letter, 10 July 1760, explaining why he had been involved in writing to the archbishop, Tennent Papers, P.H.S.

313. See, for example: 22 March 1759, James Kenny, A Journey to ye Westward [1757–1758], p. 22, H.S.P.; 12 May 1761, James Kenny, A Journey to Pittsburgh, 1761–1763, p. 4, H.S.P.; 23 December 1761, Diary of Brr. Friis and Samuel Herr, 9 November 1761–26 March 1762, Journey Collection, JA IV 1, M.A.

314. 21 January 1759, Kenny, Journey to ye Westward, p. 12, H.S.P. A Quaker book was given to a family member who expressed an interest in it

315. 1 December 1761, Kenny, Journey to Pittsburgh, H.S.P.

316. Auszug aus einem Schreiben des Herrn Pastor [Johann Friederich] Handschuchs zu Philadelphia an den Herrn Hofprediger [Friederich Michael] Ziegenhagen und Herrn Doctor [Johann Gotthilf] Francke, vom 30sten September 1757, *Hallesche Nachrichten*, II, 707.

317. *Pensylvanische Berichte*, 16 December 1755, 16 January 1756, 1 February 1756; *Pennsylvania Gazette*, 8 January 1756.

318. *Ibid.*, 21 July 1763 (first quote), 28 July 1763, 4 August 1763 (second quote).

319. Spangenberg to R. Peters, 2 December 1755, Hazard Family Papers, H.S.P. (copy).

320. Sydney V. James, *A People Among Peoples: Quaker Benevolence in Eighteenth-Century America* (Cambridge, Mass., 1963), pp. 203–204.

321. Br. Lamech and Agrippa, comps., *Chronicon Ephratense, Enthaltend den Lebens-*

Lauf des ehrwürdigen Vaters in Christo Friedsam Gottrecht, Weyland Stiffiers und Vorstehers des geistl. Ordens der Einsamen in Ephrata in der Graffschaft Lancaster in Pennsylvania (Ephrata, Pa., 1786), trans. J. Max Hark (Lancaster, Pa., 1889), pp. 236–237.

322. Norris to Charles, 29 April [1755] (postscript to a letter of 28 April 1755), Norris Papers, Isaac Norris Sr. and Jr. Letterbook, 1719–1756, pp. 70–71, H.S.P.

8. The Revolutionary Era, 1765–1783

1. *Pennsylvania Gazette*, 26 December 1765.

2. George R. Mellor, "Emigration from the British Isles to the New World, 1765–1775," *History*, n.s., 40 (1955), 68.

3. Thomas Clifford to George Stockham, 26 November 1767, Pemberton Papers, XXVIII, Thomas and John Clifford Letterbook, 1767–1773, H.S.P.

4. T. Clifford to Lancelot Cowper, 6 December 1768, *Ibid.* (first and third quotes); T. Clifford to James Russell, 7 December 1768, *Ibid.* (second quote).

5. Benjamin Fuller to Solomon Watson, 8 July 1769, Business Collection, Benjamin Fuller Letterbook, 1762–1781, p. 16, H.S.P.

6. T. Clifford to Russell, 19 November 1768, Pemberton Papers, XXVIII, Thomas and John Clifford Letterbook, 1767–1773, H.S.P.

7. Abel James and Henry Drinker to Neate, Pigou, and Booth, 14 June 1766, Drinker Papers, James and Drinker Letterbook, 1764–1766, pp. 437–438, H.S.P., quote p. 438.

8. Joseph White to John Pemberton, 13 October 1767, Cox-Parrish-Wharton Papers, XII, 32, H.S.P.

9. William Murray to Michael and Bernard Gratz, 24 April 1769, William Vincent Byars, ed., *B. and M. Gratz, Merchants in Philadelphia, 1754–1798: Papers of Interest to Their Posterity and the Posterity of Their Associates* (Jefferson City, Mo., 1916), p. 92.

10. T. Clifford to Cowper, 18 September 1769, Pemberton Papers, XXVIII, Thomas and John Clifford Letterbook, 1767–1773, H.S.P.

11. Fuller to Watson, 8 July 1769, Business Collection, Benjamin Fuller Letterbook, 1762–1781, pp. 16–17, H.S.P.

12. See Bernard Bailyn, *Voyagers to the West: A Passage in the Peopling of America on the Eve of the Revolution* (New York, 1986).

13. *Pennsylvania Gazette*, 6 October 1773, 3 November 1773, 23 March 1774, 30 March 1774.

14. "A Friend to the Poor," [Benjamin Franklin], "On a Proposed Act to Prevent Emigration," [December? 1773], Leonard W. Labaree, *et al.*, eds., *The Papers of Benjamin Franklin*, 25 vols. to date (New Haven, 1959–), XX, 522–528, quotes pp. 523, 524, 528.

15. "A Friend to Pennsylvania," *Pennsylvania Gazette*, 15 March 1775.

16. William Logan [Jr.?] to Samuel Coates, 24 January 1767, Coates and Reynell Papers, Samuel Coates Letterbook, 1763–1781, H.S.P. (copy).

17. Alexander Mackraby to Philip Francis, 2 December 1769, "Philadelphia Society before the Revolution. Extracts from Letters of Alexander Mackraby to Sir Philip Francis, from Memoirs of Sir Philip Francis, K.C.B.," *PMHB*, 11 (1887), 492.

18. Jasper Yeates to Duncan Campbell, 10 August 1770, Burd-Shippen Family Papers, Box 2 (transcripts), P.H.M.C.

19. *Pennsylvania Gazette*, 8 December 1768.

20. 13 May 1780, Christopher Marshall Papers, Remembrancer F, H.S.P.

21. 2–3 May 1778, *Ibid.*, Remembrancer E, quote 3 May 1778.

22. 18 September 1769, Theodore G. Tappert and John W. Doberstein, eds. and trans., *The Journals of Henry Melchior Muhlenberg*, 3 vols. (Philadelphia, 1942–1958), II, 423–424.

23. 29 June 1767, *Ibid.*, pp. 342–343.

24. See, for example: 30 January 1766, Gertrude MacKinney and Charles F. Hoban, eds., *Pennsylvania Archives*, 8th ser., 8 vols., *Votes and Proceedings of the House of Representatives of the Province of Pennsylvania, 1682–1776* (Harrisburg, 1931–1935), VII, 5845–5846 [hereafter Assembly, *Votes*]; 1 February 1766, *Ibid.*, p. 5848; ch. 543, 20 September 1766, James T. Mitchell and Henry Flanders, comps., *The Statutes at Large of Pennsylvania from 1682 to 1801*, 16 vols. (Harrisburg, 1896–1911), VII, 47–48 [hereafter *Statutes*]; 4 January 1769, Assembly, *Votes*, VII, 6295–6296; ch. 637, 9 March 1771, *Statutes*, VIII, 116–117; 28 January 1772, Assembly, *Votes*, VIII, 6773–6774; ch. 667, 21 March 1772, *Statutes*, VIII, 256–257; ch. 685, 26 February 1773, *Ibid.*, pp. 337–338; letter of Stephen Cottrell reporting conclusions of a meeting of the Privy Council on 19 May 1773, *Minutes of the Provincial Council of Pennsylvania, From the Organization to the Termination of the Proprietary Government*, 16 vols. (Philadelphia and Harrisburg, 1851–1853), X, 103–104 (11 October 1773) (quote p. 104) [hereafter Council, *Minutes*].

25. 5 September 1765, Minutes, Board of Property, William H. Egle and George E. Reed, eds., *Pennsylvania Archives*, 3d ser., 30 vols. (Harrisburg, 1894–1898), I, 111 (quote) [hereafter *Pa. Arch.*]; Edward Shippen to Joseph Shippen, 31 May 1769, Shippen Papers, Edward Shippen Letterbook, 1768–1772, A.P.S.; Thomas Penn to James Tilghman, 27 July 1771, Penn Manuscripts, Thomas Penn Letterbook, X, 160, H.S.P.; T. Penn and John Penn II to Richard Penn II, 30 April 1772, *Ibid.*, p. 207; 15 April 1776, *Pa. Arch.*, 3d ser., I, 407–408.

26. T. Penn to William Allen, 16 April 1768, Penn Manuscripts, Thomas Penn Letterbook, IX, 244, H.S.P.; T. Penn to William Smith, 3 March 1769, *Ibid.*, X, 341.

27. J. Shippen Jr. to E. Shippen Sr., 15 March 1771, Balch Collection, Shippen Papers, II, 10, H.S.P. (brackets in original).

28. Ch. 660, 21 March 1772, *Statutes*, VIII, 229–230, quote p. 229.

29. 17 January 1772, Assembly, *Votes*, VIII, 6756–6757, quote p. 6757.

30. Benjamin Franklin to Benjamin Rush, 22 August 1772, Labaree, *Franklin Papers*, XIX, 280; *Statutes*, VIII, 230n.

31. Nachricht von der Gemeine zu Lancaster, Johann Ludewig Schulze, ed., *Nachrichten von den vereinigten Deutschen Evangelisch-Lutherischen Gemeinen in Nord-America, absonderlich in Pensylvanien*, 2 vols. (Halle, 1787), II, 1338 [hereafter *Hallesche Nachrichten*].

32. 25–27 June 1769, Muhlenberg, *Journals*, II, 402 404, 412; Casparus Diterieus Weyberg to Richard Peters, 21 April 1772, Peters Papers, VII, 119, H.S.P.

33. W. Smith to Bishop of London, 18 December 1766, William Stevens Perry, ed., *Historical Collections Relating to the American Colonial Church*, vol. 2, *Pennsylvania* (Hartford, 1871), pp. 411–412; T. Penn to J. Penn, 17 July 1767, Penn Manuscripts, Thomas Penn Letterbook, IX, 141, H.S.P.; Thomas Barton to William Johnson, 22 July 1767, Byars, *B. and M. Gratz*, p. 81 (quote); Peters to Bishop of London, 30 August 1768, Perry, *Colonial Church*, pp. 432–433; Barton to the Secretary, 17 December 1770, *Records of the Society for the Propagation of the Gospel in Foreign Parts*, 27 reels (East Ardsley, Wakefield, England, 1964 [microfilm]), Letterbook B21, no. 23.

34. Anne Elizabeth Polk Diffendal, "The Society for the Propagation of the Gospel

in Foreign Parts and the Assimilation of Foreign Protestants in British North America" (Ph.D. diss., University of Nebraska, 1974), pp. 89–94.

35. Barton to James Burd, 2 January 1773, Shippen Papers, VII, 63, H.S.P.; J. Burd to E. Shippen Sr., 1 April 1773, Balch Collection, Shippen Papers, II, 17, H.S.P.; Yeates to J. Burd, 28 February 1774, Shippen Papers, VII, 81, H.S.P.

36. 26 November 1766, Minutes of the Presbytery of Philadelphia, 1762–1771, p. 42, P.H.S.; 11 March 1767, *Ibid.*, p. 45; 4 August 1768, *Ibid.*, pp. 59–60; 5 August 1768, *Ibid.*, p. 60.

37. Coetus of Pennsylvania to Classis of Amsterdam, 6 June 1774, William J. Hinke, ed. and trans., *Minutes and Letters of The Coetus of the German Reformed Congregations in Pennsylvania 1747–1792, Together with Three Preliminary Reports of Rev. John Philip Boehm, 1734–1744* (Philadelphia, 1903), p. 347. After the Revolution, several Christians contributed toward the costs incurred in building the first synogogue in Philadelphia. Edwin Wolf 2d and Maxwell Whiteman, *The History of the Jews of Philadelphia from Colonial Times to the Age of Jackson* (Philadelphia, 1957), pp. 143–144.

38. For example: Alexander Murray to the Secretary, 25 September 1768, *S.P.G. Letterbooks*, B21, no. 106; Barton to the Secretary, 17 December 1770, *Ibid.*, no. 23; W. Smith to the Secretary, 6 July 1771, *Ibid.*, no. 270.

39. John Andrews to the Secretary, 10 January 1770, *Ibid.*, no. 171.

40. See, among others: 7 April 1767, Muhlenberg, *Journals*, II, 325–326; 27 May 1770, *Ibid.*, pp. 441–442; Oxford Vestry to the Secretary, 27 May 1771, *S.P.G. Letterbooks*, B21, no. 129; 20 July 1775, Robert Greenhalgh Albion and Leonidas Dodson, eds., *Philip Vickers Fithian: Journal, 1775–1776* . . . (Princeton, 1934), p. 64; [15 January 1776], John McMillan, Journal, p. 24, H.S.P. (quote).

41. Robert James Gough, "Towards a Theory of Class and Social Conflict: A Social History of Wealthy Philadelphians, 1775 to 1800" (Ph.D. diss., University of Pennsylvania, 1977), pp. 447–450.

42. Inhabitants of Bristol Township to Citizens of Philadelphia, 11 April 1771, Provincial Delegates Letters, I, 19, H.S.P.

43. Original as well as Subsequent Proceedings of the order and Management of the School and Building the Concord Schoolhouse at the upper End of Germantown, 1775–1845, AM 37070, H.S.P. Other Germantown schools also provided bilingual instruction. Stephanie Grauman Wolf, *Urban Village: Population, Community, and Family Structure in Germantown, Pennsylvania 1683–1800* (Princeton, 1976), pp. 147, 152–153, 194–195.

44. 1765, [Christopher Schultz], "Historische Anmerkungen. A Schwenkfelder Chronicle," ed. Marion D. Learned, *AG*, 2 (1898), 55; Israel Pemberton to Christopher Schultz, 15 July 1765, S.L. (quote).

45. 23 July 1777, Christopher Marshall Papers, Remembrancer D, H.S.P. (quote); 13 December 1778, George Churchman, Journal, 1777–1780, pp. 52–53, Q.C.H.C.

46. Schultz to Carl Ehrenfried Heintze, [February–March 1769?], S.L. (typescript); Schultz to I. Pemberton, 29 March 1773, *Ibid.* (typescript); Anthony Benezet to Schultz, 15 July 1783, *Ibid.*

47. Philadelphia Meeting for Sufferings to London Meeting for Sufferings, 17 December 1767, 19 December 1771, Philadelphia Yearly Meeting Collection, Philadelphia Meeting for Sufferings Minutes, 1755–1775, pp. 279, 357–358, Q.C.H.C.; London Meeting for Sufferings to Philadelphia Meeting for Sufferings, 2 October 1772, *Ibid.*, p. 373 (21 January 1773); Philadelphia Meeting for Sufferings to London Meeting for

Sufferings, 25 March 1775, *Ibid.*, p. 456; Moses Brown to Benezet, 2 October 1780, Letters of American Friends, Q.C.H.C. (typescript); Benezet to John Pemberton, 29 May 1783, Etting Collection, Pemberton Papers, II, 92, H.S.P.

48. Benezet to Daniel Burton, 27 April 1767, *S.P.G. Letterbooks*, C4, pp. 54–55.

49. 4 May 1767, Philadelphia Yearly Meeting Collection, Philadelphia Quarterly Meeting Minutes, 1723–1772, p. 344, Q.C.H.C. (quote); Remonstrances of the Freemen of the City and County of Philadelphia to the Governor and Assembly, n.d., *Ibid.*, pp. 344–346.

50. Peter Miller to Franklin, 12 June 1771, Labaree, *Franklin Papers*, XVIII, 130–132.

51. Christopher Marshall to Miller, 10 August 1773, Christopher Marshall Papers, Letterbook, 1773–1778, p. 5, H.S.P.

52. 24 August 1773, Journal of a Tour from Philad^a to Bethlehem, &c. In Company with M^r and Mrs Mitchell, Miss Kitty and Miss Nancy Lawrence and Mr E. Lawrence, H.S.P.

53. 2 February 1767, H. A. Brickenstein, ed. and trans., "Sketch of the Early History of Lititz, 1742–75," *TMHS*, 2 (1886), 365.

54. 20 August 1773, *Ibid.*, p. 371; 20 August 1773, Journal of a Tour from Philad^a to Bethlehem, &c., H.S.P.; Hannah Smith to Rachel Pemberton, 1773, Pemberton Papers, XXV, 100b–101b, H.S.P.; 22 November 1773, W. J. Hinke and J. W. Heisey, eds. and trans., Extracts from the Hebron Diary Kept by the Moravian Pastors of the Hebron Church in Lebanon, Pennsylvania, p. 7, E.R.H.S.; 26 December 1774, Brickenstein, "Lititz," *TMHS*, 2 (1886), 372. The Reformed church in Lancaster purchased its organ from the same Moravian organ-builder. *Pennsylvania Gazette*, 10 January 1771.

55. Dr. Smith's Manuscript Notes, Commencement, 17 November 1767, Rev. William Smith Papers, VI, 141–142, H.S.P.

56. T. Penn to Peters, 14 March 1770, Penn Manuscripts, Thomas Penn Letterbook, X, 74, H.S.P.

57. 16 August 1773, T. W. J. Wylie, ed., "Franklin County One Hundred Years Ago. A Settler's Experience told in a Letter Written by Alexander Thomson in 1773," *PMHB*, 8 (1884), 324–325.

58. Letter 4, 4 September 1771, [Jacob Duché], *Caspipina's Letters; Containing Observations on a Variety of Subjects, Literary, Moral, and Religious.* . . . , 2 vols. (Bath, 1777), I, 74.

59. Schultz to Heintze, 6 March 1769, S.L. (typescript). The comments about Roman Catholics are particularly significant, for it was Jesuit attempts to forcibly convert Schwenkfelders to Catholicism that resulted in their emigration to Pennsylvania. Schultz to Benezet, 16 April 1768, S.L.

60. Schultz to Heintze, 6 March 1769, *Ibid.*; Benezet to George Dillwyn, July 1781, Anthony Benezet Papers, Q.C.H.C.

61. *Pennsylvania Gazette*, 25 June 1772, 5 August 1772, 9 September 1772.

62. "A New-England Man," [Benjamin Franklin], "Toleration in Old and New England," 3 June 1772, Labaree, *Franklin Papers*, XIX, 163–168, quote p. 164.

63. I. Pemberton to John Pemberton, 19 October 1774, Pemberton Papers, XXVI, 177½, H.S.P. Philadelphia Baptists, also concerned about their brethren in New England, offered their assistance in redressing grievances. 11 October 1769, A. D. Gillette, ed., *Minutes of the Philadelphia Baptist Association, from A.D. 1707, to A.D. 1807; Being the First One Hundred Years of its Existence* (Philadelphia, 1851), p. 108; 17–18 Oc-

tober 1770, *Ibid.*, pp. 114–117; 12 October 1773, *Ibid.*, p. 128; 13 October 1774, *Ibid.*, pp. 141–142.

64. James Madison Jr. to William Bradford Jr., 24 January 1774, Bradford Collection, William Bradford Jr. Letterbook, 1772–1775, pp. 23–24, H.S.P., quote p. 23.

65. Bradford to Madison, 4 March 1774, *Ibid.*, p. 25.

66. The Examination of Doctor Benjamin Franklin, before an August Assembly, relating to the Repeal of the Stamp-Act, &c., [13 February 1766], Labaree, *Franklin Papers*, XIII, 133.

67. Christopher Sauer II, "Wertheste Landes-Leute, Sonderlich in Philadelphia Bucks and Bercks-County!" [1765], Broadside Collection, H.S.P.

68. Thomas Wharton to Franklin, 14 August 1765, Labaree, *Franklin Papers*, XII, 240 (quote); T. Wharton to Franklin, 2 March 1766, *Ibid.*, XIII, 190–192.

69. [Samuel Wharton] to Franklin, 13 October 1765, *Ibid.*, XII, 316–317.

70. 5 October 1765, Muhlenberg, *Journals*, II, 273–274 (quotes); 6 October 1765, *Ibid.*, p. 274.

71. Willi Paul Adams, "The Colonial German-language Press and the American Revolution," Bernard Bailyn and John B. Hench, eds., *The Press and the American Revolution* (Worcester, Mass., 1980), pp. 181–193.

72. There was also a rush to clear land titles. With the repeal of the Stamp Act, there were lower peaks in naturalization and property transfers. Henry J. Young, "Agrarian Reactions to the Stamp Act in Pennsylvania," *PH*, 34 (1967), 25–29.

73. Examination of Benjamin Franklin, [13 February 1766], Labaree, *Franklin Papers*, XIII, 133.

74. J. Penn to T. Penn, 15 December 1765, Penn Manuscripts, Official Correspondence, X, 23, H.S.P.

75. Thomas Gage to Thomas Conway, 16 January 1766, Clarence Edwin Carter, ed., *The Correspondence of General Thomas Gage with the Secretaries of State, 1763–1775*, 2 vols. (New Haven, 1931, 1933), I, 82–83.

76. John Fothergill to James Pemberton, 10 May 1766, Etting Collection, Pemberton Papers, II, 54, H.S.P.

77. Joseph Galloway to Franklin, 13 January 1765 [1766], Labaree, *Franklin Papers*, XIII, 37 (quotes); Peter Collinson to Lord Hyde, 11 October 1765[?], Collinson-Bartram Papers, A.P.S.

78. James Pemberton to Fothergill, 7 June 1766, Pemberton Papers, Copies of Letters, 1752–1775, pp. 270–271, H.S.P.

79. Carl Bridenbaugh, *Mitre and Sceptre: Transatlantic Faith, Ideas, Personalities, and Politics 1689–1775* (New York, 1962); Frederick V. Mills, Sr., *Bishops by Ballots: An Eighteenth-Century Ecclesiastical Revolution* (New York, 1978); Elizabeth I. Nybakken, ed., *The Centinel: Warnings of a Revolution* (Newark, Del., 1980), pp. 28–72. Pleas for bishops may be found scattered throughout the *S.P.G. Letterbooks*, series A and B, and Perry, *Colonial Church*.

80. Barton to the Secretary, 16 November 1764, Perry, *Colonial Church*, pp. 366–368, quotes p. 368.

81. James Penrose to Joseph Penrose, 1 March 1766, Letters of American Friends, Q.C.H.C. Presbyterians also noted that Quakers tended to favor the establishment of episcopacy or the expansion of the Anglican church. Samuel Purviance Jr. to Ezra Stiles, 1 November 1766, Yale Photostats [Alison-Stiles Correspondence], P.H.S.

82. William Gordon to Charles Beatty, 17 January 1764, Beatty Papers, Folder 2,

P.H.S.; Allen to T. Penn, 12 November 1766, Penn Manuscripts, Official Correspondence, X, 72, H.S.P.

83. Hugh Neill to the Secretary, 19 May 1766, *S.P.G. Letterbooks*, B21, no. 125.

84. *Pennsylvania Gazette*, 3 July 1766.

85. Francis Alison to Stiles, 4 December 1766, Yale Photostats, P.H.S.

86. Alison to Stiles, 7 August 1766, *Ibid.* (quotes); Alison to Stiles, 20 August 1766, *Ibid.*; Alison, Reasons for Dissenting from the Church of England, n.d., Alison Papers, P.H.S.; Elizabeth A. Ingersoll, "Francis Alison: American *Philosophe*, 1705–1799" (Ph.D. diss., University of Delaware, 1974), pp. 286–288, 295–298.

87. Bridenbaugh, *Mitre and Sceptre*, pp. 270–287.

88. *A Letter, Concerning an American Bishop, &c. To Dr. Bradbury Chandler, Ruler of St. John's Church in Elizabeth-Town. In Answer to the Appendix Of His Appeal to the Public, &c.* ([Philadelphia], 1768), quote p. 18.

89. Deborah Mathias Gough, "Pluralism, Politics, and Power Struggles: The Church of England in Colonial Philadelphia, 1695–1789" (Ph.D. diss., University of Pennsylvania, 1978), pp. 489–503.

90. These essays have been reprinted in Nybakken, *The Centinel*.

91. Thomas Bradbury Chandler, *An Appeal to the Public in Behalf of the Church of England in America* (New York, 1767).

92. Essays by "The Anatomist," "The Remonstrant," "Irenicus," and "The Centinel," *Pennsylvania Gazette*, 8 September 1768–12 January 1769.

93. *Ibid.*, 8 December 1768.

94. "The Anatomist to the Centinel, A Card," *Ibid.*, 12 January 1769. The outcry against bishops influenced Catholic priests in Pennsylvania to discourage a proposal for a Canadian bishop to visit the more southern colonies. They feared that Protestants might react by limiting the privileges they enjoyed. John Tracy Ellis, *Catholics in Colonial America* (Baltimore, 1965), p. 386.

95. ? to Daniel Mildred, 3 January 1774, Cox-Parrish-Wharton Papers, XI, 69, H.S.P.

96. Charles Thomson to Isaac Low, 29 May 1774, Drinker Papers, Box 1, H.S.P.

97. 30 May 1774, Christopher Marshall Papers, Remembrancer B, H.S.P. A German broadside calling for observation of the fast day noted that it was called for by "many of the inhabitants of the city of most of the religious opinions." "An die Einwohner der Stadt und Caunty Philadelphia" [1774], Broadside Collection, H.S.P.

98. 31 May 1774, Christopher Marshall Papers, Remembrancer B, H.S.P.; *Pennsylvania Gazette*, 1 June 1774 (quotes).

99. Thomson to [Low], n.d., Drinker Papers, Box 1, H.S.P.; anonymous paper, n.d., *Ibid.*; Remarks from A[bel] J[ames], n.d., *Ibid.*; Benjamin Booth to Thomson, 8 June 1774, *Ibid.*; ? to ?, 9 June 1774, *Ibid.*; ? to Booth, 13 June 1774, *Ibid.*; ? to Booth, 7 July 1774, *Ibid.*; *Pennsylvania Gazette*, 9 June 1774 (correcting an item from the *Pennsylvania Packet* of 6 June 1774).

100. George Clymer to Josiah Quincy Jr., 13 June 1774, M. St. Clair Clarke and Peter Force, eds., *American Archives: Fourth Series. . . .* , 6 vols. (Washington, D.C., 1837–1846), I, 407.

101. Bradford to Madison, 4 January 1775, Bradford Collection, William Bradford Jr. Letterbook, 1772–1775, p. 37, H.S.P.

102. 24 January 1775, Christopher Marshall Papers, Remembrancer B, H.S.P.

103. Edward Biddle to Jonathan Potts, [25 February 1775?], Jonathan Potts Papers, L.C.

104. *Pennsylvania Gazette*, 15 June 1774 (first two quotes); Mildred to John Pemberton, 26 July 1774, Pemberton Papers, XXVI, 128, H.S.P. (third quote); Jack D. Marietta, *The Reformation of American Quakerism, 1748–1783* (Philadelphia, 1984), pp. 205–221; Hermann Wellenreuther, *Glaube and Politik in Pennsylvania 1681–1776: Die Wandlungen der Obrigkeitsdoktrin und des "Peace Testimony" der Quäker* (Köln, 1972), pp. 402–421.

105. *Pennsylvania Gazette*, 24 August 1774 (three articles), Postscript to 14 September 1774, 19 July 1775; Charles H. Metzger, *The Quebec Act: A Primary Cause of the American Revolution* (New York, 1936), pp. 39–44, 47–48.

106. *Pennsylvania Gazette*, 12 October 1774.

107. Christopher Marshall to H. R., 1 September 1774, Christopher Marshall Papers, Letterbook, 1773–1778, pp. 62–63, H.S.P., quote p. 63.

108. Peter Böhler to John Ettwein, 23 January 1775, Albert F. Jordan Collection, Box 3 (Translations of Peter Böhler Letters), M.A. He was slightly concerned about possible Catholic missions to the Ohio, where the Moravians were attempting to convert the Indians, but believed "we have more to fear from the Presbyterian Solemn League and Covenant than from the Catholics in America."

109. "To the Inhabitants of the Province of Quebec," 26 October 1774, Clarke and Force, *American Archives*, 4th ser., I, 932–934; William Renwick Riddell, "Benjamin Franklin's Mission to Canada and the Causes of its Failure," *PMHB*, 48 (1924), 111–158.

110. E. Shippen to John Read, 8 November 1774, Burd-Shippen Family Papers, Box 2, P.H.M.C.

111. William Reeser to Schultz, 1 May 1775, Richard K. MacMaster, Samuel L. Horst, and Robert F. Ulle, eds., *Conscience in Crisis: Mennonites and Other Peace Churches in America, 1739–1789: Interpretation and Documents* (Scottdale, Pa., 1979), p. 230.

112. 1 June 1775, John W. Jordan, ed. and trans., "Bethlehem during the Revolution: Extracts from the Diaries in the Moravian Archives at Bethlehem, Pennsylvania," *PMHB*, 12 (1888), 386–387. Moravians also presented a declaration of their beliefs about war and oaths to Congress, through their intermediary, Benjamin Franklin. Nathaniel Seidel to Franklin, n.d., "Notes and Queries," *Ibid.*, 29 (1905), 245–246; Franklin to Seidel, 2 June 1775, *Ibid.*, p. 246.

113. George Ross to Lancaster County Committee of Correspondence, 1 June 1775, Peter Force Collection, 9th ser., XII, L.C.

114. 29 May 1775, Grubb Collection, Box 1, Folder 2, Lancaster County Committee of Inspection Minutes, H.S.P.

115. Draft of the late Lancaster Committee's Letter to the Pennsylvania Delegates in Congress, 3 June 1775, Yeates Papers, Correspondence, 1762–1780, H.S.P.

116. Edward Burd to Yeates, 7 June 1775, *Ibid.*

117. 6 June 1775, John W. Jordan, ed. and trans., "Items from Letters (Relating to Early Events in Lancaster, Pa.)," *PLCHS*, 27 (1923), 96.

118. "Extracts from the Votes and Proceedings of the Committee of Observation for the County of Lancaster" [1775], Broadside Collection, H.S.P.

119. 1 July 1775, Peter Force Papers, Series 7e, Box 11, Lancaster County Committee of Safety Minutes, 1774–1777, pp. 43–44, L.C. Apparently the committee approved this proposal; it ordered a copy of the minutes to be sent to each township, and a copy of the petition as well as extracts from the minutes (above, n. 118) to be sent to Congress.

120. Petition to Assembly, 4 May 1775, Assembly, *Votes*, VIII, 7230; 5–12 May 1775, *Ibid.*, pp. 7231–7234; Petition to Assembly, 23 May 1775, *Ibid.*, pp. 7237–7240; 23 May 1775, *Ibid.*, p. 7240; Resolution of Congress, 22 June 1775, *Ibid.*, p. 7241 (24 June 1775).

121. 30 June 1775, *Ibid.*, pp. 7245–7249, quotes p. 7249.

122. Resolution of Congress, 18 July 1775, Council, *Minutes*, X, 293 (28 July 1775). Minutes of the Council of Safety of the Province of Pennsylvania are printed in the series of Council, *Minutes*, from 30 June 1775 (X, 277) to 17 March 1777 (XI, 170). Minutes of the Supreme Executive Council of the Commonwealth of Pennsylvania begin on 4 March 1777 in this series (XI, 171).

123. Petition to Berks County Committee, [September 1775], MacMaster, *Conscience in Crisis*, pp. 256–258, quotes pp. 256, 258.

124. 29 July 1775, Brickenstein, "Lititz," *TMHS*, 2 (1886), 373; 1 August 1775, *Ibid.*

125. Jacob Stoll to Alexander Mack, 21 September 1775, Donald F. Durnbaugh, ed., *The Brethren in Colonial America: A Source Book on the Transplantation and Development of the Church of the Brethren in the Eighteenth Century* (Elgin, Ill., 1967), pp. 361–362, quotes p. 362. He was responding to a query whether the money had been given "'for protection money' or 'for the needy.'" He admitted that "in part it has been given for both." *Ibid.*, p. 361.

126. York County Committee to Pennsylvania Committee of Safety, 14 September 1775, MacMaster, *Conscience in Crisis*, pp. 248–249, quotes p. 248.

127. Petition to Assembly, 27 September 1775, Assembly, *Votes*, VIII, 7259–7260 (quotes p. 7260); Committee of Safety to Assembly, 29 September 1775, *Ibid.*, pp. 7261–7262.

128. Petitions to Assembly, 20–21 October 1775, *Ibid.*, pp. 7311–7313; Petition to Assembly, 26 October 1775, *Ibid.*, pp. 7323–7324.

129. 20 October 1775, Philadelphia Yearly Meeting Collection, Philadelphia Meeting for Sufferings Minutes, 1775–1785, p. 25, Q.C.H.C.; Address of Quakers to Assembly, 27 October 1775, Assembly, *Votes*, VIII, 7326–7330.

130. 29–31 October 1775, Christopher Marshall Papers, Remembrancer C, H.S.P.; Petitions to Assembly, 31 October 1775, Assembly, *Votes*, VIII, 7334–7343.

131. Petition of Mennonites and German Baptists to Assembly, 7 November 1775, *Ibid.*, pp. 7348–7350, quotes pp. 7349, 7350. The assembly subsequently ordered a "particular Enquiry" into the contributions they had made. 24 November 1775, *Ibid.*, pp. 7365–7366, quote p. 7365.

132. Rules and Regulations for the better Government of the Military Association in Pennsylvania, Articles of Association, and Resolutions directing the Mode of Levying Taxes on Non-Associators in Pennsylvania, 25 November 1775, *Ibid.*, pp. 7369–7384.

133. 15 January 1776, "Items of History of York, Penna., During the Revolution," *PMHB*, 44 (1920), 310.

134. Petitions to the assembly from various counties and militia units, 23 February 1776, 1 March 1776, 5 March 1776, 7 March 1776, 11 March 1776, 13 March 1776, 15 March 1776, Assembly, *Votes*, VIII, 7396–7410, 7422–7426, 7429–7430, 7433–7435, 7438–7440, 7443, 7448–7449.

135. Rules and Regulations for the better Government of the Military Association in Pennsylvania, Articles of Association, Resolutions directing the Mode of Levying Taxes on Non-Associators in Pennsylvania, and Rules and Articles for the Government of the Pennsylvania Forces, 5 April 1776, *Ibid.*, pp. 7473–7503.

136. Peter Brock, *Pacifism in the United States From the Colonial Era to the First World War* (Princeton, 1968), pp. 206–209; Stephen E. Lucas, *Portents of Rebellion: Rhetoric and Revolution in Philadelphia, 1765–1776* (Philadelphia, 1976), pp. 120–122, 195–199; Marietta, *Reformation of Quakerism*, pp. 223–232.

137. Wayne Loren Bockelman, "Continuity and Change in Revolutionary Pennsylvania: A Study of County Government and Officeholders" (Ph.D. diss., Northwestern University, 1969); Wayne L. Bockelman and Owen S. Ireland, "The Internal Revolution in Pennsylvania: An Ethnic-Religious Interpretation," *PH*, 41 (1974), 125–160; Owen S. Ireland, "The Ethnic-Religious Dimensions of Pennsylvania Politics, 1778–1779," 3 *WMQ*, 30 (1973), 423–448; Robert Francis Oaks, "Philadelphia Merchants and the American Revolution, 1765–1776" (Ph.D. diss., University of Southern California, 1970), pp. 45, 47, 70–74, 78–82, 112–114, 141–145, 175, 215; Richard Alan Ryerson, *The Revolution Is Now Begun: The Radical Committees of Philadelphia, 1765–1776* ([Philadelphia], 1977).

138. Thomas Smith, Advertisement, *Pennsylvania Gazette*, 20 September 1775.

139. Rules and Regulations for the better Government of the Military Association in Pennsylvania, art. 21, 25 November 1775, Assembly, *Votes*, VIII, 7371.

140. E. Burd to ?, 15 March 1776, Shippen Papers, VII, 161, H.S.P. (quote); Adams, "German-language Press," Bailyn and Hench, *Press and the Revolution*, pp. 151–228, especially p. 173ff.

141. Henry Melchior Muhlenberg to David Grim, 22 January 1778, Muhlenberg, *Journals*, III, 124–125. Presbyterian ministers were also requested to write to their co-religionists in other colonies to encourage them to support the revolutionary movement. Philip Davidson, *Propaganda and the American Revolution 1763–1783* (Chapel Hill, 1941), pp. 89–91.

142. Petition to Assembly, 23 February 1776, Assembly, *Votes*, VIII, 7460.

143. 5 April 1776, *Ibid.*, p. 7490.

144. 24 May 1776, *Ibid.*, pp. 7520–7521 (quote p. 7521); 5 June 1776, *Ibid.*, p. 7536.

145. 19–20 June 1776, *Proceedings of the Provincial Congress. . . .* (Harrisburg, 1825), pp. 38–39.

146. Constitution, 28 September 1776, ch. 1, sect. 2, George Edward Reed, ed., *Pennsylvania Archives*, 4th ser., 12 vols. (Harrisburg, 1900–1902), III, 629 [hereafter *Pa. Arch.*]. For Penn's guarantees of religious liberty, see above, ch. 2. Penn, however, expressly granted freedom of conscience to both men and women.

147. Quoted in Wolf and Whiteman, *Jews of Philadelphia*, p. 81. Some delegates favored a more restrictive test, but those favoring complete toleration temporarily proved successful. Marshall to J. B., 30 June 1776, Christopher Marshall Papers, Letterbook, 1773–1778, pp. 191–192, H.S.P.

148. 6 September 1776, Christopher Marshall Papers, Remembrancer D, H.S.P.

149. 16–17 September 1776, Muhlenberg, *Journals*, II, 740–742.

150. Constitution, 28 September 1776, ch. 2, sect. 10, *Pa. Arch.*, 4th ser., III, 634.

151. J. Paul Selsam, *The Pennsylvania Constitution of 1776: A Study in Revolutionary Democracy* (Philadelphia, 1936), pp. 218–221. But see also the essay by "John Trusshoop" in *Pennsylvania Gazette*, 13 November 1776, that argued in support of the religious provisions of the constitution. Those opposed to allowing "Jews, Turks, and Infidels" to participate in government seem to have been using a stock phrase, with little awareness that there were actually Jews living in the colony whose rights might be infringed upon by the test. Although Jacob Rader Marcus (*Early American Jewry*,

vol. 2, *The Jews of Pennsylvania and the South, 1655–1790* [Philadelphia, 1953], p. 156) cites two newspaper articles containing anti-Jewish rhetoric, I would argue that, for the most part, Jews were simply ignored. The primary concern was the possible participation of atheists or deists.

152. Constitution, 28 September 1776, ch. 1, sect. 15, *Pa. Arch.*, 4th ser., III, 632 (first quote); *Ibid.*, ch. 2, sect. 42, p. 645 (remaining quotes). The council subsequently recommended that the assembly enact a law to protect the estates of deceased aliens, which the "rigid policy" of Britain had prevented on several occasions. 7 August 1778, Samuel Hazard, ed., *Pennsylvania Archives*, [1st ser.], 12 vols. (Philadelphia and Harrisburg, 1852–1856), VI, 685–686, quote p. 686 [hereafter *Pa. Arch.*]. A law that recognized the encouragement William Penn had given to immigration was enacted on 31 August 1778 to protect aliens who owned property. Ch. 803, *Statutes*, IX, 258–259.

153. Ch. 756, 13 June 1777, *Ibid.*, pp. 110–114; ch. 765, 12 October 1777, *Ibid.*, pp. 147–149.

154. Ch. 796, 1 April 1778, *Ibid.*, pp. 238–245. This law also dealt with those who had remained in Philadelphia during the British occupation and with men who had held offices under the Crown prior to the Revolution.

155. Ch. 822, 5 December 1778, *Ibid.*, pp. 303–308. This law neglected to disarm nonjurors, which was remedied by ch. 836, 31 March 1779, *Ibid.*, pp. 346–348. Proclamation of Pardon to Prisoners under Test Laws, 29 December 1778, *Pa. Arch.*, [1st ser.], VII, 130–131.

156. Ch. 852, 1 October 1779, *Statutes*, IX, 404–407.

157. Douglas McNeill Arnold, "Political Ideology and the Internal Revolution in Pennsylvania, 1776–1790" (Ph.D. diss., Princeton University, 1976), pp. 105–113. A revolutionary noted that "Germans in General" in his neighborhood found the abjuration objectionable because of the oath previously taken to the King. Richard Macalester to T. Wharton Jr., 28 August 1778, *Pa. Arch.*, [1st ser.], V, 559–560, quote p. 559.

158. Extracts from Assembly Minutes, 25 May 1778, *Pennsylvania Evening Post*, 23 July 1778, MacMaster, *Conscience in Crisis*, pp. 426–428; 4 June 1778, Muhlenberg, *Journals*, III, 160; [George Bryan] to Alexander McDowell, 6 June 1778, MacMaster, *Conscience in Crisis*, pp. 431–433.

159. [John Ettwein], "A Few Remarks on the Reasons of the General-Assembly of Pensilvania, for Not Granting the Petition of the Moravians, as Published in the Gen'l Advertiser 25th of May 1778," Kenneth Gardiner Hamilton, *John Ettwein and the Moravian Church during the Revolutionary Period* (Bethlehem, Pa., 1940), pp. 235–237, quotes pp. 235–236. He emphasized the Moravians' willingness to be subject to whatever government exercised jurisdiction over them.

160. Evidence in letters and petitions indicates that it consisted primarily of isolated incidents. Indirect threats of penalties or other pressure to subscribe the declarations appear to have been more frequent than imprisonment, fines, or expulsion from the state. For a general discussion of enforcement of laws enacted against the disaffected, see Anne M. Ousterhout, "Controlling the Opposition in Pennsylvania during the American Revolution," *PMHB*, 105 (1981), 3–34.

161. Annual Meeting, 1778, H. D. Davy and J. Quinter, eds., *Minutes of the Annual Meetings of the Brethren. Designed for the Promotion of Peace and Harmony of the Brotherhood. Published by Authority of the Annual Meeting, May 26–27, 1874* (Dayton, Ohio, 1876), pp. 5–6; Annual Meeting, 1779, *Ibid.*, p. 6.

162. Bryan to John Weitzel, 22 May 1778, *Pa. Arch.*, [1st ser.], VI, 541. There was

even a complaint in 1780 that in York and Northampton Counties, where large numbers of pacifists lived, collectors of militia fines had "from Motives of false Tenderness & Desire to please every one have given Indulgencies & shewn Partialities." Joseph Reed to Samuel J. Atlee, [28 or 29 April 1780], *Ibid.*, VIII, 216.

163. Resolution of Congress, 28 August 1777, *Ibid.*, V, 554–556, quote p. 555.

164. Thomas Gilpin, ed., *Exiles in Virginia: With Observations on the Conduct of the Society of Friends During The Revolutionary War, Comprising the Official Papers of the Government Relating to that Period. 1777–1778* (Philadelphia, 1848), pp. 42–43; Robert F. Oaks, "Philadelphians in Exile: The Problem of Loyalty During the American Revolution," *PMHB*, 96 (1972), 298–325.

165. H. Drinker to Elizabeth Drinker, 18 September 1777, Drinker Papers, Q.C.H.C. (first two quotes); E. Drinker to H. Drinker, 9 December 1777, *Ibid.* (fourth quote); T. W[harton] to T. Wharton Jr., 20 January 1778, Wharton-Willing Papers, Box 3, H.S.P. (third quote).

166. "A Testimony given forth from Philadelphia Yearly Meeting Held 29th Ninth Month-4th Tenth Month 1777" [1777], Broadside Collection, H.S.P.

167. 12 September 1777, Muhlenberg, *Journals*, III, 74. On 16 September 1777, however, he indicated that the "defenseless sheep" were at least partially responsible for their plight by their open criticism of a government that preserved their liberty of conscience and by their refusal to pay taxes. He also suspected that they had aided the British. *Ibid.*, pp. 75–76.

168. 1 October 1777, James Allen, Diary, 1770–1778, H.S.P.

169. James Pemberton to Phineas Pemberton, 17 September 1777, Pemberton Papers, XXX, 126, H.S.P. (quote); Oaks, "Philadelphians in Exile," *PMHB*, 96 (1972), 306–309.

170. William White, *Memoirs of the Protestant Episcopal Church in the United States of America. . . .* (Philadelphia, 1820), pp. 59–61.

171. Barton to the Secretary, 25 November 1776, *S.P.G. Letterbooks*, B21, no. 30 (quote); Barton to the Secretary, 8 January 1779, *Ibid.*, no. 36.

172. Constitution, 28 September 1776, ch. 1, sect. 8, *Pa. Arch.*, 4th ser., III, 630.

173. Ch. 750, 17 March 1777, *Statutes*, IX, 75–94; ch. 781, 30 December 1777, *Ibid.*, pp. 185–189; ch. 843, 5 April 1779, *Ibid.*, pp. 381–384; ch. 902, 20 March 1780, *Ibid.*, X, 145–173; ch. 908, 26 May 1780, *Ibid.*, pp. 192–195; ch. 916, 22 September 1780, *Ibid.*, pp. 225–227.

174. Ch. 735, 14 September 1776, *Ibid.*, IX, 22–27, declared illegal by the assembly on 26 September 1776, *Ibid.*, p. 27n.; ch. 773, 26 December 1777, *Ibid.*, pp. 167–169, repealed by ch. 872, 27 November 1779, *Ibid.*, X, 31–32.

175. Brock, *Pacifism*, pp. 196–204, 237–240, 265, 270–272, 310–313; Richard K. MacMaster, "The Peace Churches in the American Revolution," *FH*, 9 (1977), 18–20; Marietta, *Reformation of Quakerism*, pp. 236–239.

176. Pennsylvania Schwenkfelders to Silesian Schwenkfelders, 27 [June] 1779, S.L. (typescript).

177. Committee Report, 28 September 1776, Philadelphia Yearly Meeting Collection, Philadelphia Yearly Meeting Minutes, 1747–1779, pp. 356–357, Q.C.H.C.; A candid declaration of some so-called Schwenkfelders concerning present militia affairs, 2 May 1777, MacMaster, *Conscience in Crisis*, p. 312; Annual Meeting, 1781, Davy and Quinter, *Brethren Minutes*, pp. 7–8; John Ettwein, A Short Account of the Disturbances

in America and of the Brethren's Conduct and Suffering in this Connection, trans. Hamilton, *John Ettwein*, p. 163.

178. Francis Johnston to Thomas Mifflin, 21 December 1776, *Pa. Arch.*, [1st ser.], V, 125–126 (quote p. 125); Deposition respecting prisoners at Winchester, 8 December 1777, *Ibid.*, VI, 75; 7 January 1778, Muhlenberg, *Journals*, III, 119–120; 8 February 1781, *Ibid.*, p. 398.

179. Robert Pleasants to Thomas Nicholson, 5 December 1779, Robert Pleasants Letters, 1746–1797, F.H.L. (microfilm).

180. Samuel Allinson, Reasons against War, and paying taxes for its support, 13 June 1780, MacMaster, *Conscience in Crisis*, pp. 371–373, quote p. 372.

181. Benezet to Brown, 1 July 1780, Anthony Benezet Papers, Q.C.H.C.

182. James Gibbons to I. Pemberton, 19 January 1777, Pemberton Papers, XXIX, 132 (he also "intend[ed] to mention it [a collection of food for the needy in Philadelphia] to some of the Manonists in My Neighbourhood[.]"); John Wilson to Joseph Pemberton, 5 March 1781, *Ibid.*, XXXV, 97; Ann Emlen to James Thornton[?], 16 February 1782, Small Collections, F.H.L.

183. 19 March 1777, John W. Heisey, ed. and trans., "Extracts from the Diary of the Moravian Pastors of the Hebron Church, Lebanon, 1755–1814," *PH*, 34 (1967), 55; 17 March 1780, Christopher Marshall Papers, Remembrancer F, H.S.P.; 17 March 1778, Drinker-Sandwith Papers, Elizabeth Drinker Diaries, II, H.S.P. (typescript).

184. 3 April 1777, Muhlenberg, *Journals*, III, 28; 17 October 1781, Drinker-Sandwith Papers, Elizabeth Drinker Diaries, II, H.S.P.

185. Supreme Executive Council to James Young and other justices, 4 July 1777, *Pa. Arch.*, [1st ser.], V, 411–412; "A True Whig," *Pennsylvania Gazette*, 9 April 1783.

186. Some entries in these congregation diaries include correspondence with various officials. 3 December 1776–26 July 1782, Jordan, "Bethlehem," *PMHB*, 12 (1888), 391–405, 13 (1889), 71–89; 25–27 August 1777, Heisey, "Hebron," *PH*, 34 (1967), 55–56; 28 August 1777–7 February 1779, P. C. Bader, trans., "Extracts from the Records of the Moravian Congregation at Hebron, Pennsylvania, 1775–1781," *PMHB*, 18 (1894), 451–459; 1–15 May 1778, "York," *Ibid.*, 44 (1920), 314–317.

187. For example: 30 October 1777, Bader, "Hebron," *Ibid.*, 18 (1894), 454; 18 November 1777, *Ibid.*, p. 455; 28 May 1778, *Ibid.*, p. 458; Muhlenberg to Charles Magnus Wrangel, 23 October 1784, Muhlenberg, *Journals*, III, 625.

188. The advice of Anglican priest William White (later Bishop of Pennsylvania) was also sought. He believed that the matter should be deferred. 5 August 1779–11 June 1783, Muhlenberg, *Journals*, III, 253–256, 408–409, 411, 425, 427–428, 450–451, 502–504, 534, 539–540, 547; 15 June 1783, A. Spaeth, H. E. Jacobs, and G. S. Spicker, eds. and trans., *Documentary History of the Evangelical Lutheran Ministerium of Pennsylvania and Adjacent States. . . .* (Philadelphia, 1898), p. 187; 17 June 1783, *Ibid.* p 189. When an Anglican-Methodist who served an English and German congregation requested Lutheran ordination he was refused, although Muhlenberg suggested that his congregations allow him to administer the sacraments. 25 July 1782, Muhlenberg, *Journals*, III, 495.

189. Minutes of Coetus, 1779, art. 4, Hinke, *Minutes and Letters of The Coetus*, p. 368.

190. Abstract of Minutes, 18 June 1784, Gilbert Cope Collection, Society for the Propagation of the Gospel in Foreign Parts Transcripts, p. 34, H.S.P.

191. 11 December 1780, George Nelson, Diary, H.S.P.; 14 December 1780, *Ibid.*

(quote); 22 December 1780, *Ibid.* The congregation believed that their generosity would commend them to the "kind Providence of God," who would then be more disposed to "sooner suppl[y]" an Episcopalian minister. 14 December 1780, *Ibid.*

192. Atlee to Elias Boudinot, 8 September 1777, Peter Force Collection, 9th ser., XXI, L.C.

193. Rodney Atwood, *The Hessians: Mercenaries from Hessen-Kassel in the American Revolution* (Cambridge, Eng., 1980), pp. 97–99.

194. *Ibid.*, pp. 184–186; Lyman H. Butterfield, "Psychological Warfare in 1776: The Jefferson-Franklin Plan to Cause Hessian Desertions," *PAPS*, 94 (1950), 233–241.

195. Franklin to Thomas McKean, 24 August 1776, McKean Papers, I, 8, H.S.P.

196. Butterfield, "Psychological Warfare," *PAPS*, 94 (1950), 236–237. A similar plan was broached by Benjamin Rush in a letter to Richard Henry Lee, 20 December 1776, Peter Force, ed., *American Archives: Fifth Series.* . . . , 3 vols. (Washington, D.C., 1848–1853), III, 1308.

197. James H. Kettner, *The Development of American Citizenship, 1608–1870* (Chapel Hill, 1978), pp. 219–220.

198. Committee of Congress to George Washington, 28 December 1776, Force, *American Archives*, 5th ser., III, 1459; Council of Safety to Public, 31 December 1776, *Pa. Arch.*, [1st ser.], V, 146–147; Lewis Nicola to Reed, 14 July 1780, *Ibid.*, VIII, 415; James Wood to Reed, 30 June 1781, *Ibid.*, IX, 236.

199. Council of Safety to Lancaster Committee, 31 December 1776, Force, *American Archives*, 5th ser., III, 1511.

200. 31 December 1776, Muhlenberg, *Journals*, II, 771–772 (quote p. 772); 11 January 1777, Council, *Minutes*, XI, 85.

201. Council of Safety to Lancaster Committee, 3 March 1777, *Pa. Arch.*, [1st ser.], V, 251; Board of War to Reed, 21 June 1780, *Ibid.*, VIII, 343–344.

202. Printed form, William Henry Papers, I, 151, H.S.P.

203. The revocation of the college's charter was part of the attempt by the Presbyterian-dominated government to consolidate its power; the college was largely in the hands of Anglicans, many of whom were suspected of loyalist sentiments. This action was very controversial, although the appointment of a Roman Catholic trustee was not. Gough, "Pluralism, Politics, and Power Struggles," pp. 555–556; Charles H. Metzger, *Catholics and the American Revolution: A Study in Religious Climate* (Chicago, 1962), pp. 110–111, 214–215.

204. See, for example: John Clifford to T. Clifford Jr., 8 October 1783, Pemberton Papers, XXIX, Thomas and John Clifford Letterbook, 1773–1789, H.S.P.; James Pemberton to John Pemberton, 24 August 1784, Pemberton Papers, XLI, 178, H.S.P.; H. Drinker to Henry Waddy, 14 December 1784, Drinker Papers, Henry Drinker Letterbook, 1762–1787, p. 87, H.S.P.

205. 22 May 1783, Minutes of the Synod of New York and Philadelphia, William Morrison Engles, ed., *Records of the Presbyterian Church in the United States of America Embracing the Minutes of the Presbytery of Philadelphia, from A.D. 1706 to 1716: Minutes of the Syond [sic] of Philadelphia, from A.D. 1717 to 1758: Minutes of the Synod of New York, from A.D. 1745 to 1758: Minutes of the Synod of New York and Philadelphia, from A.D. 1758 to 1788* (Philadelphia, 1841), pp. 498–499, quote p. 499. This statement had been prepared in 1781 and for some reason "expunged" from the minutes in 1782. At the 1783 meeting, the Synod decided that nothing should ever be deleted from its records, and ordered the statement "revived."

206. Arnold, "Political Ideology," pp. 285–287.

207. The petition, read by the Council of Censors on 23 December 1783, is printed in Morris U. Schappes, ed., *A Documentary History of the Jews in the United States 1654–1875* (New York, 1950), pp. 63–66. The Jews also pointed to their support of the American cause during the war as a further reason why they should be allowed to participate in the government. A favorable comment from *The Freeman's Journal*, 21 January 1784, is in *Ibid.*, p. 66; one from *The Independent Gazetteer*, 17 January 1784, is in *Ibid.*, p. 66, n. 9.

9. Epilogue: The Pennsylvania Experience

1. Frederick J. Turner, "The Significance of the Frontier in American History," *Annual Report of the American Historical Association for the Year 1893* (Washington, D.C., 1894), pp. 190–227, especially pp. 215–216, 219–220.

Index